THE ABBÉ CORRÊA IN AMERICA, 1812-1820

The Contributions of the Diplomat and Natural Philosopher to the Foundations of Our National Life

Gávea-Brown Publications
Department of Portuguese and Brazilian Studies
Brown University
Providence, Rhode Island 02912

Distributed by:
Luso-Brazilian Books
538 State Street
Brooklyn, New York 11217

Library of Congress Catalog Card Number 92-81891

ISBN 0-943722-17-9

Design by Ted Ramos
Cover and illustration, portrait of the Abbé Corrêa, by Rembrandt Peale,
courtesy of the Historical Society of Pennsylvania

"The Abbé Corrêa in America, 1812-1820: The Contributions of the Diplomat and
Natural Philosopher to the Foundations of Our National Life," by Richard Beale
Davis, originally appeared in *Transactions of the American Philosophical Society*,
Vol. 45:2 (new ser.) (1955). ® 1955 by the American Philosophical Society.

Richard Beale Davis

THE ABBÉ CORRÊA IN AMERICA, 1812-1820:

The Contributions of the Diplomat and Natural Philosopher to the Foundations of Our National Life

Preface by
Gordon S. Wood

Afterword by
Léon Bourdon

Gávea-Brown

Providence, Rhode Island

This edition was made possible thanks to the generous support of the Calouste Gulbenkian Foundation, Lisbon, Portugal

CONTENTS

Foreword, by *Gordon S. Wood*

v

PREFACE

Gordon S. Wood

Joseph Francis Correa ua Serra was born in Portugal in 1750, seven years after Thomas Jefferson and one year before James Madison. Although he entered holy orders of the Roman Catholic Church and said his first mass at the Basilica of St. Peter in Rome, he became anything but a typical priest. Indeed, the Abbé Serra emerged as one of those liberal, slightly deistic, cosmopolitan polymaths of the eighteenth century Enlightenment who were at home in intellectual circles anywhere in the Western world.

The beginning of the nineteenth century was a special time in the history of the West. Despite the backsliding of the French Revolution and the confusion and bloodiness of the Napoleonic wars, a new day seemed to be dawning. Knowledge and enlightenment were everywhere increasing, and the world was becoming more comprehensible. Even in politics there was hope. Europe may have been temporarily retreating into war and darkness, but across the Atlantic a new republican nation was being created. The new United States of America held out the promise to the enlightened everywhere that free government based on the liberal aspirations of the eighteenth century was indeed possible. So in the 1790s and early nineteenth century many of these enlightened left the Old World and crossed the Atlantic to the New—liberal refugees from a confused and reactionary Europe. Among these the most prominent were Joseph Priestly, the unitarian clergyman and English scientist; Thomas Cooper, the English chemist and radical activist; Pierre Samuel du Pont de Nemours, the French philosophe and economist; and Joseph Francis Correa da Serra, the liberal Portuguese abbé botanist.

After fleeing an anti-liberal crackdown in Portugal in 1795, Correa tried living in England and then France. But as early as 1808 he toyed with the idea of migrating to the United States. It was not until 1812, however, that he did so—at the age of sixty-two. Since Correa was well-known in scientific circles throughout the Western world, he was welcomed with open arms by anxious American intellectuals eager to demonstrate their capacity for being civilized. In January 1812 before he had actually arrived in the United States he was made a member of the American Philosophical Society. Within weeks of landing he was dining with John Marshall, the chief justice of the Supreme Court, and expressing his enthusiasm for all things American. Before long he had established intimate relations with nearly every scientific figure in the United States, including former President Thomas Jefferson, whom Correa called "the great the truly great Mr. Jefferson."

Correa spoke five languages with ease, including English, and amazed everyone he met with his wit and charm. Apparently the Abbé was one of those who was never able to demonstrate his talents fully in print; it was his conversation that impressed and awed people. If even the great European scientists Cuvier and von Humboldt could be dazzled by Correa's oral displays, as they were at dinner parties in Paris, it is not surprising that provincial Americans would be overwhelmed by the scintillating talk of the learned and cosmopolitan Abbé. He seemed to know everything, from the proper consistency of cement to the difference in a ship's keel in fresh or salt water. He knew who ought to be appointed to the faculty of the new University of Virginia, and what were the proper boundaries of the Louisiana and Florida territories. The young Francis Walker Gilmer, whom Jefferson thought the best educated Virginian in the state, thought that Correa was "the most extraordinary man now living, or who, perhaps ever lived... He has read, seen, understands and remembers everything obtained in books, or to be learned by travel, observation, and the conversation of learned men. He is a member of every philosophical society in the world, and knows every distinguished man living."

Perhaps we can dismiss Gilmer's observations as the gushing enthusiasm of an impressionable and excitable young man. But then we have the views of a presumably more mature and cosmopolitan Thomas Jefferson. Correa, wrote Jefferson after his first meeting in 1813, was the "best digest of science in books, men, and things that I have ever met with; and with these the most amiable and engaging character." And Jefferson did not like priests. But than again Correa was not an ordinary priest: he, like many enlightened figures in these years, rarely mentioned Christ and often referred to God as simply "the Almighty disposer of everything". He spent a good deal of time advising Jefferson on how to avoid the evil of "clerical instruction"and how to "neutralize" the influence of "superstition and religion in the bulk of mankind." No wonder the anti-clerical Jefferson continued to believe that the Abbé was "without exception the most learned man I have met in any country." But Correa impressed nearly every American he met. He was asked to give lectures on botany, was offered university professorships, and became an important link between the enlightened in the Old and New Worlds in the exchange of ideas and plants. He advised presidents and ex-presidents on the Indians and on the loyalty of the New England Federalists, on the resources of the western territories and on General Andrew Jackson's campaign in Florida. By 1817 Henry M. Brackenridge in dedicating his book, *Views of Louisiana*, to Correa could intelligibly conclude that the Abbé was "one of the most enlightened foreigners that has ever visited the United States." Americans "like the disciples of Socrates... treasure from your lips... the profound maxims upon every subject." All Correa's contributions to America's intellectual life, said Brackenridge, entitle Americans "to claim you as one of the fathers of our country."

With this kind of praise and adoration continually sweeping over him, it is not surprising that the Portuguese exile chose to remain in the United States for nearly nine years, even after it would have been politically possible for him to return to Europe. In 1816 the king of Portugal and the Brazils appointed Correa chief minister to the United States, and thereby fulfilled his lifelong ambition to represent his country abroad as a ranking diplomat. Everyone expected the ministry to be a cushy post for Correa; it would permanently fix the Abbé in America and at the same time not interfere with what Jefferson called his "botanical rambles." Jefferson believed that the assignment would be easy because Portugal was a peaceable nation that never quarreled with its friends. "If their minister writes them once a quarter that all is well, they desire no more." For his part

Correa avowed that he loved both countries equally, "a very rare phenomenon in diplomacy." He thought that he was in the unique position of being able to bring together what he always called the two great powers of the Western Hemisphere—the United States and Portuguese Brazil.

The reality could not have turned more differently from these inflated expectations. The colonial rebellions in Latin America changed Correa's position radically. With the memory of their own anti-colonial revolution and second war with Britain fresh in their minds, many Americans naturally supported these colonial rebellions against the monarchies of Spain and Portugal. American privateersmen, bearing rebel commissions and outfitted in American ports, preyed on Spanish and Portuguese ships—even in defiance of an American neutrality act passed in 1817. Correa, like the Spanish minister, protested vehemently to the United States government, but in vain. American public opinion was against the Old World monarchies and easily allowed the privateersmen and adventures to evade the neutrality legislation.

Correa thought the privateersmen were little better than pirates, and he called Baltimore, where much of the outfitting of the ships took place, "the Algerine city," in reference to the Mediterranean pirates who plundered the shipping of the Christian world. His views of America shifted. He became increasingly disgusted with the greed and materialism of American life, and in his official protests even referred to the American people as a "most unmanageable crew." By 1820 he had had enough. He was "most heartily tired of democratic society," he told an English friend. Do not believe half of what Americans "most ostentatiously publish and say of themselves," he warned. They were full of vanity and were as money-hungry and as rotten as the European states without the civilized polish and maturity of the Old World. He told the governor of Virginia that he would be "a fool" to remain any longer in the United States. And so after spending nearly nine years in the land that was the once-great hope of the Enlightenment, the old savant sailed back to Europe.

Richard Beale Davis has told the story of Correa's stay in America with his characteristic care and erudiction. Davis was born in 1907 and died in 1981 after a productive and illustrious career. He was very much a distinguished scholar of American letters. He wrote and edited a number of important works in early American history and literature, including a massive three-volume collection entitled *Intellectual Life in the Colonial South, 1585-1763* (1978). His study of the Abbé Correa da Serra in America initially appeared in the *Transactions* of the American Philosophical Society in 1955. The purpose of that study, he said, was "to examine Correa's career in America and to indicate its form, extent, and results in his years here." But Beale did more than that. Before 1955 few general histories of the early Republic had even mentioned Correa; even many specialists had known him only as the Portuguese minister in Washington who complained of American privateering. It is perhaps not too much to say that for American audiences at least, Beale rescued the Enlightenment figure of Correa from historical oblivion. Not only did Beale write an appreciative 85,000-word essay on Correa's career in America, but he followed that up with a richly annotated collection of letters that Correa wrote to Americans, or were written to him by Americans, or concerned him during his American years. In an appendix Beale has even added a checklist of Correa's letters written to foreigners during these years from 1812 to 1820.

All in all Beale offered us a fascinating entry into the hopeful and enlightened world of Jeffersonian America. We are indeed fortunate to have this modern reprint of this distinguished thirty-year-old work.

TRANSACTIONS

OF THE

AMERICAN PHILOSOPHICAL SOCIETY

HELD AT PHILADELPHIA

FOR PROMOTING USEFUL KNOWLEDGE

NEW SERIES—VOLUME 45, PART 2

1955

THE ABBÉ CORREA IN AMERICA, 1812-1820

THE CONTRIBUTIONS OF THE DIPLOMAT AND NATURAL PHILOSOPHER TO THE FOUNDATIONS OF OUR NATIONAL LIFE

Correspondence with Jefferson and Other Members
of the American Philosophical Society and
with Other Prominent Americans

RICHARD BEALE DAVIS

Professor of American Literature, University of Tennessee

THE AMERICAN PHILOSOPHICAL SOCIETY

INDEPENDENCE SQUARE

PHILADELPHIA 6

MAY, 1955

ACKNOWLEDGMENTS

The subject of this study had a wide variety of interests, a large number of friends and correspondents, many places of residence in the United States and Europe, and withal a long life. The natural result has been that materials of the study, the letters reproduced, and the notes were gathered from and through a considerable number of institutions and persons. It is my pleasant task here to acknowledge their assistance.

A generous grant from the American Philosophical Society during 1951–1952 made it possible to spend several months in Philadelphia, Washington, and New York in the search for and examination of the majority of the basic materials used in this study. The English Department of the University of Tennessee supplied secretarial aid for the preparation of the manuscript for publication.

On the right of the heading of each letter reproduced below there is given in abbreviated form the name of the repository in which the letter is located. The writer gratefully acknowledges the permission granted by each institution or person mentioned to publish these letters.

Professor Augusto de Silva Carvalho of Correa's own Academy of Sciences of Lisbon has been kind enough to read the text of the study (though not of the letters) and make helpful suggestions. Professor Carvalho's own study of Correa's European career and his intimate knowledge of the Portuguese materials have made his checking invaluable.

My graduate students, Eleanor D. Mitchell, Elizabeth C. Phillips, Jack E. Teagarden, and James H. Justus, have rendered valuable assistance by typing many letters and other documents from microfilm or photostat.

Other individuals who have given helpful advice or information include: Percy G. Adams, Eleanor Goehring, Charles E. Noyes, Albert Rapp, Royal E. Shanks, Aaron J. Sharp, and Nathalia Wright, University of Tennessee; Francisco Aguilera and Vincent L. Eaton,

Library of Congress; Francis L. Berkeley, Jr., and Edwin M. Betts, University of Virginia; George C. A. Boehrer, Marquette University; Irving Brant; Mina R. Bryan, Associate Editor of *The Papers of Thomas Jefferson;* Lyman H. Butterfield, formerly Director of the Institute of Early American History and Culture and now Editor of the Adams Papers; Manoel Cardozo, Catholic University of America; Leonidas Dodson and Robert C. Smith, University of Pennsylvania; Harold D. Eberlein, Philadelphia; Joseph Ewan and Thomas P. Govan, Tulane University; Lewis Hanke, University of Texas; Dumas Malone, Columbia University; M. E. Phillips and Venia T. Phillips, Academy of Natural Sciences of Philadelphia; Antony E. Raubitschek, Princeton University; W. C. Repetti, S. J., Georgetown University; José Honorio Rodriguez, Ministry of Education and Health, Rio de Janeiro; Fred Shelley, Maryland Historical Society; Frans Verdoorn, *Chronica Botanica,* Waltham, Mass.

The library staffs of the following institutions have also furnished much useful information: American Philosophical Society; Library of Congress; Georgetown University; Illinois Historical Society; Kentucky Historical Society; University of Kentucky; Library Company of Philadelphia, Ridgway Branch; Massachusetts Historical Society; National Archives; New-York Historical Society; New York Public Library; Historical Society of Pennsylvania; University of Pennsylvania; Union Theological Seminary, New York; Virginia State Library; University of Virginia; Historical Society of Western Pennsylvania; Wisconsin State Historical Society; Yale University; Biblioteca Nazionale Centrale, Florence; Bibliothèque Nationale and Institute of France, Paris; British Museum, Linnean Society, and Royal Society, London; National Maritime Museum, Greenwich.

R. B. D.

ABBREVIATIONS USED IN FOOTNOTES
FOR REFERENCES MOST FREQUENTLY CITED

Almost all other items are given in full first reference and abbreviated later in obvious forms, such as short titles or author. Most periodical titles are given in full in first reference, or in instances of very long titles, in unmistakable abbreviations. C refers to Correa da Serra, and TJ to Thomas Jefferson. Other personal names are given in full at least once in each note or series of notes.

AcNatSciPhila. Academy of Natural Sciences of Philadelphia.

APS. American Philosophical Society.

Appleton's CAB. Appleton's Cyclopaedia of American Biography, edited by James G. Wilson and John Fiske, New York, 1887–1889, 6 vols.

Biog.Dir.Cong. Biographical Directory of the American Congress, 1774–1927, Washington, 1927.

Biog.Univ. Biographie Universelle, Ancienne et Moderne, [J. F. and L. G. Michaud, edd.] Paris, 1811–1847, 8 vols.

DAB. Dictionary of American Biography, edited by Allen Johnson and Dumas Malone, New York, 1928–1936, 20 vols.

DNB. Dictionary of National Biography, edited by Leslie Stephen and Sidney Lee, London, 1885–1912, 63 vols. and supplements.

Em.Phila. The Lives of Eminent Philadelphians, Now Deceased, by Henry Simpson, Philadelphia, 1859.

Enc.Brit. Encyclopaedia Britannica, eleventh edition, Cambridge, 1910, 28 vols.

HistSocPenna. Historical Society of Pennsylvania.

LibCoPhila. Library Company of Philadelphia, Ridgway Branch.

L&B. The Writings of Thomas Jefferson, edited by Andrew A. Lipscomb and Albert E. Bergh, Washington, 1903–1904, 20 vols.

LC. Library of Congress, Division of Manuscripts.

LinnSoc, London. Linnean Society, London.

List Members APS. List of Members of the American Philosophical Society, Held at Philadelphia, for Promoting Useful Knowledge . . . January 17, 1890, in *Proceedings* of the APS, **27**: 121–200.

MassHistSoc. Massachusetts Historical Society.

NatArch. National Archives.

NCAB. National Cyclopaedia of American Biography. . . , New York, 1892–1945, 32 vols.

UPennaArch. University of Pennsylvania Archives.

UVa. Alderman Library, University of Virginia.

VaHistSoc. Virginia Historical Society.

VaStateLib. Virginia State Library, Division of Archives.

I. CORREA AND THE PERIOD IN AMERICA

In the city of New York on 3 July, 1812, at a fashionable boarding house, two distinguished Europeans dined together in leisurely fashion, discussing the world situation and especially their mutual acquaintance in France and England. One of them, the thirty-two-year-old Englishman, Augustus John Foster, had already spent five or six years in the United States in diplomatic capacities and was now about to embark for London. He was departing in irritation and frustration, partly because he had failed in accomplishment of his latest mission of preventing a war between his country and America. He had traveled and observed in the young nation, and except for a small area in the northeast he had seen little he could admire, in fact almost nothing intellectually and socially. Congenital and political Tory that he was, America was to him a land of louts and boors, where the scanty remnant of an earlier colonial culture was rapidly being obliterated by the growing power of the demagogues of democracy.[1]

Perhaps something of this bitter and critical attitude was expressed in the remarks the young man made to his table companion. If so, it was met urbanely or turned adroitly aside by the gentleman addressed, for the Abbé Correa da Serra was always able to control a conversation. And with such a feeling he certainly did not agree. This venerable Portuguese, now sixty-two years of age, had arrived in the New World just a few months before and was to remain almost nine years. Among other careers he too had followed diplomacy, and he was to do so once again. Now he was a private gentleman looking long and keenly at this

---

[1] MS. "Journal," LC; and Davis, R. B., ed., *Jeffersonian America: notes on the United States of America . . . by Sir Augustus John Foster, Bart.,* San Marino, Calif., Huntington Library, 1954.

strange land. Unlike Foster, he was a liberal persecuted in his native country for his alleged religious
opinions and very recently by Napoleon for his politics.
To him the United States was a land of shining hope,
and he had come with the avowed purpose of being
useful.

The contrast between the two men could be continued on many levels. The only part of America
Foster admired Correa found least admirable. For
many years at least Correa was to be as confident of
the nation's future greatness as Foster was cynical regarding the possibility. Rawness the old Portuguese
perceived as clearly as did his young British companion, but for Correa it was the rawness of fine materials ready to be fashioned. He would assist in the
process.

So came to the single-generation-old United States
one of the remarkable figures of his age. To the boast-
ful, brawling democracy which had not yet felt Sidney
Smith's searing sneer came a sophisticated European,
wise in judgment and experience and learned in the
older continent's most ancient humanism and most recent science. For Correa da Serra was far more than
political liberal and whilom diplomat. He brought with
him an international reputation as botanist, geologist,
antiquarian, and litterateur. Trained in theology and
political economy as well as history and science, he
hoped to employ all his talents.

It is the purpose of this study to examine Correa's
career in America and to indicate its form, extent, and
results in his years here. Though in general histories
of the period his name appears scarcely at all,[2] while

---

[2] E.g., Adams, Henry, *History of the United States of America during the administrations of Jefferson and Madison,* 9 v.,
New York, Scribners, 1931; and McMaster, John B., *A history of the people of the United States from the Revolution to*

he resided in the United States and for many years thereafter he was revered, quoted, and imitated by a remarkable number of citizens of many occupations and interests.

The European traveler in earlier nineteenth-century America is perhaps better known among us now than at any time since his own. The European immigrant of the post-Civil War period is equally familiar. We are highly conscious of the impressions, literary and racial, both have left of and on our civilization. But we know much less of the cultured and even distinguished European who came to live and work among us.

In Correa we have for study of this third type an excellent case history, admittedly in certain respects an unusual one. He came between the eighteenth-century foreigners who were here to watch and assist in the birth of a nation and the later analysts and critics of the diverse schools of Mrs. Trollope, Dickens, and Tocqueville. He came with a mind trained in the latest scientific developments, with a classical learning fruitful in published monographs, and with an urbane wit which had already enlivened and stimulated the society of London and Paris. What could this man contribute to a growing civilization which combined so confusingly frontier violence and sometimes demagogic democracy with the enlightened cosmopolitanism of cities like Philadelphia and the philosophical genius of men like Thomas Jefferson?

It was to Thomas Jefferson and his kindred spirits among the gentlemen of Philadelphia that Correa bore letters of introduction, and it was with their world that he was to identify himself. When his point of view

---

the Civil War, 8 v., New York, 1883–1913. Correa's name does not appear in the indices of either of these. Of course it does appear in all the diplomatic histories. See below.

was not Portuguese or European, it was almost always Jeffersonian. He came much later than Mazzei and Lafayette, and he stayed longer than du Pont de Nemours. By birth and nature an intensely patriotic Portuguese, through long years of education and living in Naples, Rome, London, and Paris he could and did view America with relatively little national bias. Though in his diplomatic capacity later on he was necessarily to see the United States in relation to his own country, usually he considered it in its present and future relation to his whole continent, or to the whole world. This alone made him almost unique among foreign sojourners in our midst in this first quarter of the nineteenth century.

The life and accomplishments of Correa da Serra have been traced in biographical dictionaries in England, France, and Portugal, in several of the learned journals of those nations, and in a full-length volume published in Lisbon in 1948.[3] With the exception of the last, however, very little space has been devoted to his American years. And even in this recent work only his letters to Portuguese officials and a few to personal friends give us a slight indication of his activities here. Believing that the story of Correa's nine years in this country is highly significant in the complete biography of a great man and almost equally significant in its reflection of and evidence of contribution to American life, the present writer is presenting his subject in two ways. First will be traced, usually chronologically, the pattern of his activities from 1812 to 1820, with a summarizing account of his earlier and later years in Europe, and a somewhat more extensive consideration of his influence provable and probable on science, political economy, and the humanities in this

---

[3] See ch. II and those following below for references to the important biographical sources.

country. The diplomatic side of his American career, the only portion of these years already adequately treated,[4] will be discussed briefly because it sheds light upon his other activities and thus is necessary to the rounded picture of the man. Second, some hundred letters between Correa and several of his friends of the Jefferson circle have been presented. In them the whole group appears most vividly and in the end most comprehensively. Here one may see these minds at work and may judge for himself the quality and product of their labor. These letters are easily as significant to an understanding of the native Jeffersonians as to the stranger among them.

This study was begun on the basis of a known dozen or two letters between Correa and Thomas Jefferson and Francis Walker Gilmer. Further investigation has been richly rewarding. Besides those letters actually printed here, many others to and concerning Correa have been discovered in this country and have formed much of the basis for this outline of his American career. For background and occasional commentary on the United States, letters and other documents now in London and Paris have been most useful.[5] Above all, the work published in 1948 by Professor Carvalho of Correa's own Portuguese [Lisbon] Academy of Sciences has been invaluable for its presentation of otherwise inaccessible primary materials and for its rigorous examination and correction of previous statements regarding the Abbé's European career.

---

[4] Agan, Joseph, Corrêa da Serra, *Penn. Mag. Hist. & Biog.* **49**: 1–43, 1925. This article is a detailed study of Correa as Portuguese minister to the United States.

[5] The location and full identification for both American and European correspondence are given in the references below.

II. CORREA'S LIFE IN EUROPE, 1750–1811

The bent of a man's career may start at birth, or perhaps before, and so it was with Joseph Francis Correa da Serra.[1] He was born at Serpa in Portugal on 6 June 1750, the son of a physician and lawyer who was also a small landowner and research scientist, and of a mother whose family apparently were persecuted for liberal opinions.[2] In 1756 the family were obliged to flee their native country because the elder Correa's scientific activities had incurred the displeasure of the Holy Office. Soon in Naples the boy was placed under the tutelage of the already famed Abbé Antonio Genovesi, eclectic philosopher and political economist of the school of Locke. At the same time he was introduced to the study of natural history by the botanist, Luis Antonio Verney. During these years he became

---

[1] The most recent, detailed, and scholarly study of Correa's life and work is *O abade Correia da Serra,* by Augusto da Silva Carvalho, Lisbon, Academy of Sciences, 1948. Professor Carvalho had studied and weighed previous biographical sketches and corrected and added from various Portuguese archives at his disposal. Other studies of Correa referred to most frequently in the present work are D'Almeida, D. François (not a very accurate biographer), Notice sur la vie et les travaux de M. Corréa de Serra, *Mémoires du Muséum d'Histoire Naturelle, par les professeurs de cet établissement* . . . **11** : 215–229, 1824; Henriques, Júlio A., José Francisco Correia da Serra, *Boletim da sociedade Broteriana* . . . , second ser., **2** : 84–125, 1923; Griffin, Martin I. J., Sketch of the Abbé Joseph Francis Corréa de Serra, A.D. 1750–1824, *Rec. Amer. Cath. Hist. Soc. Phila.* **14** : 129–140, 1903; *idem,* Abbé Corréa, priest ambassador of Portugal. . . , *Researches Amer. Cath. Hist. Soc. Phila.* **22** : 30–43, 1905; and the article by Joseph Agan mentioned in Ch. I, note 4, above. These studies are referred to hereafter by the surnames of the authors, with the short title of the journal in which published in the case of the two by Griffin.

[2] Carvalho, 7–8, 213; Agan, 4.

vitally interested in botany, and perfected himself in Greek, Arabic, and the Romance languages other than his own.[3] From Naples the young man moved on to Rome, where he continued his studies at several institutions including the University. By 1772 he was corresponding in Latin concerning botanical problems with the celebrated Linnaeus, Swedish founder of systematic botany.[4] In Rome, he met, perhaps for the second time, his compatriot, Don John Carlos of Braganza, second Duke of Lafoens, who was then and later to be his friend and patron, a member of the Portuguese royal family tremendously interested in the sciences.[5] By 1775 the young Correa had entered holy orders as presbyter, and had said his first mass at the Basilica of St. Peter in Rome. After defending theses in canon and civil law, he was granted the degree of Doctor of Laws in 1777. His most recent biographer suspects that the concentration on ecclesiastical studies was to protect himself in his scientific researches against any suspicions on the part of the Inquisition.[6]

Thus at twenty-seven the young priest faced the world with profound learning in several fields and with a powerful and enlightened patron. Apparently it was

---

[3] Henriques, 85, from M. da Costa e Sá's 1829 [published 1848] paper before the Société Philomatique of Paris.

[4] Carl von Linné, or Linnaeus (1707–1778). See C's letters of April, 1772, 14 Dec. 1773, and 22 Jan. 1774, LinnSoc, London.

[5] Duke John (1719–1806), the son of a brother of John V of Portugal, was a friend of savants all over Europe. He had observed scientific progress in Germany, Austria, England, France, Italy, and Sweden, and he had visited Egypt and the Middle East. C's later friend De Candolle (see below) was to state that the Duke had known C or his father at the University of Coimbra, and had been a friend of the father at least for some years. See Henriques, 85, 91. The sketch of the Duke in the *Biographie Universelle* is by C himself.

[6] Carvalho, 9.

Correa's already established reputation as a botanist which drew the Duke of Lafoens to him at this time. Don John, during a voluntary but prudent exile in many courts of Europe, had studied assiduously the progress of science and was determined that his own land should profit by what he had learned. The abilities and training of his young fellow-countryman might be most useful in developing the program of scientific research, of reform in education, and of the encouragement of letters [7] which he had in mind. The result of this thinking was that both were back in Portugal at the beginning of 1778.

Correa was almost immediately established in an ecclesiastical charge in the provinces, but he did not remain there long. Soon he removed to Lisbon to the ducal palace to work with Lafoens in organizing the scientific body they thought would be most effective. Their Royal Academy of Sciences of Lisbon, continuing its work in our day, received its charter on 24 December 1779. Its organization and statutes, according to at least one authority, were almost solely the work of Correa da Serra.[8] The Duke of Lafoens was, of course, its first president. Though it has been said that at its initial meeting the Academy elected Correa its perpetual secretary,[9] actually he was first vice-secretary, then secretary, but not at this time perpetual secretary.[10] During the next several years he was busy collecting terrestrial and aquatic plants and minerals for the museum the Academy had established. He also undertook botanical research on his own account, and by

---

[7] Figueiredo, Fidelino de, *Historiá Literária de Portugal,* seculos **12–20**: 289, Coimbra, Nobel, 1944.

[8] Henriques, 86.

[9] E.g., Almeida, 216.

[10] Carvalho, 13, 214. The Almanacs of the Academy for 1783 and 1785 list C as treasurer. Apparently he was not elected secretary until 1788.

1782 at least one plant had been named in his honor.[11]
Most biographical accounts have stated that Correa
fled to Paris in 1786 because of clerical hostility after
he published for the Academy several works of a decidedly liberal character.[12] It is now known that he
left Lisbon in February, 1786, and returned on 1 April,
1788, and that he had been at Rome, whence he brought
a letter of Pelerini to the Bishop Cenáculo.[13] But there
is no sure knowledge as to other places in which he
may have stayed. All agree that he was in his native

---

[11] *Ibid.,* 14. Between 1796 and 1798, C's name was used com-
memoratively in botanical nomenclature at least three times:
(*a*) Correia, Vellozo in Roemer, Script. 106. t. 6. 1796, in a
section of a work entitled *Florae Lusitanicae et Brasiliensis
specimen* with no mention of the commemorative nature of the
name as proposed by "Vellozo." This genus is today considered
a synonym of Ouratea (family Ochnaceae) of the tropics.
(*b*) Correa, Andrews, Bot. Repository, t. 8. 1798, where the
text accompanying the colored plate states "The [genus] Correa
is a native of Port Jackson, in New Holland, and commonly
termed a Botany-bay plant: it was first raised in the year 1793,
from seeds which were given by Sir Joseph Banks, Bart. . . .
It receives its generic title from Mr. Joseph Correa de Serra,
a native of Portugal; a gentleman of very distinguished talents
as a man of science in general, and botany in particular." (*c*)
Corraea, J. E. Smith, *Trans. Linn. Soc.* 4: 219, 1798. "Locus
Australasia./In honorem amici optimi, botani doctissimi, *Josephi
Correa de Serra,* J U D, SS. Reg. et Linn. Sodalis, hoc novum
et pulcherrimum dicavi genus, cum *Correia* Vandelli *Ochnae*
species est." Professor Joseph Ewan, who supplied these references to commemoratives, points out that "Vandelli" should be
corrected to read "Vellozo." This publication seems to support
the intent of Vellozo in 1796 to honor C, though V did not
specify the commemorative nature of the name. Smith established twenty new genera in this paper, half named for his
friends in the botanical heavens. For Smith and Banks, see the
present work below.

[12] E.g., Agan, 6 (following various authorities), and Almeida,
217. Lisbon directories 1786–1791 do not list him as resident.

[13] Professor Carvalho has given me advance notice that the
evidence for this will appear in his *Os primeiros anos da Acad-*

land between 1791 and 1795, beginning the editing of the monumental *Coleccão de Livros Ineditos de Historia Portugueza,*[14] and continuing his botanical activities.

But in the latter five years everything was not going well for the Academy. Despite the tokens of royal favor still heaped upon the Duke of Lafoens, the institution he had established met with a great deal of opposition from certain ecclesiastical groups and other conservative bodies. The liberalism of many of its members, in the light of what was going on in France, alarmed these supporters of the *status quo.* Correa made his personal position dangerous by his friendship for the French naturalist Broussonet,[15] who as a Girondist had taken refuge in Portugal in 1794.[16] Correa welcomed him as a friend of English botanists with whom he had corresponded, and entertained him hospitably. It was reported that Broussonet was housed in the Academy's own building, and that the secretary was protecting him and a number of other escaped Jacobins. Amid a great hue and cry Correa and his distinguished guest, evidently in considerable danger, fled south to Gibraltar. While Broussonet embarked for Morocco, the Abbé took ship for England, though he did not carry a passport or a license to leave Portugal. This was in 1795.[17]

---

emia Real das Sciencias, to be published by the Academy of Sciences of Lisbon.

[14] Begun in 1790, by 1824 the work had run to five volumes, of which C edited the first three (of 1790, 1792, and 1793). The great collection of documents has generally been praised as a work of real scholarship, though at least one contemporary criticized it quite severely. See Carvalho, 94, 205–207.

[15] Peter Marie Auguste Broussonet (1761–1807), physician and botanist. See *Enc. Brit.*

[16] Carvalho, 22–23. Broussonet had first fled to Spain. In both Spain and Portugal earlier French emigrants of the old regime were partly responsible for his persecution.

[17] *Ibid.,* 25–30. Apparently the Duke "covered up" for C in this precipitate flight and later had it regularized.

On the last day of September the refugee reached London.[18] From his fellows of the Academy he bore letters of introduction to several British scientists, among them Sir Joseph Banks and Dr. James Edward Smith, presidents respectively of the Royal Society and the Linnean Society. Correa was welcomed heartily by both men and soon elected a fellow of both institutions. To the societies' journals he contributed several articles, and with the two naturalists he formed lifelong friendships.[19] With Banks, as he was to do so often with congenial friends in America, the exile in 1796 made a botanical and geological excursion. This expedition to the Lincolnshire coast [20] resulted in one of Correa's papers for the *Philosophical Transactions* of the Royal Society.[21] When a scientific expedition was fitted out for a voyage to New Holland, it was Correa who found and recommended to Banks the naturalist for the expedition, a young Scot named Robert Brown.[22] With the later *Sir* James Edward Smith he discussed matters botanical for thirty-eight years, from London, Paris, Lisbon, and the United States. Other English scientists also appear in the letters of this period and indi-

[18] *Ibid.*, 32.

[19] See C's letters to Smith, 1795–1823, LinnSoc, London; and Smith, Edward, *Life of Sir Joseph Banks,* 231, London, John Lane, 1911.

[20] Smith, *Banks,* 231n.

[21] On the submarine forest on the east coast of England, *loc. cit.* **89**: 145–156. The original MS. is available at the Royal Society.

[22] Smith, *Banks,* 231. See also C's On the Doryanthus, a new genus of plants from New Holland, next akin to the Agave (read before the Linnean Society, 2 Dec. 1800), *Trans. Linn. Soc.* **6**: 211–213. For other articles of C's before this society, see Carvalho, 95 (in which there are some errors in page reference). For the later fame of Robert Brown, see ch. V, below. C and Banks were still discussing Brown's achievements and general botanical matters in 1810. See Banks to C, 7 April 1810, Gray Herbarium, Harvard University.

cate a wide acquaintance and an eminently respectable position in the London intellectual world.

But Correa during these years was by no means absorbed exclusively in British friends and British science. An extensive correspondence with friends at home in Portugal, especially with D. Rodrigo de Sousa Coutinho,[23] indicates the exile's continuing and enormous interest in bringing the latest fruits of world progress to the attention of the Portuguese Academy and the Portuguese nation. New maritime maps, the methods for inoculation of the cow-pox, and agricultural husbandry were discussed at length. The latest scientific precision instruments in medicine, navigation, and astronomy in some instances were prepared for shipment; in others they were simply suggested as desirable. Long detailed catalogues of instruments, with prices attached, show that Correa was interested in procuring for Portugal such things as micrometers, theodolites, achromatic telescopes, threshing machines, various types of ploughs, and "Engines for watering gardens." The names of trees and smaller plants which might be useful appear in almost every letter. Correa's exile was thus in some measure most fortunate for Portugal.

All of Correa's friends were not out of power in Lisbon, for on 18 April, 1801, through de Sousa Coutinho, the Abbé was named Counselor of Legation and "Agente dos Negocios" for Portugal in London. Though this was a deserved recognition for his patriotic services, to Correa the appointment brought little but

---

[23] De Sousa Coutinho was an honorary fellow of the Academy, Minister of Marine, and president of the Royal Treasury. Other correspondents in this period were Bishop Cenaculo and Dr. Felix de Avelar Brotero, the naturalist. The highly interesting letters to this group are reproduced in Carvalho, 116–154, from Portugese archives.

trouble. For D. Lourenço de Lima, of a conservative family long enemies of the liberal scientist and all he stood for, was named Minister to England. After only a few months under a superior who hated him, Correa wrote to Dr. James Edward Smith:

About my Excellency and my diplomacy i cannot tell you, but there is no unluckier fatality than after being six years out of Portugal in peace, to fall again in (the) clutches of the same family who had driven me from my country, after having brought me to madness and lunacy. All the ancient hatred sanctified in their eyes by the motives you know, without any scruple about the means for the same reason, are and have been exerted by this monster of Ambassador, to effect my ruin either by sending me back to Portugal, where the Duke of Lafoens is now in disgrace, or in England if he can. I have been for many weeks al[most?] driven to madness living the greater part of my time with him, and have afterward left him and given my resignation which he did not choose to accept, b[ut?] i have sent it directly to Portugal. He is the son [of?] the Marquis of Ponte de Lima, cousin of the Grand Inquisitor. I am my dear friend in the situation of Laocoon when encircled and torn by the serpent an[d?] this is a poisonous one. . . .[24]

Correa had to struggle with his serpent for several more months, but eventually he escaped in the only way that seemed possible. On 31 March, 1802, he was still in London, but by 11 June he had established himself in Paris.[25] Here on the Seine he found a more salubrious climate, the marvelously enlarged Jardin des Plantes and the great circle of naturalists connected with it, stimulating conversation, and new sights and sounds, all together making him feel that in the Champs Elysées, near which he lived, he had indeed reached the

---

[24] C to Smith, London to Norwich, [15?] September 1801, LinnSoc, London.

[25] Two letters to de Sousa Coutinho of these dates are reproduced in Carvalho, 153-155.

Elysian Fields. "I have come to lie on your flowers," he informed his friend, the celebrated Jussieu.[26] And here too he believed that he could be even more useful to Portugal than he had been in England.[27]

Soon he was deep in a variety of researches which ranged from humanistic studies such as the history of the Templars [28] to agricultural and pure botany.[29] The circle of his friends included the immortals Jussieu, Cuvier, and von Humboldt, shining names [30] in the

---

[26] The Richmond *Virginia Argus,* 18 May 1816, 2 : no. 17, 3, col. 5.

[27] Carvalho, 155.

[28] C himself was a Knight of the Order of Christ, the successor to the Templars in Portugal, from 1807 (Carvalho, 42, 49) and was subsequently to be a Knight of two other orders (*idem,* 99). Later he was to publish Sur les vrais successeurs des Templiers et sur leur état actuel, *Arch. Litt. de l'Europe* **8** : 273 ff. For other articles by C in the *Archives* on the Arabs in Spain and the state of sciences and letters in Portugal see Almeida, 221 ff. and Carvalho, 96.

[29] The results of some of his botanical observations were published in *Ann. Mus. Hist. Nat.* and *Bull. Soc. Philom.* See Almeida, 221 ff. and Carvalho, 95–96. He contributed also to the *Magasin encyclopèdique* and the *Mem. Soc. d'Agricult.,* according to a letter to the present writer from the librarian of the French Institute of May, 1949.

[30] Antoine Laurent de Jussieu (1748–1836), professor of botany at the Museum of Natural History, issued his *Genera plantarum secundum ordines naturales disposita* . . . in 1789, the basis of modern classificatiōn. Alexander von Humboldt (1769–1859), German naturalist and father of physical geography and modern meteorology, had returned to Europe from his South American exploration in 1804 and, after several visits, settled in Paris in 1808. Except for Napoleon, he was then the most famous man in Europe. Georges Léopold Chrétien Frédéric Dagobert, Baron Cuvier (1769–1832), zoologist, was from 1799 professor of natural history in the Collège de France, in 1802 titular professor in the Jardin des Plantes, and in 1803 perpetual secretary of the National Institute in the department of physical and natural science. His five-volume *Leçons d'anatomie comparée* is a classic.

progress of modern physical and biological science. The somewhat younger botanist Augustine Pyrame de Candolle [31] relates that Correa, with von Humboldt and Cuvier, came often to his house. De Candolle watched the three at his little dinners, and noticed the deference with which the German and the Frenchman listened to the Abbé's observations. Correa, his host observed, never did his own abilities justice in print, but in oral comment he was easily and acknowledgedly superior to the greatest of his fellow naturalists.[32] Equally often Correa visited Andre Thouin,[33] keeper of the Jardin des Plantes.

To balance the scientists, the Abbé numbered among his political and humanistic friends the Marquis de Lafayette, Pierre Samuel du Pont de Nemours, and the Americans Fulwar Skipwith, Joel Barlow, and David B. Warden.[34] Correa's astonishing memory, his travels, and his amusing anecdotes and epigrams made him a remarkable social as well as scientific conversationalist. All Paris was full of his *mots heureux*.[35]

---

[31] 1778-1841. He was a Swiss who moved to Paris in 1796. His *Principes élémentaires de botanique* (1803) explained his "natural" system of classification as opposed to the Linnean or "artificial" method. Apparently its publication had been through C's encouragement (Carvalho, 105–106). He was a professor at Montpellier from 1807 and moved to Geneva in 1816.

[32] Henriques, 91, *Mémoires et souvenirs de Augustin-Pyramus de Candolle . . . ,* 163–164, Paris, 1862. See also C to Robert Brown, 30 Oct. 1811 (Carvalho, 162), in which he says Jussieu and de Candolle are of his "most habitual company."

[33] 1747-1823? See C to TJ, 6 March 1812, note 1, below. C was also gracious to visiting American naturalists. See William Dandridge Peck's Diary, 1806–1808, Widener Library Archives, item HUG 1677, Harvard U., for C's kindness to Peck.

[34] For C's relation with these men and the necessary identification of them, see letters and notes below.

[35] Almeida, 218–219.

The ten years spent in the City of Light were on the whole busy, happy ones. Recognition came from his own government in 1807 when he was made a Knight of the Order of Christ,[36] and from the French savants in his election to the Société Philomatique of Paris and, as a corresponding member, to the class of history and ancient literature of the French Institute.[37] The fruits of his studies in botany, zoology, history, and biography appeared in a variety of journals.[38] And he formed a romantic attachment with a much younger Frenchwoman, Esther Delavigne, a matter which was to be of considerable concern in his later American years.

But the Parisian Elysian Fields were not a paradise for any European liberal, for Napoleon was there. Correa's old enemies at home were actually in league with the dictator and were attempting to swing their country into his orbit.[39] As early as 1808 Correa suggested to his friend the American consul that he hoped his services might be useful to the United States, and that he would like to be invited thither.[40] Though nothing appears to have come of the suggestion then, three years later the matter was more urgent.

The events compelling his departure Correa apparently recounted to a friend in America some time later.

---

[36] See note 28, above.

[37] C was elected a correspondent of the Institute on 11 December 1807 in the class mentioned; in 1816, on the reorganization of the Institute, he was elected a correspondent of the Academy of "Inscriptions and Belles-Lettres." See letter to the writer from the Librarian of the Institute de France, May, 1949.

[38] See the bibliographies in Carvalho and Almeida, cited above.

[39] See Carvalho, 43–44. Particularly was D. Lourenço de Lima involved.

[40] C to Fulwar Skipwith, 4 Sept. 1808, below.

At the period of the third invasion of Spain and Portugal by the French in 1811, when Bonaparte was anxious to reconcile the people of the two nations to the new domination,[41] the Emperor caused it to be intimated to the exile that some essay from his pen favoring the new rule would be most agreeable. When the patriotic Abbé spurned the proposal, a second intimation was that he leave France.[42] Probably other factors entered into the departure at the end of 1811,[43] but the important fact is that he was soon ready to sail for America, a passenger on an American warship.

During the last months in France he was principally occupied in rounding up his affairs, but he did find time to contribute several sketches to the first volumes of Michaux's *Biographie Universelle*.[44] He received from his friends a bundle of flattering letters of introduction to citizens of the United States. In almost every case the European illustrious were addressing the American illustrious. As was to be expected, the French liberals and scientists wrote to kindred spirits in the New World. Thus armed, by the end of December the Abbé was aboard the *U.S.S. Constitution* [45] and on his way to a most interesting period of his career.

---

[41] The French had undertaken invasions of Portugal earlier in 1807 and 1809.

[42] The *Virginia Argus*, 18 May 1816 (see note 26 above), in an article on C's botanical lectures in Philadelphia, probably by Francis Walker Gilmer.

[43] Carvalho, 47. Augustus John Foster states (2 March 1812, "Journal," LC), however, that C "escaped from Paris."

[44] Carvalho, 44–45. See also note 5 above.

[45] Various letters of introduction give varying dates for C's departure from Paris, ranging from 11 December (du Pont to TJ, 20 December 1811, in Chinard, G., ed., *Correspondence of Jefferson and Du Pont de Nemours,* 178, Baltimore, Johns Hopkins, 1931) to 26 December (Lafayette to TJ, 26 December 1811, LC, TJ Papers). See also Carvalho, 215. For the date of actual sailing see ch. III, just below.

III. PERIPATETIC PHILOSOPHER IN AMERICA, 1812–1816

FIRST YEARS IN PHILADELPHIA

The famous frigate which carried Correa da Serra as passenger sailed straight for the Virginia capes, its first port being Norfolk, Virginia. Here on 21 February the Abbé left the ship,[1] probably proceeding at once by smaller vessel to the new capital, for it is in Washington that we have the first record of his appearance in the United States.[2] On 2 March he called upon Foster, the British minister, and within a few days was seen in the drawing rooms of General and Mrs. Samuel Smith and Madame Jerome Bonaparte, née Betsy Patterson.[3] In the same week he dined with Chief Justice Marshall and Bushrod Washington, both of the Supreme Court. But in this debut Correa was

---

[1] A list of passengers of the *Constitution* dated at Cherbourg 6 January 1812 includes C's name. The vessel did not sail until 9 January. It reached Norfolk on 19 February, and the log for 21 February shows that on that date several passengers (no names given) left the ship. Since the *Constitution* did not proceed to the Washington Navy Yard until 25 March, it may be assumed that C disembarked at Norfolk on the date indicated. See NatArch.

[2] It has been stated that C visited this country earlier, in 1797, with the Polish patriot, Kosciusko (Agan, 7; Griffin, *Records,* 129). He is supposed to have remained until 1798. Sources are not given for the statement, and actually C's letters of 23 March 1797, 31 Oct. 1797, 1 June 1798, and possibly 7 May 1798, all from London (Carvalho, 66, 117–120, 121–122, and LinnSoc, London) seem to preclude the probability or even possibility of his having visited America at this time. Nowhere has the present writer discovered references in his letters to an earlier acquaintance with the United States than that which began in 1812.

[3] General Smith (1752–1839), U. S. Senator 1804–1815, 1822–1827, had married an aunt of Elizabeth Patterson Bonaparte, the Baltimore belle. For Smith, see *DAB.*

in general disappointed by the provinciality of republican society. And when the carriage Foster had lent him overturned one night on a dark and muddy street [4] he formed an impression of Washington he was never to erase, though he admired other American cities.

But it was in the capital that he delivered the first of his credentials. Probably most important as an entree was his letter from Joel Barlow, New England poet who was the American minister in Paris, to President James Madison. Barlow observed the pattern of all these introductions in stressing Correa's "learning & science," his amiability, and his membership in "most of the learned societies of Europe." He also affirmed that he had known Correa for many years.[5] Through Madison's Secretary of the Treasury, Albert Gallatin, Correa forwarded the first letter written by himself, with an enclosure, to Thomas Jefferson.[6] For the time he retained the letters addressed to the former president from Lafayette, von Humboldt, Thouin, and du Pont.[7]

But as these last letters show that he had always planned, Correa first had to establish himself in Philadelphia. To Foster he explained that he must go there to await the orders of his king, an indication that even thus early he hoped to obtain some official diplomatic post under his own government. Of course the repu-

---

[4] For the record of C in Washington, 2–6 March, see "Journal," Sir Augustus John Foster, LC. The record of the dinner with Foster and the two Justices appears in Foster's *Jeffersonian America, loc. cit.,* 68.

[5] December 1811, LC.

[6] For Gallatin (1761–1849), see *DAB.* Gallatin's letter to TJ, 10 March 1812, LC, incloses C's of 6 March, below.

[7] Lafayette to TJ, 26 December 1811; von Humboldt, 20 December 1811; Thouin, 7 December 1811, all in TJ Papers, LC. Du Pont to TJ, 20 Dec. 1811, reproduced in Chinard, ed., *Jefferson-DuPont Corresp.,* 178.

tation of the city as a center of culture was most important in his decision to settle there. He had probably heard a great deal about it from François-André Michaux, who had botanized with his more famous father in America until 1805; from David B. Warden, the learned American consul in Paris who had succeeded Skipwith; and from J. Dauxion de Lavaysse, traveler and observer who had left America only two years before. All three of these men were anxious that Philadelphia should welcome the Abbé. Warden wrote to Dr. Caspar Wistar that Correa, already known to the physician-naturalist by reputation, should be made at once a member of the American Philosophical Society if he were not so already.[8] Lavaysse addressed the equally well known Dr. Benjamin Rush concerning his venerable friend.[9] And Michaux wrote to John Vaughan, genial and hospitable librarian of the American Philosophical Society.[10] Vaughan had also been informed earlier of Correa's coming by Henri Grégoire, Parisian revolutionist and former bishop who was a patron of many artists and men of letters.[11] It is not without significance that all three of the Philadelphians addressed were longstanding friends of Thomas Jeffer-

---

[8] 4 December 1811, APS. For C's return of the favor to Warden, see C's letters to TJ and James Madison, below.

[9] 17 December 1811, LibCoPhila. Lavaysse (c. 1770–1826) had traveled in Central and South America as well as North America. His *Voyage aux îles de Trinidad, de Tabaco, de la Marguerite, et dans diverses parties de Vénézuéla, dans l'Amérique Méridionale,* 2 v., was published in Paris in 1813. See *La Vie americaine de Guillaume Merle d'Aubigné, extraits de son journal de voyage et de sa correspondance inédite 1809–1817. Avec une introduction et des notes par* Gilbert Chinard, 144, note 91, Baltimore, Johns Hopkins, 1935. Dr. Rush died in 1813.

[10] December [1811?]. Received 10 March 1812, APS.

[11] 4 Oct. 1811, APS. For Grégoire (1750–1831) see *Enc. Brit.*

son. But they also represented various facets of their city's educational, scientific, business, and social life.

Thus favorably predisposed, the old Portuguese and the metropolis of the New World took a liking to each other which was to endure for the rest of the Abbé's life. He was cordially welcomed by everyone he met. In this city of physicians and naturalists, Quakers and Episcopalians and Catholics, merchant princes and European-born cosmopolites, he at once made himself at home. He discovered that he was already a member of America's most distinguished learned academy, for he had on 17 January been elected to the American Philosophical Society.[12]

Although Dr. Rush died the following year, in Wistar and Vaughan Correa found congenial and lasting friends. Dr. Wistar, soon to succeed Jefferson as president of the American Philosophical Society, was already known to Correa as a botanist and as Professor of Anatomy in the University of Pennsylvania.[13] His home was a rendezvous of the learned and the elegant. The two elderly scientists were soon intimate. The Abbé is said to have taken tea at Wistar's house at least once a week, whenever he was in Philadelphia, until the physician's death in 1818. Together they made several botanical excursions and a visit to Mr.

---

[12] See MS. Minutes of the APS. Unfortunately, the records do not, in this case, as they do in others, include names of sponsors or reasons for nomination. As noted above, Warden's letter to Dr. Wistar of 4 Dec. 1811 suggests that C be elected to membership if he is not already a member. Barlow's letter of 5 Dec. to Madison, however, states that C is then a member of the learned society "of Philadelphia." Presumably Barlow knew that C had been nominated for membership.

[13] See C to Wistar, 27 Sept. 1813, note 1; and 31 Dec. 1817, both below.

Jefferson.[14]   It was the Abbé who wrote, in French, a "Necrologie" of its former president for the American Philosophical Society.[15]   And it was probably Correa who suggested to Thomas Nuttall that the latter name the plant *Wistaria* in honor of their departed friend.[16]

John Vaughan, English-born librarian of the American Philosophical Society and Philadelphia man of affairs, had a genius for friendship and hospitality.[17] Though he had no real scientific achievement to his credit, he was a friend of the learned in both hemispheres.   Brother of the more famous Benjamin and William Vaughan,[18] he conversed with the Abbé about mutual friends and acquaintances in England and France.   Soon he was handling Correa's business affairs and advising him in many matters.   Relations between these two remained cordial and intimate long after Correa had cooled towards many of the more eminent.   Just a year before he died Correa was still corresponding with this Philadelphian.

Quietly the old Portuguese became a part of the

---

[14] See [anon.], The Wistar musum of anatomy, *Penn. Mag. Hist. & Biog.* **18**: 90–96, 1894; C to F. W. Gilmer, 21 July 1816, UVa; F. W. Gilmer to William Wirt, 29 August 1816, Va. State Lib.

[15] [April] 1818, now in APS.   See also C to Mrs. Caspar Wistar, 31 Jan. 1818, below.

[16] See Oberholtzer, E. P., *Philadelphia, a history of the city and its people, a record of two hundred and twenty-five years* . . . , 4 v., **2**: 115n, Philadelphia, S. J. Clarke, [1912].   C's protégé, the botanist, Thomas Nuttall, actually named the plant in 1818.   See *DAB,* Wistar and Nuttall.   Oberholtzer and others give C credit for naming it, without mentioning Nuttall.

[17] 1756–1841.   *Em. Phila.;* Sheppard, J. H., Reminiscences and genealogy of the Vaughan family, *New Eng. Hist. & Gen. Mag.* **19**: 343–356, 1865.

[18] For the two brothers, see *DNB* and letters from C and Edward Correa, 1821–1822, below.

city's life. By 20 March he was attending the meetings of the American Philosophical Society. From that time until a few days before he left America in 1820, he was a regular attendant upon its sessions.[19] Within a year he was a member of various committees appointed to comment upon or to decide the acceptability for publication of many papers read before the Society. Apparently he was considered an authority on soils, fossils, archaeological remains, and Bacon's philosophy, as well as on his favorite botany. Enthusiastic botanists like Zaccheus Collins and William Maclure became his intimates. To another society in which these latter two were much interested, the Academy of Natural Sciences of Philadelphia, he was elected on 8 February 1814. In this organization also he was most active, advising, donating to its museum and library, and often acting as presiding officer.[20] But more of these things later.

It was perhaps through these groups of professional and amateur scientists that Correa came into contact with the literary gentlemen of the city. One of his early friends was the litterateur, Nicholas Biddle, former Jeffersonian diplomatic appointee in Paris, and al-

---

[19] See Early proceedings of the American Philosophical Society . . . from the manuscript minutes of its meetings from 1744 to 1838, *Proc. Amer. Philos. Soc.* 22 (119) : 1–711, 1885. Since the dates in this printed work are sometimes inaccurate, they should always be checked by the MS. Minutes. Though C's name appears in the Minutes scores of times, he may actually have been present on other occasions, for entries frequently list as present a few names with such an additional comment as "and 11 others." References to C's activities in the Society will be to the printed version, for the sake of convenience, unless otherwise specified.

[20] See the Minutes of the Academy of Natural Sciences of Philadelphia, now in its Library, from 19 April 1814 through 3 Oct. 1820, including documents reproduced below, for a record of C's activity in the sessions of the Academy.

FIG. 2. Robert Walsh, Jr., by Thomas Sully, from the portrait in the National Gallery of Art, Washington, D. C.

most surely known to Correa in former years. Biddle had a law practice for some time, but during much of this period he was editor of Philadelphia's literary magazine, *The Port-Folio*. Correa visited the Biddle family in the city and at their country home, "Andalusia." A series of charming notes exchanged by the two men in the 1812–1815 period attests to real intimacy and warm affection on both sides, and indicates that the elderly Abbé was a favorite with both the Biddle children and Biddle's mother-in-law, the lovely Mrs. Craig.[21] To Biddle and another young literary Philadelphian, Robert Walsh, Correa was to refer as "my children." [22]

The Abbé must have met Robert Walsh, Jr., in 1812 at a "Wistar party." Both had been elected to the American Philospohical Society on the same date. Walsh, Baltimore-born Catholic who had married into the wealthy Philadelphia Catholic family of Moylan, had already made a name for himself at home and abroad as a political critic.[23] He had edited two volumes of the *American Register* (**6**, 1809; **7**, 1810) and by October, 1812, had completed the four volumes of the first standard quarterly in this country, the *American Review of History and Politics.* His political attitude up to this time was strongly Federalist, pro-British, and anti-French. Now began a relationship which was to affect both lives for the next six years. Correa contributed to the last issue of Walsh's *Review* an essay, "General Considerations upon the Past and Future State of Europe," actually at this time only a discussion of the *Past.*[24] Later, in 1813, Correa concluded his survey in "An Essay on the Future State of Europe," this time included in *Correspondence Re-*

---

[21] Nicholas Biddle (1786–1844) had served in the Paris legation 1804–1807. He married in 1811. Notes between C and Biddle, now in LC, are in several cases undated. Dated exchanges include C to NB, 28 May [1813 or 1815]; 7 July 1813; [5 September 1813]; 9 Sept. 1813; 29 Sept. 1813; NB to C, 7 July 1813. See also C to NB, 8 Sept. 1813, and NB to C, 8 Oct. 1813, both below.

[22] C to John Vaughan, 27 Sept. 1813, APS.

[23] For Walsh (1784–1859), see Sister M. Frederick Lochemes, *Robert Walsh: his story,* New York, Amer. Cath. Hist. Soc., 1941.

[24] **4**: 354–366, 1812. For further discussion, see ch. V, below.

specting Russia, between Robert Goodloe Harper, Esq., and Robert Walsh, Jun. . . ." [25]

The two were seen frequently together. James Ogilvie, Scottish orator and philosopher [26] who was visiting in Philadelphia in February, 1814, contrasts them. Ogilvie, a friend and protégé of Jefferson, may have been prejudiced by Walsh's earlier political views and continual harping on one string—the danger to the world of a particular tyrant.

By the way I cannot omit to mention, that a few days before I left Philadelphia I spent an evening at Doctor Wistar's in company with two persons who exhibited a very singular contrast, Corriere, an old Portuguese gentleman, & Robert Walsh.. Were I in possession of St. Leon's Elixir, Corriere if he pleased might empty the mystic phial, provided he would pour it down his own throat, but much as I respect him, I would not permit him to give one drop of it to Walsh. Corriere has all the wisdom of age without one particle of the garrulity; Walsh has the garrulity without the wisdom. Amongst the assembled sages of the world, Corriere would be respectable, in that assembly too Walsh would shatter & remind them that wisdom "was the gray hair of man." This little literary cuckoo has added a vanity to the "Cries of Linden" Bonaparte, Bonaparte, Bonaparte—I am sick & the public is sick of his monotonous tone. . . .[27]

Apparently Correa was not bothered by Walsh's idiosyncrasies, for the two soon made excursions together to visit Jefferson [28] and some years later were actually to live together in the same house. Gradually,

---

[25] Philadelphia, printed by William Fry. See ch. V, below.

[26] See *DAB* and Davis, R. B., James Ogilvie, an early American teacher of rhetoric, *Quart. Jour. Speech* **28**: 289–297, 1942.

[27] To F. W. Gilmer, 4 Feb. 1814, UVa, reproduced in Davis, R. B., *Francis Walker Gilmer: life and learning in Jefferson's Virginia*, 384, Richmond, Va., Dietz, 1939.

[28] Walsh also began an excursion to Kentucky with C in 1814, but was obliged to turn back when he had traveled only as far as Chambersburg, Pennsylvania. See below.

perhaps owing largely to Correa's influence, Walsh became Republican in his sympathies. He named a son for Correa, and the two names have come down together to the twentieth century.

Other friends represented other interests, and the relationships were primarily social. In these years Correa saw a great deal of William Short, Virginian who had been Jefferson's private secretary in Paris and had returned to the United States in 1810 after a brilliant but personally disappointing career as a diplomat.[29] Correa had almost surely known Short, as he had Biddle in Paris. Now the Virginian had settled in Philadelphia and was beginning to amass his great fortune through land speculation. For Correa he wrote letters of introduction to friends and relatives on the frontier, and over many years he kept Jefferson informed as to the Abbé's activities.[30]

Old Philadelphia families such as the Logans, the Merediths, and the Hopkinsons found in Correa an urbane gentleman who could hold his own in any company.[31] George Ticknor, later the distinguished Spanish scholar but then a young man on a southern tour just before his departure for Europe and German schol-

---

[29] See *DAB* and Short Papers, LC.

[30] No known letters between C and Short survive. For mention of C, see TJ and Short Papers, LC, several quoted below. For Short's kindness, see C to John Vaughan, 20 Aug. 1814, below.

[31] See Diary of Deborah Logan, 11 March 1815, Hist. Soc. Penna., for C's visit with Walsh, and Eberlein, H. D., and H. M. Lippincott, *The colonial homes of Philadelphia,* 207, Philadelphia, Lippincott, 1912. For the Merediths, see Wright, Fanny, *Views of society and manners in America by an Englishman,* New York, 1821, which describes a conversation with C. A marginal note in the LibCoPhila copy of Wright says it occurred at "Mrs. Meredith's." For the Hopkinsons' society, see just below.

arship, described a party at Joseph Hopkinson's in which the Abbé was the center of attention:

At their table I met one day a party of eleven or twelve gentlemen. Amongst them were Mr. Randolph, the Abbé Correa, Dr. Chapman, and Mr. Parish. It was an elegant dinner, and the conversation was no doubt worthy of such guests; but one incident has overshadowed the rest of the scene. The Abbé Correa—who was one of the most remarkable men of the time, for various learning, acuteness, and wit, and for elegant suave manners—had just returned from a visit to Mr. Jefferson, whom he much liked, and, in giving some account of his journey, which on the whole had been agreeable, he mentioned that he had been surprised at not finding more gentlemen living on their plantations in elegant luxury, as he had expected. It was quietly said, but Randolph could never endure the slightest disparagement of Virginia, if ever so just, and immediately said, with some sharpness, "Perhaps, Mr. Correa, your acquaintance was not so much with that class of persons." Correa, who was as amiable as he was polite, answered very quietly,—"Perhaps not; the next time I will go down upon the Roanoke, and I will visit Mr. Randolph and his friends." Mr. Randolph, who was one of the bitterest of men, was not appeased by this intended compliment, and said, in the sharpest tones of his high-pitched, disagreeable voice, "In *my* part of the country, gentlemen commonly wait to be *invited* before they make visits." Correa's equanimity was a little disturbed; his face flushed. He looked slowly round the table till every eye was upon him, and then replied, in a quiet, level tone of voice,— "Said I not well of the *gentlemen* of Virginia?" There was a pause, for every one felt embarrassed; and then a new subject was started. Many years afterwards Mr. Walsh told me that Randolph never forgot or forgave the retort.[32]

But Randolph was neither a Philadelphian nor a real Jeffersonian, and many similar dinner parties among these people Correa was to enjoy without the necessity of exercising his gift of stinging yet suave rejoinder.

---

[32] Hillard, George S., *et al., The life letters and journals of George Ticknor*, 2 v., 1: 16, Boston, 1876.

One cannot doubt the sincerity of the Abbé's remark to Dr. Wistar just a year after his arrival that "i find no spot except Paris more to my taste than your friendly city.[33]

SEEING THE UNITED STATES

Correa da Serra had lived too long and seen too much, however, to be content with knowing and doing only in hospitable Philadelphia. The first brief overland journey from Washington must have convinced him that there was much more to be observed and experienced in this great sprawling land. Thomas Jefferson, the northern lakes, the Indians, the wild frontier, a variety of climates and plants, the New England Puritan and the Southern slave-holder, these were things any European of his intellectual curiosity would yearn to know. One of the remarkable achievements of the career of this sixty-two-year-old chronic invalid —his health is mentioned in almost every other letter— is that he set out to see all these things, and did. By traveling for a few months of each of his first four years in America, despite the real hardships of the road, this stout-hearted old man saw more of the United States than all but a handful of her citizens did in a lifetime.

Quite characteristically he was attracted first by natural wonders. With a visit to Niagara as his goal, he started north from Philadelphia on 28 June 1812.[34] In the city of New York he paused for a week to enjoy again the company of Augustus John Foster, for war had been declared and Foster was awaiting the ship which would return him to England. There Correa dined with the British envoy several times, and

---

[33] 27 Sept. 1813, letter below.
[34] Z. Collins to H. Muhlenberg, 7 July 1812, HistSocPenna, and C to de Brito, 11 Oct. 1812, Carvalho, 164–166.

saw something of Richard Soderstrom, the Swedish consul general.[35] He then journeyed on through New York State and Vermont to the borders of Canada, pausing at Lake George and probably at several other beautiful or botanically interesting spots.[36] By 11 October he had returned as far as New York City again, and before the fifteenth was in Philadelphia,[37] having covered, he boasted to a friend in Paris, 346 leagues. The visit to Niagara was rendered impossible by the war, he added regretfully.[38] But he was able to report to Philadelphia botanists something of the flora of the Lake George and Ballstown regions.[39]

By early January, 1813, Correa informed these scientific gentlemen and other friends that his health was so precarious in this American climate, and his financial affairs so involved because of the war, that he had resolved to return to Europe, probably in the summer.[40] In June he was making arrangements for the voyage, but had decided to visit "the great the truly great Mr. Jefferson" before he sailed. Out of consideration for the Abbé's slender purse, Jefferson had sent him a list of inns in which he might lodge on the journey to Virginia.[41] The Abbé left Philadelphia about 9 July and had departed from Monticello on the return before 17 August.[42]

---

[35] See "Journal," LC, and *Jeffersonian America* of Sir Augustus John Foster. C remained in New York at least from 3 to 10 July.

[36] C to de Brito, 11 Oct. 1812, Carvalho, 164–166, and Z. Collins to H. Muhlenberg, 9 Jan. 1813, HistSocPenna.

[37] Z. Collins to H. Muhlenberg, 15 Oct. 1812, HistSocPenna.

[38] C to de Brito. See note 36 above.

[39] Z. Collins to H. Muhlenberg, 23 Aug. 1813, HistSocPenna.

[40] *Idem* to *idem*, 18 Jan. 1813, HistSocPenna.

[41] C to de Brito, 5 June 1813, Carvalho, 170–174. This letter, dated from New York, seems to indicate C's June visit in that city.

[42] C to N. Biddle, 7 July 1813, and Biddle to C, same date,

With him to Virginia Correa carried the letters of
introduction from Lafayette, du Pont, Thouin, and von
Humboldt. What these four had to say must have
been most interesting to the retired statesman just now
beginning to recultivate his own intellectual garden.
Lafayette and du Pont warmly recommended their distinguished friend to Jefferson's acquaintance, with a
recapitulation of the honors the Abbé had received.
Jefferson's old friend and correspondent, Thouin of
the Jardin des Plantes, added details of Correa's devotion to and mastery of botany, and the renowned
von Humboldt was unequivocal in declaring him one
of the great botanists of the century.[43] It is not remarkable that Jefferson received him with warmth.

Though this first visit was not an extended one, the
two philosophers made profound impressions upon each
other. Jefferson wrote to Dr. Wistar that Correa lived
up to all expectations, the "best digest of science in
books, men, and things that I have ever met with; and
with these the most amiable and engaging character." [44]
To du Pont and Thouin, whose letters he acknowledged
after the visit, the former President was even more
rhapsodic.[45] Correa in turn was so delighted with his
visit that Biddle reported it had "raised our country
in his estimation & will do us much honor abroad." [46]
Jefferson had parted from this new friend with regret,
for at the time he thought he should not see him again.
The two had evidently discussed anything and every-

LC; TJ to Caspar Wistar, 17 Aug. 1813, LC. C had hoped to
visit Madison on the journey, but found him ill as he went and
absent as he returned (see C to TJ, 6 September 1813, and C
to Madison, 9 Sept. 1813, below).

[43] For the dates of these letters, see note 7 above.

[44] 17 Aug. 1813, LC.

[45] To du Pont, 29 Nov. 1813; to Thouin, 14 Dec. 1813, LC.

[46] To TJ, 28 Sept. 1813, LC.

thing, and most frankly, for from this time on Correa suggested to Jefferson whatever he felt might be useful to the nation or to the man himself, from waterproof cement to new international policy.

After a few weeks in Philadelphia winding up his necessary affairs, on 11 September the Abbé set out for Boston, his port of embarkation. For a brief visit he paused at "Andalusia," Biddle's country home.[47] He was in Boston some time before 27 September, when he found that he could change all his plans. Letters from Paris and Lisbon, which he had despaired of, contained remittances which relieved his financial pressures most handsomely. Now he admitted to John Vaughan that his chief reason for deciding to return to Europe had been monetary. Since that was now removed, he would remain in the United States indefinitely.[48] Apparently involved financial affairs in Paris, and failure to receive stipends from various government and private pensions bestowed upon him during the halcyon days in Portugal, had embarrassed him intensely. These affairs were now straightened out, and he expected to return to Philadelphia by the middle of October. He rejoiced that he had such men as Vaughan and Dr. Wistar, and his "children" Walsh and Biddle to return to, "to live with for some time more and that time at rest and with easy mind." [49]

But the date of his return he had reckoned without due regard for his own curiosity concerning a new region and the hospitality of the Bostonians. Massachusetts and its capital he had probably not visited on his previous excursion; at any rate he found so much to interest him that his visit lasted almost three months.

---

[47] *Ibid.*

[48] C to Vaughan, 27 Sept. 1813, APS, below.

[49] *Ibid.* See also C to Wistar, 27 Sept. 1813, APS, below; C to Biddle, 29 Sept. 1813, LC; Biddle to C, 8 Oct. 1813, below.

Probably through the Reverend Henry Muhlenberg, the Lancaster, Pennsylvania, botanist, the old Abbé was introduced to Jacob Bigelow, M.D., a young man who was just becoming known as a botanist but who within a few years was to hold two professorships at Harvard.[50] Correa informed his old friend, Dr. James Edward Smith, in London that, Muhlenberg excepted, Bigelow was the best botanist he had found in America, and he urged Smith to open a correspondence with the Bostonian which might benefit both.[51] Bigelow informed Muhlenberg that the whole Boston group had profited by Correa's visit and hoped that the Abbé would return again in the summer.[52] Apparently Correa and Bigelow kept up a botanical exchange at least through 1819.[53]

It was probably during this visit too that the Abbé first met Ticknor and another young intellectual, Joseph Green Cogswell, both of whom were to study in Germany. On both he left a profound impression,[54] and to Ticknor at least he gave an appraisal of the state of science and letters in Europe which the young scholar found most accurate later when he was actually

---

[50] 1786–1879, *DAB*. See C to Bigelow, 7 March 1819, below; Bigelow-Zaccheus Collins correspondence, 24 Oct. 1814 to 2 July 1815, AcNatSciPhila; Muhlenberg Correspondence, HistSocPenna. The 1812 (12 Sept.) dating of a letter from Dr. Wistar introducing C to John Collins Warren of Boston may be a mistake, may represent an intention for 1812 not carried out until 1813, or may indicate that C visited Boston briefly in 1812. See C to Wistar, 27 Sept. 1813, note 1, below.

[51] C to Smith, 18 Nov. 1813, LinnSoc, London; Bigelow to Z. Collins, 2 July 1815, AcNatSciPhila.

[52] Bigelow to H. Muhlenberg, 10 Nov. 1813, HistSocPenna.

[53] See C to Bigelow, 7 March 1819, below.

[54] Cogswell to Ticknor, 18 Feb. 1816 [Ticknor, Anna E., ed.], *Life of Joseph Green Cogswell as sketched in his letters*, 44–45, Cambridge, Mass., 1874.

on the scene.[55]   Thus the wise old savant took pains to inform and to encourage young hopefuls of this new land, a practice he inaugurated with Walsh and Biddle and continued all during his years in this country.

But the alert Correa observed more in New England than a circle of promising young men who were preparing that region for its flowering.   The political leaders of this stronghold of Federalism had opposed consistently the War of 1812, and when Correa visited among them they were dangerously close to what he called open treason.   He informed Jefferson that he had seen "the sickness and the curative," but that he was genuinely alarmed, for "Treason is more to be feared in the present moment than in any epoch of your history." [56]   Though the Hartford Convention was in the offing, even when it assembled, Jefferson, who knew his countrymen better than Correa did, was not really disturbed.[57]   The old Portuguese's warning remains significant primarily for what it shows of his own attitudes towards American politics and what he conceived to be the best interests of this country.   True to his whole earlier history, he remained the philosophical liberal, but here he was especially the Jeffersonian liberal.

What he had already seen whetted Correa's curiosity to see more.   In April he was able to outline to Jefferson his plan of visiting "Kentucky and the Ohio," going through western Virginia and returning through Pittsburgh.   He planned to stop on the way at Monticello and present to its owner his *"compagnon de voyage,* Mr. Walsh."   The trip was to begin the first of May and would take about three months, he an-

---

[55] Ticknor to TJ, 14 Oct. 1815, in Long, O. W., *Literary pioneers,* 19, Cambridge, Mass., Harvard, 1935.

[56] 10 April 1814 and 20 Sept. 1814, LC, both below.

[57] TJ to C, 27 Dec. 1814, LC, below.

nounced.[58]   Before he received Correa's announcement
Jefferson had written, urging a long stay, but mentioning that he himself would be away from home during
the month of May.[59]   The latter information caused a
change in itinerary, for Correa actually went west
through Pennsylvania and Pittsburgh.

He must have delayed the beginning of the excursion until June.   Walsh started out with him, but was
obliged to turn back at Chambersburg.[60]   Correa was
at Pittsburgh before 17 June,[61] and of course paused
for a few days to converse with gentlemen interested
in science.[62]   He descended the Ohio[63] to some convenient point and then made his way to Lexington,
Kentucky, which became his center of operations for
several weeks.[64]   At Lexington he was cordially received by several members of William Short's family,
and found the frontier town fascinating.   He was much
pleased with the land, and especially the people.   He
later dwelt much upon "the probable future greatness
of the western states which he calls the real America."[65]   The soil and the potential mineral wealth of
the region he was to discuss in writing later.

Though he had planned to travel directly overland
to Monticello, he found that it was impossible to get
through the mountains, and he had to retrace his steps
to Pittsburgh.   From this point on 20 September he
informed Jefferson that he might be expected within
a reasonable period,[66] and presumably was at Monti-

---

[58] 10 April 1814, LC.
[59] 19 April 1814, LC.
[60] See Lochemes, *Walsh,* 78.
[61] Z. Collins to H. Muhlenberg, 4 July 1814, HistSocPenna.
[62] C to Madison, 10 Dec. 1814, LC, below.   C mentions Dr.
Frederick Aigster of Pittsburgh as a good mineralogist.
[63] Z. Collins to H. Muhlenberg, 4 July 1814, HistSocPenna.
[64] C to J. Vaughan, 20 July 1814, APS, below.
[65] Z. Collins to H. Muhlenberg, 30 Nov. 1814, HistSocPenna.
[66] LC, below.

cello within a week or two. This time the acquaintance ripened into the kind of friendship which only a community of interests, mutual respect, and the prospect of several years of companionship can produce. Jefferson's letter inviting Correa for the visit had rather wistfully urged that the Abbé consider Monticello a second home, especially for the summer months. From this time Correa's annual visits were looked forward to by all the family at Monticello. A room was set aside as his, and despite the hundreds of other visitors who must have occupied it on other occasions, it was referred to half a century later by Jefferson's granddaughter as the "Abbé Correa's room." It was on the front across the great hall from the master's own rooms. This bedroom and "Mr. Madison's" were the only guest chambers sharing the first floor with Mr. Jefferson's own living quarters.[67]

There was much to discuss. The British had burned Washington not long before, and all the country was shamed and indignant. And the Abbé had to recount his experiences in New England and in the West, with his usual acute observations on men and politics. The possibilities regarding national revenue from public lands in the West, about which he wrote to President Madison in detail later, he first discussed here with the former President.[68]

Here at Monticello too he formed an acquaintance with a young neighbor of Jefferson who was to be another of his protégés, as the young man was already of his host. Francis Walker Gilmer was referred to by Jefferson a few years later as "the best educated subject we have raised since the Revolution, highly qualified in all the important branches of science, pro-

---

[67] Randolph, Sarah N., *The domestic life of Thomas Jefferson*, 334, New York, 1872.
[68] C to Madison, 10 Dec. 1814, LC, below.

fessing particularly that of law." At this time he had just completed several years of legal training under William Wirt and was about to enter upon his first practice at Winchester, Virginia.[69] Gilmer, already much interested in botany, found himself at once under the spell of the Abbé's charm and erudition. Very soon he had decided to accompany Correa back to Philadelphia. Their route was via Richmond and Washington. From Richmond the young man wrote enthusiastically to his brother:

I am so far on my way to Philadelphia with Mr. Corrèa, of whom, I dare say, you heard me speak of last summer. He is the most extraordinary man now living, or who, perhaps ever lived. None of the ancient or modern languages; none of the sciences, physical or moral; none of the appearance of earth, air or ocean, stand him any more chance than the Pope of Rome, as old Jouett used to say. I have never heard him asked a question which he could not answer; never seen him in company with a man who did not appear a fool to him; never heard him make a remark which ought not to be remembered. He has read, seen, understands and remembers everything obtained in books, or to be learned by travel, observation, and the conversation of learned men. He is a member of every philosophical society in the world, and knows every distinguished man living. . . .[70]

The blackened ruins of Washington the two travelers eyed curiously, the young American with dismay. "The appearance of our public buildings is enough to

---

[69] Davis, *Francis Walker Gilmer*, xvii, 75–145; Davis, R. B., ed. *Correspondence of Thomas Jefferson and Francis Walker Gilmer, 1814–1826,* Columbia, S. C., U. of South Carolina, 1946. Gilmer states in a notebook that he first met C on 16 Oct. 1814 at Monticello. See Davis, R. B., Forgotten scientists in Georgia and South Carolina, *Geo. Hist. Quart.* **27** : 284n, 1943. Actually the letter quoted just below may indicate an earlier date of acquaintance.

[70] 3 Nov. 1814, to P. R. Gilmer. See Trent, Wm. P., *English culture in Virginia,* 37, Baltimore, Johns Hopkins, 1889.

make one cut his throat, if that were a remedy—The
dissolution of the Union is the theme of almost every
private conversation, it is not yet ventured to speak
publickly, there is great contrariety of opinion concerning the probability of the event," Gilmer informed
his brother-in-law Peter Minor.[71] But the two called
on Virginia members of Congress, and on President
Madison, who was now living in the Octagon House.[72]
Apparently here too Correa ripened an earlier acquaintance into friendship,.for a few weeks later by letter he
was advising Madison, on most familiar terms, concerning national policy in regard to revenue from public
lands.[73] His excuse for obtruding himself into internal
affairs was the "permission" the President had given
him to comment. This relationship too always remained
cordial, though never so intimate as that between Jefferson and Correa.

The travelers paused briefly at Lancaster, where
Gilmer was introduced to the botanist, Henry Muhlenberg, and then proceeded to Philadelphia.[74] Gilmer,
with such a sponsor as the Abbé and with laudatory
letters from Mr. Jefferson, found himself immediately
accepted in the city's society.[75] He was probably present at the Hopkinsons in early 1815 at the dinner scene
described by George Ticknor.[76] At any rate, during
these winter months the old Portuguese and his young
Virginia friend became so intimate that the way was
paved for another excursion for the Abbé, an expedi-

---

[71] [14?] Nov. 1814, UVa, and Davis, *Gilmer,* 77.

[72] Hunt, Gaillard, ed., *The writings of James Madison. . . ,*
9 v., **8**: 298n, New York, Putnam, 1908.

[73] 10 Dec. 1814, LC, below.

[74] Z. Collins to H. Muhlenberg, 30 Nov. 1814, HistSocPenna.

[75] Davis, *Gilmer,* 78–79.

[76] Curiously, Gilmer became a good friend of Ticknor and of
John Randolph. See Davis, *Gilmer, passim.*

tion the two were to make together, even though no definite plans were made at the time.

In June or July, 1815, Gilmer had settled in Winchester, in the Valley of Virginia, and was preparing to open his legal practice. Before he had got his affairs in shape, however, Correa, on his way to Monticello and Montpelier, appeared and induced Gilmer to accompany him.[77] First they visited Madison. Then, or a little later at Monticello, Correa petitioned the President for a recommendation to the agent with the Cherokees, an indication of the plans which were being made.[78]

At any rate, in early September, Correa and Gilmer accompanied Jefferson from Monticello to his retreat, "Poplar Forest," in Bedford County, not far from the Peaks of Otter. A few weeks later Gilmer's brother wrote that "the last account I had of you was that yourself Mr. Correa & Mr. Jefferson who travelled in a vehicle much resembling a mill hopper were taking the elevation of the Peaks of Otter and the[n] exploring the sides of them for subjects botanical."[79] They also viewed and pondered over the Natural Bridge, Jefferson's own property, and Correa encouraged the young man of the trio to try his hand at a scientific explanation of the phenomenon.[80]

Soon Jefferson bade the other two a regretful goodbye and they set forth again on the Abbé's most am-

---

[77] Gilmer to P. Minor, 28 Aug. 1815, UVa. TJ had evidently expected C, with du Pont, to visit him earlier in the summer. See TJ to C, 28 June 1815, LC. below; TJ to du Pont, 6 June 1815, Malone, D., ed., *Correspondence between Thomas Jefferson and Pierre Samuel du Pont de Nemours, 1798-1817*, 163, Boston, Houghton Mifflin, 1930; du Pont to TJ, 24 July 1815, LC.

[78] Petition, [Summer 1815], LC, below.

[79] P. R. Gilmer, 3 Oct. 1815, UVa.

[80] For Gilmer's paper read before the APS, see below.

bitious journey. Armed with the letter from President
Madison to the agent of the Cherokees, and preceded
along the road by letters of introduction from Jefferson,
they began their southwest journey down the Wilderness Road. To one old friend, Jefferson included them
both with equal warmth in his recommendation:

Two friends, who lately accompanied me to this place
[Poplar Forest] have proceeded on a tour through the
Southern Country. the one of them is Mr. Correa a gentleman from Portugal, of the first order of science, being
without exception the most learned man I have met in any
country. Modest, good-humoured, familiar, plain as a
country farmer, he becomes the favorite of everyone with
whom he becomes acquainted. he speaks English with ease.
he is accompanied by Mr. Francis Gilmer. . . , the best
educated young man of our state, and of the most amiable
dispositions. he travels with his friend Correa, as with a
Mentor, for the benefit of his conversation and the information and improvement he may derive from it; and he
will be in future whatever he pleases in either the State,
or General Government. at home in every science, botany
is their favorite. . . .[81]

Teacher and pupil proceeded slowly through what
is now southwest Virginia to Knoxville in Tennessee,
where they hoped to find Congressman John Rhea, to
whom Jefferson had directed one of his letters.[82] Rhea
was not at home,[83] and after a few days they traveled
on into the Cherokee country. Quite by accident along
the road through deep forest they encountered General
Return Jonathan Meigs, the agent to whom Madison
had written.[84] Though Meigs was headed in another

---

[81] To Governor John Milledge, of Georgia, 22 Sept. 1815, LC.
Letter quoted in full in Davis, Forgotten scientists in Georgia
and South Carolina, 271–272. This article also gives more details of this journey.
[82] TJ to C, 22 Sept. 1815, LC, below.
[83] TJ to C, 1 Jan. 1816, LC, below.
[84] R. J. Meigs to Madison, 22 Dec. 1815, LC, below.

direction, he gave them a note to his son on the Indian reservation. Here they were received most hospitably, and remained several days making all sorts of botanical observations. Gilmer's notebook containing his botanical jottings for all the journey still survives.[85] And again with Correa to encourage him, he recorded materials which he was to organize later into an interesting magazine article on "The Institutions of the Cherokee Indians. . . ."[86] His notebook also contains some five pages of Cherokee vocabulary, as well as observations on the mountain terrain.

The next pause was at Athens, Georgia, where they met William Greene, a mathematics professor in the University of Georgia who was interested in botany.[87] By 16 October the travelers had reached Augusta, already an intellectual center. They met several gentlemen there, and found among them another botanist, Thomas J. Wray.[88] After four days in Augusta they moved on to Charleston in South Carolina, arriving on 24 October.[89] Charleston had much to interest them. For years the city's botanist Stephen Elliott had been enquiring eagerly from Zaccheus Collins in Philadelphia and Henry Muhlenberg in Lancaster for news of Correa, and several times had urged that the Abbé undertake a southern excursion.[90] Correa said later that they had intended only to visit Elliott a day or two, but that this gentleman and the Rutledges threw them into such a gay whirl of dinners, clubs, and

---

[85] Now in the Duke University Library. Printed in Davis, R. B., ed., An early Virginia scientist's botanical observations in the South, *Va. Jour. Sci.* 3: 132–139, 1942.

[86] *Analectic Magazine* 12: 36–56, 1818.

[87] Davis, Forgotten scientists, 276.

[88] *Ibid.*

[89] *Ibid.*, 277.

[90] E.g., H. Muhlenberg to Z. Collins, 6 Nov. 1812, AcNatSciPhila.

concerts that they remained a fortnight.[91]   Elliott, the
Abbé later informed Jefferson, was the ablest botanist
in America.[92]   Gilmer for his part was much impressed
by the young men of Charleston, especially Robert Y.
Hayne, William C. Crafts, and above all Hugh Swinton
Legaré.[93]

Having admired everything with which they came
in contact except the climate, the two turned north
again on 8 November.[94]   After a pleasant ride through
upper South Carolina, North Carolina, and lower Virginia they reached Monticello on 6 December.   There
they found Correa's old friend du Pont de Nemours, who
was awaiting Jefferson's return.[95]   They all lingered a
few days, but were obliged to depart without seeing
their host, who had been detained in Bedford.[96]   Correa
and Gilmer reached Winchester on 15 December.[97]
After spending Christmas with Gilmer,[98] the Abbé continued north, for he had promised du Pont to spend
New Year's with his old friend at Eleutherian Mills
near Wilmington "in the Parisian manner." [99]   And on

---

[91] C to Vaughan, 17 Dec. 1815, APS, below.

[92] TJ to J. W. Eppes, 29 July 1820, UVa.   C had already
written the same thing to DeCandolle at Montpelier.   See letter
of 7 Nov. 1815 (from Charleston), Gray Herbarium, Harvard
Univ.

[93] Davis, Forgotten scientists, 279; also Davis, R. B., The
early American lawyer and the profession of letters, *Huntington Lib. Quart.* **12**: 191–205, 1949.

[94] Forgotten scientists, 279; C to Vaughan, 17 Dec. 1815,
below.

[95] Malone, ed., *Jefferson-du Pont correspondence,* 165.

[96] TJ to C, 1 Jan. 1816, LC, below.

[97] Forgotten scientists, 280.

[98] Gilmer to P. Minor, 16 Dec. 1815 [postscript of 21 Dec.],
UVa.

[99] Du Pont to TJ (Malone, ed., *Jefferson-du Pont correspondence,* 170), 20 Dec. 1815.   The quotation is in a letter from C
to Vaughan, 17 Dec. 1815, APS, below.

this note of promised gayety concluded a most remarkable journey. Though Correa was to snatch a few weeks now and then to visit Monticello, Richmond, and eastern Virginia, his official duties during the second half of his stay were to prevent such leisurely and extended excursions as this one. But he might well have rested content, for he had seen almost all of the United States.

Correa's activities in Philadelphia in the 1814–1815 period, his lectures and his activities in the American Philosophical Society and in the Academy of Natural Sciences, will be discussed below in the summary of his contributions to American life. Here have been outlined his principal physical movements during the 1812–1816 period, with some indication of the friends and acquaintances he had made. If he had returned to Europe in the spring of 1816, as he once thought of doing with Gilmer,[100] his career in the United States would still have been astonishing. But in July, 1816, when he entered another phase of it, only half his time in this country had passed, though by far the happier half.

---

[100] Gilmer to J. H. Cocke, 24 March 1816, UVa, and earlier Gilmer correspondence, UVa.

IV. ENVOY EXTRAORDINARY, 1816–1820

TEA–CUP DIPLOMACY

Though in the spring of 1816 the Abbé Correa was considering a return to Europe, his varied activity would have afforded little evidence that such an idea was in his mind. He was busy at the American Philosophical Society, investigating and reporting on botanical items;[1] he was pursuing a learned and involved correspondence with Gilmer concerning the United States' rights in the Florida boundary question, for he had urged his young friend to write an essay on the question;[2] and he was going to a great deal of trouble in gathering information for Jefferson as to the whereabouts of the manuscripts of the Lewis and Clark expedition.[3] Besides all this, he was occupied daily in preparing for a series of thirty botanical lectures to be given between 10 April and the end of June,[4] a series which would be a sequel to those he had given the year before.

But while he was thus occupied his own government in Brazil was preparing for him a new adventure, and a new duty. On 1 February, in accordance with a decree of the day before, the Prince Regent of the United Kingdom of Portugal, Brazil, and the Algarves, appointed as his Minister Plenipotentiary near the United States, the Chevalier Joseph Correa da Serra.[5] The news was apparently not received in this country until

---

[1] See, e.g., "Report on the memorial relative to the first discovery of the new genus of plants called Bartonia," 15 March 1816, MSS. APS, signed by C and Z. Collins.

[2] C to Gilmer, 8 Feb. 1816, UVa, and others for several months following, all below.

[3] TJ to C, 1 Jan. 1816, LC, and several following, all below.

[4] C to Gilmer, [27?] March 1816, UVa, below.

[5] See the letter (in Portuguese) of credence to the President of the U. S. signed by the Marquiz de Aguinar, 1 Feb. 1816, LC.

a few days before 31 May, when it was announced in the *National Intelligencer,* the Administration newspaper in Washington.[6] Even then Correa's credentials did not arrive until July, when he officially notified President Madison and Secretary of State Monroe.[7]

The Abbé was certainly not greatly surprised. As he observed to Madison, the nomination had been made long before. But he had not counted on it as his half-formulated plan of returning to Europe indicates. At any rate, the appointment gratified a lifelong ambition to represent his country abroad as a ranking diplomat. Correa's tactful letters over several years to the ministers of his government in Rio de Janeiro, and his straightforward use of what influence he could command, had not been in vain. Of course it was an unusual appointment, not because of Correa personally but because of the nature of his life during the preceding four years. And one can believe his avowal at this period that he loved both countries equally.[8]

Jefferson was delighted. He hoped this would "fix" Correa in America for life, as he informed both the new minister and Gilmer.[9] He believed too that it would not interfere with the Abbé's "botanical rambles." To Gilmer, Jefferson observed that Portugal was a harmless nation which never quarreled with its friends. "If their minister writes them once a quarter that all is well, they desire no more."[10] Never was Jefferson's natural sanguinity more mistaken, for Correa's new position was to be anything but easy, and his term in office would probably have ended in

---

[6] Agan (15) gives 15 May in the *National Intelligencer.*
[7] C to Madison, 10 July 1816, LC, and to Monroe, 10 July 1816, NatArch, both below.
[8] To Gilmer, 21 July 1816, UVa, below.
[9] To C, 5 June 1816, LC, below; to Gilmer, 7 June 1816, UVa.
[10] Letter of 7 June quoted in Agan, 15.

war had Portugal possessed the strength to wage it.[11]

All the trouble was undreamed of, however, when Correa addressed his letters to Madison and Monroe informing them officially of his appointment. He really expected "the Portuguese minister to be a sort of family minister." [12] For some years there had been only a Portuguese consul general, and before that a Minister Resident.[13] Now the diplomatic representative would bring together the two great powers of the Western Hemisphere, as Correa always called them.

For a time the new minister was able to keep up his former way of life. He and Gilmer visited Jefferson in August 1816,[14] and he then accompanied his younger friend back to Winchester.[15] By the middle of October he was in Philadelphia attending personal affairs,[16] and by 1 December had settled in Washington,[17] ready for business. First, however, he had to make himself as comfortable as possible and renew acquaintances, for friendship was vital to him.

This first winter in the capital he spent at Mrs. Wilson's boarding house, in the Seven Buildings group, where he had two connecting rooms and at least one liveried servant. The Virginia member of Congress, Henry St. George Tucker, a friend of Gilmer, described Correa's domicile and added:

But his simplicity does not desert him notwithstanding his florentine breeches and black silk stockings. He was kind enough to express his thanks for my immaterial agency

---

[11] *Cf.* Agan, 15.
[12] C to Madison, 10 July 1816, LC, below.
[13] Cipriano Ribeiro Freire, 1794–1799. See *Reg. Dept. of State.* . . , 119 etc., Washington, 1874.
[14] Gilmer to William Wirt, 29 Aug. 1816, VaStateLib; C to Dashkoff, 7 Sept. 1816, UVa, below.
[15] Gilmer to P. Minor, 23 Sept. 1816, UVa.
[16] C to Monroe, [18?] Oct. 1816, NatArch.
[17] C to da Barca, 2 Dec. 1816, Henriquez, 115–116.

about his establishment here and promised to call & see me which promise he performed this morning. I was from home but met him at the house where we had some conversation in relation to this political anomaly (the District of Columbia) on which subject he appeared as well informed as if he had been the framer of the Constitution. He is certainly a remarkable man and his unassuming manners make him appear yet more extraordinary. He certainly reminds me very strongly of the monk of the Sentimental Journey, and Sterne himself would recognize his resemblance to his picture—[18]

On the same day Tucker made these observations Mrs. Samuel Harrison Smith, wife of the editor of the *National Intelligencer,* described the Abbé as she had seen him the night before at a brilliant drawing room. Though she was impressed by his learning and the five languages he spoke perfectly, then and later she was as often bored as enthralled by his conversation.[19] Apparently many of his subtle witticisms escaped her. The men seemed to appreciate him more, whatever the reasons may have been. A few days after Tucker had given his first impressions of Correa to Gilmer, he added further details:

Monday evening he came over to our lodgings in his carriage & pair, (handsomely lighted with lamps) & spent the whole Evening with us. The company, consisting among others of M[ess]rs. Brown and Robertson from Louisiana [.] the Abbe had a fair opportunity of exhibiting in his unostentatious way his minute acquaintance with the geography, soil, natural productions and climate of a country that most of us know nothing about. He had moreover some good jests, and fine witticisms and the afternoon

---

[18] H. St. George Tucker to Gilmer, 5 Dec. 1816, UVa. The Seven Buildings were located at Pennsylvania Avenue and Nineteenth Street. For C's address, see *Congressional Directory* for 1816.

[19] Hunt, Gaillard, ed., *The first forty years of Washington society. . .* , 135, 138, 139, 142, New York, Scribners, 1906.

passed off delightfully. He compares the State of Pennsylvania to the Sphynx whose head and bosom (Philadelphia) is most beautifully finished, while the residue of its frame is disgusting & deformed. . . .[20]

Actually the Abbé's remark about Pennsylvania was mild compared with what he said about the raw capital on the Potomac. He is given credit for calling Washington "the city of magnificient distances," [21] but another saying of his concerning it was more popular in his day. Like many others, Correa felt the location was unfortunate. He could be sure his audience would laugh with him.

The Portuguese resident minister (an old monk) says, "Every man is born with a bag of folly which attends him through life. Washington was born with a small bag, which he kept to himself, and never imparted any of it to the world, until the metropolis of the nation was founded, when he emptied the whole of it in this city." [22]

But with all this jollity Correa had settled down to official business at once. The cloud no larger than a man's hand was on the horizon, and he was conscious of it. South American provinces had been in ferment against their European masters for some years, though most or all the revolutionists were of the Spanish possessions. But a revolt in Uruguay under José Artigas was feared by Portuguese authorities, for the rebels might invade the nearest Brazilian province. Don John ordered a fleet to blockade Montevideo, ignoring

---

[20] 11 Dec. 1816, UVa. For the same story about Pennsylvania, see Griffin, *Researches,* 34 (who quotes it from Michael Chevalier's *Society manners and politics in the United States, 1834–1835* [Paris, 1836; Am. transl., Boston, 1839]).

[21] See Griffin, *Researches,* 43; Hunt, ed., *First forty years,* 135n.

[22] Hubbard, Robert J., Political and social life in Washington during the administration of President Monroe, *Trans. Oneida Hist. Soc. Utica, N. Y.* **9**: 59, 1903.

Spanish protests of interference, and Artigas had recourse to privateering in order to free himself. Commissions signed in blank were sold to adventurers in foreign parts, especially Baltimore. From that port vessels which never saw Uruguay sailed out to harry Portuguese commerce.[23]

Such tactics had already been employed for years by revolting Spanish colonies, but protests to the United States government from Spain's envoy, De Onis, had been profitless. De Onis had asked that these privateers flying foreign flags not be allowed to violate neutrality by entering American ports, but in 1815–1816 Secretary Monroe's reply had been unsatisfactory, though several persons were prosecuted and some ships libeled.[24] The Spaniard was still reporting violations when Correa came into office.

During the fall of 1816 the new minister learned that a Captain Fisk, of the ship *Romp,* flying the flag of Buenos Aires with instructions to cruise against Spanish commerce, had been further instructed to proceed against Portugal if his alleged government became involved in the Uruguayan matter. This was before Artigas' ships had appeared. Correa's letter to Secretary Monroe of 20 December, his first move in this affair, was a tactful and yet pointed one.[25] Though he had no personal or national love for Spain, as his earlier activities in the Florida boundary matter give evidence, here that nation's interests and Portugal's coincided. He enclosed a copy of instructions given by Thomas Taylor of Baltimore to Fisk for the *Romp,* and named several other ships and their captains in the same situation. These were clearly criminal acts. He was sure, he said, of the American government's disposition to

---

[23] Agan, 17.
[24] *Ibid.,* 18.
[25] NatArch.

deal properly with these men.[26]   The fault was entirely in the inadequacy of existing laws and the opportunities they afforded for the evasion of neutrality.   Only the enactment of the necessary legislation would justify this nation in the eyes of the civilized world, he added. He did not ask for punishment of a few individuals, but hoped that Congress would remedy the situation. He concluded by tactfully referring to the friendliness of Don John and Portugal, especially during the late war with Great Britain, when Portuguese subjects maintained a strict neutrality.

Monroe replied on 27 December that the recommendation had been accepted and would be communicated to Congress by the President.[27]   Evidently many concerned looked favorably upon it, for already Congress was debating neutrality.   At any rate, on 3 March 1817, "An Act more effectually to preserve the neutral relations of the United States," better known as the Neutrality Law of that date, was passed.   On 13 March Acting Secretary Rush sent a copy to Correa, with a note to the effect that the President hoped the Portuguese sovereign would perceive in "the spirit and scope of its provisions a distinguished proof of the desire which animates this nation to maintain with his dominions and subjects the most harmonious relations." [28] In 1820, when the privateering question was even more acute, Monroe recalled to John Quincy Adams that the credit for the Act was due to Correa.[29]   After redefinition in 1818, this neutrality law came down to our own day.[30]   Thus the Abbé had a part in the determination of American foreign policy.

---

[26] Cf. Hill, Lawrence F., *Diplomatic relations between the United States and Brazil,* 16, Durham, N. C., Duke, 1932.

[27] NatArch.

[28] NatArch; quoted in Agan, 20.

[29] Agan, 30; Monroe, *Writings* 6: 147.

[30] Agan, 27.

This act, supplementing old statutes of 1794 and 1797, was aimed directly at conditions in the southern portions of the hemisphere. Among other things it prohibited cruising under commission of "any colony, district, or people," terms intended to include unrecognized governments of Spanish America.[31] But despite severe penalties for violation, these clauses of the law accomplished little. The *Zeitgeist* was against them. Though the new Portuguese minister had distinguished himself as a diplomat and patriot, for the first time in his long career he was throwing himself, perhaps originally not by his own choice, into the camp of conservatism. What he could sympathize with in the United States as a nation, he could not condone in the rebellious subjects of his own ruler. In short, Correa showed himself first loyal subject-patriot and, distinctly second, liberal. As time went on, the liberal was to become more and more submerged. But he was growing old, and increasingly sick, and the grossly materialistic side of American civilization was to loom darker and darker before him.

South America after all was but following in the footsteps of her northern neighbor, and there was no doubt that there was sympathy even in Congress for the revolutionists. Two presidential neutrality proclamations besides the several laws on the subject were issued at various times during the South American wars for independence, but popular sympathy in the United States did not hold aloof. Protected by this sympathy of the country generally, and impelled undoubtedly more urgently by greed, adventurers fitted out ships with American crews to prey upon Spanish and Portuguese commerce. The whole 1815–1825 decade is a record of evasions after trial or before, of

---

[31] Hill, *Diplomatic relations,* 16; *United States statutes at large* **3** : 370.

robberies, and of other crimes of these freebooters.[32]

Baltimore was the base of operations for many or most of these privateers. Local officials were weak or venal, and the distinguished William Pinkney was attorney for the privateering interests. The scholarly diplomat representing Portugal found himself in a nest of hornets when he complained, naming names, and offering to bring suit in Baltimore. His last three years in office particularly were a series of vexations and vain protests on his part, and angry recriminations from the citizens partaking of the freebooters' profits.

Correa certainly made some mistakes, particularly when he tried to appeal directly to the American people through the *National Intelligencer* without going through diplomatic channels, and he probably issued some misleading and premature statements.[33] But the provocation was enormous.

President Madison, who retired from office soon after Correa's assumption of the diplomatic role, was always friendly. So at the beginning was President Monroe, whom the new minister had already come to know personally quite well. But in May, 1817, the Pernambuco affair, mentioned in so many of Correa's letters to the Administration, produced in its effects a coolness between them.[34] Alarmed that the United States might recognize possible envoys from the revolutionists of this Brazilian province, Correa had antagonized Acting Secretary Rush by protesting against and denouncing *possible* future action.[35] Correa's later explanation that he had the good name of the United

---

[32] Agan, 21.

[33] *Ibid.*, 25.

[34] *Ibid.*, 23.

[35] See exchange of notes from 13 May 1817, NatArch; and Rush to Madison, 18 June 1817, HistSocPenna, really a defense of the Administration's action, probably with the idea that C had given a different view of the affair to the former President.

States at heart was accepted by the Secretary, but the minister had shown what seemed unwarranted presumption. From this time, apparently, Monroe showed a growing coolness toward the Abbé.[36]

John Quincy Adams, who became Secretary of State in the autumn of 1817, gives the most discerning picture of Correa as diplomat. On the whole, Adams was quite sympathetic with the minister's claims and often believed that the President did not do them or the minister justice.[37] Monroe determined about this time to keep foreign representatives at arm's length, possibly with the idea of avoiding the embarrassment of his former intimacy with Correa.[38] Seeing this avenue to personal discussion closed to him, and certainly genuinely attracted to the new Secretary, Correa fell into the habit of calling upon Adams in the evening informally,[39] in addition to making the usual official visits to the Department of State. Adams, by no means taken in, was like most sophisticated men much taken with the Abbé. He returned the calls at Hieronimus' Hotel, where Correa then lived, once finding the Abbé "dressed like ourselves, and not in the full court suit." [40] Like everyone else, Adams found the conversation delightful, and the wit sparkling.

By candor apparent or actual, by occasional hints, by analogies from situations he knew of elsewhere in the world, the Abbé strove to make his points. Officially he still sent protests and documented evidence of depredations, and he demanded indemnities. Some-

---

[36] See Adams, C. F., ed., *Memoirs of John Quincy Adams* . . . , 12 v., **4**: 22–24, Philadelphia, 1875–1877.

[37] *Ibid., passim.*

[38] *Ibid.* **4**: 22 (20–21 Nov. 1817). For evidence that C's conversational skill occasionally overcame this at levees, see *ibid.* **4**: 314.

[39] *Ibid.* **4**: 57–58 (27 Feb. 1818) ; 60 (6 March 1818), etc.

[40] *Ibid.* **4**: 81–82

times officially or personally he went too far, as when he called Americans a "most unmanageable crew;"[41] but when Adams replied stiffly the Abbé was adept in his explanation, which was not really apology. Eventually Adams came to understand and sympathize with Correa's position on the depredations to such an extent that he explained and defended it to other foreign ministers who cast aspersions on their colleague.[42]

When on 8 April, 1819, Correa called to take leave for the summer, he and Adams discussed old European friends, botany, and America's future wealth in Florida. After the visit, the Secretary analyzed his caller:

The Abbé Correa is a man of extensive and general literature, of profound science, of brilliant wit, and of inexhaustible powers of conversation. He is so much of a philosopher as to have incurred the vindictive pursuit of the Inquisition, and to have obtained the friendship and patronage of my old friend Araujo, the late Count de Barca, by whom he was appointed to the mission here. He is insinuating and fascinating in his manner and deportment, and though sixty-eight years of age, as lively as if he were twenty-five. His temper, however, is not remarkable for equanimity: it is quick, sensitive, fractious, hasty, and, when excited, obstinate. Yet he is timid and easily cast down. An attack upon him last spring, in some of our newspapers, drove him almost into a fit of melancholy madness. . . .[43] The Abbé's diplomatic ability consists principally in affecting to be anything but a diplomat. He introduces himself as a familiar acquaintance, to talk literature and philosophy, as a domestic inmate, to gossip over a cup of tea. Mr. Monroe saw through this, but, having no relish for literature and philosophy, and no time to listen and laugh at jokes, he always kept the Abbé, as it was and is his principle to keep all foreign Ministers, at arm's length. Mr. Madison and Mr. Jefferson always received and en-

---

[41] *Ibid.* **4**: 133–135 (17 Oct. 1818).

[42] *Ibid.* **4**: 173 (17 Nov. 1818).

[43] See *National Intelligencer,* 29 April, 12, 19, 22, 24 May 1817 for C's statements and *one* of the attacks; also Adams, *Memoirs* **4**: 85–87 (1 May 1818).

couraged the Abbé's social visits, and I have always done the same, always avoiding any distinction between him and any others of the foreign Ministers.[44]

Much as he sympathized with the Abbé's troubles, Adams thought Correa's oft-repeated allusions to Portugal and the United States as the two great American powers mere "romancing." At the last the Secretary thought the minister's whole task had been most disagreeable to him, but that Portugal had real grounds of complaint, and that if the case had been reversed we should have declared war without hesitation.[45] Adams' final mention of Correa's mission aptly sums up the whole case:

I received a letter from the President recommending that a note should be written to the Abbé Correa positively rejecting his proposal for the appointment of Commissioners to concert and adjust with the Portuguese Ministers the complaints of Portuguese subjects against the pirates under Artigan colors fitted out from the United States. I immediately made a draft of the note, and wrote a short letter to the President, enclosing it for his revisal. The Abbé's notes have, I think, given us advantages in this controversy independent of the merits of our cause. The President is more anxious than I should be to make the most of the Abbé's bad management. I do it with reluctance; I think we have something to answer for to Portugal in this case on the score of justice, and that we shall answer for it, soon or late, by our own suffering.[46]

Though neither Adams nor Correa could foresee what would happen forty years later when another Adams held Correa's position near the Court of St. James's, the statement was remarkably prophetic. As for Correa, he had concluded his career as diplomat by losing a just cause for which he fought hard and long. The excuses for his growing irritation and therefore

---

[44] *Memoirs* **4**: 325–326.
[45] *Ibid.* **5**: 176–177 (19 Sept. 1820).
[46] *Ibid.* **5**: 180–181 (26 Sept. 1820).

curt and sometimes bungling notes are not hard to find. At his best, in the earlier years, he was an able tactician. Even towards the end he often acted with real finesse. See, for example, his note to Monroe hailing a new year of the President's administration, which ends with an adroit reference to his own problem.[47] Some developments noted below will shed light on the Abbé's other activities during this 1816–1820 period. It is safe to say that whatever he might have done as minister, his cause would have been lost. Right in itself, it stood athwart the destiny of the hemisphere —and man's greed.[48]

A NEW FRANKLIN

Much as his diplomatic problems worried Correa, they did not consume all his time, even when they were most complex and harassing. He was never to spend more than about half the year in Washington, dividing the remainder of his time between long sojourns in Philadelphia and shorter visits to Virginia and New York City. The year 1817, for example, before his official trials began to burden him almost intolerably, must have been one of the most pleasant of his stay in America. Already known from Boston to Charleston for his personal qualities, his new official dignity added an éclat which in combination with his known abilities, brought a deference he could not but relish. He became the most renowned wit and epigram-maker of his age.[49] Books were dedicated to him. In this republican society he was the oracle of the learned and the spark of the fashionable.

---

[47] 1 Jan. 1820, LC, below.

[48] For a more detailed study of the Portuguese-American relations in this period, see Agan, *loc. cit.*

[49] Hunt, ed., *First forty years,* 135n.

FIG. 3. Correa da Serra, by C. B. Lawrence, from the portrait in the American Philosophical Society. Courtesy of Frick Art Reference Library.

After spending the spring of 1817 at his duties in Washington, Correa made Philadelphia his headquarters from June [50] until the opening of Congress in the late fall. He attended many sessions of the scientific academies to which he belonged, and managed to make two extensive excursions. In July he was in New York

---

[50] Walsh to Gilmer, 3 June 1817, UVa.

City, planning to spend the summer in the State of New
York and in New England, "where i can fill many
chasms that remain in my knowledge of these parts of
your country." [51]   The Pernambuco affair interfered,
however, and he was soon back in Philadelphia.[52]   But
he had by now many friends in New York and must
have enjoyed his week or two there.   It was possibly on
this visit or earlier that he engaged in the only religious
discussion recorded in this country, a discussion remembered and printed a generation later.   The narrator is
the noted New Yorker, Dr. John W. Francis.   He describes the Abbé's conversation in a "literary circle"
with the Reverend John M. Mason, eminent divine and
from 1810–1816 Provost of Columbia University:

[Correa] was interrogated by Dr. Mason on the government and ecclesiastical polity of the Pontifical Church.
Armed at every point, the learned and profound Abbe vin-
dicated the claims of his order and the wisdom of the
Romish policy, in which he had been disciplined with the
astuteness and dexterity of the ablest Jesuit, while the calm
conversational tone and courteous diction which flowed between these two champions won the admiration of the company, and afforded the happiest proof of the benignity of
intellectual culture.   The angular points of Scotch Presby-
terianism seemed in the discussion to be somewhat blunted
by the expression given the Romish church, and I was led
to the conclusion that a religion whose fundamentals were
charity and love depended more upon the conformity of the
heart to its saving principles, and less upon nonconformity
to established rituals.[53]

In Philadelphia, before the Abbé started South for
Monticello and later Washington, two new honors
awaited him.   Edward Everett, another young Boston

---

[51] C to TJ, 12 July 1817, MassHistSoc, below.
[52] C to Gilmer, 21 Aug. 1817, UVa, below.
[53] Francis, J. W., *Old New York,* 60–61, New York, 1858
and 1886.

intellectual Correa had probably known in that city, enclosed to John Vaughan a "diploma" for him from the University of Göttingen.[54] And Henry M. Brackenridge, who had published portions of his attitudes on the Louisiana-Florida boundary questions in various newspapers and in Walsh's *Register*,[55] dedicated to "His Excellency" the 1817 edition of his *Views of Louisiana,* a work inspired in part by Correa,[56] as Gilmer's earlier study of the Florida boundary question had been. This dedication [57] is perhaps the best literary expression of the admiration of American intellectuals, young and old, for this foreigner in their midst. Though much of it had already been said by Jefferson and a dozen others, certain phases are indicative of something more: "Sir, your amiable simplicity of manners, and communicative temper, restore to us our Franklin . . . and for your interest in all phases of our life, we claim you as one of the fathers of our country." The whole statement is well worth reading.

But Correa did not live entirely upon praise from his fellows, even though he may have thrived best on communion with some of them. Once more he prepared to visit Monticello, this time with Walsh as his companion.[58] The visit confirmed the latter in his recent leaning towards the Republican point of view and produced in him a profound admiration for his host.

---

[54] 11 May 1816, APS.

[55] 1: 128 ff., 1817.

[56] There had been an earlier edition, without a dedication, published in Pittsburgh in 1814. The 1817 (Baltimore) edition with the dedication to C is considerably modified and reorganized. It was encouraged by C, who may have suggested revisions and certainly saw the appropriateness of making information concerning the great territory more widely available.

[57] Printed in its entirety below.

[58] C to TJ, 20 Sept. 1817, LC, below; Gilmer to P. Minor, 18 Oct. 1817, UVa.

As the two friends returned north they spent a day with the recently retired Madison, who was most pleasant. It would have been impossible, Walsh reported, for anyone "to be in better spirits or a more communicative mood than the ex-President." [59]

In Washington, Walsh, who was now editing a new *American Register* and needed to be near the fountainhead of politics, proposed that his family and Correa form a ménage.[60] The proposal was agreeable to the homeless old diplomat, and they all settled in the Brent house, across the street from Correa's friend, Mrs. S. Harrison Smith.[61] Mrs. Walsh, a "jolie femme," became official hostess for the Portuguese mission, attended diplomatic dinners and levees, and generally enlivened Washington society.[62] Correa romped with the Walsh children,[63] as he had with those of Biddle and of friends of Gilmer in Winchester. The only sour note of the moment was John Randolph's, who called on the Walshes but refused to leave his card for a minister who "boarded out." [64]

But this carries us into 1818, a year which was in many respects a turning point in Correa's career in the United States. Increasingly ill from what was apparently earlier a mild chronic diabetic condition, worried by the turn of Portuguese-American affairs, each of these troubles aggravating the other, the old Abbé's temper grew shorter and his spirits lower. He became a sharp critic of America and Americans, and gradually estranged many of his friends.

His first quarrel, in this instance partially motivated

---

[59] Walsh to Gilmer, 4 Nov. 1817, UVa.

[60] *Ibid.*

[61] Hunt, ed., *First forty years,* 142. Mrs. Smith observes that they are her new neighbors in a letter of 23 Nov. 1817.

[62] Lochemes, *Walsh,* 86–87.

[63] Walsh to Gilmer, 23 Dec. 1817, UVa.

[64] Hillard, *Ticknor* **1**: 16.

by other things, was with Walsh. Its whole basis is mysterious, for Walsh destroyed or effectively concealed from most of his contemporaries the papers he collected regarding this "shocking affair." Two letters from Walsh to Gilmer late in 1818 give several hints but no details.[65] According to Walsh, Correa confessed an act of moral "turpitude" which he knew would cause Walsh to lose his respect for him. He also confessed to a hearty dislike for Walsh. Walsh elaborates upon this betrayal of a family which had cherished Correa for six years. The two men were never again to be on speaking terms, as one letter of Correa's published below indicates.[66]

Gilmer had obtained some inkling of the affair and had written Walsh for information. He received in reply the letters referred to and the "papers" of "proof," which were to be returned. Perhaps the details are mercifully lost in the mists of the past, but the matter must be mentioned to complete the record. In Correa's defense are at least two strong facts. Gilmer read the documents and did not diminish in the least his own affection for or companionship with the Abbé. And we know from Ogilvie's picture of Walsh given above and other contemporary testimony that the gifted little man was vain and excitable. Correa's expression of dislike, undoubtedly brought on by too great propinquity, must have wounded Walsh deeply. Whatever the trouble was, we may be fairly sure that the "little Cuckoo" exaggerated it.

---

[65] 4 Nov. 1818 and 7 Nov. 1818; also see Oct. 1819, all UVa.

[66] C to Vaughan, 27 March 1818, APS, *below.* This letter, of course, shows that the quarrel occurred before this date. Walsh's letter of 12 March 1818 to Gilmer, UVa, apparently when on good terms with C, sets the earliest possible date for the rift. For knowledge of the rift, see Adams, *Memoirs* 4: 325–326.

Correa's health was now a matter of intense concern to him. A little while before the quarrel Walsh had noted a very alarming change in his appearance,[67] and John Quincy Adams observed it a little while later, stating that the Abbé was "highly hypochondriac." [68] At all events, in March, 1818, Correa hurried off to Norfolk in Virginia, where lived a Portuguese physician, a Dr. Fernandes, whom he had probably met at Monticello the year before.[69] Fernandes, a friend and correspondent of Jefferson, was said to be the only physician in America Correa trusted. The Abbé remained six weeks, combining medical treatment with observation of the flora of this region he had not before visited.[70] By 24 April he was back in Washington at Hieronimus' Hotel,[71] professing himself much recovered.

As official troubles multiplied in his last three years in the United States, the Abbé continued to find his escape in his friendships, his botanical researches, and his travels, naturally often combining the three. The new friendship of particular interest in this last period is that with the English-born Thomas Cooper, a man as versatile in his interests as Correa himself. These two born in the same decade [72] had a remarkable number of things in common. Cooper, educated at Oxford, various medical schools, and the Inner Temple, had been in England chemist, barrister, liberal pamphleteer, a champion of individual freedom and of the French Revolution. In the British reaction of the

---

[67] Walsh to Gilmer, 12 March 1818, UVa; to TJ, same date, LC.

[68] *Memoirs* 4: 81–82 (27 April 1818).

[69] TJ to Dr. Fernandes, 17 July 1816, LC. For Fernandes, see C to John Vaughan, 27 March 1818, note 1, below.

[70] See his letters from Norfolk of 24 March, 10 April, below.

[71] C to J. Q. Adams, 24 April 1818, NatArch.

[72] Cooper was born in 1759.

1790's he was bitterly attacked, and in 1794 had come
to America with his friend, Joseph Priestley, much as
Correa had been compelled to leave his native soil.
Soon Cooper and Priestley were attacked by Cobbett
and the Federalist press, and about the same time
Cooper not unnaturally emerged as a strong Republican, writing many essays in the cause and going to
prison for one of the most extreme of them. By 1801
he was a correspondent and friend of Jefferson himself.
Successively he was judge of the third Pennsylvania
district and professor of chemistry at Carlisle (later
Dickinson) College, all the while continuing his political and scholarly publications. By January, 1816, he
had resigned at Carlisle to accept the professorship of
chemistry in the liberal arts college of the University
of Pennsylvania.[73] It was probably at this time that
Correa first knew him.

By September, 1817, they were fairly intimate,[74]
and the friendship developed rapidly. On 31 October,
1817, Correa wrote to Jefferson concerning the possible loss of Cooper as a faculty member of the incipient University of Virginia, for Jefferson had for
some time been working to have Cooper there. Failure
to secure him, Correa wrote, "would be an irretrievable
loss to your seminary."[75] Though certain parties in
Philadelphia were endeavoring to procure for Cooper
the more lucrative post of professor in the medical
school of the University of Pennsylvania, Correa always supported Jefferson in trying to get the great
scholar for Charlottesville.[76] Though the Presbyterian

---

[73] For Cooper, see Malone, Dumas, *The public life of Thomas
Cooper,* New Haven, Yale, 1926; *DAB;* and Smallwood, William M., and Mabel, S. C., *Natural history and the American
mind,* 244–248, New York, Columbia, 1941.

[74] Cooper to TJ, 19 Sept. 1817, UVa.

[75] C to TJ, 31 Oct. 1817, LC, below.

[76] See letters between TJ and C, beginning in November

element in Virginia, alarmed at Cooper's "atheism" and alleged intemperance, eventually thwarted all their efforts, Correa continued to take a deep interest in Cooper's welfare. In 1818 they visited Virginia together, Cooper meandering mineralogically while Correa browsed botanically.[77] Correa once at least assisted Cooper in a geological lecture at the University of Pennsylvania.[78] Later the Abbé appears to have been influential if not instrumental in obtaining Cooper's appointment as professor in the South Carolina College,[79] where the venerable fighter in many causes was to make his last campaigns, eventually as the institution's president. Correa claimed that Cooper was "taking this road" by his advice.[80] And most interesting and puzzling of all, Correa's only known sacerdotal function performed in this country was his christening in St. Joseph's Catholic Church in Philadelphia, of "Maria Anna" and "Helena," children of Thomas Cooper, and his wife Elizabeth, on 17 September, 1820, at the very end of his stay in America.[81] Was this last act a symbolic gesture of the brotherly love between the liberal yet loyal Catholic and the sturdy old freethinker?

One more human relationship was to bring comfort to the Abbé in these American years, this time with one of his own blood. In 1818 his son by Esther Delavigne, the fifteen-year-old Edward Joseph Correa da Serra, reached this country.[82] In a letter of 27

1817, concerning this matter, all below. See especially C to TJ, 26 Sept. 1818, LC; and C to Gilmer, 10 Oct. 1818, UVa.

[77] C to Gilmer, 10 Oct. 1818, UVa, below.

[78] C to Z. Collins, [Sept. 1819], AcNatSciPhila, below.

[79] See Cooper to TJ, 3 May 1820, UVa; C to J. Poinsett, 20 Oct. 1819, APS below; C to Gilmer, 11 Oct. 1820, UVa, below.

[80] C to Gilmer, 11 Oct. 1820, below.

[81] See Parish Register, Old St. Joseph's and Griffin, *Records,* 137. The latter includes some serious errors in transcription.

[82] Carvalho, 75, 78, 79–80 ff.

March, Correa mentioned that Edward was now in an American college very much like that the boy had attended at Belleville in France.[83] The appearance of this lad on the scene must have been surprising to many of Correa's acquaintances, but the Abbé himself had been deeply concerned for the welfare of the boy and his mother ever since he reached this country in 1812. As regularly as possible he had sent remittances through Benjamin Delessert, millionaire botanical gardenist, for the two,[84] and always enquired anxiously from his friend in Paris, the Minister de Brito, concerning them.[85] Once he had to thank de Brito for lending Madame Delavigne money, when his own funds had not arrived in time.[86] To de Brito too he confessed that these two represented for him the sum total of human happiness.[87] Friends like Jefferson must have known of their existence at least some time before the boy's arrival, for once Jefferson, in inviting the Abbé to Monticello, insisted that he make it his home until he should have a "wife and family" to settle in the neighborhood.[88]

At all events, Edward's name occurs frequently in the letters after early 1818. Officially his father's nephew or secretary, the boy came to know Correa's Philadelphia friends quite well; it is probable that he spent his school holidays in that city. Later from

---

[83] C to Vaughan, APS, below. St. Mary's College (Sulpician) in Baltimore. See note 3 of letter.

[84] See C to LeRoy, Bayard & McEvery, 28 April 1814, HistSocPenna; to Delessert, 1813, 1814, 1821, Library Institute de France. For Delessert (1773–1847), see *Biog. Univ.* For C's contributions to Delessert's botanical garden, see Lasègue, Antoine, *Musée botanique de M. Benjamin Delessert. . .*, 51, 464, 505, Paris, 1845.

[85] Carvalho, 75–76, 164–166, 170–174, 174–177.

[86] 6 June 1813, Carvalho, 175.

[87] 11 October 1812, 5 June 1813, Carvalho, 165, 173.

[88] TJ to C, 25 Nov. 1817, LC, below.

Europe Edward wrote quite sprightly letters back to his American friends giving news of himself and of his father until at least a year or two after the Abbé's death,[89] and indicating that he was a worthy son of that intelligent man.

In the last years we get two conflicting pictures of the Abbé. Not only the politicians in Washington, but old acquaintances like William Short felt that Correa's troubles had soured him irretrievably. And quite clearly Short was sympathetic in this letter to Jefferson:

. . . I have spoken to Corea about his visit to Monticello. He tells me now that it is postponed until the winter, & that he has written to you on the subject. He seems quite unsettled in all his plans, even his going to Washington: his dissatisfaction with the directers there, I fear will do him injury in their eyes, although he certainly has great right to be dissatisfied. To be obliged to be the witness to the fitting out of privateers in our ports with the evident & acknowledged purpose of going to plunder & pillage the vessels of his nation—to hear the boasting of these patriotic pirates when they have been successful in seizing rich Portuguese ships—to be able to give a list of these pirates parading our streets, & to receive no redress from Government must indeed be too much to be borne by any one; & our friend is of nothing less than a bearing disposition. This situation has depressed his spirits manifestly—& this again seems to have sensibly diminished his *Èsprit*. His conversation which was formerly so brilliant *s'en repent,* & is often now heavy & dull. I fear that his judgment has also suffered as well as his *esprit*—for he has decided not only to quit this country but to return to Rio Janeiro, & thus place himself again in the hands of the *prétaille* who will probably end by placing him in the hands of the inquisition. Hitherto when I have heard him hint at such an intention I have thought it was a mere *Contade* arising from his dissatisfaction with this government; but I find it is more serious, & I am really sorry for it. . . . He has been named of the Council of State, & this *eau benite de cour* is probably the source of his [delusion? decision?]. . . .[90]

---

[89] See Edward Correa's letters, 1821–1824, below.
[90] Short to TJ, 1 Dec. 1819, LC.

A very different view is given in this same year of 1819 by the famous English visitor, Fanny Wright, who met him at the home of a Mrs. Meredith in Philadelphia. The writer begins by quoting from Brackenridge's dedication to "our Franklin" and then comments that these are the terms "universally applied" to Correa da Serra.

After such testimonies from those who can boast an intimate personal acquaintance with this distinguished European, the observations of a stranger were an impertinent addition. I can only say that as a stranger, I was much struck by the unpretending simplicity and modesty of one to whom the unvarying report ascribes so many high gifts, vast acquirements and profound sciences. The kindness with which he spoke of this nation, the admiration that he expressed of its character and of those institutions which he observed had formed the character and were still forming it, inspired me, in a short conversation, with an equal admiration of the enlightened foreigner who felt so generously. As he walked home with me (for your character is not here fastened to a coach as Brydone found his was in Sicily) I chanced to observe upon the brilliancy of the skies, which, I said, as a native of a moist and northern climate, had not yet lost to me the charm of novelty. He mildly replied: "And on what country should the sun and stars shine brightly, if not on this? Light is every where and is each day growing brighter and spreading farther." [91]

But one must admit that Short's observation is more typical for these last years than Fanny Wright's. A few months after Short had made the remarks quoted above, he found that Correa had lost *all* his former warmth and was cold and distant "as far as I allow him to be." [92] Even with his intimates, Jefferson and Gilmer, the tired old man could not maintain his cheerful attitude. Optimistic and glowing as he had earlier been to Gilmer regarding the future of America, by

---

[91] Wright, Fanny, *Views of society and manners in America by an Englishman,* 129, New York and London, 1821.
[92] To TJ, 2 May 1820, LC.

1818 he was afraid that "the weeds may spoil the crop." [93] On perhaps his last visit to Monticello, Correa astonished his host with his irritability and excitement when discussing the whole privateering affair.[94] Walsh wished he would leave the country, because of his "bitter sarcasm at the expense of the nation and its government." [95]

So by 4 July, 1820, Correa could be weary and disillusioned enough to comment to an English friend:

i am tired of five years of this laborious mission, and most heartily tired of democratic society. Rational Liberty can be fully enjoyed under other forms, do not believe half of what is said in Europe of this country, and of what they most ostentatiously publish and say of themselves. They have the vanity of believing it all, but except in eagerness for money. . . , they are not yet comparable to ripe European nations, and they are not less rotten.[96]

As indicated above, by 1819, Correa had been named a Counselor of State for Brazil and soon received his orders to report to the court there.[97] Though he may have been foolhardy, as Short indicates, he was certainly glad to go. At first he expected to sail in June, 1820,[98] but he was delayed until late autumn. In July he paid his farewell visit to Jefferson, Madison, and Monroe [99] and then went on to Richmond to bestow

---

[93] C to Gilmer, 28 Dec. 1818, UVa; also C to TJ, 12 Oct. 1820, LC, both below.

[94] Adams, *Memoirs* 5: 176–177.

[95] Oct.[?] 1819, UVa.

[96] C to R. A. Salisbury, LinnSoc, London.

[97] C to J. Q. Adams, 25 Nov. 1819, NatArch; C to Gilmer, 2 March 1820, UVa, *below;* Adams, *Memoirs* 5: 170 ff. Among the 13 letters of 1818–1820 from C to his government now in the Ministério da Educaçao e Saude, Rio de Janeiro, those of 29? March and 14 May 1819 discuss his having been admitted Councelor of Fazenda.

[98] C to Gilmer, 2 March 1820, UVa, below.

[99] TJ to J. W. Eppes, 29 July 1820, UVa; Adams, *Memoirs* 5: 170 (21 Aug. 1820).

his adieus upon Gilmer.[100]   The parting scene, which Gilmer describes in his letter to Dabney Carr reproduced below, shows with what genuine affection the Abbé parted from this American friend.   Gilmer's own deep emotion is perhaps best indicated in an entry in his personal notebook immediately below the date and hour of Correa's departure: "I ne'er shall see his like again." [101]

John Quincy Adams found Correa in their final conversations vivacious and witty, and particularly amiable after his last visits in Virginia.[102]   One remembers that he had Adams' sympathy as well as that of Jefferson and Madison.   Correa was actually leaving America with the friendship of four presidents of the republic, and an active sympathy for his cause on the part of three of them.   His final gracious tributes to Virginia, which he thought would always be the France of America, are of course largely due to his high opinion of the two "philosophical Presidents" [103] and their young protégé, Gilmer.

But if Virginia was the great American "country," Philadelphia was the great city.   Full of honors as he was, the Abbé could not but be gratified by the resolutions of respect tendered him by the American Philosophical Society and the Academy of Natural Sciences.[104]   In the last days in the city he was still, characteristically, corresponding with Jefferson regarding the University of Virginia, and, less than a week

---

[100] Gilmer to P. Minor, 3 Aug. 1820, UVa (which shows that C visited Gilmer both going and returning from Monticello) ; Gilmer to D. Carr, 10 Aug. 1820, UVa, below.

[101] Davis, Forgotten scientists, 284.

[102] Adams, *Memoirs* **5**: 170 ff. (1 Sept. 1820).

[103] C to Gilmer, 9 Nov. 1820, UVa, below.

[104] AcNatSciPhila, 26 Sept. 1820, below (his reply of 3 Oct. also below) ; Early proceedings APS, 498 (1 Dec. 1820).

before he sailed, attending a meeting of the American Philosophical Society.[105]   On the day before his embarkation in New York, the old savant addressed deeply appreciative letters to his two close friends, Gilmer and Vaughan, and through them his farewells to the remainder of the Jefferson circle in Virginia and in Philadelphia.[106]   On 10 November, with Edward and his servant Adam Cain, the Envoy Extraordinary and Minister Plenipotentiary of H.M.F. Majesty sailed aboard the packet *Albion*.   He was bound for England and the last round of adventures of his career.[107] Jefferson summed up his feeling in a letter to Madison: "no foreigner I believe has ever carried with him more friendly regrets." [108]   Even then the sage of Monticello had not said his final word on the Abbé.

---

[105] 3 Nov. 1820.

[106] 9 Nov. 1820. UVa and APS, respectively. C also addressed an official letter to J. Q. Adams (NatArch) on this date.

[107] See Carvalho, 75 and *New York Evening Post,* 11 Nov. 1820.

[108] 29 Nov. 1820, LC.

V. CHANNEL OF ENLIGHTENMENT: CORREA AND AMERICAN INTELLECTUAL LIFE

About such a man as Correa da Serra one great natural question presents itself. What real impression, if any, did he leave upon the intellectual life of the youthful nation in which he spent nine busy years? If an impression, of what kind? Was it ephemeral or enduring? Concrete or specific influences are always difficult to determine, especially from a man who held no formal educational position, founded no school of thought, and wrote no book. The only possible answer here is to summarize Correa's activities in various fields of knowledge, point to some of the persons and things affected by them, and let the reader draw his own conclusions as to their permanent effect.

The Abbé arrived in this country at a period in American history when the nation generally was withdrawing itself from the European world and assuming a degree of isolation which was to last for a generation. It was the beginning of the age of the Monroe Doctrine, of the natural resentment against travelers like Basil Hall and Mrs. Trollope, of a growing nationalism and provincialism to be modified sharply only after the Civil War. Yet it was the period when Ticknor and Everett and Longfellow studied abroad and brought back Germanic philology and pan-European song and story. It was the age of expanding ideas in curriculum and subject matter in the institutions of learning. Jefferson was founding the first real university, and the older and greater colleges were developing into universities. And as Correa saw too well, it was the age of growing corruption and greed in politics and business enterprise, the moment when the utilitarian idealism of the Enlightenment of the founding fathers was giving way to the more cynical and hard-bitten governmental spoilers, the popular democrats of the Jackson variety.

It was in this dawn of conscious aspiration, despite the presence of elements he refused to appreciate and in truth did not always fully understand, that the old Abbé was very glad to be alive. Ideologically he always remained the agrarian liberal of the century in which he was born; but one recalls that his own great age believed implicitly in progress through dissemination of knowledge. He had informed the American consul in Paris some years before he embarked for the New World that he could be useful to the United States in several ways. He wished to employ his talents. And these talents reached into almost as many fields as did those of his admired friend, Mr. Jefferson.

BOTANY

A listing of Correa's European correspondence would include a beadroll of the immortals of botanical science for a full century, though he himself lived less than three-quarters of the period. For in 1772 [1] Correa as a promising young student was sending his observations to Linnaeus, the father of modern taxonomy, who had published his *Systema Naturæ* in 1737. In the years following among his particular friends were Jussieu, father of modern "natural" classification; the elder de Candolle, Jussieu's great disciple and modifier; and Sir James Edward Smith, who adopted the Linnean system and was responsible for its introduction and long continuance in English schools. And the Abbé's last known letter addressed abroad was to Robert Brown, Correa's own "discovery," and his long-time correspondent, the first *English* botanist to advocate the "natural"

---

[1] See his three Latin letters of 1772, 1773, and 1774 to Carl von Linne, LinnSoc, London.

system, with far-reaching consequences.[2] Brown was doing his best work just about a century after Linnæus had published the *Systema Naturæ*. Besides these, the naturalists less specifically identified with botany but certainly contributors to its development, men like Sir Joseph Banks and the Baron von Humboldt, and the lesser-known botanists of his native Portugal, were his intimates.

Thouïn, in his letter introducing Correa to Jefferson, had spoken of the Abbé's many herborizations in all parts of Europe and his friendship with the eminent of the botanical world. The others, said Thouïn, made botany a "metier"; to Correa it was a divinity whose mysteries he delighted in making known to his contemporaries.[3] Correa's words in 1820 near the end of his life expressed his devotion somewhat differently, in terms of personal satisfaction, though still with something of the tone of Rousseau: "Dear botany has been to me a treasure of sweet and innocent pleasures, and i owe to her the best moments i have enjoyed in my life." [4]

But Correa was neither a Rousseau nor a William Bartram rhapsodizing on the beauties of nature. His letters regarding plants alone and those concerning the place of the science in the university curriculum show that he believed botany should be *useful*. To one correspondent he was sceptical concerning all Bartram's observations on natural life in Georgia. In a letter to Smith less than two years after he arrived in the United States, he showed his opinion of the state of science

---

[2] See ch. II, note 22, above. Brown (1773–1858) was called later by von Humboldt "Botanicorum facile princeps." See Botany, *Enc. Brit.* **4**: 300; also von Sachs, Julius, *History of botany* (*1530–1860*), 139–144, Oxford, 1890. C's last letter to Brown was dated 16 April 1823 (Carvalho, 200–201).

[3] 7 Dec. 1811, LC.

[4] 18 Nov. 1813, LinnSoc, London.

here and of some of those who professed devotion to it.

Botany is still in her infancy in America; some amateurs are scattered throughout this continent, and some european rather traveling gardeners than real botanists, are collecting plants and shrubs and trees for the gardens of European rich men, or for the nurseries.[5]

His own excursions over the United States, during which he examined thousands of plants, were certainly not of the nature of those he describes here. In the first place, his purpose in these long journeys was never purely botanical observation. Geological formations, general terrain, peoples, climates, governments, these also were interesting. He could and did describe a few plants in the New York region to his Philadelphia friend, Zaccheus Collins,[6] but from the long western excursion he brought back no plants,[7] and on the expedition to the Cherokee country he permitted his young companion, Gilmer, to do the noting and the collecting.[8] From these observations he could draw general conclusions, but he wisely left the detailed description and annotation to the capable local scientist who had the time to do it accurately.

No, these travels aided the development of Correa's favorite science in quite another way than by his personal recordings. His ramblings put him into personal touch with the "amateurs," some of whom he came to regard quite highly; and he could make suggestions to them. His unusual capacity for combining friendship with science was here most effective. Through his exercise of it he was able to make what was perhaps his greatest contribution to botany in this country and in Europe at the same time.

---

[5] C to Dr. J. E. Smith, 18 Nov. 1813, LinnSoc, London.

[6] Z. Collins to H. Muhlenberg, 23 Aug. 1813, HistSocPenna.

[7] *Ibid.*, 30 Nov. 1814, HistSocPenna.

[8] See above, ch. III, notes 81 and 85.

REDUCTION

OF ALL

THE GENERA OF PLANTS

CONTAINED IN THE

CATALOGUS

PLANTARUM AMERICÆ SEPTENTRIONALIS,

OF

THE LATE DR. MUHLENBERG,

TO

THE NATURAL FAMILIES

OF

MR. DE JUSSIEU'S SYSTEM.

FOR THE USE OF THE GENTLEMEN WHO ATTENDED THE COURSE
OF ELEMENTARY AND PHILOSOPHICAL BOTANY
IN PHILADELPHIA, IN 1815.

PHILADELPHIA:

PUBLISHED BY SOLOMON W. CONRAD,

NO. 87, MARKET STREET.

1815.

FIG. 4. Title page of Correa's *Reduction of all the Genera
. . . ,* Philadelphia, 1815.

As noted above, Correa's first real acquaintance in America was among the group of Philadelphia gentlemen interested in science. Some of this group were professional scientists, like Dr. Caspar Wistar, and others men of differing occupations; but all were interested in botany at least as an amusing avocation. A few made genuine contributions in the field. Correa was right in calling them all amateurs, though some proved remarkably proficient ones. From these men came our first real botanists.

Among Correa's particular friends from the first month to the last of his stay in America was "the over modest Mr. Collins," as the Abbé called him.[9] Listed in the Philadelphia Directory merely as "gentleman," [10] Zaccheus Collins was a member of the American Philosophical Society and vice-president of the Academy of Natural Sciences.[11] Highly regarded in the Philosophical Society, he and Correa frequently comprised a committee reporting on the publication-merits of botanical essays submitted. Collins was highly regarded too by the Reverend Henry Muhlenberg, as their long correspondence on matters botanical would indicate.[12]

Muhlenberg, the able but rather lonely botanist who lived at Lancaster, Pennsylvania, was regularly informed by Collins of the Abbé's activities from the first month of Correa's stay in Philadelphia. Almost the first mention of the Abbé by Collins to Muhlenberg is accompanied by the remark that Correa knew of Muhlenberg's work before he came to America.[13]

---

[9] C to Vaughan, 13 Jan. 1822, APS, below.

[10] Directory of 1819. His address was 29 North Second. Merchants, physicians, usually lawyers, etc., are described by occupation.

[11] *Jour. Acad. Nat. Sci. Phila.* 1: list of officers, 1818; *List of members APS,* 23 (elected 1804).

[12] See their letters, HistSocPenna and AcNatSci Phila.

[13] 10 April 1812, HistSocPenna; see also Collins to J. Bigelow, 28 May 1815, AcNatSciPhila.

Through three years, until Muhlenberg's death in 1815, Collins gave him news of Correa's excursions, carried or mailed books and specimens between the two, and probably introduced them personally.

Very soon Correa was performing for Muhlenberg a service he was to render many times to other Americans. He forwarded to a major European botanist, with an introductory letter, a communication from Muhlenberg asking for information or confirmation regarding certain of his observations.[14] The man addressed was Chrétien-Henri Persoon, an authority on cryptogamic plants.[15] Thus the Abbé was the channel of communication for scientific observation in the two hemispheres.

A little later he did the same sort of thing for the young Bostonian, Jacob Bigelow, who was introduced to Dr. James Edward Smith in terms which indicate Correa's purpose:

He will be i am confident an illustrious botanist if he is put in correspondence with the chiefs of the science in the doubts that he may encounter. I am persuaded i do a great service to botany as well as to him by introducing him to you our venerable patriarch. By fostering his efforts, and by resolving his doubts, you will i am sure in a few years bring forth more thorough knowledge of North American plants, than we have hitherto had. He will write to you and send this little memorandum. . . .[16]

The correspondence was inaugurated, for by 1815 Bigelow had received a letter from Smith.[17] In 1819 Correa urged Bigelow to correspond with Professor Lamouroux of Caen, a marine biologist.[18] How much

---

[14]Muhlenberg to Collins, 5 June 1812, AcNatSciPhila; Collins to Muhlenberg, 7 July 1812, HistSocPenna.

[15] 1770–1836. Persoon later was elected a member of the Linnean Society of Philadelphia. *Biog. Univ.*

[16] 18 Nov. 1813, LinnSoc, London.

[17] See Bigelow to Collins, 2 July 1815, AcNatSciPhila.

[18] C to Bigelow, 7 March 1819, MassHistSoc, below.

Bigelow's later real distinction as a scientist, including publications such as the *American Medical Botany,* owed to these communications would take a separate investigation as long as this paper to indicate. We know that Correa performed a similar office for George Ord of Philadelphia [19] and for Gilmer, the latter of whom was "set to corresponding" with de Candolle on subjects botanical.[20] And the Abbé did the same thing for Stephen Elliott of South Carolina (whom he was finally to call the greatest American botanist)[21] and probably certain others of the Philadelphia brotherhood.

Correa himself acted for these men as an authority who could resolve their doubts. Muhlenberg, Collins, Elliott, Bigelow, Gilmer, and many of the less proficient brought their problems to him.[22] They did not always accept his judgment. Gilmer, when he found by checking in published works that the Abbé was wrong, pointed out the fallacy, and found that correction was always accepted with affable grace. But the important thing to these Americans was that here in the "wilderness" they possessed an authority as revered as any in the world. They could and did appeal to him.

In 1815 the Abbé was asked to give lectures on botany. In informing his friend and correspondent, da Barca, of his plans, Correa mentioned that he in-

---

[19] C to Sir J. E. Smith, 9 May 1820, HistSocPenna, below. This letter introduces Ord to Smith. For Ord, see Allen, Elsa G., *The history of American ornithology before Audubon,* in *Trans. Amer. Philos. Soc.,* new series, **41**: 561–565, Philadelphia, 1951.

[20] Davis, *Gilmer,* 144.

[21] TJ to J. W. Eppes, 29 July 820, UVa; C to de Candolle, Charleston to the University of Montpellier, 7 Nov. 1815, Gray Herbarium, Harvard U.

[22] See Muhlenberg and Collins letters, *loc. cit.;* Baldwin, William, *Reliquiae Baldwiniana: selections from the correspondence of the late. . . ,* Philadelphia 1843; letters of 14 Jan. 1813 and 31 Oct. [1812?], Muhlenberg-Elliott Correspondence, Arnold Arboretum, Harvard U.

tended to give a private course in botany out of gratitude to this country, which had been so kind to him.[23] It was to begin on 4 May, he stated. The thirty lectures were concluded some time before 24 July.[24] Though they were delivered independently of the University of Pennsylvania, in another part of the city at the American Philosophical Society, the absence of the University's professor of natural history, Benjamin Smith Barton, because of illness had been a major reason for giving the series. The Abbé was well paid, for he received $1,050 for the course.[25] Apparently his audience was composed of the learned, the students, and the fashionably interested. The following year, upon urgent request, he gave another series under the same conditions and stipend. At the end of the first series, Correa reported that the University people begged him to assume their chair of natural history, but that he had declined without absolutely saying no.[26] The appointment as minister of course put an end to his consideration of the proposal. But he would probably have declined positively anyway, for in June, 1816, he reported to Jefferson that the second series had been given under handicaps. "Under severe rheumatic pains, i have lectured almost every day in the afternoon, and gone to the fields in a gig every morning to collect the necessary plants." [27] This latter course must have been widely attended, however, for it was commented upon favorably in newspapers as far away as the Richmond *Virginia Argus*.[28]

---

[23] 26 April 1815, Henriquez, 114–115; Carvalho, 53.

[24] Du Pont to TJ, 24 July 1815, LC. Du Pont states that C leaves him to set out for Monticello.

[25] C to daBarca, 9 Feb. 1816, Carvalho, 182. For more of C's relation to B. S. Barton, see C to TJ, 12 Feb. 1816, notes below.

[26] C to daBarca, 9 Feb. 1816, Carvalho, 182.

[27] 16 June 1816, LC, below.

[28] See this newspaper, 18 May 1816, 2: no. 17, p. 3, col. 5.

Of the content and method of presentation of these lectures we know little. We have an occasional inkling, as the report of one friend of Jefferson's that Correa had commented upon the impracticability of hedges in this country.[29] For more than this, one must turn to the little handbook Correa prepared for the use of his "students," the *Reduction of all the Genera of Plants contained in the Catalogues Plantarum Americae Septentrionalis, of the Late Dr. Muhlenberg, to the Natural Families of Mr. de Jussieu's System. For the Use of the Gentlemen who attended the Course of Elementary and Philosophical Botany in Philadelphia, in 1815.*[30] In the preface the author states that

The difficulty of procuring in America, books relative to natural families, has induced the person who in this summer has given a course of elementary and philosophical botany in Philadelphia to offer to his subscribers instead of a common *syllabus,* this reduction to natural families of all the American genera of plants, contained in the late Dr. Muhlenberg's Catalogus Plantarum Americae Septentrionalis.

This modest sixteen-page pamphlet probably marked the first appearance of Jussieu's system in America, the first attempt to group our plants by the "natural" system.[31] It was published separately and as an appendix to the second edition of Muhlenberg's *Catalogus* isued in 1818.[32] The latter form may indicate that considerable importance was attached to it.

---

[29] J. C. Cabell to TJ, 4 July 1816, *Early history of the University of Virginia as contained in the letters of Thomas Jefferson and Joseph Cabell,* 62–64, Richmond, Va., 1856.

[30] Philadelphia: Published by Solomon W. Conrad, No. 87, Market Street. 1815. See iv, 5–16.

[31] *Cf.* Harshberger, J. W., *The botanists of Philadelphia and their work,* 8, Philadelphia, 1899.

[32] *Ibid.* I have examined the separate edition. The AcNatSciPhila has a copy of Muhlenberg's 1813 edition in which C's

While he was minister Correa continued to manifest his interest in his favorite science by his attendance and advice at the two Philadelphia academies, and especially by sponsoring one quite ambitious observational excursion by a young professional botanist, Thomas Nuttall.[33] Correa and some of his friends furnished the financial means through which in 1819 this Englishman explored the Arkansas country.[34] Nuttall, a promising young man, had already published in 1818 his *Genera of North American Plants and a Catalogue of the Species to 1817* and dedicated it to Correa.[35] His expedition set out in October, 1818, and returned in 1820. In 1821 Nuttall published *Journal of the Travels into the Arkansa Territory During the Year 1819. . .* , dedicated to Correa, Zaccheus Collins, William Maclure, and John Vaughan, in that order.[36] It has been stated that no other explorer of botany in North America has made so many personal discoveries as did Nuttall.[37] The botanical dictionaries certainly abound in the names he gave plants, includ-

---

pamphlet has been laid, with a note signed by C: "Having been requested by Mr. Finley to give my opinion of Dr. J. E. Smith's Introduction to Botany which he is about to republish, I have no hesitation to say that I believe it to be an excellent work, perfectly well suited to the purpose of instructing those persons who wish to study botany and to know the science in its present state of perfection." The 1822 New York edition of J. E. Smith's *A grammar of botany . . .* also contains [213 ff]. C's pamphlet in somewhat revised format followed by colored illustrations with tables. Page v includes the statement that the *Reduction* was added at the suggestion of Dr. Mitchill.

[33] 1786–1859, *DAB;* also see letters from T. Cooper to TJ, 21 June 1819, and 28 July 1819, both UVa.

[34] C to Bigelow, 7 March 1819, MassHistSoc, below.

[35] Philadelphia, 2 v.

[36] The dedication and the book itself are reprinted in v. 14 of Thwaites, R. G., ed., *Early western travels, loc. cit.*

[37] *DAB.*

ing, as we have noted above,[38] the *Wistaria*. This work of his of 1821 is one of the major records of western exploration.

Though he never held a professional chair in America, the Abbé did advise two universities in regard to their offerings in botany. His letter to a member of the board of trustees of the University of Pennsylvania regarding its proposed Faculty of Physical Science and Rural Economy, given below, indicates the Abbé's profound sense of the usefulness of botany and his definite conceptions as to its proper relation to kindred subjects.[39] It will be noted again under Correa's relation to American education.

In 1826, three years after Correa's death and within a few months of his own, Jefferson outlined for the first Professor of Natural History at the University of Virginia his old friend's plan for a botanic garden for that institution. Jefferson apparently approved highly of this plan (quite characteristically with his own modifications), though probably for financial reasons it was never carried out.[40]

Such things as these cannot be evaluated in exact terms. Correa, "who preferred an amalgamation of the methods of Linnaeus and of Jussieu to either of them exclusively," [41] had presented his methods and his ideas to the citizens of the United States, except in a few instances, orally. But by presenting an international rather than a provincial standard of judgment in determining the value of botanical papers presented before the Philadelphia academies, he aided these Americans in establishing criteria in their research.

---

[38] Ch. III, note 16.

[39] C to [Wm. Rawle], 14 March 1816, UPennaArch.

[40] Letter from Dr. Edwin Betts, editor of Jefferson's Garden and Farm Books, to the writer, 4 Jan. 1952. See TJ to Dr. J. P. Emmet, 27 April 1826, LC and UVa, below.

[41] TJ to Emmet, 27 April 1826, below.

To him competent botanists from Boston to Charleston appealed as higher authority. Above all he was the medium through which other men on both sides of the Atlantic exchanged plants and ideas.

OTHER SCIENCES

"At home in every science," Jefferson had said in describing the Abbé to Governor Milledge.[42] In general Correa's participation in American observation and research in the natural sciences other than botany followed very much the same pattern it had in his favorite. In the sessions of his two academies he recommended for publication or commented upon papers on such subjects as "An Osseus Fragment from Big Bone Lick" or "The Geological Formation of the Natural Bridge of Virginia," [43] or he informed the gentlemen of mammoth bones recently found in several places in South America.[44]

His letters mention fossil remains a number of times, partially because of their revelations of prehistoric plant life. And the correspondence also shows his interest in mineralogical or geological formations. His only scientific paper read before the American Philosophical Society was that on the soil of Kentucky on 3 March, 1815,[45] a few months after his return from the western expedition. This seven-page essay states and supports the theory that the soil of the "Elkhorn Tract" in Kentucky, rich, deep, and dark, is the last of the deposits of a receding inland sea. This is a soil similar

---

[42] See ch. III, note 81.

[43] Early proceedings of the APS, 461, 16 Feb. 1816.

[44] Minutes AcNatSciPhila, 22 Feb. 1820.

[45] MS. Minutes APS. This "communication" was accepted for publication on 21 April 1815 (MS. Minutes), but not published until 1818. See C to Madison, 5 Sept. 1818, LC, notes, below.

in its vegetable matter, general characteristics, and manner of formation to the coal buried under several "superincumbent strata" in western Pennsylvania, western Virginia, and Ohio. "Only thus can we explain the depth of the Kentucky mould," he concludes. It is a lucid argument, parallelling his early reports before the Royal Society on the submerged forests of Lincolnshire.

As noted above,[46] in 1819 Correa spoke of assisting Cooper in a geological lecture at the University of Pennsylvania as though it was the kind of thing he did fairly frequently.[47] Besides these evidences of interest in geology and geography, the observations Gilmer made under Correa's direction of the terrain and climates of the South,[48] Correa's letter to Madison concerning the saline deposits in the West,[49] and his favorite topics of conversation recorded by his contemporaries, are further indications of his alert consideration of many other forms of earth than her flowers.

EDUCATION

In 1821 Jefferson remarked that "Mr. Correa's approbation of the plan & principles of our university flatters me more than that of all it's other eulogists; because no other could be put in a line with him in science and comprehensive scope of mind." [50] When one considers Correa's part in Jefferson's University of Virginia he is again faced with the intangible and the tenuous. The letters given below, from 9 December, 1814, to 12 October, 1820, indicate the Abbé's enormous interest in his friend's plans and also Jefferson's desire to have his criticism. Correa advised on

---

46 Ch. IV, note 78.
47 C to Z. Collins, [Sept. 1819], AcNatSciPhila, below.
48 See ch. III, note 85, above.
49 10 Dec. 1814, LC, below.
50 To Dr. Fernandes, 28 May 1821, LC.

choice of professors and method of choosing them, on curricula and on general aims. He urged that the mediocrity of New England's export of intellect should not be allowed to control and stunt this institution at its beginning.[51] He fought long to get Cooper for the University, and probably he also recommended Elliott and other first-rate men for its chairs.[52] His advocacy of a professorship of theology or religion, in which he differed from Cooper, was the result of his belief that an educated clergy could not be a bigoted clergy.[53] And he outlined the botanical garden for the University which Jefferson later proposed, as we have noted above.[54]

No evidence remains that Jefferson was wholly indebted to Correa for any single facet of his educational theory or practice. The plan of sending to Europe for professors to avoid New England mediocrity, for example, may indicate Correa's influence, but it had been in Jefferson's mind for years before he knew Correa.[55] That the agent who was so successful in procuring competent Europeans was Correa's protégé Gilmer is interesting, but Gilmer was Jefferson's protégé too, and the appointment as agent was made after Correa's death.

These letters do indicate, however, that long conversations on the subject of Jefferson's project had taken place at Monticello in this 1814–1820 period, when the father of the University of Virginia was crystallizing out and perfecting the details of his plans.[56]

---

[51] To TJ, 22 March 1819, LC, below.
[52] TJ to J. W. Eppes, 29 July 1820, UVa.
[53] C to TJ, 9 Dec. 1814, LC, below.
[54] Ch. V, note 40.
[55] Davis, *Gilmer*, 193–236.
[56] See Honeywell, Roy J., *The educational work of Thomas Jefferson,* 66 ff., Cambridge, Mass., Harvard, 1931; Bruce, P. A., *History of the University of Virginia,* 5 v., 1, New York, Macmillan, 1920.

The exalted opinion Jefferson held of Correa's abilities would indicate the likelihood of employed advice, and certainly Correa's approval generally of his friend's ideas must have been most encouraging to their author.

Despite his age, Correa himself was considered for or was invited to occupy professorships in American institutions. Jefferson and Madison had in 1816 or earlier urged the Abbé to accept a chair in the national university they hoped to establish in Washington.[57] At the very end of the story in 1822, Jefferson still hoped Correa might return to a professorship at Charlottesville.[58] As we have seen, the University of Pennsylvania in 1815 had wished him to occupy its chair of natural history and botany,[59] and his two series of lectures must have been given at least partially under the sponsorship of that institution.

Correa's long letter to William Rawle given below, an answer to a request for advice on a proposed new Faculty of Physical Science and Rural Economy in the University of Pennsylvania, is perhaps the most enlightening extant record of the Abbé's belief in the essential usefulness of those sciences to which he was devoted, and certainly of what he considered their proper relation in a curriculum. Again it is difficult to determine whether he actually affected the University's plans, but as the notes to this letter indicate, it seems very likely that he did.[60] The letter shows also to a remarkable degree his familiarity with such curricula in a number of European universities.

---

[57] C to daBarca, 9 Feb. 1816, Carvalho, 182–183. See also the Annual Messages to Congress 1810, 1815, and 1816 proposing this institution, in Hunt, G., ed., *Writings of James Madison* **8**: 127, 342, 379.

[58] TJ to General Dearborn, 31 Oct. 1822, LC, quoted at end of ch. VI below.

[59] See just above, ch. V, note 25.

[60] C to [Wm. Rawle], 14 March 1816, UPennaArch, below.

One young scholar who had been a tutor at Harvard was convinced that the Abbé was the kind of man, or the man, that institution needed if it was to grow from a college into a university. Joseph Green Cogswell, later himself to study at European universities and as a great teacher to have part in preparing New England for her flowering, in 1816 wrote from Marseilles to George Ticknor, then at Göttingen:

It is time for Cambridge to take a rank above a mere preparatory school, and to do this she must call to her aid all the talents she can command. . . . Such men as Correa no one would suppose would be of any service to boys in their forms, but no university can ever attain a reputation without them; the limits which a student fixes for his attainments, are not confined to what is taught him, but to what the most learned of his professors is supposed to know; so that Correa, if, as you say, he should do nothing, would be a more powerful excitement to ambition, and the means of producing a greater number of fine scholars, aye, ten to one, than the most laborious drudge.[61]

Perhaps Cogswell had the key to much of Correa here. The Abbé wished to be and was a powerful excitement to intellectual ambition.

POLITICS, POLITICAL ECONOMY, AND SOCIOLOGY

Correa's earliest recorded training had been under the political economist, the Abbé Genovesi, at Naples. Undoubtedly he felt both before and after his nomination as envoy that he could be useful to the United States as a governmental advisor. His letters to Jefferson and Madison contain many items of candid, yet usually tactful, and often perceptive advice concerning American affairs. Exactly what plan he had for bringing New England back to "loyalty" in 1814 is not entirely clear, but it is evident that he expounded it to Jefferson[62] and perhaps to Madison in conversation.

---

61 [Ticknor, Anna E., ed.?], *Cogswell*, 44–45.
62 C to TJ, 10 April 1814, 20 Sept. 1814; TJ to C, 27 Dec. 1814, all LC, all below.

The Indian problem, most acute in his time, he apparently had commented upon after his visit to the Cherokees in 1815, for he drew up probably for Jefferson, "The Case of the Brazilian Indians," [63] at once a request for advice on the South American native problem and a series of hints that what had already been done there might well be heeded by this country. He concluded, "Our wish is to move them to be in fact, what they are by law, a real augmentation of the class of white subjects."

The Abbé's advice to President Madison concerning means of securing a "domanial branch of revenue" for the nation, a plan which suggests the exploration and development of saline and other mineral resources controlled by the government in the western territories, would appear good liberal doctrine in our day as well as in his.[64] Even though he stated that it had already been tried in Europe, the Abbé felt that he must apologize for his enthusiastic scheme as romantic "rhapsody." Our generation, which has known the TVA and has seen the progress of the liberal socialistic state, might take him more seriously than evidently he took himself. In the same letter he presents a straightforward proposal as to the way our government should conduct its campaign in Florida under General Jackson: we should disavow territorial aims, and then our best "retaliation" for recent British outrages would be to state officially that despite all irritations, we would stick to the rules of civilized warfare. This, Correa thought, would prejudice all Europe in our favor and thus aid us at the peace tables. Though this advice was not followed, many Americans of the time, including members of the cabinets of Madison and later Monroe, would almost surely have agreed with the policy enunciated.

---

[63] LC, 3 pages MS.
[64] C to Madison, 10 Dec. 1814, LC, below.

The whole series of letters to Gilmer in 1816 concerning the Florida-Louisiana boundary question [65] probably sprang from the mixed motives of bringing to the United States what "belonged" to her by treaty or by destiny, of hitting back at Portugal's traditional enemy, Spain, a nation he never loved, and of aiding Gilmer to make a name for himself. The encouragement of H. M. Brackenridge's published views on the same subject in 1816 and 1817 [66] must have sprung from the same complexity of motives. The Neutrality Law of 1817, or rather his train of reasoning which led to it, seems again the result of his desire to aid the United States and his own country at the same time. This was perhaps the last of such efforts of his to influence government policy for mutual benefit, for the privateers were almost upon him.

Correa's two-part essay published through Walsh, "General Considerations upon the Past and Future State of Europe," [67] should also be here considered, for it is a concise presentation of political history to an American public just then (in 1812–1813) anxious about the future state of the civilized world and of the American part in it. Part One, suggesting that the best way to divine the future is by the past, argues that the present conflagration in Europe started more than

---

[65] 6 Feb. to 21 July, all below.

[66] See ch. IV, notes 55 and 56, above; also Brackenridge, H. M., *Views of Louisiana; containing geographical, statistical and historical notices of that vast and important section of America. . .* , Baltimore, 1817; and *idem,* The Florida question stated, *American Register* 1: 128–148, 1817.

[67] The "Past State," published under the more general title given above, appeared in Walsh's *American Review* 4: 354–356, 1812; the second part, "The Future State," as an appendix to *Correspondence respecting Russia, between Robert Goodloe Harper esq., and Robert Walsh, jun. . .* , 121–139, Philadelphia, 1813.

three centuries before. Tracing the major factors in European history as Christianity, the Roman Code, and the Balance of Power, it suggests that the endless circle of revenue for military might and military might for revenue had become the momentous concern of European cabinets. Prussia at length set the example of armed proscription, not dangerous in that secondary power, but when taken up by France caused Vesuvius to erupt. In Part Two, on the present state of Europe, Correa recapitulates by concluding that at the dawn of the Napoleonic era, through the events of thirteen centuries, Europe formed "a republic of monarchical states of different strengths and size." In defining "republic," incidentally, he refers to Jefferson's *Notes on Virginia*. The European republic may become, if the continent is conquered, one universal monarchy of a single capital, an empire marked by heavy taxes, degeneracy, oppression, and the banishment of the clergy from education.

The balance of power for more than two centuries, he feels, turned chiefly on the jealousy of France and the House of Austria, with the older English-French rivalry still a factor. The next great axes might be Russia and Austria. "Strange as it may appear, it is nevertheless probable, that France will be the support of the house of Austria, and England the natural ally of Russia." The Abbé concludes with a question he leaves unanswered—what will be the state of affairs if Europe is left, after the present wars, partially but not wholly conquered? Altogether it is a suggestive essay which displays a comprehensive understanding of the forces which had made its author's world, and incidentally an inferred belief in the clergy as the great educating force.

One specific "welfare" project the Abbé engaged in, something which had interested him in his European days. He was one of the founders of the Pennsylvania

Institution for the Deaf and Dumb. Along with Bishop White, Jacob Gratz, William Meredith, and others, he was instrumental in establishing in 1820 this school for the indigent and handicapped. The systems employed were those followed in Paris. Correa pronounced them equally effective here in Philadelphia.[68]

HUMANE LETTERS

In the final considerations of Correa's place in American intellectual life, we again are reminded strikingly of his friend, Jefferson. For to the master of Monticello and to the Abbé, as to many another child of the Enlightenment, the humanities were valued as they were useful. In Correa's case two instances well illustrate the point.

Among the many American Philosophical Society papers which Correa was asked to judge critically for their potential publication value, one especially will interest all students of American literature. Actually it was not an essay read before the Society at all, but a manuscript volume which had found its way into the Society's library at some earlier time. It was William Byrd's "Secret History of the Dividing Line between Virginia and North Carolina," probably the earlier of two versions of what is now regarded as a classic of our colonial literature.[69] Correa was chairman of a committee of which his friends, Peter S. DuPonceau and Dr. Wistar, were the other members. On 22 May, 1816, they submitted the terse report:

---

[68] Oberholtzer, *History Philadelphia* **2**: 128; Rebecca Gratz to Maria Gist Gratz, 4 April 1820, Philipson, David, ed., *Letters of Rebecca Gratz,* 28, Philadelphia, Jewish Pub. Soc. Amer., 1929.

[69] See Boyd, William K., ed., *William Byrd's histories of the dividing line betwixt Virginia and North Carolina,* xvi, Raleigh, North Carolina Hist. Com., 1929.

The journal of the Commissioners to fix the limits between Virginia and North Carolina from the Library of the Late Colonel Bird, is well worthy being published for the important and curious information it affords, not only on the object of the operation, but more particularly on the state of civilization of these states about the middle of the last century.[70]

The interesting things here are the report's emphasis on the historical usefulness of the work as a picture of a period culture, and the fact that had this recommendation been acted upon, American literature would have had one of its most noted productions available more than a century before it actually was published. The "Secret History" did not appear until 1929, when Professor Boyd edited it in a parallel text edition with the longer and quite different "History of the Dividing Line," the latter itself not published until 1841.[71]

In another project within or just approaching the realm of letters the Abbé's encouragement produced more concrete results. In January, 1819, Father Peter Babad, who taught Spanish and Portuguese in St. Mary's Seminary, Baltimore, where Edward Correa was a student, planned to publish the first grammar of the Portuguese language composed in this country. In 1820 it was published, a prospectus states, through "the liberality of his excellency the Portuguese minister." [72] Apparently in his various visits to Baltimore the Abbé had come to know the French Sulpicians in Paca Street quite well.[73] Father Babad dedicated his book to Correa, and indicated how considerable a part the Abbé had had in its publication.

---

[70] APS, MS. Minutes, etc.

[71] In *The Westover manuscripts.* . . , edited by Edmund Ruffin, Petersburg, Va.

[72] Quoted in Smith, Robert C., A pioneer teacher: Father Peter Babad and his Portuguese grammar, *Hispania* **28**: 337, 1945.

[73] *Ibid.,* See also C to Vaughan, 27 March 1818, note 3, below.

Your kindness in encouraging the project . . . in order to facilitate to the young students of this country and to the public at large, the acquisition of the beautiful language of Camoens, Vieyra, Theodora [*sic*] de Almeyda, &c; your generous condescension in guiding my trembling steps in this intricate and arduous undertaking; your constant benevolence in resolving all my doubts and difficulties, have strongly induced me to hope that you will not blame me for the liberty I take in placing under your patronage this little work, the existence, publication, and general utility of which, are to be principally attributed to you.[74]

The author adds that he consulted men of letters conversant with the "genius and rules of the Portuguese language, and especially the learned minister plenipotentiary of H.M.F.M. Mr. Corrêa de Serra." [75] Thus as advisor and sponsor of Babad's unpretentious little book as well as in his encouragement of European study for George Ticknor, Correa had his finger at least *upon* if not *in* the beginnings of the serious study of the modern European languages in this country.

VI. LAST YEARS IN EUROPE, 1821–1823

After a rough and uncomfortable passage from New York, Correa and his son and his servant, Adam Cain, disembarked at Liverpool on 5 December, 1820.[1] He had expected to proceed within a short time to Brazil, but he found that a rapid succession of events might alter his plans. In the summer and autumn of 1820 a bloodless revolution had taken place in Portugal. It had been aimed among other things at removing the country from subservience to Brazil and from English military influence, and at re-establishing the ancient Cortes. Loyalty to John VI was the unifying factor among rebels with otherwise varying aims. Correa's

---

[74] *Ibid.,* 337–338.
[75] *Ibid.,* 338.
[1] Carvalho, 74–75, 199–200; and letters below.

own Academy of Sciences wished to have a Cortes of the traditional type with nobles, ecclesiastics, and commoners. A demand for nation-wide suffrage, however, resulted in a November election in which the deputies, mostly middle-class liberals, were elected without trouble. They were to meet on 24 January, 1821, and select a new regency and debate a future constitution.[2] In such a fluid situation Correa could do nothing but wait or carry out orders from Brazil. In a sense he did both.

The Abbé had written to his superiors the day after landing,[3] but before they had opportunity to receive his messages he had received earlier orders to undertake a mission to Paris. In December and in January he was in London renewing old acquaintances.[4] But for a period of a month he was back in the French capital, where he was received most cordially.[5] He was old, sick, and disappointed, however, and according to William Short, who passed the news on to Jefferson, he was so "dictatorial, impatient of contradiction" that he soon antagonized all his old friends there, became himself disgusted, and returned to England.[6] Correa's own account indicates that he remained in Paris long enough to accomplish his mission and then returned to await further orders. He probably saw Esther Delavigne for the last time on this journey, perhaps with their son.[7]

---

[2] Livermore, H. V., A history of Portugal, 406–409, Cambridge, Eng., Cambridge U., 1947.

[3] To Snr. T. A. Vila Nova Portugal, 6 Dec. 1820, Carvalho, 199–200; MS. in Ministério da Educaçao e Saude, Rio de Janeiro.

[4] C to Sir J. E. Smith, 1 Jan. 1821, 2 Jan. 1821, 10 Jan. 1821, 20 Feb. 1821, LinnSoc, London.

[5] Agan, 39, quoted from Lavradio, 219.

[6] 5 Dec. 1821, LC. Short received the news second or third hand.

[7] Carvalho, 75. Actually she is not mentioned in the known

In England he saw and corresponded with his friends, Sir James Edward Smith, R. A. Salisbury, and Robert Brown.[8] But he was restless, for much was happening. A sympathetic revolution in Rio de Janeiro had supported that in Portugal, and the necessity of the King's accepting the parliamentary regime became urgent. By 28 April, John had agreed to swear to the constitution and had decided to return to Portugal. On 4 July the King landed at Lisbon and a day later took the oath. A projected constitution had been printed on 30 June, 1821, but debates on it lasted until September, 1822. In the meanwhile in July, 1821, with some misgivings, Correa sailed from Falmouth for Lisbon.[9] With him were his son Edward, aged eighteen, and his servant, Adam Cain, aged twenty-eight.[10] At long last on 6 August the venerable exile set foot in his native land.[11]

When Correa stepped ashore, some of his compatriots were mildly shocked to observe that he was dressed like an American gentleman. Always sensitive to public opinion, the Abbé soon abandoned this costume for his cassock.[12] He was received immediately with great favor at court, and honors were heaped upon him. His earlier appointment as Counselor of Fazenda in Brazil did not apply in the new situation, but at the King's request he was named to the same position in Portugal. He was reimbursed for funds due and also given new pensions.[13] Already the King

---

correspondence of this period. It seems possible that she died about the time Edward went to America.

[8] See letters of the period in LinnSoc, London, especially to Sir J. E. Smith, 20 Feb. 1821; to Salisbury, 3 Sept. 1821; also Smith to Prof. Hosack, 30 May 1821, HistSocPenna.

[9] C to Sir J. E. Smith, 23 July 1821, LinnSoc, London.

[10] Carvalho, 75.

[11] *Ibid.*

[12] *Ibid.*, 77.

[13] *Ibid.*, 78 ff., 81; see also letters of C and Edward C, below.

had placed under his charge all the royal establishments of arts and sciences.[14]   In 1822 he was elected a deputy of the Cortes, where he seems to have done little save make one speech defending the Academy of Sciences.[15]   He was named to one commission after another by the King,[16] apparently remaining in high favor at court until the last.

But all this was aggravating the already grave diabetic condition.   The Abbé wrote what was probably his last letter abroad to his old protégé, the by now renowned botanist, Robert Brown, on 18 April, 1823.[17] Already in 1822 he had petitioned the King that his son, Edward, be legitimized and made his legal heir, and by a decree of 5 February the request was granted.[18]   But the ancient antagonism against the Academy and himself was flaring afresh, and the old man's troubles were becoming intolerable.   These last troubles came as a part of the counter-revolution of May, 1823, which overthrew the Cortes and restored for a time a degree of absolute monarchy,[19] a political move which may have been the *coup de grace* to the hopes and spirit of the old liberal patriot.   For at the end it is apparent that, whatever his attitude in America, he remained with the liberals.   From his youth he had considered them his country's only hope.

---

[14] C to Sir J. E. Smith, 2 Jan. 1821, LinnSoc, London.

[15] Carvalho, 84–86.   C resided in Lisbon and placed third and last of those elected, receiving 1,371 votes.   See *Diario das Cortes Gerais da nacao Portugueza, segunda legislatura,* tomos I–III, 1822–1823.   The *Diario* (which has been examined for me by Professor George C. A. Boehrer of Marquette University) contains notices of C's activities, including speeches and motions, through the spring of 1823.   Apparently he was a moderate, not an extreme liberal.

[16] Carvalho, 81, 84–85 ff.

[17] *Ibid.,* 89, 200; also LinnSoc, London.

[18] Carvalho, 80–81.

[19] Livermore, *History of Portugal,* 412–414.

In the meanwhile, probably in the summer of 1822, Edward Correa had moved to Paris. The young man admitted that his disgust at conditions in Portugal and his desire to finish his education inspired this step,[20] and he may also have wished to see his mother. In August, 1823, one of the lonely Abbé's last recorded acts was to see that Peter DuPonceau of Philadelphia was elected a corresponding fellow of the Portuguese Academy,[21] but he did not appear personally at the session. He was probably already trying as a last resort the baths at Caldas da Rainha, for it was at Caldas that he died on 11 September. Because of the political bitterness of the period he was buried without recognition from the nation for which he had labored so long and so faithfully.[22] For years no one dared pronounce a eulogy upon him even at the Academy. Costa e Sá's paper was read there in 1829, but no one had the courage to publish it until 1848,[23] though France had long before given him recognition.[24] A bitter end to a "longa vida de martiro," [25] to a life about as varied and as interesting, and one is tempted to say as useful, as a man can live.

But what thoughts had Correa of America in these last harried years? The bitterness toward the government of the United States remained with him to the end. Even the warm personal friendships to which he himself had attested so graciously in his final American letters were neglected. Apparently he never wrote a word to Jefferson, Madison, or Gilmer, probably partially because they represented to him the govern-

---

[20] E. Correa to Vaughan, 8 Jan. 1823 and 1 July 1823, below.
[21] Carvalho, 89.
[22] *Ibid.*, 90.
[23] *Ibid.*
[24] Almeida, 1824. See ch. II, note 1, above.
[25] Carvalho, 90.

ment—the Virginia dynasty—which had not supported his claims to his satisfaction.[26] Even to his Philadelphia friends he wrote rarely. During the whole of 1821 one letter by Correa and one by Edward appear to have been all they addressed to this country.[27] In December of that year William Short observed to Jefferson that almost nothing had been heard from the Abbé:

This as regards Vaughan is more than neglect—it is downright ingratitude. His silence observed towards his friends here proceeds probably in some degree from his aversion to writing; but it is also, I apprehend, not without some kind of Jesuitical calculation.[28]

In 1822 Correa did write pleasant letters to Vaughan and to DuPonceau, and Edward also gave news of his father to Vaughan.[29] In 1823 Edward wrote twice to Vaughan,[30] but apparently his father was too ill and busy and indifferent to write to anyone in America.

Meanwhile his American friends had not forgotten him, and except for Short were quite generous in all references to him. Whenever Jefferson got news of Correa's activities, he passed the information on to mutual friends.[31] Even Walsh grew more understanding. In one letter to Jefferson he remarked that

All the happiness of M. Correa was destroyed by his appointment as minister. He became fretful, suspicious, valetudinary, and has been more or less wretched ever since. So much for reaching the summit of our wishes. All his philosophy vanished before the *reason[s?] of state*. Your example ought to have had a salutary effect upon his mind, when he enjoyed your society. . . .[32]

---

[26] TJ to Walsh, 5 April 1823, UVa.

[27] C to Vaughan, 23 April 1821; Edward C to Vaughan, 26 June 1821, both APS, both below.

[28] 5 Dec. 1821, LC.

[29] C to DuPonceau, 12 Jan., AcNatSciPhila; to Vaughan, 13 Jan., APS; Edward C to Vaughan, 19 Jan., APS, all three below.

[30] 8 Jan. and 1 July, APS, both below.

[31] E.g., TJ to Walsh, 5 April 1823, UVa.

[32] 14 April 1823, LC.

In 1822 General Henry Dearborn, United States minister to Portugal, was attempting to negotiate a commercial treaty with that country. Correa was appointed by the King to act for Portugal; the Abbé declined on the ground that as a member of the Cortes he should not do so,[33] but perhaps because he wished to have nothing to do with America. Though the treaty was never signed, the failure was from reasons stronger than Correa's hostility.[34] One biting comment of his on America survives from this period and is indicative of his feeling. When he saw the Portuguese constitution for the first time, he remarked that Portugal as a monarchy had more real democracy, and more republican institutions, than the United States ever did.[35]

But the now ailing old gentleman who lived at Monticello and had loved the Abbé was always understanding of his friend's trials of time and spirit. He ignored the neglect. In a letter to Dearborn which was communicated to Correa in February, 1823,[36] and to which there seems to have been no reply, we have the last testimonial of a remarkable friendship. Jefferson wrote on 31 October, 1822, asking for information concerning the Abbé. The tone is tender and wistful.

I have a friend, of Portugal, in whose welfare I feel great interest; but whether now there, or where I know not. it is the Abbe Cor[rea who p]ast some years in the US, and was a part of the time th[e minister] of Portugal at Washington—he left it under an appointm[ent to the c]abinet—council of Rio Janeiro, taking his passage th[i]ther by way of England. while at London or Paris he would h[ave] heard that the king & court had returned to Lisbon; and what he did next is unknown here. he writes to none of his friends, & yet there is no one on

---

[33] Agan, 41; Lyman, Theodore, Jr., *The diplomacy of the United States,* 2 v., 230, Boston, 1828 (2nd ed.).

[34] Agan, 41.

[35] Carvalho, 77.

[36] Agan, 41.

whose behalf his friends feel a more lively solicitude or wish more to hear of or from. if at Lisbon, and it should ever fall your way to render him a service or kindness, I should consider it as more than if done to myself. if things go unfavorably to him there, he would be received with joy into our University, and would certainly find it a comfortable & lucrative retirement. should he be in Lisbon, be so good as to say it to him. . . .[37]

VII. "OUR SOCRATES"

"Our Socrates" Walsh once affectionately called the Abbé,[1] perhaps referring half humorously to Brackenridge's word for Correa in the dedication to the *Views of Louisiana.* The Abbé, realizing that the future of a youthful nation lay in its youthful citizens, had from the very beginning of his stay in America been the encourager of young men. What he had done for the botanists in putting them in touch with the great men in their field in Europe we have seen. Sometimes, as in the case of Ticknor and Lardner Vanuxem of Philadelphia, whose parents could afford to send them to Europe for study, he advised as to universities and countries in which their particular fields of interest were most flourishing.[2] Again, he was an agency in

---

[37] 31 Oct. 1822, LC. Material in brackets is conjectural restoration of letters or words which are illegible or obscured by the seal of this letter.

[1] Walsh to Gilmer, 12 March 1818, UVa.

[2] C to TJ, 12 Nov. 1820, LC, below, and Vaughan to TJ, 24 March 1821, UVa. Vanuxem became professor of mineralogy in Cooper's South Carolina College, and was recommended for a professorship in the University of Virginia. He was a member of the APS (List of members APS, 29) and of the AcNatSciPhila (*Jour. Acad. Nat. Sci. Phila.* 1 (1): 82, 182, 214–216, 1817–1818). He had studied at Paris "under the recommendation of Mr. Correa." For Ticknor, see Ticknor to TJ, 14 Oct. 1814, *loc. cit.*

turning the young conservative critic, Walsh, towards liberalism and Jefferson. On the long journey to the South in 1815, he talked more to Gilmer of American governmental problems than he did of botany, for he felt that in this young man he was counseling one of the future leaders of the republic.[3] The list is long, and it is unnecessary to rename all those to whom the Abbé's "communicative temper" brought stimuli to thought and action. In a country necessarily occupied principally in laying the foundations of its national life, a distinguished foreigner who could in kindly fashion offer suggestions of improvements in the structure as it arose should have been a welcome guest. That he generously put the builders in contact with the experts in the architecture of a civilization already nearing completion should have made him even more greatly appreciated. And as in the man himself was embodied a remarkable assemblage of the best qualities of a ripe culture, he afforded to the Jeffersonians more than a glimpse of what their nation and its citizens might become in maturity. As Fanny Wright said, Brackenridge was but expressing a general approbation when he called Correa da Serra "one of the fathers of our country."

VIII. THE LETTERS

The letters reproduced below are all from, to, or concerning Correa da Serra in his American years, though they begin with one written three years before he came to this country and conclude with others written three years after his departure and almost two years after his death. These letters are mainly representative of his personal interests, activities, and friendships in the United States. For reasons noted above and below,

---

[3] C to TJ, 12 Feb. 1816, LC, below.

only a few key items of his official correspondence as Portuguese minister have been included. A few brief items have been omitted because they are repetitious of matters also present in those printed. Even these, however, are referred to in the text above or the notes to letters below. Letters of this period to European or Brazilian correspondents have been quoted or referred to above but have not, with one exception, been reproduced.

All letters retain the spelling, capitalization, and punctuation, though not the spacing, of the originals. Words or phrases in brackets are occasionally inserted for intelligibility, for at times, especially in his later years, Correa's English idiom is awkward or difficult. Other bracketed insertions complete text originally present but now indecipherable because of the condition of the manuscripts. *Sic* has been employed sparingly and only when it was felt to be really necessary. For the idiosyncrasies of Jefferson's text, see Julian P. Boyd, *et al.,* edd., *The Papers of Thomas Jefferson* 1: xxx–xxxii, Princeton, 1950. In the letters written in French, or partly in French, Correa is quite unorthodox by modern standards, and somewhat so by standards of his own time, in the matter of accents and spelling. The accents have been reproduced exactly as he wrote them, and the spelling as exactly as the editor can decipher it. Correa is not, of course, always consistent in his unorthodoxy, even in his signature.

As a heading for each letter, at the left, are given the names of the writer and the addressee. The name is given in full above the first letter with which it is concerned, and after that only as surname. The exception is that the full name of Correa's son must be given to distinguish him from his father. On the right of the heading is given, in abbreviated form, the name of the repository in which the letter is located.

For the use of other students of Correa, a checklist of his extant letters to foreign correspondents during his American years is given as an appendix to the letters reproduced. With one exception, the texts of these foreign letters are not given in the present study.

TO

HIS EXCELLENCY

THE CHEVALIER

JOSE CORREA, DE SERRA

MINISTER PLENIPOTENTIARY

OF

H. M. F. Majesty

THE KING OF PORTUGAL AND

THE BRAZILS.

A PLAIN republican, to whom high names, official dignities, or vast riches, command no awe or veneration, but who willingly acknowledges as his superior, the man of mind, whatever may be his station, humbly DEDICATES, his performance, unworthy as it is, TO ONE OF THE MOST ENLIGHTENED FOR‑EIGNERS THAT HAS EVER VISITED THE UNITED STATES.

The giddy world, too often assigns the highest places in the temple of fame, to mighty conquerors and war‑riors, who are more frequently the enemies, than the friends of mankind, while its real benefactors, are but slowly, are never fully appreciated. The few, on whom nature has bestowed the choice gift of a capacious mind, which they have stored with knowledge for the good of their fellow creatures, should ever be regarded as bless‑ings to the people among whom they have been cast.

They are to be received like the angel of Milton, who came down to instruct our first parents in wisdom and virtue.

As an American, I am proud that my country has been the choice of a sage, acknowledged both by Europe and America, as one of the most enlightened of human kind; who after having gathered from every field of science in the old world, has brought his ample store as a present to the new.

Sir, your amiable simplicity of manners, and communicative temper, restore to us our Franklin; in every part of our country, which you have visited (for you have nearly seen it all) your society has been as acceptable to the unlettered farmer as to the learned philosopher: the liberal and friendly manner, in which you are accustomed to view every thing in these States, the partiality which you feel for their welfare, the profound maxims, upon every subject, which like the disciples of Socrates, we treasure up from your lips, entitle us to claim you as one of the fathers of our country.

To none, therefore, could I with more propriety dedicate my *"Views of Louisiana,"* than to you whose favourite study is the American government, manners, and soil; and who (I say it without hesitation) have in the short space of five years, acquired a knowledge of this country, as critical and extensive, as any of its most intelligent citizens. But if any additional motive were necessary, to justify the liberty I have presumed to take in thus addressing you, I could allege a sense of gratitude, for the commendations you were pleased to bestow upon this work, while yet in the shape of newspaper essays;

Pollio amat nostram, quamvis est rustica musam,

and it is in a great measure owing to these commendations, that it has assumed its present form.

Accept, sir, the expressions of the high veneration of one who esteems it as among the most felicitous circumstances of his life, to have personally known you, and to be able to subscribe himself,

Your sincere and
ardent admirer,
disciple, and friend,

H. M. BRACKENRIDGE.[1]

CORREA TO FULWAR SKIPWITH [2]   [*Hist.Soc.Penna.*]

Paris 4th. Septr. 1808.

Dear Sir

I take the liberty of addressing to you these few lines, as a final memorandum of the business, you know by our conversations i have so much at heart. to live in America is the utmost of my wishes, you know the only

---

[1] This dedication occupies pages 3–6 of the 1817 edition of Brackenridge's *Views of Louisiana; Containing Geographical, Statistical and Historical Notices of That Vast and Important Portion of America,* published in Baltimore. See ch. IV, notes 55 and 56, **above.**

[2] Agan, 9, gives the date of this letter as 1805, "Skipworth" as the name of the addressee, and the latter as "a friend in Philadelphia and former American consul at Paris." Actually Fulwar Skipwith (1765–1839) was still in Paris at this time. A Virginian whose brother, Henry, had married a sister of TJ's wife, he had held various consular posts in the French capital. He was consul general to 1796, commercial agent 1802–1809, and consul again in 1815. Skipwith also was to have a considerable part in the West Florida manoeuvers several years after 1809. See MS. List of U. S. Consular Officers by Posts, Dept. of State Records, NatArch; also James A. Padgett, The West Florida revolution of 1810, as told in the letters of John Rhea, Fulwar Skipwith, Reuben Kemper, and others, *La. Hist. Quart.* **21**: 78 ff., 1938.

means of doing it and of getting rid of all *contrarietis* [*sic*] is to be invited by the government of the U. States, and my passport to be asked officially by their minister. You know how useful i can be to them, i neither ask nor need any salary or emolument for my services, and indeed you are acquainted with my circumstances, to be necessary for me to enter into further explanations. If per accident any detail shall be required about my litterary caracter you may remit them to the Philosophical Transactions, those of the Linnean Society Les Annales du Museum d'hist. Naturelles, Les Archives Litteraires, in which collections many of my essays have been published, and to the several works of the Royal Academy of Lisbon,[3] whi[ch] i know are to be found at Philadelphia in the Library of the Philosophical Society.[4] Perhaps al[l] that may be unnecessary, and i believe it useless to mention any more of this business to you who are so well acquainted with all particulars by our conversations. I will only repeat the aknowledgements of the perfect esteem and real friendship with which i am

Sir

Your most sincere friend
Joseph Corrèa de Serra

You are sensible of what real service i can be to the U.S. when once got home.

---

[3] For not exhaustive bibliographies of C's writings see Carvalho, 93–107, and Almeida, 221 ff. Many of these and others are mentioned in the present study above. C in the present instance refers to his publications in the journals of the Royal and Linnean Societies and of various French learned groups, as well as those in the series of the Portuguese society of which he had been a founder.

[4] Of course the APS. C's knowledge of the presence of these scientific periodicals in America probably was derived from correspondence with members of the APS, or from conversation with Parisian members, or simply from the policy of exchange of journals among learned societies of the period.

[Note in a different hand:]

The abbé Correa, whom I knew very well & who has often been at my house, was the founder of the Academy of Sciences at Lisbon—The Inquisition twice compelled him to fly his Country—From 1816 to 1819 he was Portuguese Minister at Washington, & when I went to England in 1817 he gave me letters of introduction to several of the literati of Paris (by whom he was highly esteemed & respected) as well as to the Marquis Palmella,[5] Portuguese Minister in England, who had been his pupil. He was recalled to Portugal, & afterwards appointed Minister to Brazil. He was a great botanist, and published many literary & scientific papers in the transactions of Philosophical Societies in America & Europe. He died in 1823.

R Gilmor [6]

This letter was sent to me by Mr. Custis [7]

CORREA TO THOMAS JEFFERSON   [L.C.]

Washington city 6 March. 1812

Sir

When i left Europe two months ago, several of your correspondents and friends in that part of the world

---

[5] Dom Pedro de Souza Holstein, Marquis and Duke of Palmella (1786–1850), Portuguese statesman, was minister plenipotentiary, representing his country at the Congress of Vienna in 1814, in 1815–1816 minister to England, and in 1816 head of the ministry of foreign affairs in Portugal. *Biog. Univ.*

[6] Robert Gilmor (1774–1848), wealthy Maryland merchant and patron of arts and letters, member of the APS from 1803, was a frequent visitor in Europe. He numbered among his acquaintances many leading figures of both continents. *NCAB; List of Members APS*.

[7] Gilmor's brother, William, had married Mary Ann, daughter of Isaac and Elizabeth Custis (Teakle) Smith. Elizabeth Custis Teakle was the daughter of Thomas Teakle and his wife, Elizabeth, daughter of John Custis. Of course the prominent Custis

favoured me with letters of recommendation [8] to you, knowing how ardently i wished the honour of your acquaintance. Mr. Thouin [9] gave me also his last publication on grafting,[10] that i might present to you on his part. Not having the advantage of finding you in this place as i was led to believe in Europe, and being obliged to go as soon as possible to Philadelphia where i intend to reside, i send you Mr. Thouin's book, that you may not be deprived of the pleasure of reading it, and keep the letters with me, which i shall have the honour of presenting to you in the course of this summer when i intend to undertake the pilgrimage of Monticello. The

---

living in 1808 was George Washington Parke Custis. The Warden Papers in the Maryland Historical Society show that Eliza Parke Custis knew Skipwith and Correa. See *Ancestral records and portraits,* Colonial Dames of America, 2 v., 1 : 288–291, New York, Grafton, 1910, for a rough genealogy without dates, of the Gilmor family.

[8] The letters to TJ are those from André Thouin, Alexander von Humboldt, Pierre S. duPont de Nemours, and the Marquis de Lafayette, cited in chapter III, note 6, above. Since TJ did not reply to these French friends until the autumn of 1813, it is clear that the letters were not delivered until the summer of that year, rather than 1812, for C for some reason delayed his first visit to Monticello. Apparently the present letter "and work" were enclosed to TJ in a note from Gallatin of 10 March 1812 (LC).

[9] André Thouin (1747–1823), distinguished naturalist, had in 1792 relinquished his "public agriculture" post in the French cabinet to become chief of the Jardin des Plantes. Like C, Thouin was a member of most of the learned societies of his day, including the French Institute, and was a founder of the Linnean Society of Paris. *Biog. Univ.*

[10] The first edition of a *book* with the title . . . *Monographie des greffes; ou, description technique, des diverses sortes de greffes employées pour la multiplication des vegetaux* is 1821 [Paris]. From 1808 to 1824, however, Thouin had published a number of studies of grafting in *Annales du Museum d'histoire naturelle.* It may be to one of these that C refers.

present letter and Mr. Thouin's book i leave here at the care of Mr. Gallatin.[11] I am most devoutedly

>Sir

>>Your most obedient he. Servt.
>>Joseph Corrêa de Serra

JEFFERSON TO CORREA   [*L.C.*]

>Monticello   Apr. 17. 12.

Sir

Your favor of Mar. 6 was duly recieved, & with it the pamphlet of M. Thouin on the subject of engrafting,[12] for which be pleased to accept my thanks.   should your curiosity lead you to visit this part of the US. as your letter gives me reason to hope, I shall be very happy to receive you at Monticello, to express to you in person my great respect, and to recieve from yourself directly the letters of my friends beyond the water introducing me to the pleasure of your acquaintance. to my much valued friend M. Thouïn especially I am indebted for frequent attentions, and particularly in the transmission of foreign seeds, which I place always in the hands of the best gardeners of the US. with a view of having them indigenated here, and of thus fulfilling his benevolent intentions of disseminating what is useful.   should you be in correspondence with him, you would do me a great favor in giving a place in your

---

[11] Albert Gallatin (1761–1849), from 1801 to 1814 Secretary of the Treasury, wrote to TJ as noticed in note 8 above, that this "interesting and learned Portuguese" was recommended by Barlow, Humboldt, and others.

[12] See letter just above, C to TJ, 6 March 1812, notes 9 and 10.

first letter to the assurances of my affectionate remembrance of him. for yourself be pleased to accept the assurance of my high respect and consideration.

Th. Jefferson

M. Correa de Serra.

CORREA TO JEFFERSON   [*L.C.*]

Philadelphia 6 Septber. 1813 [13]

Sir

Together with this letter i forward to you by the post office the book of Senator Fossombroni.[14]   The 1st. part of the book is wholly antiquarian, and though highly curious to Italian readers, is of little interest to any other; the second part will give you an idea of that ingenious and experimental practice.   If it was judged proper to familiarize the Americans with it then it would be necessary to extract and translate what relates to it, in Fossombroni's memoir on this matter (which is printed in the 3d. vol. of the transactions of the Italian society [15]) and in the tracts of the Florentine collection

---

[13] "1813" is apparently in a lighter hand than the rest of the date line.

[14] Count Vittorio Fossombroni (1754–1844), politician and scientist, had published several books on hydraulics and Roman agriculture.   The particular work here presented is almost certainly . . . *Memorie idraulico-storiche sopra la Val-di-Chiana,* Firenze, 1789, for a book of this title (though without place or date published) is listed in the library TJ sold to Congress. *The catalogue of the library of the United States.   To which is annexed a copious index.   Alphabetically arranged.* 119, item 237, Washington . . . , 1815.

[15] Fossombroni was a Fellow of the Società italiana delle scienze, which published *Memorie di matematica e fisica.*   Vol. 3 of this periodical contains Fossombroni's "Sopra la distribuzione delle alluvioni."

of hydraulic books.[16]

Permit me to expose an idea which came to my memory in reading the unlucky accident of the two schooners upset in Lake Ontario in these last cruizes of Comre. Chauncey.[17] In the time of Suwarow's campaign,[18] the English assisted the house of Austria in building a flotilla of war in the Lake of Constance, and sent an English officer of the name of Williams to command it.[19] As it was the first instance of a lake navy in the actual state of naval improvement, i heard many interesting observations, made by competent judges, and particularly on the necessity of making alterations in the construction, because sea water being considerably heavier than fresh water, seemed to indicate that at least the prominence of the keel ought to be in an inverse ratio to the weight of the water, in order to give steadiness to the ship, and safety to its navigation. That a merchant ship had not the same necessity of hazardous manoeuvres, and consequently less occasion of feeling

---

[16] The Director of the Biblioteca Nazionale Centrale di Firenze is unable to locate such a collection. There was a later *Nouva raccolta di autori italiani che trattano del moto dell'acqua,* Bologna, 1823–1845.

[17] The *Hamilton,* Lieut. Winter, and the *Scourge,* Mr. Osgood, were capsized in a squall on or about 7 August, 1813. James Fenimore Cooper, *History of the Navy of the United States of America,* 2 v., 2: 419, London, 1839.

[18] Alexander Vasilievich Suvárov, Count Suvárov Rimniksky, Prince Italysky (1729–1800), had in 1799 fought against the French revolutionary armies in Italy. In the Alps and in Switzerland his Russians fought alongside of the English rather than the Austrians, with whom they could not agree. *Enc. Brit.*

[19] No information can be obtained on this matter from the British Museum nor the National Maritime Museum, Greenwich, though the latter states that the movements of a Captain Robert Williams, R.N., at this period are not made clear in one of the main sources of naval history, Marshall's *Naval Biography.*

the necessity of such an alteration. Has this been attended to, by your naval constructors in the lakes?

When i returned to Washington with Col. Randolph [20] we missed to [sic] meet Mr. Madison. [21] I write to him as is my duty in leaving this continent, but i remember you of Mr. Warden's title of Consul general, [22] about which you were so good as to promise me your interest. I have learned since i am in Phila-

---

[20] Thomas Mann Randolph (1768–1828), Jefferson's scholarly son-in-law, lived much of the time with his family at Monticello. He and C were always firm friends. In his letters to F. W. Gilmer (UVa), Randolph shows the great esteem in which he held the venerable Portuguese. See above, and *DAB*. For three letters of C to Randolph, see below.

[21] See C to President Madison, 9 September, 1813, just below.

[22] David B. Warden (1772–1845), Scotch-Irish by birth and education, had come to the U. S. in 1799. Admitted to citizenship in 1804, in that year he accompanied General John Armstrong, newly appointed minister, to Paris. In 1810 he returned to the U. S. and secured an appointment as consul at Paris and as agent for "prize causes." In 1814 he was removed from office on the ground that from the death of Joel Barlow (in 1812) to the arrival of the new minister, Crawford, he had acted as consul-general, for which he was not officially invested. TJ in a letter to Madison of 8 December 1810 (*L&B* **19**: 176–178) gives an interesting character appraisal of Warden, who had just visited at Monticello. Another letter of TJ to Madison (7 April 1811, *L&B* **18**: 268–270) shows that Armstrong had opposed Warden's appointment even as consul with the argument that the position required "a man of business, as well as a gentleman." TJ belittles Armstrong's criticism and defends Warden stoutly. Warden received the consular appointment.

Warden, author and book collector, member of the APS and many European learned societies, included among his personal friends, TJ, John Quincy Adams, Lafayette, Talleyrand, Jared Sparks, Nicholas Biddle, and Rembrandt Peale, as well as C. As noted above (ch. III, note 8), Warden had written a letter of introduction for C to Dr. Wistar (4 December 1811), suggesting that if C were not already a member of the APS he should be elected at once. Evidently now C was attempting to

delphia that Mr. Sylvanus Bourne had the same title in Holland when that country enjoyed a government of its own.[23]

In a few days i go to the northern ports in order to find embarkation for the Peninsula.[24] Whatever occasions there or elsewhere may occur of obeying your commands, Mr. Vaughan [25] will forward them to me. I will profit of the leave i obtained of writing to you if i meet with, or think any thing worth your notice, but do not exact any answer but what you will think fit. I hope you will find me always

Most sincerely yours

Joseph Corrêa de Serra

P. S. I enclose Mr. Cuvier's paper,[26] and write to him, that if it is possible to have the objects, it will be by your means and care.

---

return the favor by aiding him in procuring an official title which would give him prestige as well as authority in Paris. Apparently the attempt was not at this time successful. *DAB* and TJ Papers, LC. For mention of C to and by Warden see the Warden Papers, Md. Hist. Soc. These contain letters from TJ, A. Bruce, Thomas Cooper, and Eliza Curtis to Warden referring to C, 1815–1818.

[23] Bourne was vice-consul, 1794–1815, consul-general, 1815 until his death in 1817, at Amsterdam. Perhaps the appointment as consul-general has been made by the time C writes, though Bourne was not confirmed by the King until June, 1815. Actually C must have been in error, for in one sense Holland had had no free government since 1794. See MS. List of U. S. Consular Officers by Posts, Dept. of State Records, NatArch.

[24] For C's plan of returning to Portugal in 1813, for reasons of health and economy, see ch. III, above.

[25] For John Vaughan (1756–1841), C's closest American friend of approximately his own age, see ch. III, note 17, and many other later references, above.

[26] Among the TJ Papers, LC, is an undated note in which "M. Cuvier prie M. Corréa" that the latter procure for "the Museum" the cranium of an American buffalo, and of a musk ox of Canada, the skin and skelton of a mink, etc. See TJ to C, 19 April 1814, below.

CORREA TO NICHOLAS BIDDLE [27]   [*L.C.*]

Philadelphia   8 September 1813.

Dear Sir

Saturday last i wrote to you,[28] to inform of my intended departure and how sorry i am the occasion affords so little time, that takes away the the possibility of seeing you before my departure. I entreated you also to present my respects and feelings of the highest esteem to Mrs. Craig [29] and to your family. No body being found in your house in town, the letter was forwarded to your father, and i am sure it will reach you if it has not done so already. Permit me to speak to you about the steam boat papers.[30] I leave Philadelphia for Boston saturday next 11th. of the month early in the morning, if the papers do not go with me it is very uncertain if they will ever reach me, in the present state of the world; a large cargo has greater facility of arriving than a parcel of

---

[27] For Biddle, see ch. III, note 21 above. He had returned to America from France in 1809. C almost surely first knew him in Europe.

[28] See C to NB, [5??] September 1813, LC.

[29] Margaret M. Craig, widow of John Craig, was NB's mother-in-law. She died in 1814 in the fifty-third year of her age. According to Professor Thomas Govan of Tulane University, NB's biographer, she was one of the charming women of the day. The obituary notice by NB in the *Port-Folio,* 3rd ser., **3**: 284–289, 1814, recalls her great personal beauty, masculine judgment, fine mind, and familiarity with the French language and literature.

[30] Presumably a reference to some of NB's left-over legal business, for he was now retired from the law and devoting almost all his time to the editorship of the *Port-Folio.* But David Warden and Fulwar Skipwith, consuls in Paris, and General William Lyman, consul in London, had sent NB a great deal of legal business between 1807 and 1810, when he gave up practice. Because some of these affairs remained incomplete, NB continued correspondence concerning them for some time afterwards.

papers, which captains or passengers easily forget or miss. If it was possible to have them in my hands to-morrow or friday, it will do me a great pleasure and save uneasiness and uncertainty[.]

You will soon hear from me, and wherever i shall exist you may be sure of having a real friend, and a man who knows your worth.

Most sincerely yours

J. Corrèa de Serra

P.S. You must have received a letter from Mr. Jefferson,[31] about a Mr. Peter Allen [32] who wrote to him asking information as the real editor of Lewis' travels.

[addressed: Nicholas Biddle Esq

by Holmesburgh   Andalusia

Penn

[on reverse of address:

Mr. Waterman will oblige the writer of this letter if he will cause it to be delivered in the course of today;—Mr. Biddle will pay a messenger [our?] thanks wednsdy morng

---

[31] TJ to Biddle, 20 August 1813, LC. It begins: "In a letter from mr Paul Allen of Philadelphia, I was informed that other business had obliged you to turn over to him the publication of Govr. Lewis's journal of his Western expedition; and he requested me to furnish him with any materials I could for writing a sketch of his life." TJ sent the material to NB, for the latter was entitled, TJ felt, to decide what shall go into the edition. A letter for Allen is included in that to Biddle. Evidently TJ was a little suspicious of Allen's claims.

[32] Paul Allen (see note 31 above), who did not edit but did see through the press the Lewis and Clark edition prepared by NB. At this time Allen was NB's assistant on the *Port-Folio*. The edition, which appeared in 1814, bore on its title-page, "Prepared for the press by Paul Allen, Esquire." See Thwaites, Reuben G., ed., *Original journals of the Lewis and Clark Expedition 1804–1806* . . . , 8 v., 1: xlii–xliii, lxxvii, New York, Dodd, Meade, 1904–1905, and TJ to C, 26 April 1816, below.

CORREA TO JAMES MADISON [33]   [*L.C.*]

Philadelphia 9th. September. 1813.

Sir

Being about to leave this continent, and return to Europe,[34] i consider it my duty to express to you my grateful acknowledgements for the goodness and civility with which you were pleased to receive me when i had the honour of presenting myself to you. Unluckily this year the state of your health, did not allow me the pleasure of seeing you in my passage through Washington to Monticello, and when i returned, you had just left that city. The only equivalent i can find to this disappointment, is to tender you my ready compliance with any commands you will honour me with, whenever or wherever you may judge that i can be of any service to you, and which you may forward to me by Mr. J. Vaughan of Philadelphia[.]

At Monticello i asked Mr. Jefferson on the propriety of speaking to you, about a concern of Mr. Warden your Consul at Paris,[35] he not only approved of it, but kindly promised to interfere in it. i dare consequently expose the matter to you in the inclosed paper, not from any application from Mr. Warden, but because i esteem and love the man, as every body does in Paris who is acquainted with him.

I shall consider myself very happy to find occasions of showing to you the sentiments of respect and high esteem with which i am

> Your Excellency's
>
> > Most humble obedient servant
> > J. Corrèa de Serra

---

[33] Of course the President of the U. S.

[34] See ch. III, and C to TJ, 6 September 1813, above, and C to J. Vaughan, 27 September 1813, below, for C's decision to leave the U. S. at this time.

[35] See C to TJ, 6 September 1813, note 22, above.

CORREA TO JOHN VAUGHAN   [*A.P.S.*]

Boston. 27, Septr. 1813.

Dear Sir and respected friend

From every thing which has happened to me in this journey i am disposed to be a greater believer in novels than i was before. So long was i without letters from Portugal, so little did i know the state of my affairs, that my impatience had got the better of me. As soon as i left Philadelphia the letters have flocked from every unexpected quarter. You sent me some from Philadelphia, Mr. Kantzow [36] just disembarked from England in New York gave me others very important ones. Mr. Sampayo [37] whose residence is in New York, was not there but in Boston, gave me here some others. Finally the ships lately arrived from Lisbon brought me (recommended to him that fortunately had delayed his staying here more than he intended) not only letters but bills of change for 987 pds. sterling, and the certainty of 450 pds. st having been sent to Paris to pay great part of what i owed. Together with this the certainty of recovering what remains due to me, and of putting in regular order the future payments of every part of my little revenue. You can easily conceive that the best thing i can do, is to remain with you at least till next summer. By the middle of October i intend to be in my dear Philadelphia, and finish the promised

---

[36] Baron Johan Albert de Kantzow was minister resident of Sweden and Norway in the U. S. from 28 October 1813 to 24 April 1817. See MS. Foreign Representatives, Dept. of State, NatArch.

[37] Apparently an agent for British commercial interests in this country. For example, on 20 April 1812, Sampayo, or Sampago, had called on the British minister, Augustus John Foster, concerning flour shipments. See Foster Diary, LC.

paper for the Phil. society.[38]   I write to my children
Walsh [39] and Biddle, and to my excellent friend Dr.
Wistar.[40]   God be praised that i have such men as you
and they, to live with for some time more and that time
at rest and with an easy mind.   You may tell Miss
Drake [41] that i am a steady boarder, and that she may
reckon with my calling there; but to take care of my
english trunk wich [sic] is fitter for voyages, instead
of which she will have the largest of the american trunks
that i bought, which is fitter for a sedentary life.   My
health is not yet good, but i have hopes it will be much
mended by a few weeks rest.   Farewell my worthy and
revered friend.   I am

Most sincerely yours.
J. Corrêa de Serra

You can tell the friends
my resolution of coming back
and the cause of it.[42]

---

[38] The only paper C ever read before the APS was on the
soil of Kentucky (3 March 1815), which territory he had not
even visited by 1813.   See C to James Madison, 5 September
1818, note 269 below.

[39] Robert Walsh, Jr., for many years C's friend and disciple.
See above, ch. III, note 27, and ch. IV, notes 66, 67, 68; also
Lochemes, *Walsh, passim.*

[40] See letter to Dr. Wistar immediately below, and ch. III,
notes 13–16, above.

[41] There are many references in C's and Edward Correa's
letters, given below, to the Misses Drake.   From 1814 to 1819
Miss Margaret Drake conducted a boarding house at Little
George and 7th Street, and after that period another at 128
Pine Street.   See Kite's *Phila. Dir. 1814;* Paxton's *Ann. Phila.
Dir. 1816;* 1819; and Whitely's *Phila. Dir.* 1820.

[42] Addressed to No. 107 South Front Street, Philadelphia.

CORREA TO DR. CASPAR WISTAR [43]   [*A.P.S.*]

Boston 27. Septr. 1813

Dear Sir and respected friend

The best thing i can do, after what has happened since we parted, is to go back to my dear Philadelphia, and pass my time in the enjoyment of company such as yours. I was going with impatience to meet my affairs, and they are come to meet me in the most novel-like manner at Boston. There is no necessity, nor there will be so soon very likely, of my going to Europe, and looking on the globe i find that no spot except Paris is more to my taste than your friendly city, and you must take to yourself a good part of its fitness to my taste. In my letter to Mr. Vaughan i have told him something of this adventurous journey, that has put my mind at rest, and gives me the occasion of again personally testifying to you the sentiments of high esteem and real friendship with which i am

Most sincerely yours.

J. Corrêa de Serra

BIDDLE TO CORREA   [*Nicholas B. Wainwright*]

Anda.[44]   Octr. 8, 1813

I cannot express to you my dear Sir, how much I am delighted at the happy change in your prospects and our own which your letter of the 29th of Sepr has just

---

[43] For Dr. Wistar (1761–1818), especially as C's friend, see ch. III, notes 13–16, above. Wistar had written a letter of introduction for C to John Collins Warren, professor of anatomy in Boston, 12 September 1812 [actually 1813?]. See Edward Warren, comp., *The Life of John Collins Warren, M.D.*, 2 v., **1**: 125-126, Boston, 1860.

[44] "Andalusia" was Biddle's summer home in Bucks county, Pennsylvania.

announced to us. Not having heard from you I concluded that the bustle of preparation had not left you time to tell us of your sailing but that you were now very far on your route to Lisbon. On this supposition we have often spoken of you at our fireside as of a friend whom we should never perhaps again see, & lamented that we should have known you so late. Judge then of the pleasure with which we hear of your intended return. Your letter was so wholly unexpected that it has quite electrified all the family every member [45] of which anticipates the satisfaction of your company during the winter. I am rejoiced to hear of the improvement of your health. When you were about sailing you took leave I presume of your old American companion the bumble bee, and he has no longer any claim on your acquaintance. We have not yet fixed the period for our return to town, but if you arrive whilst we are at Andalusia, I wish that you would either stop at the Tavern near us, or make the steam boat put you on shore here or at any rate spend some time with us.

Mrs Craig & Mrs Biddle desire their most particular & kind remembrance & charge me to express their great pleasure at the hopes of seeing you once more.

I defer till I see you all mention of what is passing in the world, & I need scarcely say how sincerely I am

Yrs
N.B.

Mr Correa de Serra
Boston

---

[45] That Biddle's children were very fond of the Abbé is made evident in B's letter to C of 7 July 1813, LC.

CORREA TO JEFFERSON   [*L.C.*]

Sir

Mr. Short [46] tells me that you intend to give me an invitation to visit you at Monticello, for which i give you my sincere thanks, because no moments of life can i consider more precious than those i would pass in your company. In the summer or in the fall i will attempt to profit of your kindness. In the meantime as i am determined to visit Kentucky and the Ohio, an excursion which i presume will take about three months, i intend to begin it about the first of May, and enter Kentucky by Virginia, to return afterwards by Pittsburg. In this manner i shall be able by stopping a day at Charlottesville to pay once more by respects to you, and of presenting to you my *compagnon de voyage* Mr. Walsh,[47] whose name you know by its first productions, which were rather of another hemisphere, but there has been a gradual and great change in his ecliptic; as will naturally happen to every man who is *avant tout* a good and sincere American. Such men easily find the high road, only by observing the deviations of party spirit, which are to well meaning persons equivalent to a demonstration *ad absurdum*[.]

---

[46] William Short (1759–1849), protégé of TJ and formerly a diplomat in Europe, was now settled in Philadelphia, building his great fortune through land speculation. He and C had almost surely first become acquainted in Paris, where Short occupied an "enviable position" in society. The profound attachment between Short and Alexandrine Charlotte de Rohan-Chabot (Rosalie, wife of the Duc de la Rochefoucald) lasted for fifty years. For Short, see *DAB, Em. Phila.;* ch. III, above.

[47] Robert Walsh, Jr. (1784–1859), critic and editor, earlier a strong anti-Jeffersonian, had by 1814 assumed a friendly tone towards the Republicans. It was certainly partially through C's influence. For Walsh, see *DAB;* Lochemes, *Walsh, loc. cit.;* ch. III, notes 22–27, above; letters reproduced below.

I dare entreat your favour for an object about which i feel the greatest curiosity. There grows in Louisiana a tree called by the French *Bois d'arc,* and by the Americans Bow wood.[48] I am sure a word from you to Govr. Claiborne [49] can obtain for me a young branch of it or two, pressed in brown paper with their leaves, and both the male and female flowers, also some of the fruit, either dry, or in a mixture 1/3 wiskey, 2/3 water, also in the proper season some ripe seeds. All this i will consider as a very great favour. I ta[ke] the liberty of reminding you of the Louisiana springs being very early.

My three months residence in New England have afforded me occasion of studying both the sickness and the curative,[50] you will best judge when i meet you, if

---

[48] *Maclura pomifera,* or the Osage-orange, is a thorny tree with large, yellow, somewhat orange-like fruit. Its hard, strong, flexible wood was used by the Osage and other Indians west of the Mississippi for bows and war clubs; hence its vulgar names. I's botanical name apparently was bestowed by Thomas Nuttall (see above, ch. V, and below) in honor of William Maclure, president of the AcNatScPhila, and one of the co-sponsors with C of Nuttall's Arkansas expedition (see ch. V, above). C sent the seed, or some of them, to Lord Bagot, who had two fine trees in his conservatory. See Thwaites, ed., *Early western travels . . .* , in Travels in the Interior of North America, by Maximilian, Prince of Wied . . . , 22: 186, note 96; and *Enc. Brit.*

[49] William Charles Claiborne (1775–1817) was the "proconsular representative" of TJ and Madison in Louisiana. *DAB.*

[50] For C's New England excursion, see ch. III, above. Unlike many British travelers, he did not like the northeast more than, or even as much as, the middle and southeastern states. His reference here is probably to the New England opposition to the War of 1812 culminating later in the near-treasonable Hartford Convention of 1814.

my view of the matter is correct. I expect i will be so happy as to find Col. Randolph at Monticello,[51] but wherever he may be, my most sincere respect and good wishes are for him.

I am Sir with the highest consideration
Your most faithful obedient servt.

Joseph Corrèa de Serra

Philadelphia   10 April.
   1814

JEFFERSON TO CORREA   [L.C.]

Monticello Apr. 19. 14.

Dear Sir

Mr. Randolph first, and latterly mr Short have flattered me with the hope that you would pay us a visit with the returning season. I should sooner have pressed this but that my vernal visit to Bedford [52] was approaching, and I wished to fix it's precise epoch, before I should write to you. I shall set out now within a few days, and be absent probably all the month of May; and shall be very happy to see you here on my return, or as soon after as may be. it will give me the greatest pleasure, and our whole family joins in the invitation. if, consulting your own convenience and comfort, you would make as long a stay with us as these should permit. you know our course of life. to place our friends at their ease we shew them that we

---

[51] See C to TJ, 6 Sept. 1813, note 20 above. Randolph spent a portion of his time on his own estate of "Edgehill." In 1813 he had been on active military duty as colonel of the 20th U. S. Infantry and had participated in the Canadian campaign. *DAB*.

[52] TJ spent several months each year in Bedford county, Virginia, at his hideaway, "Poplar Forest."

are so ourselves; by pursuing the necessary vocations of the day, and enjoying their company at the usual hours of society. you will find the summer of Monticello much cooler than that of Philadelphia, equally so with that of the neighborhood of that place, and more healthy. the amusements it offers are such as you know, which, to you, would be principally books and botany. mr Randolph's resignation of his military commission [53] will enable him to be an associate in your botanical rambles. come then, my dear Sir, and be one of our family as long as you can bear a separation from the science of the world. since Bonaparte's discomfiture I wish much to see you, to converse with you on the probable effect that will have on the state of the world, of it's science, it's liberty, it's peace & prosperity, and particularly on the situation of our literary friends in Europe. percieving the order of nature is be [sic] that individual happiness shall be inseparable from the practice of virtue, I am willing to hope it may have ordained that the fall of the wicked shall be the rise of the good.

I can readily fulfil M. Cuvier's request [54] for the skin & skeleton of the mink. I have procured a fine skin, and can at any time get the entire subject. the difficulty will be to find a vessel which would receive so large a subject, and preserve the spirits in which it would be immersed. but this shall be an article of consultation when you are with us. the cranium of the buffalo cannot be procured but from the other side of the Missisipi. there I can readily obtain it. but it must go thence by the way of New Orleans, which cannot well be till peace. I have done for mr Warden what you and himself wished as to his commission.[55] it's effect with the government I have not learned. I also suggested to the

<hr>

[53] See TJ to C, 10 April 1814, note 51, just above.
[54] See C to TJ, 6 September 1813, note 26 and letter, above.
[55] See *ibid.*, note 22.

government your observation on the difference of structure in vessels which the difference of specific gravity between salt & fresh water might render useful. Accept my thanks for Fossombroni's book,[56] which tho topographical, presents circumstances of curiosity. I salute you with sincere affection and respect.

Th.Jefferson

JEFFERSON TO CORREA   [L.C.]

Monticello Apr. 25. 14.

Dear Sir

Your favor of the 10th. by the delays of our winter post, is but just received and mine of the 19th. I presume reaches you about this time. They have passed each other by the way. I am sorry that your visit to us will be delayed until your return from Kentucky; [57] mais tout ce qui est differé n'est pas perdu; and it will then and will always be welcome. you promise also to call on us en passant. should I have set out on my journey to Bedford, you will find mr & mrs Randolph [58] here who will recieve you with the pleasure your society gives us all; as they will also your companion mr Walsh— his visit I should lose personally with real regret, entertaining equal esteem for his worth and tal-

---

[56] See *ibid.*, note 14.

[57] C's western tour did not take place until August–September, 1814. As usual with him, he got away later than he had originally planned. For the tour, see C to John Vaughan, 20 August 1814 (from Lexington, Kentucky), and C to TJ, 20 September 1814 (from Chambersburgh, Pennsylvania), below; ch. III, above.

[58] Martha Jefferson Randolph (1772–1836), TJ's older daughter, a highly educated and intelligent woman, had been with her father in France and was his hostess during his Presidency.

ents. it is still however possible that I may be detained some days longer than I expect; as my departure hangs on certain circumstances not within my controul. should you therefore have left Philadelphia on the 1st. of May as you propose, and make no stay at Washington, I do not entirely despair of participating of your company here, altho' you may not have recieved this letter apprising you of the possibility.

The first Western mail shall carry a letter to Govn. Claiborne, or perhaps to a friend in Natchez [59] more conversant in Botanical researches, to engage an execution of your request as to the Bow-wood. not entirely without a hope of seeing yourself & mr Walsh here, but in every case wishing you a pleasant journey & safe return, I salute you with affection & respect.

Th.Jefferson

M. Correa de Serra.

CORREA TO VAUGHAN   [*A.P.S.*]

Lexington [Kentucky] 20 August, 1814.

Dear Sir

Three weeks ago i received your very friendly letter of the 14th. last, and am very grateful for the expressions of kindness and interest for my welfare which it con-

---

[59] Dr. Samuel Brown and TJ were regular correspondents. See TJ to Brown, 28 April 1814 (TJ Papers, LC), and *idem,* 14 July 1813, *L&B, 13*: 310–312. In the former letter TJ repeats the request of "an European friend, M Correa de Serra" almost word for word, including the directions for packaging. TJ added: "Mr Correa is . . . setting out on a visit to Kentucky. he is perhaps the most learned man in the world, not merely in books, but in men & things, and a more amiable & interesting one I have never seen altho a stranger to no science, he is fondest of Botany. should you have gone to Kentucky as your

tains. It would have required a more expedite answer if we were on terms of greater etiquette, but you who know my remissness in writing when travelling, will i am sure easily forgive me. This place has been for me a center of operations, and from it i have made by incursions to see whatever could interest me a radium of from twenty to thirty miles. Now i will take the road to Monticello through the mountains, and from hence you will hear from me. If Mr. Walsh is in Philadelphia, be so kind to tell him that from Monticello i will direct to him a long letter. I hope to be there by the 6 or 7 of September the distance being *430* miles. In the whole i am pleased with what i have seen in this western new world; we shall talk at my return. It is impossible to be more cordially treated than i have been by Mr. Short's family.[60] Mr. Wilkins [61] gave me the letters from Paris that you sent, and has furnished me with recommendations for the parts of the country that i have visited. These woods afford great occupation to a botanist. The news from Europe are not so good as you suppose it is only a new face of this Proteus like

last letter seemed to contemplate, take him to your bosom, and recommend all the attentions to him by which our brethren of Kentucky can honor themselves."

[60] William Short had made extensive purchases of land in Kentucky after his return to America in 1810, and several members of his family were settled in the region. His brother, Peyton Short (1761–1825), had moved to Kentucky in 1789 and had become a large landowner. A sister, Elizabeth (d. 1822), married Dr. Frederick Ridgely, professor in Transylvania College, Lexington, and another sister, Jane (d. 1821), married Dr. Charles Wilkins, a member of the faculty of the same institution. See the Short Papers, LC.

[61] Besides the Professor Charles Wilkins mentioned just above, another or the same Charles Wilkins was a prominent Lexington merchant in this period. See Worsley & Smith, *Almanac, Directory of 1818* for Lexington, Kentucky. Also see C to James Madison, 10 December 1814, below.

revolution.[62] Let us see. If there are any letters for me be so good to send them together with your commands to Monticello. My best compliments to all my friends, and i entreat Dr. Wistar and Mr. Walsh to take part in this letter.

I remain most sincerely yours

J. Corrèa de Serra

CORREA TO JEFFERSON   [L.C.]

Chambersburgh. 20 Septr. 1814

Sir

After having visited your western states, and attempted in vain to pass through the mountains directly from Lexington (Ky) to Monticello, i have been obliged to come back to Pittsburgh and to this place, from whence as soon as i receive an answer from Philadelphia, that is to say in two or three days i will proceed to pay my respects to you. In the mean time i address to you these few lines, because the moments are precious in these circumstances, and i entreat your forgiveness for the impatience of my American feelings.

Last year i passed three months in the eastern states from whence i did not return to Philadelphia but in winter, i lived with all parties but chiefly with the lead-

---

[62] On 11 April 1814 Napoleon had abdicated at Fontainebleau and on 5 May Louis XVIII entered Paris. The Treaty of Paris was signed on 30 May by the powers who had overthrown Napoleon. Louis did not restore the institutions of pre-revolutionary France, but on the contrary retained those of Napoleon of the year VIII. Though the return of the king was accompanied by a grant of a "charter" and "representative government," C as a liberal apparently eyed these moves, as well as the later (September) Congress of Vienna, with considerable question.

ers of the opposition. I am convinced that though many of them are so by party feelings, or by private interests, still there is among them more treason than from what i remember of our conversations, you seemed aware of.[63] Among their followers the greater number by far is composed of dupes whom the leaders keep together by manyfold artifices, but who are at the bottom very good americans. Treason is more to be feared in the present moment than in any epoch of your history. the only talent ever known in Lord Castlereagh was that of an artful and succesful intriguer.[64] This last French catastrophe [65] is a striking proof in all its details, and what is more surprising though less important, he has in the same time outwitted the Pope and his cardinals, and by his artifice has rendered them irrevocably his tools to sow discord among the Irish R. Catholics.[66]

---

[63] TJ and Madison never appear to have been too seriously alarmed at the idea of New England secession, though the Hartford Convention a few months after the date of this letter convinced the whole country of this near-treason. See Mc-Master, *History of the people of the United States* 4: 245–252, for a view somewhat sympathetic toward the Convention. See also Dwight, Theodore, *History of the Hartford convention* . . . , New-York, 1833, by the secretary of the Convention; and Adams, *History of the United States of America from the first administration of Thomas Jefferson, loc. cit.*

[64] Robert Stewart, 2nd Marquis of Londonderry (1769–1822), British statesman known to history as Lord Castlereagh (he did not become Marquis until a year before his death). Why Correa uses the past tense here is somewhat puzzling, for Castlereagh was at this moment quite active.

[65] C probably refers to the Congress of Chatillon (5 February to 10 March 1814) and the surrender of Paris, which led to Napoleon's abdication on 11 April. In the month in which C was writing Castlereagh was at Vienna for negotiating the peace, and was making a secret treaty for Great Britain with Austria and France to protect Western Europe against the plans of Russia and Prussia.

[66] C may be referring to the controversy over the Quarontotti

Would it not be this a fit moment to give rise in the eastern states to committees of public safety? They are an american institution. It seems that if they were prudently instituted and directed they could do much good and prevent the execution of much treasonable plans and practices. You may expect that the leaders and their trumpets will cry aloud but even that might be made to recoil on them. Party name ought not to exclude any one from being members, all are to be invited as in common danger, but noted party men are too be excluded. I am persuaded that this thing wisely executed will separate from their ranks a vast number of followers. Moments of danger and invasion are the proper time for such institutions, because all the sincere of whatever party agree in them by the presence of danger; the guilty alone are against them, and they lose the dupes who followed them. You and the actual government know better the properer steps to be taken, but i expect your pardon for thus meddling in your public affairs. In every case i entreat you to destroy this note because a Portuguese is in circumstances worse than if he had sworn allegiance to the crown of Great Britain.

My best compliments to Mr. and Mrs. Randolph, and may all sort of happiness fix itself in Monticello.

I am with the greatest veneration

Sir

Your most obedient servt.

Joseph Correa de Serra

Rescripts, the contents of which were announced in England at the end of April, 1814, or to the negotiations which took place between Cardinal Consalvi and Castlereagh in the summer of that year. The Irish Catholics, particularly the clergy, were much disturbed over the rescripts, and the Irish hierarchy in a meeting at Maynooth voted that they were not binding. See Ellis, J. T., *Cardinal Consalvi and Anglo-Papal relations 1814–1824*, Washington, D. C., Catholic U., 1942, especially chapters II and IV.

CORREA TO JEFFERSON   [*L.C.*]

Philadelphia   9 Decr. 1814.

Sir

I am in Philadelphia returned again to my old train of life, that is reading and walking. From the inclosed you will see that i have not forgotten the cement for your cisterns.[67] That alone would have occasioned this letter, but i have matter of much more importance to communicate to you. The last arrivals have brought english and french papers, pamphlets and letters which i wish i could put under your eyes, to give you a just idea of what is going in Europe. No favourable result is to be expected from Vienna; [68] war is adjourned. So far you know already and from better sources, but what is very important and remarkable, and which only an attentive lectures of a great number of the above materials can show, is that the only ally that you have now in Europe, and a powerful one, if properly seconded, is public opinion, which has sprung again in Europe immediately after the pressure of circumstances has disappeared wishing for rest and deprecating ambition. Your enemies with their papers and pamphlets strive to persuade Europe that this country is the nest of anti-monarchical jacobinism and this government the [tool?] of Bonaparte, to be severely chastized and crushed like him. It seems as if they wished to raise a crusade against this country. The papers of the continent sympathize with you, and consider you as a nation wronged by a piratical and ungenerous mode of warfare. The british government writers speak of

---

[67] See letters below, C to TJ, 12 February 1816; C to TJ, 16 June 1816 [enclosure]; TJ to C, 20 July 1816; and TJ's reply to the present letter, 27 December 1814.

[68] The European peace conference in progress from September, 1814.

american *insolence* the necessity of punishing this country, and the *interest of Monarchs*. The continental papers seem far from partaking this opinion, and even in England i see from the opposition papers many people do not partake it. As you are remained alone on the theatre all the eyes are turned on you and your contest. A dignified resistance without imitating what the continent highly disapproves in them, and causes their feelings to be on your side is the only means to conserve this advantage of public opinion, which is in this case what the weather gage is in naval combats. Such line of conduct and pinching trade are the only means of bringing honorable peace.

You intended to write to the President on an object which was incidental in a conversation.[69] I earnestly entreat you now to employ all your influence to suspend it. In the present moment it must have a deleterious effect instead of doing good, it could serve to excite the fellow feelings of many powerful people, and give pretext to excite an ill will where it does not exist. The same capital employed on the trade would be more profitable and without inconvenient. I know at present from good authority that the two points in question have not been neglected in the last obstinate law suit as they were before, but for personal reasons have been much contemplated. This is so natural, that i wonder the possibility of it did not occur to the gentleman that mentioned them, together with the natural reflection that sixteen years might bring very material changes. All this i submit to your wisdom, i dare not give advices to such a man as you, but i make just and friendly representations.

Most sincerely yours

J. Corrèa de Serra.

---

[69] See TJ to C, 27 December 1814, below. The subject is obscure.

[P.S.]
I have read with attention and ruminated your plan of school,[70] and as you are above compliments i will only tell you that i would have been proud of having planned it, so much i find it porportionate to the actual degree of improvement of human mind, and to the present state of your nation. I differ nevertheless in one point from you, which is the Theological branch, not for the reasons of Dr. Cooper,[71] because persuaded as i am that superstition and religion in the bulk of mankind must always exist, they being the natural result of the inequal proportion with which the different mental faculties are generally coupled in the human nature, it is much better to neutralize them, than to leave them alone to work according [to] their caustic nature. You have done much in America to neutralize them, by withdrawing any support from government, and breaking their old alliance, but that is not yet all; the best means of neutralizing them is by learning infused in their ministers[.]

The question is; if it is best to have the clergy of the most considerable sects, composed of gentlemen or vulgar people? of learned or ignorant men. David Hume has in some manner resolved the first question,[72] and there may be no doubt as to the second. If they are

---

[70] TJ had probably sent C the same plans for his projected university which he had earlier submitted to Dr. Thomas Cooper (10 Sept. 1814 and 7 Oct. 1814) and which Cooper had commented upon (22 Sept. 1814). See Malone, *Cooper*, 227–228 and notes; *L&B* **14**: 200; TJ Papers, LC.

[71] Thomas Cooper (1759–1839), scientist, educator, liberal, later president of the South Carolina College, and soon to be one of TJ's candidates for a professorship in his incipient university, was at this time professor of chemistry in (later) Dickinson College at Carlisle, Pennsylvania. See notes just below.

[72] David Hume (1711–1776), Scottish philosopher and historian. The general tenor of Hume's *History* is in favor of gentlemen, for he treats the regular clergy with some respect

learned they will in proportion be liberal minded and neutralize the absurdities incidental to their creeds, if ignorant they will go on deeper and deeper into fanaticism and nonsense, which as you know are and will always be very epidemic and dangerous diseases.

I wish therefore that there may be an opening left in the University in order to have learned clergymen, but their studies there to be real things, in which all sects agree (to avoid the just objections of Mr. Cooper to Theology and ecclesiastical history [73]) and of such nature that not only neutralize fanaticism, but protect important branches of learning which otherwise will have no support amongst you.

1. Natural theology, which pretending to ground on reason the principles of general religion, makes them conversant with metaphysics and the philosophy of human mind

---

but never ceases to ridicule the self-appointed preachers among the Puritans. No specific source has been found. Hume does give a long disquisition on the characteristics of the clergy generally in his philosophical works. See Green, T. H., and T. H. Grose, edd., *The philosophical works of David Hume,* 4 v., 3 : 245–247 n, London, 1898.

[73] In his letter of 22 Sept. 1814 Cooper said: "I reject the Department of Theology: for reasons numerous and I think very weighty, but which need not be repeated. Where there exists a rational system of religion there ought to be a church establishment to support it, and regular seminaries in which should be taught the dogmata and their [illegible] which the nation has thought fit politically to adopt [.] If religion be politically necessary, then teach it without regard to the truth of the adopted system : but if you are to teach theology in your university on the ground of its truth, who is judge which system is true?"

Cooper also observed that ecclesiastical history could be read as well at home, and asked whether it is fair to teach the "Evidences" of Christianity without the objections to it. See TJ Papers, LC.

2. Hebrew and its relation with oriental languages and oriental literature, in order to understand the Bible; the greek is already in the plan of the college. 3. What is called *Eruditio Biblica*. That is to say the knowledge of facts and things necessary or useful to understand the Bible. It is incredible what number of capital books exist on this object. Two works of the first eminence in natural history are the Hierozoican of Bochart [74] and the Hierobotanas of Celsius,[75] on the animals and plants of the Bible. This branch of learning carries a man to the deep recesses of the history of the Asiatic world, and to what remains of the first ages of mankind. The critical history of the books of the Bible, must make one of the chief articles of this branch.

All these studies have the natural effects of neutralizing fanaticism and enlarging the mind, to the contrary of what elements of Divinity and ecclesiastical history, whatever they may be must naturally have.

These few words are sufficient for you who will see in a moment the consequences. As for the other objections of Dr. Cooper,[76] they have put me in mind of many a rich atlas full of precious maps some minutely topographical, others geographical in different scales, but wanting a Mappemond in which they are found in their relative proportions. and positions.

---

[74] Samuel Bochart (1599–1667), *Hierozoicon, sive, bipertitum opus de animalibus s. scripturae, cujus pars prior libris iv. De animalibus in genera, & de quadrupedibus viviparis & oviparis . . . , Cum indici Septuplici. Ed. 3. Ex recensione Johannis Leusden.* Title for edition of Leyden, 1692. The original edition had appeared in London in 1663.

[75] Olof Celsius, *Hierobotanicon, sive de plantis sacrae scripturae dissertationes breves. . . .* 2 parts, Upsala, 1745 etc.

[76] See note 73 above.

CORREA TO JAMES MADISON   [*L.C.*]

Philadelphia 10 Decr. 1814

Sir

According to the permission you gave me i send you from this place my guesses on the branch of revenue which the U. S. could have in domains belonging to the union. But in looking to the subject with attention i have found another instance of what you so justly observed to me, and what i have myself often experienced viz. that a foreigner who visits a country is apt to believe that what he does not yet see in it, does not exist. Indeed if Mr. Jefferson when i mentioned to him the necessity of a domanial branch of revenue had followed the conversation, which took a different turn, i would have known that the principle had been adopted long ago, though very little acted upon. I could have recollected that Messrs. Wilkins and Morrison of Kentucky [77] had told me of having rented many years the saline of the U. S. in the Illinois territory. I will therefore only add a few things which may perhaps be also known to government, but in this case there is no harm in recalling them to memory.

---

[77] On 3 March 1803, the U. S., which had retained title to all salt springs and licks within the Illinois territory, authorized the Secretary of the Treasury to lease these salines for the benefit of the government. In 1811 a Captain Isaac White sold his interest as lessee in the salt works to three men, Jonathan Taylor of Randolph county, Illinois, and Charles Wilkins and James Morrison of Lexington, Kentucky. Morrison, a banker, and Wilkins, a merchant, were in 1818 shown at the same business address in Lexington, the corner of Short and Upper Streets. This Wilkins was probably the brother-in-law of William Short (*q.v.*). See Worsley & Smith, *Almanac, Directory of 1818,* Lexington, Kentucky; and George W. Smith, The salines of southern Illinois, Illinois State Historical Society *Transactions* 9: 248–249, 1904.

The principle once adopted that the tracts where plenty of mineral and fossil substances are found, are to be marked for their exploitation, and to be rented, instead of being alienated for ever, the following tracts may be remarked.

Immediately after the acquisition of Canada, the English were informed of the extraordinary quantity of copper found in the southern shores of Lake superior now belonging to you. A company was formed of very respectable persons even lords for the purpose of exploiting these mines. The want of population and wild state of the country fifty years ago was the only obstacle, the riches of the mines was verified and the attempt left for another more favourable epoch. I have read the book of Mr. Henry [78] one of the persons they sent, who afterwards fixed himself at Montreal.

Amongst the western people many informed me that they had had accounts from the Canadians of many different ores in several places from Lake Superior to the Mississipi, and in all the country to the north of the Missouri. This appears very natural even in a geological point of view.

In the United States, lands between the Alleghany and the Mississipi a great and strong probability exists of rich iron ores in several places.

Up the Arkansas a very great probability exists of finding silver, because some of the richest spanish mines exist in the ridge from which these waters flow.

The lead mines of the Missouri territory are too obvious a reference, but i was told that the principal occupation of the Canadian inhabitants is to exploit them in an uncontroulled manner. They may contain as is

---

[78] Henry, Alexander (1739–1824), *Travels and adventures in Canada and Indian territories between the years 1760 and 1776* . . . , 2 parts, New York . . . , 1809, etc.

often the case in lead mines some silver which may increase their value.

To explore these and other unknown or unsuspected things is the first step. This nation is no more in the necessity of calling proper persons from Europe to explore such objects. The U. S. possess already two men advantageously known even in Europe for their mineralogical science. Dr. Bruce of New York [79] and Dr. Silliman of New haven,[80] the first particularly has received there great encomiums for his American Mineralogical journal. There is at Pittsburg a german called Mr. Aigster [81] very good mineralogist and chemist who could be a useful person in this line. The expense of such a visit would be trifling, and foundation would be laid for national riches as well as future revenue, which would proportionally diminish for the future the pressure of other taxes.

I do not bring to memory the infinite quantity of salts, the consumption of which will increase with the population, and which are in Europe a capital branch of revenue—If the salines which in the West belong

---

[79] Archibald Bruce (1777–1818), physician and mineralogist, was professor of materia medica and mineralogy in the College of Physicians and Surgeons of the State of New York, 1807–1811, and editor of the *American Mineralogical Journal* in 1810, "the first purely scientific journal in America." *DAB.*

[80] Benjamin Silliman (1779–1864), professor of chemistry and natural history in Yale College, 1802–1853, later a renowed scientist. *DAB.*

[81] Frederick Aigster, M.D., physician and chemist, had lectured as early as 1811 three times a week on chemistry to the students of the Pittsburgh Academy and to townspeople. From these lectures grew the Pittsburgh Chemical and Physiological Society, which maintained a cabinet of mineralogy and some experimental apparatus. See Riddle, James M., *Pittsburgh Directory for 1815* (Pittsburgh, Colonial Trust Co., 1905); and Starrett, Agnes L., *Through one hundred and fifty years: the University of Pittsburgh,* 48, Pittsburgh University, 1937.

to private owners were the property of the Union, what handsome revenue would they already afford! The past cannot be revoked, but the resources for the future are an immense store, not to be in the same manner alienated.

You will find inclosed in a bit of paper the calculation of which i spoke to you of the sum of money for which all your unlocated lands can be security if they were to be mortgaged for money to be lent on them.

In taking your time with the above rhapsodies i have made use of your indulgence, but in what i am now to take the liberty of writing to you i wish you may see a proof of the real interest i take in the happiness of this nation and the prosperity of his government, and very real indeed because i have nothing to ask or to hope from either. I am an old man, have lived sixty years in Europe, and not with shut eyes, i will only state things and submit them to your wisdom. The last arrivals have brought a number of English and continental papers and pamphlets, to all which i have given the greatest attention. If the war there seems adjourned another ally and a powerful one is there working for you, and can do wonders if properly seconded. Public opinion one of the great rulers of the European world, has arisen with a wonderful strength from the grave where the revolution kept it. An universal surfeit of violence and ambition pervades Europe, which France employs most dexterously to her ends with the show of moderation. The English court papers already complain that the Emperor of Russia is gone to that side and system on which they look with horror. Their papers and pamphlets which i wish i could submit to your eyes are raising hue and cry against this nation as the nest of jacobinism, they speak of antimonarchical insolence, and of the interest of Monarchs in crushing you as a dangerous people. The continent on the contrary seems to sympathize with you as the victims of a pirati-

cal and vindictive warfare. As you are remained alone
in the theatre all the eyes are open on you. A dignified resistance without imitating in the least what the
continent highly disapproves in them, on the contrary
following the French plan of making show of moderation and self possession, will ensure and rivet in your
service all the continental feelings and force them to
make peace. The disappearance of the *sine qua non*
is already an effect of this state of things[.] This together with pinching their trade for which the people
of Europe have no fellow feeling will have a wonderful
effect. Give me leave to afford some instances. General Jackson it is said has entered Pensacola. In the
old european stile which Talleyrand is now preaching
with such effect, an official communication would have
been made to the foreign ministers, that you enter that
territory only to expel your enemies and leave everything as it is to the actual possessor, and let every civil
thing go in his name and by his officers, and such a
declaration to be published in the papers. A thing
which would have a wonderful effect in Europe would
be something like a general instruction to all your com-
manders, that though this government is sure that very
little out of rule has been done by his armies, as the
secretary of state has demonstrated to admiral Cochrane,[82] still as many causes of irritation daily occur you
again recommend to your officers the strictest adherence
to the old rules of civilized warfare, and to leave to
your enemies all the merit of transgressing them. This
sort of retaliation is what in the present state of european minds and feelings, will attach them all to you,

---

[82] A reference to Vice-Admiral Sir Alexander Forrester
Inglis Cochrane (1758–1832), British officer in command of
the North American station, 1814–1821. No record of Secretary of State James Monroe's "demonstration" survives among
the state papers in LC or NatArch.

and put them against them, and the force of such a general opinion is in the present moment incalculable and will for a while continue so. Retaliation in kind is now very dangerous and out of season[.] it could perhaps in a manner or other serve the purposes of your enemies. If you bind yourselves close to the present ruling ideas of Europe, which England sees clearly (because her papers and pamphlets allow it) are levelled against her by skilful hands, you will soon have peace or allies to weather the storm. I do not ask pardon for speaking so freely and candidly to the chief of a great nation, on the contrary i consider it as the highest compliment i can pay to his personal qualities, and a proof of the high esteem and veneration with which i am

      Sir

        Your most obliged humble servant

          J. Corrèa de Serra

[Enclosure:]

Sum of money for which all the unlocated lands of the U. S. can be security if they were to be mortgaged for money lent on them

The price and value of things are fixed by the demand which exists of them

The price and value of unperishable things which will be in demand only at future stated periods is actually equal to the common price of the thing deducting from it the interest of the money till the time the thing will be in demand, and clear the money it is worth

It follows that a thing worthy two dollars when demanded, cannot command actually more than 1.88. cents if it is to be delivered at the end of a year. An acre of land if supposed of the value of two dollars delivered in this moment, will be worthy 188 cents in this moment if to be delivered at the end of a year.

176. if delivered at the end of two years
164 3
152 4
140 5
128 6
116 7
104 8
 92 9
 80 10
 68 11
 56 12
 44 13
 32 14
 20 15
  8 equal to two thirds of a year

That is to say that a man who would advance 8 cents, for an acre to be delivered at the end of 16 years would be a loser.

In the supposition of the annual sale being of 400,000 acres, in the moment they are delivered worth two dollars each—he may give for them 800,000 dollars; for those to be delivered at the end of a year 752,000 dollars, and by above scale of depreciation the money he could advance would be only 7,072,000 dollars

But there is an infinitely more advantageous point of view, in the hypothesis that the interest is secured elsewhere, and the lands mortgaged only as a security of a sinking fund proportionate to the annual sales—In this hypothesis your lands could be by fair and evident calculations brought to be sufficient security for vast sums.

JEFFERSON TO CORREA   [*L.C.*]

Monticello Dec. 27. 14.

Dear Sir

Yours of the 9th. has been duly recieved, & I thank you for the Recipe for imitating Pursolane;[83] which I shall certainly try on my cisterns the ensuing summer. The making them impermeable to water is of great consequence to me.[84]   That one chemical subject may follow another, I inclose you two morsels of ore found in this neighborhood, & supposed to be of antimony. I am not certain, but I believe both are from the same peice: and altho' the very spot where this was found is not known, yet it is known to be within a certain space not too large to be minutely examined, if the material be worth it.   this you can have ascertained in Philadelphia where it is best known to the artists how great a desideratum antimony is with them.

You will have seen that I resigned the chair of the american Philosophical society,[85] not awaiting your fur-

---

[83] I.e., porcelain (given in *L&B* **14**: 222, as *purrolani*).   Actually the French word, used by C, was *pouzzolane* (C to TJ, 12 Feb. 1816, below), "Terre volcanique rougeâtre, qu'on mêle avec de la chaux pour en faire un mortier qui se durcit dan l'eau" (*Dictionnaire de L'Académie Française,* Sixiéme Edition, 2 v., **2**: 478, Paris, 1835).

[84] In a letter of 19 June 1808, TJ had mentioned in a letter to Christopher Colles (*L&B* **12**: 74) that he had heard that in France there was "a cement used as a lining for cisterns and aqueducts, [which] renders them impermeable to water." Evidently he had asked Correa to procure the formula, or at least information concerning the process, for him.

[85] TJ had been elected president of the APS in January 1797 and held the position until 23 November 1814, when he resigned on account of his age.   In two letters of the latter date to Robert M. Patterson, secretary of the APS, TJ begged to be permitted to resign the chair, stating that he had wished to do so some time before but had continued at Patterson's urgent request.   See *L&B* **14**: 209, 210–211; **19**: ix.

ther information as to the settlement of the general opinion on a successor, without schism. I did it because the term of election was too near to admit further delay.

On the subject which entered incidentally into our conversation while you were here, when I came to reflect maturely, I concluded to be silent.[86] to do wrong is a melancholy resource, ever where retaliation renders it indispensably necessary. it is better to suffer much from the scalpings, the conflagrations, the rapes and rapines of savages, than to countenance and strengthen such barbarisms by retortion. I have ever deemed it more honorable, & more profitable too, to set a good example than to follow a bad one. The good opinion of mankind, like the lever of Archimedes, with the given fulcrum, moves the world. I therefore have never proposed or mentioned the subject to any one.

I have recieved a letter from mr Say,[87] in which he expresses a thought of removing to this country, having discontinued the manufactory in which he was engaged; and he asks information from me of the prices of land, labor, produce etc. in the neighborhood of Charlottesville, on which he has cast his eye. it's neighborhood has certainly the advantages of good soil, fine climate, navigation to market, and rational and republican society. it would be a good enough position too for the reestablishment of his cotton works, on a moderate scale, and combined with the small plan of agriculture, to which he seems solely to look. but when called on to

---

[86] On the now-lost subject of this conversation, see C to TJ, 9 Dec. 1814, above.

[87] Jean Baptiste Say (1767–1832), French economist, had written to TJ on 15 June 1814, a letter received on 9 December (see *L&B* **19**: 248, TJ's letter to Say of 14 May 1817). A reply was written on 2 March 1815 (*L&B* **14**: 258–267), sent to C for his perusal (see TJ to C, 6 March 1815, just below), to be conveyed by George Ticknor, who may never have delivered it, TJ was to think.

name prices, what is to be said? we have no fixed prices now. our dropsical medium is long since divested of the quality of a measure of value; nor can I find any other. in most countries a fixed quantity of wheat is perhaps the best permanent standard. but here the blockade of our whole coast preventing all access to a market, has depressed the price of that, and exalted that of other things, in opposite directions, and, combined with the effects of the paper deluge, leaves really no common measure of values to be resorted to. This paper too, recieved now without confidence & for momentary purposes only, may, in a moment be worth nothing. I shall think further on the subject, and give to Mr Say the best information in my power. to myself such an addition to our rural society would be inestimable; and I can readily concieve that it may be for the benefit of his children & their descendants to remove to a country where, for enterprise & talents, so many avenues are open to fortune and fame. but whether, at his time of life, & with habits formed on the state of society in France, a change for one so entirely different will be for his personal happiness you can better judge than myself.

Mr. Say will be surprised to find that 40 years after the developement of sound financial principles by Adam Smith and the Economists, and a dozen years after he has given them to us in a corrected, dense & lucid form,[88] there should be so much ignorance of them in our country: that instead of funding issues of paper on the hypothecation of specific redeeming taxes, (the only method of anticipating, in a time of war, the resources of times of peace, tested by the experience of nations)

---

[88] Say's *Traité d'économie politique* appeared first in 1803 and in a revised edition in 1817. In a letter of 14 May 1817 (*L&B* **19**: 248–250) to Say, TJ notes that the book is beginning to be read in the U. S.

we are trusting to tricks of jugglers on the cards, to the illusions of banking schemes for the resources of the war, and for the cure of colic to inflations of more wind. The wise proposition of the Secretary at war too for filling our ranks with regulars, and putting our militia into an effective form,[89] seems to be laid aside. I fear therefore that, if the war continues it will require another year of sufferance for men and money to lead our legislators into such a military and financial regimen as may carry us thro' a war of any length. but my hope is in peace. the negociators at Ghent are agreed now on every point save one, the demand and cession of a portion of Maine. this, it is well known, cannot be yielded by us, nor deemed by them an object for continuing a war so expensive, so injurious to their commerce & manufactures, & so odious in the eyes of the world. but it is a thread to hold by until they can hear the result, not of the congress of Vienna, but of Hartford.[90] when they shall know, as they will know, that nothing will be done there, they will let go their hold, and complete the peace of the world, by agreeing to the status ante bellum. indemnity for the past, and security for the future, which was our motto at the beginning of this war, must be adjourned to an-

---

[89] Monroe as secretary of war had proposed a plan to the preceding Congress for keeping the army at a good strength, a plan of which TJ heartily approved. See TJ to William H. Crawford, 11 Feb. 1815, *L&B* **14**: 242.

[90] The Congress of Vienna (1814–1815) was concerned with the disposition of Napoleon's empire by the four powers who had overthrown him—Austria, Prussia, Russia, and England. Naturally the settlement of European troubles would enable Britain to concentrate on her American war. But TJ was quite right in feeling that the Hartford Convention of malcontent New Englanders (meeting 15 December 1814, though called much earlier) would come to nothing, and thus would indicate to the British that there was no hope of American disunion. The rest of this letter is remarkable long-range prophecy.

other, when, disarmed & bankrupt, our enemy shall be
less able to insult and plunder the world with impunity.
this will be after my time. one war, such as that of
our revolution, is enough for one life. mine has been
too much prolonged to make me the witness of a second, & I hope for a coup de grace before a third shall
come upon us. if indeed Europe has matters to settle
which may reduce this hostis humani generis to a state
of peace and moral order, I shall see that with pleasure,
and then sing; with old Simeon, nunc dimittas Domine.[91] for yourself cura ut valeas, et me, ut amaris,
ama.[92]

> Th.Jefferson

JEFFERSON TO CORREA   [L.C.]

> Monticello Mar. 6. 15.

Dear Sir

I mentioned to you in a former letter that Mr Say
had asked of me information relative to the price of
lands etc in the neighborhood of Charlottesville with a
view to the removal of his family to this country.[93] in
the inclosed letter [94] I have given him the best and full-
est information I could, of every circumstance which
might influence his judgment and final determination.
altho' I have endeavored to confine myself vigorously

---

[91] *Nunc dimittis servum tuum, Domine.* . . . Luke 2: 29.

[92] *Cura ut valeas,* but not the rest of the Latin, appears in
several places in Cicero, *Ad Familiares.* Of course the whole
is a normal complimentary conclusion between friends, and
variants of the whole appear at several places in Cicero's letters
generally. The remainder of the Latin in the construction as
it appears is probably TJ's.

[93] See TJ to C, 27 Dec. 1814, and note 87 above.

[94] TJ to Jean Baptiste Say, 2 March 1815 (*L&B* 14: 258-
267).

t[o] matters of fact, yet aware of our natural partiality to our own country, and even our own neighborhood, I am afraid I may have given an aspect influenced by that. of this a foreigner would be a better judge than a native, and none better than yourself. I have therefore left the letter open, and request you to peruse it, and if you find any thing which ought to be corrected, that you will be so good as to note it in a letter to mr Say with whom I believe you are particularly acquainted. when perused be so good as to stick a wafer in it, and also in the envelope to mr Ticknor, and commit it to the mail, with as little delay as you can, as mr Ticknor will sail for Europe very soon.[95]

We all rejoice at the peace,[96] and most especially as we closed the war with such a sample to England of our character as an enemy, in proportion as we advance in the exercises of war. Yet it is but a truce, unless in the interval of general peace, she settles amicably the business of impressments. the first american citizen she impresses will be a declaration of war. I am not without apprehensions that the late change in the condition of Europe may tempt you to leave us. if this be necessary for your happiness, as is but too probable, our friendship for you would require us to submit to the sacrifice. if you continue with us a while longer, I shall hope for your passing at Monticello as much of the summer as you can. the cession of my library to Congress [97]

---

[95] George Ticknor (see TJ to C, 27 December 1814, note 87 above) was about to sail for Europe to prepare himself for "a literary career" at Göttingen and other universities. See Davis, *Gilmer*, 82–83; *idem*, The early American lawyer and profession of letters, *loc. cit.*, 12: 191–205, 1949; Long, *Literary pioneers*, 9 ff.

[96] The Treaty of Ghent was signed on Christmas Eve, 1814. See McMaster, *History of the U. S.* 4: 273.

[97] Learning through the newspapers of the British vandalism and destruction of the first Library of Congress, TJ in a letter

will have left you that resource the less for your amusement with us. but the season for botanizing will in some measure supply it. accept my affectionate and respectful salutations.

Th.Jefferson

M. Correa de Serra

JEFFERSON TO CORREA   [*L.C.*]

Monticello June 28. 15

Dear Sir

When I learned that you proposed to give a course of Botanical lectures in Philadelphia,[98] I feared it would retard the promised visit to Monticello. on my return from Bedford however on the 4th. inst. I recieved a letter from M. Dupont flattering me with the prospect

---

of 21 Sept. 1814 to Samuel H. Smith offered to sell his own library of between nine and ten thousand volumes to the nation as a nucleus for the new library Congress would need. As Professor Gilbert Chinard points out (*Thomas Jefferson, apostle of Americanism,* 477, Boston, Little, Brown, 1929), this was not a forced sale, but the generosity of an American who knew his fine library would be of more value than any collection which could be made for years to come. TJ placed his books "at the disposal of Congress . . . the act of a public spirited citizen unable to make an outright gift and yet unwilling to make any profit on the public treasury." That Congress haggled and finally paid him much less than the library was worth was regarded even by an anti-Jeffersonian Britisher, Augustus John Foster, as one of the most shameful acts of the American legislative body. See Foster Journals, LC.

[98] For C's lectures, see ch. V, notes 23–32, above. He also delivered lectures the next summer, 1816, for he speaks of his troubles in obtaining specimens (see letter below, C to FWG, 27 March 1816, and C to TJ, 16 June 1816). And a laudatory notice of his intention to give the lectures appears in the *Virginia Argus,* 18 May 1816 (2 (17) : 3, col. 5), with a quotation from a "Philadelphia paper" of 14 May concerning the matter.

that he and yourself would be with us so soon as my return should be known.[99] I therefore in the instant wrote him of my return, and my hope of seeing you both shortly. I am still without that pleasure, but not without the hope. Europe has been a 2d time turned topsey turvey since we were together, and so many strange things have happened there that I have lost my compass. as far as we can judge from appearances Bonaparte, from being a mere military Usurper, seems to have become the choice of his nation; and the allies, in their turn, the usurpers & spoliators of the European world. the right of nations to self government being my polar star, my partialities are steered by it, without asking whether it is a Bonaparte or an Alexander towards whom the helm is directed. believing that England has enough on her hands without us, and therefore has by this time settled the question of impressment with mr Adams,[100] I look on this new conflict of the European gladiators, as from the higher forms of the amphitheatre, wondering that Man, like

---

[99] Pierre Samuel duPont de Nemours (1739-1817), distinguished French scholar, philosopher, and politician, who had come to America in 1815, was a good friend of both TJ and C. He had on 20 December 1811 written a letter of introduction for C to TJ (see Chinard, ed., *Jefferson-duPont correspondence*, 178 ff.), and ch. III, notes 7 and 45, above. On 26 May 1815 duPont had informed TJ that he hoped with C to spend several days at Monticello when they learned that TJ had returned (see Malone, ed., *Jefferson-duPont correspondence*, 162, and ch. III, note 95, above).

[100] John Quincy Adams (1767-1848), later secretary of state in C's time in the U. S., had at this period just returned from Ghent as one of the commissioners for that treaty. He had seen in Paris the return of Napoleon from Elba, and was now in London, where with Henry Clay and Albert Gallatin he negotiated (1815) a "Convention to Regulate Commerce and Navigation." Soon after this he became U. S. minister to Great Britain, returning to America in the summer of 1817. See ch. IV, notes 37 ff., above.

the wild beasts of the forest, should permit himself to be led by his keeper into the Arena, the spectacle and sport of the lookers on. nor do I see the issue of this tragedy with the sanguine hopes of our friend M. Dupont.[101] I fear, from the experience of the last 25 years that morals do not, of necessity advance hand in hand with the sciences. these however are speculations which may be adjourned to our meeting at Monticello, where I will continue to hope that I may recieve you with our friend Dupont, and in the mean time repeat the assurances of my affectionate friendship and respect

Th. Jefferson

M. Correa

CORREA TO PRES. OF U. S.[102]   [L.C.]

[Summer 1815?]

Petitions of [J.?] Correa to the President of the U.S.

1. A recommendation to the agent with the Cherokees [103]

2. Some perfect fruits of Bow wood from Louisiana, and some perfect seeds of the same═the fruits if they are spoiled by drying, can be put in a Liquor half spirits half water.[104]

---

[101] In a letter of 26 May 1815 duPont had expressed his belief that military despotism would not long maintain itself in Europe, that Bonaparte was but a step toward genuine republicanism, and that Germany, Italy, and England would eventually renounce their kings and royalty generally. See Malone, ed., *DuPont-Jefferson correspondence,* 159–161.

[102] A letter to James Madison apparently intended to prepare for C's projected southern excursion and to obtain certain items for himself and Cuvier already mentioned to TJ. See C to TJ, 10 April 1814, and TJ to C, 19 April 1814, above.

[103] See Return J. Meigs to James Madison, 22 Dec. 1815, below. C planned to visit the Indian country of Tennessee.

[104] See C to TJ, 10 April 1814, above.

3. A perfect skull of Buffaloe.

These objects if sent to Genl. Mason [105] at Washington who has continual intercourse with the West and Indian nations, will safely come to M. Correa's hands and he will indemnify the expenses to Genl. Mason

JEFFERSON TO CORREA   [L.C.]

Poplar Forest Sep. 22. 15.

Dear Sir

I arrived here the morning after we parted, to wit, yesterday morning, and I have this day written by mail to mr Rhea [106] and Govr. Milledge: [107] but I have thought it also safe to inclose in this letter a duplicate of that to Govr. Milledge, and put both under cover to mr Rhea, lest any miscarriage should happen to that sent by mail. there is no person in Georgia who can be so useful to you as mr Milledge; & particularly as to plants, altho' not a regular botanist, he has been always uncommonly attentive to them. I shall leave this the 1st day of October & be here again from the 1st to the middle of November, and shall hope to see you

---

[105] General John Mason, son of George Mason of Revolution fame, was a prominent citizen of Georgetown in the District of Columbia at this time.

[106] John Rhea (1753--1832), Irish-born resident of Knoxville, Tenn., a Princeton graduate, was a Democratic member of the U. S. House of Representatives from 1803 to 1823, except during 1815–1817. *DAB; Biog. Dir. Cong.*

[107] John Milledge (1757–1818), U. S. Senator and Governor of Georgia, had in 1809 retired from all public office. For TJ's letters of introduction to him and the journey made with Francis Walker Gilmer, see Davis, Forgotten scientists in Old Virginia, *Va. Mag. Hist. & Biog.* **46**: 97–111, 1938. Forgotten scientists in Georgia and South Carolina, *Geo. Hist. Quart.* **27**: 271–284, 1943; *Francis Walker Gilmer, loc. cit.,* 75–92.

on your return either here or at Monticello, and to keep you as long as as the science and society of Philadelphia will permit. I should envy mr Gilmer [108] his botanical enjoyments with you had not long avocations of a different character first lessened my little stock in that science, and the decay of memory and decline of strength for rambling, frobidden me to think of renovating it. mr Gilmer while with you cannot be better employed. he will be enlarging the foundation on which his own fame and the hopes of his friends and country are to be raised. to the serious occupations which these will reserve for him his physical science will add ornament and comfort, but he must not expect that we shall permit him to devote to ornament & comfort alone the solid utilities we expect to derive from him. I salute you both with affectionate friendship and respect

Th. Jefferson

Mr. Correa.

CORREA TO VAUGHAN   [*A.P.S.*]

Winchester. 17. Decber. 1815

Dear Sir and Friend

After a long and laborious campaign here i am resting for a few days [109] and as young Kinloch told me in

---

[108] For Francis Walker Gilmer (1790–1826), see *Gilmer, loc. cit., DAB,* and ch. III, notes 69–98, above. Gilmer was a young Virginia essayist, amateur botanist, and practicing lawyer of great promise. TJ called him the best educated citizen Virginia had produced since the Revolution, and predicted for him a great career in state and nation.

[109] C and Gilmer, returning from their Southern excursion, reached Monticello on 25 November and Winchester on 15 December. *Forgotten scientists in Georgia and South Carolina, loc. cit.,* 280.

Charlestown [110] that Walsh was in Baltimore i intend
to remain with him for some days, and then thence go
to Wilmington to fulfill my promise to my old friend
Dupont de Nemours of passing with him the New
Year's day in the Parisian manner.[111]   So i shall be
in Philadelphia the 2d or 3d. of January, and i hope
to find you in the most perfect health, according to my
best wishes.   What [a] great man you are in Charlestown!   Gentlemen and ladies all asked me about your
health, many told me that you ought to pass the winters
with them.   What excessive hospitality that of the Caro-
linians!   I intended to pass incognito, and pay only a
visit to the botanist Mr. Elliott [112] and the plants of the

---

[110] They had left Charleston on 8 November. "Young Kinloch" may have been Cleland (1798–1823) or Francis (1798–
1840) Kinloch, twin sons of Cleland Kinloch, prominent South
Carolina planter, or Frederick Rutledge Kinloch (1791–1856),
who was in the U. S. army 1813–1816. The South Carolina
Kinlochs were relatives of Gilmer through the marriage of
Margaret, daughter of Colonel John Walker of Albemarle
county, Va., to Francis Kinloch (1755–1826). See Bull, H. D.,
Kinloch of South Carolina, *Sou. Car. Hist. & Geneal. Mag.*
46: 65–67, 159–165, 1945.

[111] The travelers had spent an evening with duPont at
Monticello between 25 November and 6 December. See Forgotten scientists in Georgia and South Carolina, 280.

[112] Stephen Elliott (1771–1830), a native South Carolinian
and a Yale graduate, was already a noted amateur botanist.
He had in 1812 moved to Charleston from Beaufort, S. C., in
connection with his duties as first president of the Bank of the
State of South Carolina, and had immediately become identified
with the social and literary life of the city.   The Henry Muhlenberg-Elliott and the Henry Muhlenberg-Zaccheus Collins correspondence of 1812–1813 mentions several times Elliott's anxiety
to have C visit Charleston.   Elliott was not to publish his monumental *Sketch of the botany of South Carolina and Georgia*
until 1821–1824 (2 v.).   See Muhlenberg-Elliott Correspondence, Arnold Arboretum of Harvard U., and Botanical Corres.
Z. Collins, AcadNatSciPhila.; Letters of the Rev. Henry Muhlenberg, Hist.SocPenna.; *DAB*.

neighborhood, but he and the Rutledges [113] threw me into such a whirlpool of invitations to dinners, suppers, clubs, concerts that only at the end of a fortnight, by a strong pull i could disengage myself, and even then their hospitality pursued me to the frontiers of South Carolina, and i was obliged to follow a route which they prescribed to me from plantation to plantation to admire their oriental and magnificent hospitality. But above all i must praise their good manners, and good breeding, i wish i was a powerful Fairy to bestow on them a better climate, and a higher soil. I am

Most sincerely yours,

J. Correa da Serra

RETURN J. MEIGS [114] TO MADISON   [*L.C.*]

Cherokee Agency
22nd December 1815.

Sir

On my return to Nashville on the 2nd. of October last, I met in the road leading through the woods Mon-

---

[113] The famous Rutledge family, which included a signer of the Declaration of Independence and several governors of the state, was large and naturally prominent. Gilmer, himself only twenty-five at the time, lists as the "Young men of Charleston" who particularly impressed him, "Haine," William C. Crafts, Hugh S. Legaré, and Frederick Grimké. Legaré was to remain Gilmer's correspondent over many years. See The early American lawyer and the profession of letters, *loc. cit.*

[114] Three men of this name are sketched in the *DAB*. The first, General Return Jonathan Meigs (1740–1823), is the author of this letter. He was appointed agent to the Cherokees in 1801, who named him "The White Path." He was commissioner to negotiate several treaties between the U. S. and the Indian nation, and one between the state of Tennessee and the Cherokee. At eighty-two he insisted on giving up his quarters to a visiting Indian and moved into a tent. He contracted pneumonia, died, and was buried in the Cherokee agency in Tennessee.

sieur Carrea [*sic*] De. Serra in a Carriage with Mr.
Wilmer [115] [*sic*], after passing the Carriage, a lad
passed, who informed them, of my name they stopped
and called to me : when by the hands of Monsieur De.
Serra I had the honor to receive your letter.—As I
had appointed to meet the Cherokees within a few
days. I could not turn back—I sat down in the road
& wrote in the same letter to my son at the place of
this Agency ; and we parted. On my return home, having been absent 11 days.—The Gentlemen stayed at my
sons house several days. My son [116] informed me that
he had the satisfaction of apparently making their stay
very happy.—Monsieur De Serra was constantly busy,
examining the vegetable productions of nature here and
informed my son & daughter of the qualities of a number of plants of which before they had not known.—

My son sent a young man with the Gentlemen as a
Guide & Interpreter, who went with them nearly to the

---

[115] This was of course Francis Walker Gilmer. For an incomplete list of the plants C and FWG observed in the Cherokee
country, see Davis, An early Virginia scientist's botanical observations in the South, *loc. cit.,* 132–139, and forgotten scientists in Georgia and South Carolina, *loc. cit.*

[116] Meigs presumably refers here to his son, Timothy (1782–
1815), who died during the month in which his father wrote
this letter, December, 1815. Timothy was the only one of
RJM's children to settle in Tennessee. Soon after 1807, when
the Cherokee Agency was moved from Southwest Point to
Hiwassee garrison, at the mouth of the Hiwassee river, Timothy
opened a store at the garrison which did a flourishing business
with the Indians even long after his own death. His business
partner was John Ross, later the great chief of the Cherokees.
Timothy's wife, evidently the "daughter" referred to here, was
Elizabeth Holt, daughter of a farmer who had emigrated from
Virginia. See McClung Papers, Notes on Various Families,
Lawson-McGhee Library, Knoxville, Tenn., and Penelope John-
son Allen, Leaves from the family tree. Return Jonathan
Meigs . . . , Chattanooga *Times,* January 28, 1934.

Georgia line. Monsieur De. Serra requested of my son to let him have your letter to me; saying that he would carry it to France: to show with what facility he could pass through an extensive country here; observing that to make such a tour in France it would require perhaps a hundred applications to be made on the route. I ask leave sir to avail myself of the opportunity afforded on this occasion, just to say that I am one amongst the millions of our Country who rejoice that you have had the very great happiness of conducting the nation though an arduous struggle, that in despite of foreign power and domestic faction we have gained every thing we wished—and it is not the least, that a restless faction must now be convinced of its own nonimportance. I have the Honor to be

with the greatest respect

Your Obedient servant

His Excellency
James Madison
President of the
United States

Return J. Meigs

Dec. 22, 1815

CORREA TO JEFFERSON   [*L.C.*]

[enclosure] [117]

[Before 1 Jan. 1816]

---

[117] Apparently the lost recipe, later recovered, referred to in the letter of 1 January 1816 just below, and TJ to C, 20 July 1816, below. It is (like that given in C to TJ, 12 Feb. 1816, below) a condensation of the several recipes C mentions in *Cours complet d'agriculture théorique, pratique, économique, et de médecine rurale et vétérinaire . . . ou dictionnaire universel d'agriculture . . . ,* 10 v., Paris, 1793–1800. This particular edition C used is a set then as now in the Library of the Philadelphia Society for Promoting Agriculture (at present housed in the library of the Veterinary College, University of Pennsylvania).

In the Cours complet d'Agriculture edited by the Abbè
Rozier and written by the Frenchmen, the more deeply
versed in each of the branches, in the second edition,
in the article Citerne, and the articles Tonneau and
Foudre,[118] in which all the details are given for building the cisterns for the keeping and conservation of
wine, the following cements are described:

1°. Brique pileé et tamisée fine melée a la chaux
vive au lieu de gravier

2°. What they call, Cendrèe de Tournay, ciment de
chaux et cendres de charbon de terre, bien melees ensemble jusques a ce que le ciment pese un quart de plus
que la chaux simple=Il durait sous l'eau et devient plus
dur que les pierres qu'il lie

3. Dans les angles et dans les jointures du mur, ou
les crevasses sont plus aisement faites, on employe pour
les lier davantage et les rendre impermeables, le ciment
suivant—Eteignez une pierre de chaux vive, avec du
song de bœuf chaud, avant d'avoir caillè, melez et fouet-
tez longtems jusques a consistance de colle epaisse.

By all the details given in this book, it seems that every
cement employed in cisterns must be employed in slight
layers successively patiently and carefully applied with
the aim of making them a solid and tight body without
any the slightest vacuity.

JEFFERSON TO CORREA   [L.C.]

Monticello Jan. 1. 16.

I learnt, my dear Sir, with inexpressible concern, on
my arrival at home, that my detention in Bedford had
lost me the pleasure of your visit here. having heard

---

[118] For this edition and the set C used, see note 117, just
above, and C to William Rawle, 14 March 1816, below.

nothing from you since our parting on the Natural bridge,[119] I had supposed your return longer delayed than you had expected, and that even possibly your course might be shaped as to take Poplar Forest in your way. I hungered for your observations on the country you had passed over, and should not probably have been mistaken in your estimate of it. it was additionally unlucky that when you were at Monticello my family did not observe the letters for you lying on my table. some of them had been recieved a considerable time before, but not knowing your exact trajectory, or in what part of it they might light on you, I was afraid to risk them in the attempt. I now inclose them and add a letter I wrote you under cover to mr Rhea, expecting it would get to Knoxville by mail before your arrival there, as it probably did : but mr Rhea being unfortunately absent on a journey to the Westward, you failed in the receipt of it. as in the benefit you might have derived from his friendly attentions. he lately returned it to me with expressions of his regret at having lost the opportunity of being useful to you; and I now inclose it only to shew that the failure did not proceed from want of attention in me. not knowing whether you may have arrived at Philadelphia when this gets there, I put the whole under cover to mr Vaughan.

The death of Dr. Barton [120] revives my anxiety to

---

[119] On their journey south C and Gilmer had with TJ explored the Natural Bridge and the Peaks of Otter. In February, 1816, Gilmer's article, On the geological formation of the Natural Bridge of Virginia, was read before the APS in Philadelphia (*Trans. Amer. Philos. Soc.,* new ser., **1**: 187–192, 1816).

[120] Benjamin Smith Barton, M.D. (1766–1815), physician and naturalist, had died on 19 December.

recover the MS. journals of Capt Lewis,[121] for the satisfaction of his family; [122] and may at the same time facilitate it. he had promised me sacredly that he would see to it's restoration; and as you were so kind as to say you would attend to it on your return to Philadelphia, I now earnestly entreat your aid for this object, knowing nothing of what is doing, or intended to be done as to the publication of the papers respecting the natural history & geography of the country, you will oblige me by any information you can obtain on this subject. the right to these papers is in the government, as may be seen by the instructions to Capt. Lewis. they were left in his hands that he might derive to himself the pecuniary benefits of their publication, on the presumption they would certainly be published. if that presumption is to fail the government must reclaim them; and it is to put this object into an effective course that I wish for information what is doing, or likely to be done. I know I should have the concurrence of Genl. Clarke [123] in this, were he within the timely reach of consultation; and I shall not fail to advise with him as soon as I can do it understandingly.

---

[121] Several letters below discuss this matter of the Lewis journals of the expedition to the Pacific. For a detailed outline of their history, see Thwaites, Reuben G., ed., The story of Lewis and Clark's journals, *Annual report of the American Historical Association for the year 1903,* 2 v., 1: 105–129, Washington, U. S. Govt. Printing Office, 1904; *idem, Original journals of the Lewis and Clark expedition, 1804–1806* 1: xxxiii–xlix.

[122] Captain Meriwether Lewis (1774–1809), a Virginian and TJ's secretary 1801–1803, had been commissioned to lead the expedition to the Pacific (1803–1805). He had died mysteriously at Nashville, Tenn., in 1809. *DAB.*

[123] William Clark (1770–1838), another Virginian and brother of the more famous George Rogers Clark, was asked by Lewis in 1803 to be co-leader of the expedition. Clark was a brigadier-general of militia for the Louisiana territory from 1807. In 1813 he had been made governor of the Missouri territory. *DAB.*

I am ashamed to ask whether your observation or information as to the cisterns of Charleston [124] can facilitate the perfecting those I have constructed because by some accident which I cannot ascertain I lost the paper you were so kind as to give me at Dowthwaite's.[125] You recollect our situation there. I was shaving, changing linen, opening and doing up my baggage on the bed, when you put that paper into my hands. I thought it certain that I put it into my pocket; but when I got back to Poplar Forest I could not find it. whether it was lost out of my pocket, or laid & left on the bed, I cannot say; but being lost, I am thrown again on your goodness to replace it if you can.

What effect will the apparent restoration of the Bourbons have on your movements? will it tempt your return? I do not see in this a restoration of quiet. on the contrary I consider France as in a more Volcanic state than at any preceding time. there must be an explosion, and one of the most destructive character. I look forward to crimes more fierce and pitiless than those which have already distinguished that bloody revolution. these are not scenes, my dear friend, for you to be thrown onto [*sic*]. they have no analogies with the tranquility of your character. true we cannot offer you the scientific society of Paris. but who can enjoy science, or who think of it, in the midst of insurrection, madness and massacre? besides, you possess all science within yourself. from others you can get nothing new, and the pleasure of communicating it should be

---

[124] For more of the cement for cisterns, see letters below of 12 February, 16 June, and 20 July 1816. The recipe TJ lost (ard later recovered) is given just above this letter.

[125] Probably a Mr. Dowthwaite mentioned by TJ in a letter to Archibald Stuart 30 October 1794 (original in Stuart Papers, VaHistSoc.). There is no real identification of the man. The letter is printed in *Va. Mag. Hist. & Biog.* **8**: 120, 1900, and *Wm. & Mary Quart.*, 2nd ser., **5**: 288, 1925.

greatest where it is most wanting. stay then with us. become our instructor. help us on in the paths of that science which is wanting to our ripening character. you know how much you are beloved and desired every where, welcome every where, but no where so cordially as at Monticello. come and make it your home then the place of rest & tranquility, from which, as your priè-des-tal, you can make what excursions you please. you will find it's summers as moderate as those of Philadelphia, and it's winters more so. had I arrived before your departure, I should have pressed your trial of it the present winter. a comfortable room, in a country of fuel, for retirement when you chose it, and a sociable family, full of affection & respect for you, when tired of being alone, would have made you forget the suspension of the season for botanical rambling. turn this subject in your mind, my good friend, and let us have as much of the benefit of the result as shall be consistent with your own happiness, and in all cases be assured of my warm affection & respect.

Th.Jefferson

CORREA TO FRANCIS WALKER GILMER [126]   [*U.Va.*]

Philadelphia 6 Febry. 1816

Dear Sir

The moment for your Florida essay is come; [127] it ought to appear before your public begins to forget Mr.

---

[126] Francis W. Gilmer (1790-1826) had accompanied C to the Cherokee country, Georgia, and South Carolina. See ch. III, above, and many letters above and below.

[127] As a letter from Gilmer to TJ of 16 February 1816 (Davis, ed., *Correspondence of Thomas Jefferson and Francis Walker Gilmer, 1812–1826,* 34–37) indicates, Gilmer had been gathering material for an essay on the subject since "last winter." Then he had secured from a secretary of Don Luis de Onis (1762–1827) the whole outline of the Spanish cause, which he found very weak.

Onis's letters.[128]   You will find here the facts i promised you to ascertain.   They serve to prove that the
Louisiana such as the French Kings possessed it was
chiefly on the east side of the Mississippi.

1°.   From the journal of the discoveries of Chevr. de la

---

[128] Onis, who had arrived in America in 1809, had not been
received as minister for six years because the U. S. by general
policy would recognize no representative of either of the rival
governments in Spain. He had been sent to gather information on the movements and policies of the U. S. towards the
"South," and if possible to formulate a boundary treaty which
would halt further encroachments on "Spanish" territory. The
years 1809–1815 he spent in gathering information, occasionally
making a protest against American policy through the British
minister, until his credentials were accepted by Monroe, Secretary of State, on 19 December 1815. Onis began his official
term as minister with a steady stream of notes to the State
Department, the first demand being that West Florida be returned to Spain pending the settlement of its title (the section
west of the Perdido having been claimed by the U. S. with the
Louisiana Purchase). Some of the letters which passed between Monroe and Onis were published in various newspapers
throughout the country. For a detailed discussion of this
highly involved problem, see Preston C. Brooks, *Diplomacy and
the borderlands: the Adams-Onís Treaty of 1819,* Berkeley,
U. California, 1939.
Though there are several other letters here between C and
Gilmer on the subject, and though Gilmer gathered what material he could from TJ and William Wirt (Davis, *Gilmer,*
99), there remains no evidence that he ever published the essay,
though he did "finish" it. At the time Gilmer was just recovering from protracted illness, and may have lacked the
energy to go into the matter as he knew it warranted. This
correspondence on the Florida question is more significant as
an indication of C's enormous interest in all things American,
his desire to encourage and to increase the reputation of a potential statesman, and his essential sympathy with the American
point of view. Although this last may have been inspired in
part by Portugal's own rivalry with Spain then and in the
past, all other evidences point to C's enthusiasm for and faith
in (at this period) the greatness and righteousness of the U. S.
It also shows his very considerable knowledge of world history.

Salle published by Chevr. Tonti his companion, republished (after many preceding editions) in the 2d. vol. of the Collection of the New York hist. soc.,[129] we see that in the first year of the discovery of Louisiana (1679) the French settlement was on the [Minois? Missouri?]; they settled afterwards St. Joseph near the Lakes, and it is proved by the subsequent hist. of Louisiana that they had occupied it on the east of the Mississippi many years before they attempted any settlement to the west of it.

2°. From the journals of Mrs. de Bienville et d'Iberville who in 1701, discovered Louisiana by the South, we see that the French first settlement was at Biloxi and at Mobile, both on the east of the river far from it. New Orleans itself was founded only about 1720.

3°. The French writers quote the treaty of Cambray [130] between France and Spain (which treaty must have been about 1714) in which it was stipulated that Rio perdido should be the limit of Louisiana and Florida. The great point is to show that the meaning of the phraseology of the treaty of St. Ildefonso [131] was that something more was to return to the French than what

---

[129] An Account of Monsieur de la Salle's Last Expedition and Discoveries in North America, Presented to the French King, and published by the Chevalier Tonti, Governour of Fort St. Louis. . . . Reprinted from the London edition of 1698 . . . , *Collections of the New-York historical society for the year 1814* **2**: 217–341, 1814.

[130] The Treaty of Cambray was formulated in 1724–1725.

[131] By the secret treaty of San Ildefonso, 1 October 1800, Spanish Louisiana had been retroceded to France at the demand of Napoleon. If Gilmer could show what the meaning of the phraseology of the treaty was as to whether West Florida was included in the retrocession, he would have been a cleverer diplomat than the professionals who argued the case for many years. The ambiguity is clearly present. See Brooks, *Diplomacy,* 4–5, 119–120, and C to Gilmer, 8 February 1816, below.

they had given Spain in 1762, because otherwise no such forms were necessary, nor Spain had entered into any treaty with foreign powers about the country west of the Mississippi and the now so called island of New Orleans, which are the countries they had received from France.

Mr. Campbell [132] is at Washington, i have called three times at his house nobody is there, the windows are shut, and your letter is with me.

Poor Walsh [133] has been very dangerously sick these two months past, but is now on the recovery, he is still here with his family.

As for myself, the snow overtook me immediately after Harper's Ferry and i am still surrounded with it. My health has suffered much, and it is only this last week that i have felt some amendment with exercise. I begin to feel my existence, and my intellectual faculties begin to thaw.

I wish your lot of health has been better than mine, and that your incommodities have had a stop. The news of Paris [134] are gloomy and discouraging far beyond what you may read in the newspapers, and the stormy weather of Europe promises to be of long duration.

---

[132] This may be George Washington Campbell (1769–1848), Scottish-born U. S. Senator from Tennessee, a Princeton graduate, later secretary of the Treasury and minister to Russia. *DAB*. Gilmer and C may have made his acquaintance in Tennessee.

[133] For Robert Walsh, see ch. III, notes 22 ff., and C to J. Vaughan, 27 Sept. 1813, above.

[134] C probably refers to the treaty signed in Paris 20 November 1815, which showed the victorious allies greedy for compensation for their services in securing peace in Europe. They decided to exact indemnities, etc. On the same day a treaty of alliance was signed in Paris by Great Britain, Austria, Russia, and Prussia. Six articles of this latter treaty seemed to assure the allies a throttle-hold on Europe.

May you enjoy every sort of happiness, according to the best wishes of

Your most sincere friend

J. Corrèa de Serra

P.S. Everything to the West of the Mountains was Louisiana in the time of the French Kings, till the war of seven years. The treaty to which they allude in St. Ildefonso's Treaty is that by which Spain recognizes the U.S. and consequently the alienation of that part which fell within their limits.

CORREA TO GILMER   [*U.Va.*]

Philadelphia 8. Febr. 1816

Dear Sir

Your letter of the 2d. of this month, with the paper for the Philos. S. is just come to my hand. Your paper will be read the 16th at the stated meeting.[135] I am very sorry to see that your health has not mended so soon as i expected; we must hope a milder season will be more favourable to both, my mind is nearly as frozen as my body. You will not i hope take it amiss, if i add to your paper some other facts that support your explanation.

Two days ago i wrote to you on the Florida business, now i must add that in the Democratic press of yesterday evening a disquisition[136] on the same subject has begun, written by Judge Cooper, it is on the opposite

---

[135] See TJ to C, 1 Jan. 1816, note 119, above. Gilmer's paper, On the geological formation of the Natural Bridge of Virginia, was read before the APS on 16 Feb. 1816. See Davis, *Gilmer,* 275.

[136] This two-and-a-half column article appears in the *Democratic Press* (Philadelphia), as C states, in the issue of 7 February 1816. Except for a two-paragraph introduction, it

side of the question, but it promises to be very learned and full of facts. It must be very useful to you to see it. The great point and most substantial for you to state in order to explain the sense of the phraseology of St. Ildefonso's Treaty,[137] is the following viz. that if it was meant to restore to France only what she had given, that phraseology is unintelligible and superfluous. The only reasonable sense is obviously that Spain was to restore so much of old Louisiana as then was in their power and not acknowledged to belong to others by any treaty of hers with any foreign power. Now by her treaty with England in 1783 she had the country to the west of Perdido,[138] the rest of Louisiana on this side of the Mississipi she had acknowledged to belong to the

---

is in outline form under specific dates of treaties and other pertinent printed documents, 1673–1803. Most of it is merely condensed summary of facts, as C suggests, and it should have been useful to Gilmer. Under the 1685 and 1763 entries, however, the writer, "Viator," interprets his data as supporting the Spanish claims regarding the boundary. He concludes by summarizing the American contention and the Spanish contention, as though his previous data had been presented impartially and objectively, and says that this is enough for the present. No further discussion of the matter in this paper by this writer has been discovered. The only internal evidence pointing to Cooper as author is under the date 1685, where the writer compares the border disputes with similar disputes in Pennsylvania courts, in which Cooper (see immediately below) had recently been a judge.

In September, 1815, Dr. Thomas Cooper (1759–1839), already a noted liberal, former jurist, and distinguished scientist, had resigned his position as professor of chemistry at Carlisle (later Dickinson) College and had returned to Philadelphia. A friend of both C and TJ, Cooper has a considerable place in the correspondence given below. John Binns, editor of the *Democratic Press* (Governor Simon Snyder's organ), was a good friend of Cooper despite some political differences. See Malone, *Cooper, passim.*

137 Compare C to Gilmer, 6 Feb. 1816, note 131, above.
138 Spain had regained the Floridas from England by the Treaty of 1783. See Brooks, *Diplomacy,* 3, 111.

U. S. by recognizing their independence. The ambiguity left in the terms by the French whom no body can suppose to be dupes in a moment when they were the paramount power, is relative to the uncertainty of the northern boundaries of W. Florida, which notwithstanding the King's decree which we have read in the laws of Georgia was extended to a line drawn much higher by the lat. of the Yazous river, which line, is marked in Arrowsmith's Map of the U. S.[139] I cannot find the decree or order by which it was so altered, but *de facto* the Governors of W. Florida extended their power so far, and as the treaty of peace between Spain and England in 1793, ceded the Floridas to Spain without any mention or reference to the treaty between England and the U. S. signed at the same epoch, this was the reason of Spain keeping so long Natchez and the Walnut hills. By this interpretation the French would have been enabled in time to wrest fr[om] the U. S. all the waters of the Alabama and Tallapoosa &c. which had been in old times possessed by the French who had these settlements such as Fort Toulouse &c. If i find in these few days other things of which i am in quest you shall have

---

[139] *A map of the United States of North America drawn from a number of critical researches by A. Arrowsmith, hydrographer to H.R.H. the Prince of Wales. No. 10 Soho Square* [variant: *Charles Street, Soho Square*] [1796]. There are three copies of the 1796 engraving of this map in LC, apparently in two or three states or issues. The "No. 10" address map does not show at all the line C refers to, but the other two bear a dotted line from the mouth of the Yazoo due east to the Appalachicola as he indicates. In one of these this line, and the course of the Appalachicola southward to the Florida line, is traced in red "boundary" ink similar to that of the general Georgia boundary indicator; in the other there is nothing more than the dotted line of the basic engraving. A study of the relative dates of the states of the map might throw some light on the historical claims regarding the boundary.

them. But i recommend to you very earnestly that no body may know that i have the least part in these things. I know all the rascality of the Spanish Agent [140] and our court in the Brazils is now in the greatest intimacy with Spain, and on the eve of a still greater by marriages.[141]

No doubt you have written to Dupont, whom i left very much disposed to give you any information you could desire from him.[142]

As to the horse i acquiesce readily in whatever you chuse to do, i will not want money but by the middle of next month.

Take care of your health, and may you enjoy all the prosperity i wish you.

Most sincerely yours
J. Corrèa de Serra

CORREA TO GILMER
[U.Va.]

[1816?] [143]   [No date]

Besides what Mr. Gallatin had recorded,[144] the following things must be considered.

---

[140] Presumably Luis de Onís (1762-1827). See C to Gilmer, 6 Feb. 1816, notes 127 and 128, above.

[141] C refers to the marriages of the Portuguese princesses, Maria Isabel and Maria Francisa (second and third daughters of King Dom João VI), to the King of Spain, Fernando VII, and his brother, the Infante Don Carlos María Isidro de Borbón, respectively. These two marriages took place in Madrid in a joint ceremony in September, 1816. See Mendes, Fernando, *La dinastia de Bragança* 5: 30, Lisbon, J. Romano Torres, 1910; de Vasconcellos, A. A. Teixeira, *Le Portugal et la maison de Bragance,* 616, Paris, 1859.

[142] Though Gilmer and duPont corresponded in 1816-1817, it was not on the subject of Florida. See Davis, *Gilmer, passim.*

[143] Though this fragment is without date and repeats some of the information in the two letters preceding, it probably follows them. C is apparently in Washington or New York on a brief excursion.

[144] Albert Gallatin (1761-1849), Swiss-born Secretary of the

That there is not the least doubt about what concerns the country West of the Mississipi except some uncertainty about the limits with Spain which make not part of the question.

That it is clear from the wording of the treaty of St. Ildefonso that something more was to be given by Spain, than the Louisiana such as France had given to her—which was everything to the W. of the Mispi. and the island of N. Orleans.

That it is equally clear that every other part which the Kings of France had before possessed and was now in the hands of Spain, is meant by the words of the treaty.

The French had possessed or claimed under the name of Louisiana vast countries to the East of the Mississipi. Indeed all the three successive seats of their government there were on the East of that river. 1st when they first discovered it by the North Chevr. dela Salle established the colony near the Wabash (vide La Salle's discoveries in the New York Historical coll.) [145] 2d when they attempted the settlement by the Gulph of Mexico, the colony was fixed at Biloxi which is now reckoned Florida. 3d when they transferred it to N. Orleans it was equally on the East, because the supposed island of N. Orleans

---

Treasury, 1801–1813, was in Paris from 1816 to 1823 as minister to France. As early as 1803–1805 he was giving considerable thought to the Florida boundary question and was advising TJ and Madison in the matter (see Adams, Henry, ed., *The writings of Albert Gallatin,* 3 v., 1: 109–110, 241–253, etc., Philadelphia, 1879). In 1803 his On the amicable settlement of the limits of the State of Georgia (Yazoos claims) was published in the State Papers (see *ibid.* 1: 125–132; 3: 618 ff.). C probably refers, however, to Gallatin's able summary of American rights in Introduction to the collection of laws, treaties, and other documents having operation and respect to the public lands. . . . Published under Act of Congress of 27th April 1810 (originally printed 1810; reproduced in *Writings* 3: 207–229).

[145] See C to Gilmer, 6 February 1816, note 129, above.

is an invention of the treaty of peace of 1763 between England and France because the river Iberville which is supposed to make the Island had no water but in the great freshets of the Mississipi, the water of which is generally ten or twelve feet lower than this outlet called Iberville.

The French not only possessed Mobile, but claimed according to the European general usage all the waters of it. They had a settlement on the Alabama at Fort Toulouse &c. They claimed all the waters going into the Missipi. and the actual Nashville was one of their indisputed colonies.

By the wording of the treaty Spain was to give back everything which had in her power of all that was before claimed by the French, and which she had not alienated to other powers. The country to Rio perdido is in this case otherwise the words of the treaty are unnecessary and absurd.

The reason why clearer specification was not used is because Spain by her treaty with England of 1783 pretended to have rights to all the lands to the parallel of the mouth of the Yazous from which *de facto* the Americans had expelled her. Vide Ellicott's work on the line of the Southern frontier [146] and the French without

---

[146] Andrew Ellicott (1754–1820), mathematician and surveyor, had in 1796 been commissioned to survey the Florida-U. S. boundary and serve on a joint Spanish-U. S. commission to lay out this boundary along the thirty-first parallel from the Mississippi eastward to the Appalachicola (Chattahoochee) River. The Spanish, hoping the Western Country might be detached from the Union, employed a delaying action using the old arguments C here suggests. See *The journal of Andrew Ellicott, late commissioner on behalf of the United States during part of the year 1796, the years 1797, 1798, 1799, and part of the year 1800: For determining the boundary line between the United States and the possessions of His Catholic Majesty in America, containing occasional remarks on the situation, soil,*

doubt wished to take it also, it being included also in the ambiguous words of St. Ildefonso's treaty.

I will send you from Philadelphia clearer details on the treaty of 1793.

[Unsigned]

CORREA TO JEFFERSON   [L.C.]

Dear Sir

I have found at my return in Philadelphia near a month ago, your kind letter for which i would have immediately returned my most grateful thanks if it did not contain two articles to which it was my duty to answer, viz. the cements for cisterns,[147] and the papers of Captain Lewis. As to the first, the books containing the prescriptions were not at hand, and i could attain them with some difficulty, but having after unavoidable delays had sight of them, i am able to send you the contents.[148]

1. Cendrèe de Tournay, ciment qui a la proprieté de se consolider dans l'eau et de devenir aubout dequelques annèes plus dur que les pierres au quelles il sert de liaison.

Melez dela chaux pure avec la cendre du charbon de terre jusques a ce que le melange pese $\frac{1}{4}$ de plus qu' un egal volume de chaux pure — Il est necessaire d' ecraser la cendrèe jusques à ca qu' elle fasse une páte unie et douce, et par la seule force du frottement, et sans y

---

rivers, natural productions, and diseases of the different countries on the Gulf of Mexico, with six maps comprehending ... the whole of West Florida, and part of East Florida ... , Philadelphia ... , 1803. For the spelling "Yazous" River employed by C see the map before p. 25 of this work.

[147] See TJ to C, 27 December 1814, note 84, above, and C to TJ [before 1 Jan. 1816], and TJ to C, 1 Jan. 1816, and 20 July 1816, note 197, below.

[148] Essentially a condensation of the recipes from the Cours complet d'agriculture already given TJ in late 1815 (see fragment of before 1 Jan. 1816, and TJ to C, 1 Jan. 1816, above).

mettre plus d'eau qu' il n'en faut pour 1 eteindre.

2d. Imitation de pouzzolane dont l'efficace est prou-vèe—Prenez une moitie chaux, un quart brique pilèe bien pulverisée et passèe ou tamis un quart [macheser?] egalément bien pulverisè.

3d. Ciment pour les jointures des citernes particu-lierement de celles destinèes a garder du vin — Prenez une pierre de chaux, que vous [leisserez?] éteindre à l'air prenez du sang de bœuf, avant qu'il ait caillé, c' est a dire encore chaud; melez ces deux substances, en les fouettant longtems ensemble, jusques a ce qu'elles aient la consistance d'une colle epaisse, enduisez en toutes les jointures.

General observations for the construction of good cisterns— 1°. to avoid any gravel or stony nucleus of any size whatever in the cement—2°. to spread the ce-ment which must cover all the inside (l'enduit) in thin strata successively and equally. It is a work of prac-tice and attention, which is well repaid by the excellence of the cistern.

I am sorry the cisterns of Charleston did not occupy my attention, but i have strong reasons to suspect, they are not well constructed. The water of Charleston is far from being so good as rain water generally is, and dif-fers from it so much in taste and in salubrity, that it is more than probable that in so low a situation and so surrounded by water as Charleston is, the cisterns ad-mit by filtration other waters. Now what they take in there, would be let out if they were situated in a high and dry ground.

Now for Captain Lewis's papers, i have found it a difficult work, but you may rely on my zeal and assidu-ity to fulfil your wishes. Several times have i called on Mrs. Barton [149] and twice on Mr. Pennington her

---

[149] Dr. Benjamin Smith Barton had married in 1797 Mary, a daughter of Edward Pennington (1726–1796), of Philadelphia.

brother,[150] who has great influence on her, and assists her in the arrangement of her affairs, but i am not more advanced than in the beginning. The Dr has left such an immense heap of papers, and in such disorder; the reclamations for papers and books are so many, that i conceive how the poor lady is embarrassed how to do. It seems that for a great number of years the Drs. Library and cabinet followed the same law that Dante has inscribed on the gate of hell

[Yesbe?] di Speranza o voi che entrate.[151]
But i hope there will be an end to this suspence; you will know the result.

The Letters you directed to Knoxville i have also received here, and cannot but blush at the excessive praises, which your goodness bestows on me, but as to the danger of Mr. Gilmer catching from me an immoderate taste for ornamental knowledge, you may well change your opinion, and he will tell it himself.[152] Curious and strange as it may seem, he has received from me during all the voyage more hints and disertations about what i conceive to be the real interests of his country and the means of her reaching the high destinies to which it seems destined by nature, than even about the plants we were meeting. He must have wished to find many of his countrymen so zealous on that subject as his european companion; as i love the country and like

---

[150] A second Edward Pennington (see note immediately above) was elected a member of the APS 16 January 1808, and died 16 March 1834, aet. 68.

[151] Dante, Inferno, Canto Terzo, 1. 9, reads "Lasciate ogni speranza, voi ch' entrate." C himself assisted in preparing the Barton Library for sale by classifying and arranging. See Francis R. Packard, 190th annual report, the Pennsylvania Hospital, 6–18, Philadelphia, 1941.

[152] C and Gilmer had probably discussed the Florida and other American problems as they rode through the country.

his mind and his heart, my grand point was to help him with whatever was in my power to do that good which i myself would have attempted, and fit him to *se mergere civilibus undis* [153] with glory to himself and his country. I come lastly to the kindness you show to me, in the interest you take in the future steps of my life. As long as i live i feel your goodness, and keep a grateful sense of so much kindness. Your judgement of European present and future affairs, is what myself think; but i see little chance of escaping the necessity of returning there. What i can do is not rashly to chuse Paris for my residence, till i see the turn things take. As long as i shall remain on this continent i will perform with devotion and gratitude my annual pilgrimage to Monticello, and when in Europe i will turn very often my eyes to the West and think of the real greatness and dignity of the man who has laid such a claim to my respect and heartfelt gratitude.

I am most feelingly and sincerely yours

J. Correa de Serra

Philadelphia 12. Feby.
1816

CORREA TO GILMER   [*U.Va.*]

Philadelphia 10 March 1816

Dear Sir and friend

Immediately as i received your letter, i called on Dr. Wistar and gave him what you had written to him about the state of your health.[154] He answered me after some

---

[153] Horace, *Epistles,* I, 1, 16, "nunc agilis fio et mersor civilibus undis" ["Now I become all action, and plunge into the tide of civil life" (Loeb transl.)].

[154] Gilmer had been in serious ill-health during the winter of 1815–1816, perhaps an early stage of the tuberculosis and other ailments which were to cut his life short in 1826.

consideration that he would think maturely because as much as palliatives would be easy, as much a radical cure such as he wished required attention on his side and perseverance on yours. He tells me now that he has written to you and sent his opinion two days ago. I am very sorry to see by your letter that your spirits are low, but important as your case is, no immediate danger exists, and nothing according to the Dr. that you are not able to get rid of both for the present and the future.

What i wrote to you about Florida i am afraid was confuse, because my mind has been frozen by the bad season which we have experienced. Now an argument occurs to me — That the bare mention of treaties of Spain with other powers carries the dispute to the east of the Mississipi, she having entered into none for the countries to the West — that there exist only two senses, either that she must give up what she acquired by these treaties, or keep it — Now if this last is the sense, there is no occasion to stipulate retrocassions which in this case would not exist, nor of mentioning the word treaties.†

The verses you gave for Washington's monument are not of Tibellus, they are of Claudian in the poem de Laudibus Stiliconis.[155]

I have received many letters from Europe, and see clearly that there exist no hopes of rest, the volcano is burning and smoaking, God knows what sort of eruptions and how many there will be.

Walsh is recovering slowly he is now in Baltimore, but i expect him here next month. Mr. Vaughan [156]

---

[155] C probably refers to two lines in Claudian's On Stilicho's Consulship, I, 89-90, "Felix arbitrii princeps, qui congrua mundo / iudicat et primus censet, quod cernimus omnes." Loeb transl.: "Happy our emperor in his choice; he judges and the world agrees; he is the first to value what we all see."

[156] John Vaughan. See C to TJ, 6 September 1813, note 25,

will forward Tickenor's [157] letters for you, if any comes to his hand directly to your address in Winchester. If it is not inconvenient for you to settle the business of the horse, it would do to me great pleasure i had already prevented you that in this month of March i would be in want of money.

Expecting confidently better news of your health, i remain

Most sincerely yours

J. Correa de Serra

† because there is not an inch of ground on the east of the river, which if this last was the sense, she ought to give up or France to receive from her.

CORREA TO [WILLIAM RAWLE?] [158]

[U.Penna.Archives]

---

and ch. III, note 17, above.

[157] George Ticknor (1791–1871) and Gilmer had become good friends in Philadelphia in the winter of 1814–1815. Ticknor had sailed for Europe in April, 1815, and wrote Gilmer several letters from Göttingen and other places. See Davis, *Gilmer,* 82–83, 109–110; Trent, *English culture in Virginia,* where the letters are included in the appendix; and Davis, The early American lawyer and the profession of letters, *loc. cit.,* 191–205.

[158] This letter does not bear the name of the person to whom it is directed, but the index which accompanies the University of Pennsylvania papers for this period indicates that it was addressed to William Rawle. Additional evidence is the fact that another letter, also giving advice on the proposed new faculty, was addressed specifically to Rawle on 6 March 1816 by N. Chapman (see UPennaArchives). Rawle was a member of the committee of the University Board of Trustees appointed to investigate facilities and to formulate plans for the proposed Faculty of Physical Science and Rural Economy. This committee was appointed 6 February 1816. For this and some other information given below I am indebted to Dr. Leonidas Dodson, University of Pennsylvania Archivist. For more of Rawle, see note 160 below.

Dear Sir

Receive my thanks for the communication of the report to the trustees about the new faculty.[159]   It gives

---

[159] On 6 Feb. 1816, the Trustees' Minutes report, William Rawle moved, and the resolution was made, that a Faculty of Physical Science and Rural Economy be established. This Faculty was to consist of the following professorships: (1) Botany, (2) Zoology, (3) Geology and Mineralogy, (4) Comparative Anatomy and Veterinary Arts, (5) Agriculture and Horticulture. A committee was appointed to investigate and make plans.

At the Trustees' meeting of 5 March 1816, the committee reported its findings and suggestions. The report is not contained in the Minutes. There is, however, a notation that one hundred copies were to be published. Presumably this is the report to which C refers (though no copy has been found). The organization C criticized may be the one outlined or an intermediary one. At any rate, the Board recommended on 4 October 1816 an organization of professorships of: (1) Botany and Horticulture, (2) Natural History, including Geology, Zoology, and Comparative Anatomy, (3) Mineralogy and Chemistry as applied to Agriculture and the Arts. At the next meeting, on 5 November, an additional professorship of Comparative Anatomy (separately) was recommended. Perhaps at some unrecorded meeting the fifth professorship, Natural Philosophy, was added, for in 1821, in summarizing earlier recommendations for such a faculty, a report signed by Rawle and Zaccheus Collins (pamphlet, *At a meeting of the trustees of the University Tuesday, January 1, 1821,* copy in UPenna-Arch) states that *five* professorships had been the 1816 plan: (1) Botany, (2) Natural History, including Geology, (3) Natural Philosophy, (4) Mineralogy and Chemistry, as Applied to Agriculture and the Arts, (5) Comparative Anatomy. Thus the organization of this Faculty remained for many years, the Archivist reports.

C's proposal is, of course, somewhat different from that finally adopted. Since the printed report on which he commented is unavailable, one cannot determine whether he had any real influence. It will be noticed, however, that the Veterinary is abolished. C's suggestions of references to authorities on various phases of the subject may also have influenced certain regroupings.

me great satisfaction, and find it the work of enlightened good will and good sense. The only thing which seems to me worthy reconsideration is the division or rather distribution of the matters to be treated in some chairs; for instance (Comparative anatomy and veterinary). You know better than anybody what comparative anatomy must be.[160] Its aim is to know how the same or analogous vital functions may be performed by quite different organizations, and to reduce the essential principles or attributes of Life, and the animal functions to the simplest and truest idea. To obtain this end all the tribes of animal creation without exception, either vertebrated or invertebrated, solid or molluscs must be compared, a single one left out would impair the nature of the science. All this, important as it is, is perfectly useless to the veterinary, our domestic animals being very few, and all included in a simple series of the vertebrated structure. Veterinary by itself, is more than enough to occupy a whole course, inasmuch as the professor to be useful, must enter in the details, and that this art is not of those which can be treated a priori[.]

Again, i am perfectly satisfied that comparative anatomy, if treated professedly and to its whole extent, is a refinement of science for which your establishments of instruction are not yet ripe. But taught as the key of Zoology and blended with its stamina, as it is now practiced in Paris and Gottingen, it gives a solid and

---

[160] William Rawle (1759–1836), distinguished Philadelphia lawyer, litterateur, and amateur botanist, was an active member of the APS and the Society for Promoting Agriculture, as well as an honorary member of the Linnean Society. *DAB; Em. Phila.* Why he should know comparative anatomy so well is puzzling, and brings up the question as to whether the letter here was in the *first* instance addressed to Rawle at all. Actually it may have been addressed to C's and Rawle's friend, Dr. Wistar, or some other member of the medical faculty, and transmitted by him to the Board through Rawle.

more important basis to this last science, and takes it from the low station of nomenclatural science and mere inventory of species formed from external characters, where it had been reduced by the Linnean school. I say the Linnean school, because that great man [161] himself thought otherwise, he made what little was known of comparative anatomy eighty years ago, the basis of his classification, as we see in his Systema Naturæ. But his followers have been to him, what the Arabs and the scholastics were to Aristotle. Comparative anatomy is even more allied to real Zoology than Mineralogy to Geology.

The fractionary parts of natural history which the report throws together with Zoology, can be no other but meteorology and hydrology. This last you know has disappeared for ever in the hands of the chemists and the first belongs much more naturally to the professor of natural philosophy. The chairs it seems would then be. Botany — Geology and mineralogy — Zoology founded on compar. anatomy — Veterinary — Agriculture and rural economy. Because i perfectly agree that this last by itself is enough to fill a course. That depends from [sic] the details in which the professor is to enter. In most of the South European universities, the principles of vegetable physiology, and those of the diseases and culture of plants &c which constitute the foundation of agriculture are explained by the professor of botany, but they are very compendiously thaugt [sic]. In Paris in Padua and in a few other cities it occupies a whole chair, and a garden of experiments.

This is all i have to say, and you see it is but little.

---

[161] Carl von Linné (or Linnaeus) (1770–1778), Swedish physician-naturalist and the founder of systematic botany, had been a friend and correspondent of C when the latter was a young man in Italy. See the letters of the two of April 1772, 14 Dec. 1773, and 22 Jan. 1774 in the Linnaean Society, London.

Permit me now a digression occasioned by an expression which i do not clearly understand. It is subjoined to the chair of agriculture that the professor is to have a necessary licence to explain the principles of chemistry and their application to his science — What does this mean? Is Chemistry or any science the exclusive property of any professor? Cannot the others when it is necessary to their business recur to it? Agriculture as scientific art cannot be taught without frequent recourse to Chemistry and to Botany, perhaps more to this second, i say real Botany and not the simple nomenclature of plants—foliis ovalibus or foliis ovato lanceolatis. To you a word of comparison will be enough. Agriculture stands to these two sciences in exactly the same relation that Medicine stands to Chemistry and Anatomy. Chemistry helps to the knowledge of the nature of remedies, very seldom to that of diseases. Anatomy shows the body itself that is to be treated, and what change organization receives in each disease. You will feel the justness of the comparison, and i need not carry it farther.[162]

I left four years ago Europe divided between chemical and botanical agriculture, and as always happens the division was according to the different interests of the countries. In the very northern ones, where new

[162] C's comments on giving each professor liberty to teach what he pleased *may* have borne some sort of fruit at the 4 October 1816 meeting of the Board of Trustees, where the new faculty was formally recommended, and the recommendations followed by a resolution embodying the clause, "That the right of the professor of Chemistry in the Medical Faculty to treat of such parts of the subjects of the new professorships as he may deem necessary, shall not be impaired by the establishment of the professorships." This is, of course, declaring freedom of action for the other party, and is designed primarily to avoid jealousies and certain questionings from the medical faculty.

cultures could not be easily introduced and the soil is not of the best sort, the manures and amendments of the soil were of course the great objects and chemical agriculture took the lead. The first book ever published on this subject was that of Wallerius [163] about fifty years ago in Sweden. Recently Davy's work [164] has given to it celebrity in England, but the case of England being not absolutely so much in the case of Sweden (though its soil and climate according [to] David Hume are inferior to that of France Spain and Italy [165]) the English have found that manures and amendments of soil the only objects in which chemistry is paramount, were still short of the improvements they could attain. Their reviews show that the work did not satisfy their expectations. Countries which from their soil and climate have a wide range of useful vegetables to introduce or to bring into culture are chiefly for botanic agriculture, as you can see in the works of French Italian and south German authors, chiefly in the

---

[163] Wallerius, Johan Gottskalk, *Elemens d'agriculture physique et chymique, traduits du Latin de M.W.*, Yverdon, 1766.

[164] Sir Humphry Davy had published *The analysis of soils as connected with their improvement,* London, 1805; *Conversations on chemistry . . . fixed alkalis,* New Haven, 1813; *Elements of agricultural chemistry . . . ,* Philadelphia, 1815, to cite only some of those C was thinking of. These three do not show Wallerius as a source, but C may mean only that Davy's work revived interest in the subject and therefore in Wallerius.

[165] "It may seem an odd position, that the poverty of the common people in France, Italy, and Spain, is, in some measure, owing to the superior riches of soil and the happiness of climate; yet there want not reasons to justify this paradox." Since the preceding paragraphs have to do with England, "superior to England" must be the sense here rather than just "above average." See *Philosophical works of David Hume,* Green, T. H., and T. H. Grose, edd., 4 v., 3: 298, New Impression, London, 1898.

famous = Cours complet d'agriculture, by a society of naturalists and land owners, of which you have here a copy in the library of the agricultural society.[166] Common sense dictates that what is good be taken from either side, as the circumstances require it. I am persuaded that Pennsylvania is so situated as to be capable of deriving profit from both. At all events if ever you have a botanic garden, it would be worth while to appropriate some acres of ground to try the naturalization of useful vegetables from abroad, or domesticate the wild ones of the country which may give hopes of turning of utility. But i perceive that i am digressing too far, but you wish to have my opinion on the report, and i am apt to run into digressions when telling you my mind.

Most sincerely yours.

J. Corrèa de Serra

Thursday 14 March
    1816

CORREA TO GILMER   *[U.Va.]*

Philadelphia 27 March 1816

Dear Sir

Both your letters of the 15 and 22 March are arrived in proper time. The first would have been immediately answered if my eyes had been better, but the madness of the climate in these last weeks, had caused an in-

---

[166] *Cours complet d'agriculture théorique, pratique, économique, et de médecine rurale et vétérinaire . . . ou dictionnaire universel d'agriculture . . . ,* 10 v., Paris, 1793–1800. For the particular set C used, see C to TJ, fragment or enclosure [date "Before 1 Jan. 1816"], note 117 above.

flammation in them which has hindered me from writing and what is worse from reading for many days. I am now better, but there is no trusting to your calendar. Sansom Street [167] is still filled with the snow fallen twice in last week.

I must thank you for your kind offers of money, but as i have lived long, and the narrowness of my finances obliges me to calculate beforehand, i know that there will be no occasion of want after the end of April, because i had provided for that. What you have sent and what remained in my power is more than sufficient to fill the gap, to the whole of my possible expenses. What you notice in your last letter of the 17$ you had paid for me at Winchester i was surprised not to find in your first and shows the hurry in which you then wrote. That account shall be settled when we meet, and the horse sold or before if there is occasion. I shall treasure in my mind your kindness, though there is no occasion of making use of it.

The apparent contradictions of epochs about the Louisiana Treaties, may perhaps be settled; that whatever they were, the execution of them shows their true spirit. Now the first treaty between Spain and France was a secret one in 1762, before East Louisiana and Florida were ceded to England, it was not known and executed, but in 1765, when already east Louisiana and Florida were in possession of England. In the treaty of peace in 1763, it is the King of France who ceded east Louisiana to England, and the King of Spain ceded Florida. As to the proclamation of the division of Florida in East and West being of October 1764 and their occupation in Novber. following, that meant nothing, the treaty of peace by which they were ceded being of

---

[167] A narrow street parallel to and lying between Chestnut and Walnut Streets.

a much earlier date in the same year.[168]

Much pleasure has given me the convalescence of little Louisa,[169] being a child i take much more interest in her, than nature makes me capable of feeling for any grown person who is not of my intimate acquaintance.

I am very much pleased also with your success in the bar,[170] though i never doubted of it. Go on ascending by this ladder, but remember that a genius like yours must not make it the only business of his life, but employ the ascendancy he gets by that means, to better the mental situation of his nation, which is still in this respect magis absque vitiis quam cum virtutibus.[171]

In the end of June i finish the course[172] which i am to begin in a fortnight, till then i cannot stir from Philadelphia, immediately after i hope i shall have the pleasure of seeing you in Winchester perfectly reestablished in health. What will happen after that, i do not yet know, but there is the greatest possibility that i will recross the Atlantick.

I am with real friendship

Most sincerely yours

J. Corréa de Serra

---

[168] *Cf.* Brooks, *Diplomacy,* 4–5. C appears to have had details here not generally available.

[169] Evidently the child of one of Gilmer's friends in Winchester, Virginia.

[170] *Cf.* Davis, *Gilmer,* 96–97. Gilmer's reputation as a trial lawyer was rising rapidly.

[171] C apparently had in mind Tacitus, *Hist.* 1: 49, 11: "magis extra vitia quam cum virtutibus." Loeb transl.: "being rather free from faults than possessing virtues."

[172] The course in botany given at APS. See TJ to C, 28 June 1815, note 98, above, and ch. V, above, as well as C to TJ, 16 June 1816, below: also the notice in the *Virginia Argus* of 18 May 1816.

CORREA TO JEFFERSON   [*L.C.*]

Philadelphia 29 March. 1816

Dear Sir

At last Mrs. Barton has sent me a little morocco bound volume, part of Capt. Lewis journal containing his observations from April 9 of 1805 to February 17 1806, and the meteorological observ. for July August September. 1805, together with the drawing of a quadruped which he calls the Fisher.[173]   As the chaos of this library begins to clear, by the separation of printed books which are sold to the hospital [174] i doubt not the remaining papers of Capt. Lewis may be found, but you could help me much by sending me a description of their external appearance, and their probable volume, because Mrs. Barton who acts in all this very honestly (but does not permit any body to search the papers of her husband, but by what i understand only herself and her brother who is also a very honest person) will be much helped in finding them.   In the mean time i expect your directions about what i am to do with the volume i have yet, and the others that may appear.

I hope you have enjoyed perfect health, and your winter probably has not been so capricious as in Pennsylvania, where after very pleasant weather, we have felt two rather severe snowstorms since the middle of the month.

---

[173] The drawing is now in MS. Journals and Miscellaneous Papers, Lewis and Clark, APS, Philadelphia, 7.   The volume of observations referred to is now Codex P, Lewis and Clark Papers, and the meteorological observations, Codex O, the same.   See also Thwaites, ed., *Original Journals* 7 : 420 ff.

[174] Barton's natural history books are today at the Pennsylvania Hospital in Philadelphia.   See Packard, *op. cit.,* C to TJ, 12 February 1816, note 149, above.

Marshall Grouchy [175] has been here a few days in the same hotel with Mr. Short [176] whose acquaintance he is. I have spoken with him, and he did not seem to me very sanguine in his expectations about what is going in Europe. From his account Bonaparte's talents did not shine in the last years of his political existence.

I remain with the highest respect and esteem

Most sincerely yours

J. Corrèa de Serra

JEFFERSON TO CORREA

[A.P.S. (here printed) and L.C.]

Poplar Forest   April 26. 16.

Dear Sir

Your favor of Mar. 29 was recieved just as I was setting out for this place. I brought it with me to be answered hence. since you are so kind as to interest yourself for Capt. Lewis's papers, I will give. you a full statement of them.[177]

1. ten or twelve such pocket volumes, Morocco bound, as that you describe, in which in his own hand writing, he had journalised all occurrences day by day as he travelled. They were small 8vos. and opened at the end for more convenient writing. every one had been put into a separate tin case, cemented to prevent

---

[175] Emmanuel, Marquis de Grouchy (1766-1847), marshal of France, was court-martialled for his partial failure at Waterloo and was exiled to America, where he remained until 1821. On his return to France he was reinstated as general.

[176] William Short (q.v.) had of course known Grouchy during his years in Paris.

[177] All the materials TJ knew of and describes here were not collected until Professor Thwaites located them in various places when he prepared his edition. See *Original journals* 1: xxviii–lvi.

injury from wet. but on his return the cases, I presume, had been taken from them, as he delivered me the books uncased. There were in them the figures of some animals drawn with the pen while on his journey. The gentlemen who published his travels must have had these MS. volumes, and perhaps now have them, or can give some account of them.[178]

2. Descriptions of animals and plants. I do not recollect whether there was such a book or collection of papers, distinct from his journal; altho' I am inclined to think there was one: because his travels as published, do not contain all the new animals of which he had either descriptions or specimens. mr. Peale, I think, must know something of this, as he drew figures of some of the animals for engraving, and some were actually engraved.[179] Perhaps Conrad, his bookseller, who was to have published the work,[180] can give an account of these.

3. Vocabularies. I had myself made a collection of about 40 vocabularies of the Indians on this side the Mississipi, and Capt Lewis was instructed to take those of every tribe beyond, which he possibly could. The

---

[178] Nicholas Biddle and Paul Allen. See C to Nicholas Biddle, 8 Sept. 1813, notes 5 and 6, above, and descriptions of the edition in Thwaites, ed., *Original journals* 1: lxxvii. Biddle did have many of the papers.

[179] Charles Willson Peale (1741–1827), artist and founder of the Pennsylvania Academy of the Fine Arts and the Peale Museum, must be the person referred to. The engravings, however, are unknown today. Mr. Charles Coleman Sellers, author of a two-volume biography of Peale, knows nothing of them. The American Philosophical Society and the Pennsylvania Academy of the Fine Arts have no record of the engravings or of Peale's connection with these things.

[180] John Conrad, who had planned to publish the Lewis and Clark journals before his bankruptcy in 1811, had taken a great interest in securing another publisher for the work. See Thwaites, ed., *Original journals* 1: xli.

intention was to publish the whole, and leave the world
to search for affinities between these and the languages
of Europe and Asia. he was furnished with a number
of printed vocabularies of the same words and form I
had used, with blank spaces for the Indian words. he
was very attentive to this instruction, never missing an
opportunity of taking a vocabulary. After his return,
he asked me if I should have any objection to the printing his separately, as mine were not yet arranged as
I intended. I assured him I had not the least; and I
am certain he contemplated their publication. but
whether he had put the papers out of his own hand or
not, I do not know. I imagine he had not: and it is
probable that Doctr. Barton, who was particularly curious on this subject, and published on it occasionally,
would willingly receive and take care of these papers
after Capt. Lewis's death, and that they are now among
his papers.

4. his observations of longitude and latitude. he
was instructed to send these to the war office, that
measures might be taken to have the calculations made.
whether he delivered them to the war office, or to Dr.
Patterson,[181] I do not know; but I think he communicated with Dr. Patterson concerning them. These are
all important: because altho', having with him the Nau-
tical almanacs, he could & did calculate some of his
latitudes, yet the longitudes were taken merely from

---

[181] Probably Robert Patterson (1743–1824), Irish-born professor of mathematics in the University of Pennsylvania and
member of the APS (its president in 1819). Or possibly his
son, Robert M. Patterson (1787–1854), professor of natural
philosophy from 1813 and of mathematics from 1814 (succeeding his father) in the same institution. See *NCAB; Em.
Phila.* Biddle thought the astronomical observations were in
the hands of Ferdinand Hassler, Swiss mathematician and surveyor, who gave up the calculations in despair. See Thwaites,
ed., *Original journals* 7: 405–406.

estimates by the log line, time and course. so that it is only as to latitudes that his map may be considered as tolerably correct; not as to it's longitudes.

5. his map. This was drawn on sheets of paper, not put together, but so marked that they could be joined together with the utmost accuracy; not as one great square map, but ramifying with the courses of the rivers. the scale was very large, and the sheets numerous, but in perfect preservation. this was to await publication, until corrected by the calculations of longitude and latitude. I examined these sheets myself minutely, as spread on a floor, and the originals must be in existence, as the map published with his travels must have been taken from them.[182]

These constitute the whole. they are the property of the government, the fruits of the expedition undertaken at such expence of money and risk of valuable lives. they contain exactly the whole of the information which it was our object to obtain for the benefit of our own country and of the world. but we were willing to give to Lewis and Clarke whatever pecuniary benefits might be derived from the publication, and therefore left the papers in their hands, taking for granted that their interests would produce a speedy publication, which would be better if done under their direction. but the death of Capt. Lewis,[183] the distance and occupations of General Clarke, and the bankruptcy of their bookseller, have retarded the publication, and rendered necessary that

---

[182] Clark, the recognized draughtsman of the party, appears to have done all the maps. They were secured by Professor Thwaites from the Clark family, and are reproduced with others TJ evidently did not know about in *Original journals* **8** (Atlas). The map TJ speaks of was among the material Biddle turned over to the APS. See *Original journals* **7**: 406.

[183] Lewis' mysterious death at Nashville, Tennessee, occurred in 1809. General William Clark (1770–1838) was from 1813 Governor of the Missouri Territory.

the government should attend to the reclamation & security of the papers. their recovery is now become an imperious duty. their safest deposit as fast as they can be collected, will be the Philosophical society, who no doubt will be so kind as to recieve and preserve them, subject to the orders of government; and their publication, once effected in any way, the originals will probably be left in the same deposit. as soon as I can learn their present situation, I will lay the matter before the government to take such order as they think proper. as to any claims of individuals to these papers, it is to be observed that, as being the property of the public, we are certain neither Lewis nor Clarke would undertake to convey away the right to them, and that they could not convey them, had they been capable of intending it. yet no interest of that kind is meant to be disturbed, if the individual can give satisfactory assurance that he will promptly & properly publish them. Otherwise they must be restored to the government; & the claimant left to settle with those on whom he has any claim. my interference will, I trust, be excused, not only from the portion which every citizen has in whatever is public, but from the peculiar past I have had in the design and execution of this expedition.

To you, my friend, apology is due for involving you in the trouble of this enquiry. it must be found in the interest you take in whatever belongs to science, and in your own kind offers to me of aid in this research. be assured always of my affectionate friendship and respect.

Th. Jefferson

CORREA TO JEFFERSON   [*Mass.Hist.Soc.*]

Philadelphia 12 May 1816

Dear Sir

Your letter from Poplar forest reached my hands last week, and with it i am enabled to follow with more cognisance the research of Capt. Lewis's papers. The only part which i had recovered i had forwarded to you by your excellent grand daughter when she was here.[184]

Colonel Jones of the Guards who is going to Kentucky to dispose of his lands there will present this to you.[185]   He wishes to have the honour of seeing you and conversing with you. I assure you that he is worthy of it. He is the whiggest of all whigs i have met, and bears a highly honourable character.

Be so kind to remember me to Mrs. and Colonel Randolph, and receive the assurance of the sentiments with which i am

> Sir
>
> > Your most obliged obedt. servant
>
> > J. Corrèa de Serra

JEFFERSON TO CORREA   [*L.C.*]

> Monticello June 5. 16.

I had determined, my dear Sir, to have withdrawn at the close of this year from all subscriptions to news-

---

[184] Ellen Wayles Randolph (1796–1876), daughter of Martha and Thomas Mann Randolph (*q.v.*), once engaged to Francis W. Gilmer and later married to Joseph Coolidge, Jr., of Boston. On 25 April 1816, TJ wrote to Elizabeth Trist (letter in Mass. Hist. Soc.) that "Ellen past the winter at Washington, with Mrs. Madison, and has taken a flight to Philadelphia, with Mr. Dallas's family."

[185] Unidentified. See TJ to C, 5 June 1816, below, mentioning him.

papers, and never to read another. but the National Intelligencer of the 1st. inst.[186] has given me so much pleasure that I shall defer for a year longer my resolution. it announced your appointment from your new king, to be his minister to this country. if this is acceptable to you, I congratulate you sincerely, but still more my countrymen to whom I know it will be most acceptable. I hope this fixes you with us for life, and that you will continue to visit your old friends as before; and be contented that we recieve and treat you as our friend, keeping out of sight—political character. particularly I hope it will not disappoint [us in?] the visit we should shortly have expected. I leave this f[or] Bedford [187] on the 20th. inst. and shall return the 1st week of July, in the hope of the expected pleasure of recieving you here at your own convenience.— my grandaughter delivered me the MS. volume of Capt Lewis', journal, & I hope the others, & most specially his observations of Long. & Lat. will be found. Colo. Jones passed a few days with us, and did justice to your recommendations. we found him a plain candid man, knowing all our European acquaintances, able to give us their history & present situation, and to give us new information of the many characters which have figured on the wonderful drama of our day. I have rarely met with a more interesting or agreeable acquaintance, and he left us with impressions which will follow him thro' life. I salute you with constant & affectionate esteem & respect.

Th. Jefferson

Mr. Correa.

---

[186] The announcement of C's appointment as minister from Portugal appeared originally in the Washington *National Intelligencer* of 31 May. A notice also appeared in the Philadelphia *Port Folio,* fourth ser., **2**: 85, 1816. See ch. IV, above.

[187] TJ's estate of Poplar Forest in Bedford county, Virginia.

CORREA TO JEFFERSON   [*L.C.*]

Philadelphia   16. June. 1816.

Dear Sir

Your kind letter of the 5 of this month reached me in due time, and i must entreat your forgiveness for not answering it sooner; neither my health, nor the hurry to finish the botanical course in which i was engaged without defrauding my hearers of any of the promised lectures have given me a moment's rest.[188] Under severe rheumatic pains, i have lectured almost every day in the afternoon, and gone to the fields in a gig every morning to collect the necessary plants. I feel very sensible to your congratulations, as to every sign of kindness from you, as to the thing itself though i must value it, does not make a great impression on me. It is somewhat like persimmon fruit, comes late, and has been ripened by hard frosts. One of the clear advantages i find in it, is that by keeping me in America, it ensures me a greater number of pilgrimages to Monticello. Three other pocket books of Capt Lewis have been found among the papers of Dr. Barton, and that was all that existed in the Drs. hands. but all his remaining papers concerning that expedition i have found deposited with Mr. Nicholas Biddle, who tells me he is ready to give them, on receiving an intimation to do so, from Genl. Clarke from whom he had them.[189] You see that i have done every thing in my power to satisfy your wishes, and you may be sure that will be the case in every occasion to serve you.

---

[188] For these lectures, see C to FWG, 27 March 1816, note 172, and ch. IV, both above.

[189] TJ wrote to Clark, received permission to deposit the materials with the APS, and the APS accepted the trust on 19 Nov. 1817. As noted above, Mr. Thwaites in 1903 found still more papers in the hands of the Clark family. See *Original journals* 1 : xlvi–xlviii, li–liv; 7 : 397–410.

Lately, litterary presents, from Paris, after long delays, have at last reached my hands, in them i have found the prescription of a new impenetrable cement, which i enclose in this letter.[190] Mr. Blainville has published a little memoir of ingenious conjectures to show that your Megalonyx is the Grisly Bear of the Missouri.[191] What he says is very cleaver, but not sufficient to bring conviction, and he himself avows it. This memoir is printed in the journal de physique, and is not among the presents i received, otherwise i would have sent it to you. My best respects to Mrs and Mr Randolph, and souvenirs to all your family. I expect to be able to renovate them personally in a few weeks.

I remain with the highest esteem and respect

Most sincerely yours

J. Corrèa de Serra

CORREA TO MADISON   [*L.C.*]

Philadelphia. 10 July. 1816

Sir

You know too well my respectful, and i beg leave to say friendly sentiments towards you, and my personal

---

[190] See letters 1815–1816, between TJ and C, above, for discussion of the cement.

[191] Henri Marie Ducrotay de Blainville (1777–1850) was apparently the author of an unsigned article, Note sur l'ours d'Amerique, *Journal de phisique, de chimie et d'histoire naturelle* **81**: 416–419, 1815, which makes the suggestions C mentions. For a good account of TJ's work and this aftermath, see George Gaylord Simpson, The beginnings of vertebrate paleontology in North America, *Proc. Amer. Philos. Soc.* **86**: 151–157, 1942, and Martin, Edwin T., *Thomas Jefferson, scientist,* 107–111, New York, Schuman, 1952.

feelings towards the nation of which you are the head, to be persuaded without difficulty, that of all the diplomatic missions in which my Soveraign would employ me, none would have such allurements to me, as that near the United States. You have long ago known my nomination to it, and i have already to thank you for the kind expressions which i am informed, you have manifested on that occasion. A few days ago i received via England my nomination and my credentials, and would have immediately set out for Washington and Montpellier, if a fit of rheumatism of which i flattered myself to have got the better, had not redoubled with encreased severity. As soon as i will be able to move with less pain, i will hasten to go and pay my respects, and as credentials have not yet passed, you will i hope permit [me] to come in the same unceremonious philosophical friendly manner, as in my last visit, and treat me in the same manner, as nothing can be more flattering to me than your personal friendship. As for the future, i have the fond expectation that (during my mission at least) the Portuguese minister will be found for the United States a sort of family Minister. Our nations are now in fact both American powers, and will be always the two paramount ones, each in his part of the new continent. I have the conscience also that no foreign minister ever came to the United States with such heartfelt attachment to this nation as myself, nor is it likely that any such, will come for ages.

I entreat you to present my best respects to Mrs. Madison, and to accept the assurance of the high esteem and respect with which i am

      Sir

        Your most obedient humble servant

          Joseph Corrèa de Serra.

CORREA TO JAMES MONROE [192]   [*Nat.Arch.*]

Philadelphia   10 July. 1816.

Sir

A few days ago i received via England, the dispatches
of my government including my nomination as Minister
Plenipotentiary near these United States, which was already known to you by the dispatches of Mr. Sumpter.[193]   I would have immediately set out for Washington to pay my respects to you, and to know when and
in what form my Credentials are to be presented, if a
severe fit of rhumatism, of which i was persuaded to
have got the better, had not redoubled with increased
pain.   In this circumstance i cannot but participate it
to you, that you may not think, that my delay in beginning my correspondence with this Government, was
owing to improper negligence.   My sentiments towards
this nation and this Government, are i am confident,
already too well known to you, to want any new assurance from me.   I hope in some days i will be in state
of feeling motion with less pain, and will either go to
Washington, in case you still remain there   or if as it
is reported you move towards the North, i will consider
it my duty to meet you in your journey, at the place
and time that you will judge most convenient to you.
I beg you will accept the assurance of the high respect
and [es]teem with which i am

                    Sir
              Your most obedient humble ser[vant]
              Joseph Corrèa de Serra

---

[192] Of course at this time Secretary of State.

[193] See TJ to C, 5 June 1816, note 186, and ch. IV, both above.
Thomas Sumter (1768–1840) of South Carolina was minister to
Brazil, 1810–1821. He is not to be confused with his father,
General Thomas Sumter (1734–1832). See Gregorie, Anne K.,
Thomas Sumter, passim, Columbia, S. C., R. L. Bryan, 1931.

MONROE TO CORREA [194]   [*Nat.Arch.*]

Mr. Joseph Corrèa de Serra   Department of State.
   Minister Plenipotentiary   July 18. 1816.
of Portugal, Algarves, Brazil.

Sir

I have had the honor to receive your letter of the
10th., informing me of your appointment, by your
Sovereign, his Minister Pleniptotentiary to the United
States, and that you were prevented by indisposition
from coming to this City to ascertain when and in what
form it, would be proper for you to present your letter
of credence.

I very much regret that you have been prevented by
indisposition from making a visit to this City, as it
would have been very gratifying to me to have seen
you. For the purpose however of entering on the duties
of your office, it will not be considered as indispensible
by the President, that you should attend him in person.
If you will have the goodness to transmit to me a copy
of your letter of credence, it will be agreeable to him,
that I should communicate with you on affairs interesting to our respective governments, in the same manner,
as if you had been received in the usual form. The
President will return to this City in the month of October, at which time, I shall have the honor of presenting you to him.

It gives me great pleasure to state that the appointment of a gentleman so well known and so much es-

---

[194] Like that of C to JMon, 10 July, above, this is one of the
dozens of letters and notes exchanged by Monroe and C, and
John Quincy Adams and C, in official capacities. Since most
of them are concerned entirely with diplomatic problems of a
highly technical and political nature which have been considered
in detail by Joseph E. Agan in his article, *loc. cit.,* only a few
representative items from the group will be reproduced in this
volume. The correspondence may be seen in NatArch.

teemed in this country, has afforded to the President great satisfaction, and he sees in it, a strong proof of the desire of your Government to cherish the friendly relations which now so happily exist between the two Nations.

I have the honor to be &c.

James Monroe.

JEFFERSON TO CORREA   [*L.C.*]

Monticello   July 20. 16.

Dear Sir

I returned from Poplar Forest about a week ago, and found here your favor of June 16. I learn with sincere regret your rheumatic indisposition; and the more as it strikes so directly at your summura bonum of botanical rambles. would it not be well to direct these towards the Augusta springs, which we consider as specific for that complaint? they are but about 80. or 90. miles from Monticello. but of this we will say more when we have the pleasure of seeing you here; which from the 'few weeks' of your letter of June 16. we daily hope. mr Gilmer is also daily expected by his friends. I am very glad to learn that 3. more of Capt Lewis's volumes are found, and hope the rest will reappear in time, as no one could think of destroying them. as to the astronomical observations & the vocabularies, I will write to Genl. Clarke to obtain his order for their delivery to the war office, to which they belong.[195] besides the notoriety of the fact that the ex-

---

[195] On 7 Nov. 1817 TJ informed Peter S. DuPonceau, chairmen of the proper committee of the APS, that he had waited long without avail for the appointment of a new Secretary of War, and that now he would ask that the APS be made the general depository for all the Lewis and Clark material. For Clark's letter to TJ of 10 Oct. 1816 on the subject of the material, see *Original journals* 7 : 397–399.

pedition was under public authority, at public expence. & for public objects and consequently that all it's results are public property, in the xivth page of the life of Capt Lewis prefixed to the History of his expedition,[196] it will be seen that the astronomical observations were expressly directed to be rendered to the War office for the purpose of having the calculations made by proper persons within the US. if on these considerations mr Biddle would think himself authorised to deliver these papers to the order of the Secy. at war, I will sollicit such an order to be given in favor of such person as the secretary may engage to make the calculations. but if mr Biddel has any scruples of delicacy with respect to Genl. Clarke I shall not press it, but wait an answer from him, which will only add 3. or 4. months to the delay already incurred. I hope my anxieties and interference in this matter will be excused, when my agency in the enterprise is considered, and that the most important justification of it, still due to the public depends of these astronomical observations, as from them alone can be obtained the correct geography of the country, which was the main object of the expedition.

I thank you for the new recipe for the cement.[197] I think it more easily practised than the former one, which, by the bye I have recovered. I had stuck the paper into a little Cornelius Nepos [198] which I had in

---

[196] The "life of Captain Lewis" appears in **1** : vii–xxiii of the two-volume first edition of *History of the expedition . . . of Captains Lewis and Clark . . .* , Philadelphia, 1814.

[197] Apparently a pamphlet "recipe," or transcript of one, no longer extant.

[198] TJ, C, and Gilmer had explored the Natural Bridge in September, 1815, when C and Gilmer were on their way south. Poplar Forest, as noted above, was TJ's second home (hideaway) in Bedford county. The Cornelius Nepos may have been a volume from TJ's "petit-format" library, a group of small-size books kept especially for his family circle. Among the books which TJ had turned over to the U. S. in 1815, how-

my pocket at the Natural Bridge, and had replaced the volume on it's shelf at Poplar Forest without observing the paper.

I am in the daily hope of seeing you, and the more anxiously lest the recurrence of my calls to Bedford should repeat the last year's misfortune. but as the next visit to that place has nothing to fix it to the day, it can be accomodated to your movements if known without the least inconvenience   ever & affectionately yours

Th. Jefferson

CORREA TO GILMER   [*U.Va.*]

Philadelphia   21 July 1816

Dear Sir

Perfectly at rest about the opinion you must entertain of my friendship and regard for you, i have indulged my laziness to write letters and have delayed answering your two last letters. But the epoch is come that i must return to the circulation of the world, giving more attention to letters than even to books, and i begin by paying my debts.

I am astonished that your plant was an Orobanche; [199] from the description i believed it was probably some

---

ever, the year before this letter was written, was a copy of *Cornelii Nepotis excellentium imperatorem vitae,* Glasgow, Robert and Andrew Foulis, 1761, a copy now in the Rare Book Division, LC. The books he acquired later in life were offered at auction in 1829, and in the *Catalogue* published by Nathaniel P. Poor (Washington, 1829), entry 33 is for "Cornelius Nepos, Foulis." This may indicate that the 1761 edition, a handy-size octavo, was that which TJ had with him.

The recovered recipe is printed above, under date of "before 1 January 1816."

[199] Orobanche, broom-rape, a parasitic herb of purple and brown color without green foliage growing on the ground or attached to the roots of other plants.

Pinguicula,[200] of which several species are found in America. I am very glad that your Florida work is finished,[201] at Winchester i will peruse it, and we will find some means of having the original words of the treaties. You must try to have at hand the supplement to the description which accompanies the new Map of Louisiana by Mr. Darby,[202] because it contains many important facts, relative to the original limits of that country, in support of your opinion. I have cut out new work for you, about which we shall speak when we meet.

Saturday next i will be in Bethleem,[203] where Dr. Wistar will meet me and we shall go together by Winchester on our way to Monticello, where i hope you will rejoin me.[204] Our voyages this year cannot be

---

[200] Pinguicula, butterwort, small acaulescent herbs of carnivorous habits, with pretty long-spurred flowers something like a snapdragon.

[201] So far as is known, Gilmer's work was never published.

[202] William Darby's *A geographical description of Louisiana . . . being an accompaniment to the map of Louisiana . . .* appeared first in Philadelphia in 1816, and a second edition in New York in 1817. It includes extensive general geographical descriptions, and sections on "That Part of West Florida included in the State of Louisiana" and the useful "Progressive Geography of Louisiana" (a chronological survey). The author urges the claims of the U. S. to a territory to the Perdido as the east boundary of Louisiana (limit between Louisiana and Florida) and to the Rio Grande del Norte on the west (p. xvii, first ed.). Among the subscribers to the first edition were C's Philadelphia friends, Zaccheus Collins and Thomas Cooper.

[203] Bethlehem, Pennsylvania?

[204] Gilmer wrote to J. H. Cocke on 1 August 1816 (Cocke Coll., UVa) that he would not be able to accompany the two savants to Monticello because of his law courts. Yet he succumbed to the temptation, for on 29 August he informed William Wirt (VaStatLib) that he was spending a few days in Albemarle with C and Wistar. C at least returned with him to Winchester (Gilmer to Peter Minor, 23 Sept. 1816, UVa).

very long, either to the Springs and the Kanhaway,[205] or to Lake Champlain and the state of Vermont, this last excursion is the most probable, but we shall decide in proper time. Neither of the two can take more time than three weeks or a month.

I thank you for your felicitations at my nomination, what i prize the more is that i will be able to be useful to both countries, as i love them equally, which is a very rare phenomenon in diplomacy, but of which you know so well my sentiments are already fully convinced, as well as that i am

Most sincerely yours

Joseph Corrèa de Serra

My best compliments to Judge Carr [206] and Judge Holmes,[207] and some others who were kind to me, but whose names i cannot find, though their figures are present to my memory. You know them all.

CORREA TO MONROE   [*Nat.Arch.*]

Philadelphia   22 July. 1816.

Sir

I have the honor of receiving your letter of the 18th. and in conformity to your direction i transmit to you the copy of my letters of credence, which you assure me will be deemed sufficient for the moment. I feel

---

[205] The Kanawha Falls, Fayette County, now West Virginia.
[206] Dabney Carr (1773–1837), nephew of TJ, was chancellor of the Winchester judicial district.
[207] Judge Hugh Holmes of Winchester was later one of the commissioners appointed by the Virginia legislature to choose a site for the University.

much obliged to the President for this instance of kindness, but still believe myself in duty bound to present myself to you and to him, the sooner that the state of my health will allow it, though the epoch of my having the honor of being presented by you to him in my public capacity, be differed as you inform me to October next.

The flattering expressions of your and the President's satisfaction at my appointment, will operate on me as additional motives to endeavour by all means to deserve the good opinion, you are both so kind to entertain of me.

> I have the honor to be with great consideration and respect
>
> Sir
>
> Your most obedt. humble servant
>
> Joseph Corrèa de Serra

CORREA TO ANDRÉ DASCHKOFF [208]   [*U.Va.*]

Charlottesville 7. September. 1816.

Monsieur et ami

Je viens de recevoir votre lettre du 25 du mois dernier, qui est arriveè a Monticello tandis que j'etois alle chez le President une seconde fois d'après son invitation. Je suis fachè que vous ayez la moindre cause de chagrin, et que la distance m'empeche, d'employer a votre ser-

---

[208] André Daschkoff, Russian Envoy Extraordinary and Minister Plenipotentiary (15 November 1811 to 6 March 1819), had earlier (11 July 1809 to 24 June 1810) served as Chargé d'Affaires and Consul General. See MS Foreign Representatives, Dept. of State, NatArch. This is one of several letters to members of the diplomatic corps which show C on the best of terms with them.

vice, les moyens quelconques qui seroient a ma porteè, mais pour vu qe la chose qui semble vous affliger, puisse attendre quelques jours, je compte etre a Philadelphia dans dix ou douze jours au plus tard, et je serai enchantè de pouvoir vous etre d'une utilitè quelconque, car vous pouvez franchement compter sur mon attachment pour vous.

Je vous prie de presenter mes respects a Madame Dashkoff, et de compter sur les sentimens d'amitie, de respect, et de consideration avec les quels j'ai l'honneur d'etre

Monsieur,

Votre tres attache et obeisst. serr.

Joseph Corrèa de Serra

a S. Exce. Mr. de Dashkoff

CORREA TO VAUGHAN [209] *[Georgetown U.Arch.]*

Washington City. 7 Dec. 1816.

Dear Sir and Friend

This moment i receive your letter of the 5th with the enclosed copy of the protest. It is very unpleasant but you shall not lose a cent. It is a necessary consequence of the distance which kept me unacquainted with the direction the payments had taken and the bad intelligence but natural enough that i gave to the advice from the treasury at Rio Janeiro. I see through all this a spite and an appearance of ill will. Tomorrow i will

---

[209] John Vaughan (*q.v.*) remained C's correspondent until the latter's death. See ch. III, above. Vaughan was later Portuguese vice-consul for Pennsylvania, Delaware, and West Jersey under C. See C to Acting Secretary of State, 14 December 1818 (Dept. of State Papers, NatArch), when Vaughan was nominated.

call on the Secretary of the Treasury,[210] but above all send me word what is the sum to be paid, and i will put it ready. I believe we might make use of the credit they opened with Leamy, they can not refuse payment. At all events tell me what is to be done, and i shall do it. It is a fortnight that i am here and i ought to have written to you many times, but the time has been taken with visits and much ado about nothing. I will write to you what happens with the Secretary of the Treasury, and expect you will write me also all the details of what is to be done, that I may directly do it, and that you may not have the least uneasiness. It is the least i am bound in conscience to do for you as

a Sincere Friend and Servant

J. Correa de Serra.[211]

CORREA TO MONROE   [*N.Y.P.L.*]

Sir

I delayed sending you the office you had read, because i had expected the mails could bring further information from New York, from whence i expect it every day. If it comes i will communicate it to you for what usage it may be.[212] If you find it convenient either in your receipt, or in your dispatches to Mr. Sumpter pay

---

[210] Evidently Vaughan was handling certain monetary affairs for C and the Portuguese government. Since the records of the Treasury Department for this period were destroyed by fire, no definite light can be thrown on C's problem here mentioned.

[211] A note on the back of this letter reads: "Relative to bill of £ 666. 13. 4."

[212] See Agan, 19–20, and ch. IV, above. Presumably this letter, slight in itself, concerns one of the most interesting phases of C in America, his part in or responsibility for the Neutrality Law of 1817. On 20 Dec. C had written to Monroe, informing the Secretary of State that a Captain Fisk, under the flag of Buenos Aires, had been commissioned to cruise against Spanish subjects and commerce, and if necessary against Por-

some compliment to H. Mr.[213] It will do very well for the good work we intend to do. But on this i leave it intirely to your judgement and experience and remain with the highest esteem and real friendship

Your most obedient servt.

J. Corrèa de Serra

22d. December. 1816.

JEFFERSON TO CORREA   [*L.C.*]

Dear Sir   Monticello June 14. 17.

No one could recieve greater pleasure than I did at the proof that your sovereign set a due value on your

---

tuguese. Already Artigas, leader in the Uruguayan struggle for independence, had commissioned privateers (most of them from the U. S.) to prey on Portuguese commerce, for Portugal had besieged Montevideo (over Spanish protest), claiming it feared invasion of Brazil.

C's letter, after describing the open manner in which these ships of Artigas and the others were being fitted out in Baltimore, and declaring his faith in the U. S. government's strict neutrality, pointed out the deficiencies in the existing neutrality law which allowed loopholes for such acts, and requested the President to ask Congress to enact a new law to meet the situation. For Monroe's reply and credit given to C for the new law, see ch. IV, above. In the present letter C seems to be referring to the actual evidence he would supply to the U. S. government of violations of neutrality.

[213] Dom João VI had assumed the throne in March, 1816, soon after he appointed (when he was regent) C as minister. He was still resident in Brazil, but was to return to Portugal on 3 July 1821. Described by some as a "weak-minded fool," he had his "virtues," which included generosity and a lavishness in distribution of sinecures, titles, and decorations (see C's honors mentioned above). See Gribble, Francis, *The royal house of Portugal*, 113, London, E. Nash, 1915; Cunha, V. Bragança, *Eight centuries of Portuguese monarchy*, 122, London, S. Swift, 1911; and [Browne, John Murray], *An historical view of Portugal, since the close of the Peninsular War . . . , by an eye-witness*, [London], 1827, *passim*.

merit, as manifested by the honorable duties assigned to you with us. but into this sentiment a little spice of egoism also thrust itself. as the appointment was to fix your residence almost in our vicinity, it gave me hope of more frequently seeing you here. I trust that this hope will be verified at the ensuing season, when health as well as leisure will recommend a visit to us. and that I may not, as before, lose the advantage of it by my frequent and long visits to Poplar Forest, I will take the precaution of mentioning to you that I shall be at that place during the latter part of this, and the beginning of the next month, say to the 10th. and again thro' the months of August & September the last of which I shall visit the Natural Bridge for being but 28 miles from Poplar Forest, which may be rode in [3?] hours, I think. I shall be disposed to make it an annual visit while strength enough remains. the President [214] expected to be about two months on his Northern tour, and will then find it prudent to exchange Washington for Albemarle, until the arrival of frost. I am in hopes you will take measures to have a meeting here with mr Gilmer, whose visit will be equally welcome and desirable to us all. That you may have many and long years of honors, health & happiness is the prayer of yours affectionately.

Th. Jefferson

M. Correa de Serra

CORREA TO JEFFERSON   [*Mass.Hist.Soc.*]

New York. 12. July. 1817

Dear Sir

Your very kind and esteemed letter of the 14th. of last month was directed to Washington, which place i left

---

[214] Presumably TJ refers to the new President, James Monroe.

the 3d of that month for Philadelphia,[215] and after a short stay had left that city also to ramble through parts of the country which i had not yet visited. At last it has reached my hands, and i hasten to thank you for all your friendly dispositions toward me which i duly prize. Every circumstance well weighed i believe the best epoch for my pilgrimage to Monticello this year will be the latter part of September, and i will apprize Mr. Gilmer of your wish of his being of the party, and concert with him the details of the journey. The summer i intend to pass in the state of New York and in New England where i can fill many chasms that remain in my knowledge of these parts of your country. If it was not contrary to my duty i would also peep into Canada but that may be done perhaps in other time if my life and strength continue. In the mean time receive the assurances of my most cordial respect and friendship

Your most obedient servt.

Joseph Corrèa de Serra

---

[215] The reading of the *seven* in the dateline is slightly in doubt, but in general the evidence bears it out as proper. On 3 June 1817 Robert Walsh, Jr. wrote to Gilmer (letter UVa) that "Mr Correa gave us a mere call yesterday [in Baltimore], and proceeded to Pha. in the Steamboat." C was not to pass the summer as he here planned. Notes exchanged between him and Richard Rush, acting Secretary of State, on 18 and 23 July (NatArch) indicate that he spent most of the summer in Philadelphia and Washington, busy with the affairs of his office. See also C to Gilmer, 21 Aug. 1817, below.

CORREA TO GILMER   [*U.Va.*]

Philadelphia 21 August, 1817

Dear Sir and friend

Yesterday I put in the hands of Judge Holmes [216] a small packet for you containing a few ounces of Sainfoin [217] come from Italy, not that i have any hopes that this vegetable so appropriate to the country you live in, may find favour with your farmers, but for the discharge of my conscience, and for the good will i feel for America.   It might be sown at the same epoch with wheat.

Mr. Jefferson wrote me in June, that the end of September would be the most proper time for paying a visit to Monticello, and he expects my visit; i accepted the invitation.   He wished to see you together with me and bids me to settle the business with you, i expect therefore that you will send me a word about the precise time in which you will be able to leave Winchester that i may be there and procede together to Albemarle.

I wish to introduce our friend Mr. Walsh [218] to Mr. Jefferson, but Mr. Walsh cannot stay so long as probably we shall, and my wish of introducing him is subordinate to my wish of avoiding appearance of intrusion. You can advise me about the best manner of doing it.

My summer has been busy and is still a little so.   Instead of going to see the falls of the Kanhawa,[219] I have

---

[216] Judge Hugh Holmes (*q.v.*) of Winchester, Virginia, friend of C and Gilmer.

[217] Sainfoin, or Saintfoin (*Onobrychis viciaefolia*), Holy Clover, a perennial plant grown for forage.   In the U. S. grown chiefly in the southern states, it has never become agriculturally important here.

[218] Robert Walsh, Jr. (*q.v.*), apparently now turning from Federalism to Jeffersonianism, was the editor of several periodicals and an essayist of reputation.   See ch. III, above.

[219] The Kanawha Falls, in Fayette County, now West Vir-

been inspecting the intrigues of the company of Pernam-buco.[220]   The activity of our present cabinet has not-withstanding the immense distance of the metropolis, as distant as St. Mary from Nova Scotia very soon put an end to it.   Notwithstanding the sanguine expectations of some at the end of 77 days all was absolutely over, because the articles of the newspaper put by the Per-nambuco emissary cannot give existence to what does not exist.[221]   For my part i have made it a rule never to stoop to give the least intelligence to newspaper edi-tors.   Facts are stubborn things and the reality will prevail in the end.   To the Brazils it has been exceed-ingly useful, to me here prodigiously so; it has been like a survey of the coast, i am a little acquainted with channels and shallow grounds.

Judge Holmes has suffered much of his sickness as well as of *ennui*.   To stay in Philadelphia when the city is deserted by its best inhabitants is somewhat irk-some, even to me who am partial to it.   He has told me of several new babies, that have made their appear-ance in Winchester.   I shall see all this new people,

---

ginia, was certainly not the destination C had suggested earlier to TJ, when he mentioned New England rambles as a summer excursion.

[220] The Pernambuco "company" was the group of revolution-ists at Pernambuco, in northern Brazil, who had on 6 March proclaimed a republic.   The provisional government had sent representatives to seek recognition and aid of the U. S.   See Agan, 23–24.

[221] As C suggests, the Pernambuco government was destroyed in a few months.   But C had antagonized acting Secretary of State Rush by suggesting that the U. S. show Europe that it was not sponsoring such rebellions in South America.   See Rush to Madison, 14 June 1817, HistSocPenna.   C's comment that he never gave newspaper editors information may be an indirect defense of himself or denial of a charge that he had caused unauthorized and misleading information regarding the Brazilian situation to be inserted in the *National Intelligencer*. See Agan, 25.

but i will retain my steady attachment to my little sweet heart on the hill and i beg of her father to recommend me to her good graces, which i shall endeavour not to loose by any negligence or misconduct of mine.

You have lately been in Richmond i am told. I have heard of great improvements, which i am afraid may prove as many deteriorations. God grant it be otherwise. Tell me your opinion.

I remain with high esteem and sincere friendship.

Most devotedly yours

J. Corrèa de Serra

CORREA TO JEFFERSON   [*L.C.*]

Philadelphia 20th. Septber. 1817

Sir

According to the wishes you expressed in your letter of June last, i have invited Mr. Gilmer to come with me to Monticello and to keep himself ready by the end of this month, in order to leave Winchester, when I should pass by. He writes to me that the courts are sitting there almost all October, and that he will be in the impossibility of quitting the town till November. He seems to be entirely *mersus civilibus undis,*[222] and i cannot disapprove him, though i am disappointed in this occasion, and must content myself with seeing him at my return, if i take that road.

I trust to your goodness, that you will not find it too presumptuous, if i fill the place that Mr. Gilmer leaves vacant, by taking with me one of the most interesting young Americans, whom you know by his works, and who wishes to have the honor of your acquaintance,

---

[222] Horace, *Epistles* 1: 1, 16. See C to TJ, 12 Feb. 1816, note 153 above.

Mr. Walsh the author of the American review &c [223]
He began his youthful career with the federalists but
was brought to better ways of thinking by the excesses
of the Boston stamps during the war. This explanation is indeed unnecessary, since i know how you soar
above minutious party feelings. The 25th i shall leave
Philadelphia, and stopping a day in Washington to
greet the President for his happy return, hasten to pay
you my respects once more.

I beg you to remember me to Mr. and Mrs. Randolph, and the whole family, the little ones not excepted. I remain with the highest esteem and veneration

     Sir

    Your most obedt. servt.

     J. Corrèa de Serra

CORREA TO JEFFERSON   [*L.C.*]

Philadelphia 31. October. 1817.

Sir

You must not be offended if your central college [224] is
in some measure become one of my hobby horses. The

---

[223] *The American Review of History and Politics* was edited
through eight numbers by Walsh in 1811–1812. He also edited
The American Register in 1809 and in 1817. See Lochemes,
Walsh, 229.

[224] The Central College, from which the University of Virginia was to evolve, was at this time the cherished active project of TJ. On 5 May 1817, the Trustees (Board of Visitors)
of the Central College (established from Albemarle Academy
by an act of the state legislature in February, 1816) had approved a plan for a lottery, the money from which would supply
funds for the building of the college, and accepted TJ's now-
famous plans for the structures to be erected. On 7 October
1817 the Trustees made allowance for a "French House" to be
occupied by a respectable French family, in which the boarders

prospect of seeing a seminary for the American youth unshackled from the trammels of clerical influence and direction, and where really useful sciences may be induced into young minds is a vision so congenial to my feelings, that i cannot abstain from frequently reminding it, and taking a hearty interest in its success. As soon as i reached this city, i made proper inquiries about a fit professor of French litterature, and i find that in the actual circumstances the difficulty will be rather in choosing than in finding. The great obstacle is in determining any body to search a place, which will not be in existence but two years hence. It is very probable that none of those which could suit your seminary will enter into any engagement or promise for so distant a period, consequently the best thing that can be done, is to store the informations, in order to supply to the best possible, at the proper epoch. I am afraid that this same lateness of opening your school may produce a much worse effect by depriving it of Judge Cooper's assistance,[225] which would be an irretrievable loss to your seminary. There is a party now in this city (and powerful enough) who are striving to obtain from the

---

would speak only French at meals. Among the professorships was to be one of "languages, belles-lettres, rhetoric, oratory, history and geography." See Bruce, *History of the University of Virginia* 1: 94 ff., 178 ff.; Honeywell, *The educational work of Thomas Jefferson, passim.*

[225] Dr. Thomas Cooper (*q.v.*) was elected professor of chemistry and law in TJ's university on 7 October. Within a few months he was a candidate for the professorship of chemistry in the medical school of the University of Pennsylvania, a position he did not secure. He had been since December, 1816, professor of chemistry and mineralogy in what we would call the college of liberal arts of the University of Pennsylvania. See Bruce, *History* 1: 195; Cabell, N. F., *Early history of the University of Virginia as contained in the letters of Thomas Jefferson and Joseph C. Cabell,* 396–399, Richmond, 1856; Malone, *Public life of Thomas Cooper,* 243 ff.; Honeywell, *Educational work,* 90.

University some thing, of which i believe he would be satisfied, and if they succeed, of which there is probability enough also, the attractions of this residence, would particularly for his family, make up for any little diminution in the profits, from what he would receive in your central school.

If the legislature grants what you have every reason to expect, this could be avoided, by opening your school next year in some building in Charlottesville, to be transferred the year after to the buildings about to be erected.[226] Another advantage, and a very material one in my opinion would follow from this arrangement, that of your inspection and assistance to this establishment for a year more. The first moments of existence decide of the future sort of every new thing, and i am convinced that there is not a person in America to supply your place on this subject. Though i will say to you *serus in cœlum redeas diuque lœtus intersis* [227] and hope as i wish it will be so, still a year is a year, and a year in the beginning is worth a great many in the future age of this establishment.

Permit me to pass from such a serious subject to entertain you with two very trifling ones, but which i have at heart. A gentleman living in his farm near this city has a young tree of Marrons de Lyon,[228] they are as good as in France. i have taken from his tree nine ripe marrons, and i will send them to Monticello, by the first occasion recommended to Mrs. Randolph, to be sown where they may thrive. These marrons being american born will no doubt prosper in a milder

---

[226] Year after year TJ hoped to open the doors of his institution, but it did not offer instruction until 1825.

[227] Horace, *Carminum* 1: 2, 45. Loeb transl.: "late mayest thou return to the skies and long mayest thou be pleased to dwell [here]."

[228] The marron or maroon, a large kind of sweet chestnut native to southern Europe.

climate than that in which they were produced. At Tinsleyville i was shown by Mrs. Tinsley [229] a Turkey hen with a beautiful tuft of fine feathers in her head; the good lady told me she destined it to the Richmond museum.[230] In a civilized country they would profit of the phenomenon in order to perpetuate if possible this new variety. All the beautiful varieties in the domesticated species of animals have been obtained in this manner. This would be a new Virginian variety of Turkeys. You best know what could be done to save it from impending destruction. Old Duke John of Braganza,[231] my good patron in my early life, used to say that a peculiar character of my conversation and compositions was to mix with the most serious objects some microscopic observation. You have a fair specimen of it.

I remain with heartfelt esteem and respect

     Sir

        Your most obedt. servt.

        J. Corrèa de Serra

---

[229] Tinsleyville was listed in 1813 as in Goochland County, Virginia, and John Tinsley (d. 1814) is shown as its postmaster. His wife, Ann, died in 1836, a woman of considerable property. See *Table of post offices in the United States . . . 1813;* Goochland County Deed Book 31, 1836–1839 (Virginia State Library), 11–13. C may have visited in Goochland on journeys between western Virginia and Richmond.

[230] The Richmond Museum was opened in February, 1816, after the state legislature granted James Worrell permission to erect a building for the purpose on Capitol Square at Twelfth Street facing F. It was stocked with all the curiosities Worrell could secure, but it lasted only a few years. See Richmond *Enquirer,* 1 Jan. 1818; Christian, W. A., *Richmond, her past and present,* 95, Richmond, L. H. Jenkins, 1912.

[231] Don Jon of Braganza, Duke of Lafões (1719–1806), nephew of King John V of Portugal and patron of science and arts, had like C lived in France, Italy, and England. For his part with C in the founding of the Royal Academy of Sciences of Lisbon, see above, ch. II. The sketch of Duke John in the *Biog. Univ.* was written by C himself.

JEFFERSON TO CORREA   [*L.C.*]

Poplar Forest   Nov. 25. 17

Dear Sir

I am highly gratified by the interest you take in our Central college, and the more so as it may possibly become an inducement to pass more of your time with us. it is even said you had thought of engaging a house in it's neighborhood. but why another house? is not one enough? and especially one whose inhabitants are made so happy by your becoming their inmate? when you shall have a wife and family wishing to be to themselves,[232] then the question of another house may be taken ad referendum. I wish Doctr. Cooper could have the same partialities. he seems to have misunderstood my last letter. in the former I had spoken of opening our Physical school in the spring of 19. but learning that that delay might render his engagement uncertain the Visitors determined to force their preparations as to recieve him by midsummer next, and so my letter stated. in one I now write I recall his attention to that circumstance. but his decision will no doubt be governed by the result of the proposition to permit the medical students of Philadelphia to attend him. I can never regret any circumstance which may add to his well-being, for I most sincerely wish him well. that himself and mrs Cooper will be happier in the society of Philadelphia cannot be doubted. it would be flattering enough to us to be his second choice. I find from his information that we are not to expect to obtain in this country either a classical or mathematical professor of the 1st. order and as our institution can-

---

[232] Perhaps a reference to some oral expression of C's to TJ to the effect that eventually he would bring Esther and his son, Edward, to the U. S. See ch. IV, and references to and letters from Edward Correa below.

not be raised above the common herd of academies, colleges etc. already scattered over our country, but by supereminent professors, we have determined to accept of no mediocrity, and to seek in Europe for what is eminent.[233] we shall go to Edinburgh in preference, because of the advantage to students of recieving communications in their native tongue, and because peculiar and personal circumstances will enable us to interest Dugald Stewart [234] and Professor Leslie [235] of that College in procuring us subjects of real worth and eminence. I put off writing to them for a classical & mathematical professor only until I see what our legislature, which meets on Monday next, is disposed to do, either on the question singly of adopting our college for their university, or on that of entering at once on a general system of instruction, for which they have for some time been preparing. for this last purpose I have sketched, and put into the hands of a member a Bill delineating a practicable plan, entirely within the means they already

---

[233] As early as 1783 and 1791 TJ had expressed interest in bringing eminent European professors to America. Actually at the time of this letter TJ had already attempted or was about to attempt to secure the services of several distinguished or promising Americans, as Nathaniel Bowditch, George Ticknor, and of course Dr. Cooper.

[234] Dugald Stewart (1753–1828), Scottish common-sense philosopher, had been TJ's friend and correspondent since the days in Paris, 1784–1789. TJ admired the Scot's various works, which he received from the author as they appeared. See Koch, Adrienne, *The philosophy of Thomas Jefferson,* 48–53, New York, Columbia, 1943; *DNB.*

[235] [Later Sir] John Leslie (1766–1832), mathematician and natural philosopher of Edinburgh, offered in 1824, when Gilmer was in Britain searching for professors for the University of Virginia, to go to America and inaugurate the new institution by himself giving a series of lectures. Leslie had spent the year 1789 in Virginia as tutor to two young Randolphs. See Davis, *Gilmer,* 215–217; Davis, ed., *Jefferson-Gilmer correspondence,* 96 etc.; *DNB.*

have on hand, destined to this object.[236] my bill proposes 1st. Elementary schools in every county, which shall place every householder within 3 miles of a school. 2, district colleges which shall place every father within a day's ride of a college where he may dispose of his son. 3. an University in a healthy and central situation, with the offer of the lands, buildings & funds of the central college, if they will accept that place for their establishment. in the 1st. will be taught reading, writing, common arithmetic, and general notions of geography. in the 2d. ancient & modern languages geography fully, a higher degree of numerical arithmetic, mensuration and the elementary principles of navigation. in the 3d. all the useful sciences in their highest degree. to all of which is added a selection from the elementary schools of subjects of the most promising genius whose parents are too poor to give them further education, to be earned, at the public expence thro' the colleges & university. the object is to bring into action that mass of talents which lies buried in poverty in every country, for want of the means of developement, and thus give activity to a mass of mind, which in proportion to our population shall be the double or treble of what it is in most countries. the expence of the elementary schools for every county is proposed to be levied on the wealth of the county, and all children,

---

[236] TJ's bill for general education, with an alternate clause for the adoption of the Central College as the university then talked of, was submitted to the legislature in the winter of 1817–1818. It was thrown out at this session, but a substitute authorizing a state university and commissioners to decide on its location was passed. For text of the general bill see Honeywell, *Educational work,* 223–243. See also Bruce, *History* **1**: 206–208, and Adams, H. B., *Thomas Jefferson and the University of Virginia, passim,* Washington, 1888.

rich and poor to be educated at these 3 years gratis.[237] the expence of the colleges and University, admitting two professors to each of the former, and 10 to the latter, can be compleately & permanently established with a sum of 500, 000 D. in addition to the present fund of our Central college. our literary fund has already on hand & appropriated to these purposes a sum of 700, 000 D and that increasing yearly. this is in fact and substance the plan I proposed in a bill 40 years ago, but accomodated to the circumstances of this, instead of that day, I derive my present hopes that it may now be adopted from the fact that the H. of Representatives at their last session, passed a bill, less practicable and boundlessly expensive, and therefore alone rejected by the Senate. and printed for public consideration and amendment,—mine, after all may be an Utopian dream, but being innocent, I have thought I might indulge in it till I go to the land of dreams, and sleep there with the dreamers of all past and future times.

I have taken measures to obtain the crested turkey,[238] and will endeavor to perpetuate that beautiful & singular characteristic, & shall be not less earnest in endeavors to raise the Maronnier. God bless you, and preserve you long in life and health, until wearied with delighting your kindred spirits here, you may wish to encounter the great problem, untried by the living, unreported by the dead.

Th. Jefferson

---

[237] TJ's first plan for free education in the state was submitted in June, 1779, his "Bill for the More General Diffusion of Knowledge" (in Boyd, Julian P., et al., edd., The papers of Thomas Jefferson 2: 526-535, Princeton, U. Press, 1950). See Honeywell, Educational work, 19 ff. for a comparison of the 1779 and 1817 bills.

[238] Nothing more has been ascertained concerning this rare bird.

CORREA TO DR. WISTAR [*Gray Herbarium, HarvardU.*]

Washington. 31 December 1817.

Dear Sir and Friend

I cannot in conscience see a new year approaching fast, and let the occasion pass unnoticed of marking to you the sentiments of attachment and true friendship which bind me to you, and expressing my hearty wishes that you and your family may enjoy all happiness and health. In a little time i will pay a visit to Philadelphia and renew personally my respects to you; now we are here very busy about nothing, and waiting very anxiously for no body knows what. This congress composed chiefly of recruits does not yet manoeuvre with deliberation, nobody knows yet what talents it contains nor what spirit will dominate in it.

Your Philadelphia Naturalists going to Florida [239] have passed by this city without taking any notice of me. It is not well done on their part, i had spoken to several members of the southern states in order to procure them introductions and instructions. all my labour lost.

My best compliments to your Lady and Mrs. Morris,[240] and many blessings to my two young friends.[241] I remain

Most sincerely yours

J. Corréa de Serra

---

[239] C probably refers to the Florida expedition of George Ord, Titian Peale, Thomas Say, and William Maclure to Georgia and Florida. See C to Sir J. E. Smith, 9 May 1820, note 360, below.

[240] Unidentified.

[241] Probably Richard M. (1805–1883) and Mifflin (1811–1875), sons of Caspar and Elizabeth Mifflin Wistar. Elizabeth (1816–1834), the Wistar's youngest, was probably too young to have been considered. See *The Wistar family, a genealogy* . . . , Philadelphia, 1896.

CORREA TO GILMER [*U.Va.*]

Washington 8 January 1818

Dear Sir and Friend

Several times i have been on the point of writing to you, but other things intervened which diverted my sight. Just now i have read the letter you have written to Mr. Walsh [242] in which you seem to wish that i tell you my opinion about the residence you are to chuse in leaving Winchester, whether Baltimore or Richmond; I am decidedly for this last.[243] You will be incomparably better among your natural friends the Virginians than among the Baltimoreans; the reputation which your skill and talent have acquired in Winchester will follow you at Richmond, and have no doubt will be little regarded in Baltimore. As for pecuniary rewards i believe Baltimore has little advantage over Richmond, witness the number of eminent lawyers who are become rich there, and the future prospect is still more brilliant. Richmond in spite of the present inhabitants must forcibly become one of the first cities in the Union. You understand me — Moreover according to my wishes and your powers you are not to content yourself with wealth you are to aspire to something above it and that you will better obtain in your native state, which you may very usefully serve, and both wants and deserves it. These are my reasons. Think for yourself.

---

[242] As Robert Walsh, Jr., had written Gilmer on 4 November 1817, he and the Abbé had taken a house together in Washington for six months (see Davis, *Gilmer,* 115–116, and ch. IV, above). Young Gilmer, restless in the small town of Winchester, now wished to pursue his legal career in a larger city.

[243] From a letter of William Wirt of 20 January 1818, one learns that Gilmer had already decided upon Richmond as his future home, though Wirt, a native Marylander, was in favor of Baltimore. See Davis, *Gilmer,* 118–119.

I have had the pleasure of seeing here Mr. Wirt, and of reading his book,[244] it put me in mind of a definition i heard once from the Italian Pythagoras the Abbe Genovesi.[245] Some books said he prove the subject, others prove the talents and ability of the writer. Mr. Wirt's book is of this second class. He has paid very ably and ingeniously a splendid sacrifice to his object of present Virginian idolatry, *mais il n'en pas le dupe* and whenever posterity wonders at the fashionable idol of this day they will find in the book proofs enough that his historian knew him as well.[246]

You have sent me the copy of Pursh [247] for which i must thank you, i am not sure of having paid you the price, and have only a notion that when i settled ac-

---

[244] William Wirt (1772–1834), Attorney-General of the U. S., had married as his first wife Gilmer's sister. Wirt had made his name as a lawyer and litterateur in Virginia, to which he had gone as a young man. His *Life of Patrick Henry* had appeared in 1817. See Kennedy, J. P., *Memoirs of the life of William Wirt,* 2 v., Baltimore, 1849, and Davis, *Gilmer,* 41–119.

[245] Antonio Genovesi (1712–1769), Italian writer on philosophy and political economy, had like C originally studied for the Church and had taken orders. He drifted away from ecclesiastical life, became an advocate, and eventually a student and professor of philosophy at Naples, where C studied under him. Though not highly regarded as a philosopher and bitterly opposed by partisans of scholastic routine, as a disciple of Locke he did introduce the new order in Italy. See *Enc.Brit.*

[246] Wirt's eulogistic biography was criticized severely even by many contemporaries, though its reception generally was favorable. Wirt certainly attempted to depict Henry as the orator was. See Kennedy, *Wirt, passim.* C perhaps shared with TJ a considerably qualified esteem for Henry the reactionary.

[247] Frederick Pursh, *Flora Americae Septentrionalis; or, a systematic arrangement and description of the plants of North America, containing, besides what have been described by preceding authors, many new and rare species, collected during twelve years travel and residence in that country . . . ,* 2 v., London, 1814 [second ed., with no alteration of text, 1816, with

counts with you i left the price with you. In case i be wrong tell me how much it is, and i will give it to Genl. Tucker [248] to remit to you.

With all my laziness in point of writing letters, you have here a proof that when your real interest is concerned i do not delay my answer.

I remain with true friendship

Most sincerely yours

J. Corrèa de Serra

CORREA TO MRS. CASPAR WISTAR [*Hist.Soc.Penna.*]

Washington 31 Janry. 1818

Madam

If a letter from me could have afforded you consolation, i would have written to you the first moment that the certainty of the loss of my never to be forgotten friend [249] reached me. But in such awful dispensations of Provi-

---

colored or uncolored plates]. Professor Joseph Ewan has called to the editor's attention in the APS a field journal of Pursh (first published by Thomas P. James in 1869) with a title-page in the handwriting of C, reading: "Journal of a Botanical excursion in the North Eastern parts of Pennsylvania & in the State of New York. By an unknown person who appears to have been a German & a friend of the late Dr. Benj. S. Barton. Found among the Books of Dr. Barton after his death in 1817." Of course 1817 is a slip for 1815. The identity of Pursh as the author has been established.

[248] Henry St. George Tucker (1780–1848), then member of the U. S. House of Representatives and a brilliant lawyer, had served as a volunteer officer in the War of 1812. On 3 Jan. 1816 he had been elected brigadier-general by the state legislature. See *DAB; Appleton's CAB; Calendar Va. St. Papers* **10**: 428.

[249] Dr. Caspar Wistar (*q.v.*), professor of anatomy in the University of Pennsylvania and from 1815 president of the APS, had been C's good friend and companion on various botanical excursions (see ch. III, above). Botanist, inspiring

dence no human consolation is of any avail, it can only come from above, in the consideration of another and better life, and in a resignation to the will of the Almighty disposer of every thing. I thrust in your principles that this support you have found in this moment, which no human words howsoever friendly can give. My letter therefore is not to condole with you in a complimentary way, but to assure you that the sentiments which i entertain for the memory of Dr. Wistar, will always render your family sacred and dear to my heart, and make me sollicitous of every occasion of being servicable or useful to you all — As long as i remain in this low world you may be sure of finding in me always a

> Most respectful sincere and attached
>
> friend and servant
>
> Joseph Corrèa de Serra

CORREA TO JEFFERSON   [*A.P.S.*]

Sir

I must thank you for the two plants which you forwarded to me in the name of Mr. Girardin.[250] You may tell him that they are both plants common both to the North of Europe, and from what i see to the mountains of Virginia. That with a reddish blossom is a variety of the *spirea ulmaria*.[251] The other with a slen-

---

teacher, and friend of all those who live by knowledge, he was one of the eminent Americans of his day. He died on 22 Jan. 1818.

[250] Louis Hue Girardin (1771–1825), whose real name was Louis Francois Picot, a correspondent of TJ over several years, was then living at Staunton, Virginia. See Philips, Edith, *Louis Hue Girardin and Nicholas G. Dufief and their relations with Thomas Jefferson,* Baltimore, Johns Hopkins, 1926.

[251] *Spiraea ulmaria,* or *Filipendula ulmaria,* Queen of the Meadows, a feathery beautiful herb three to five feet high, a

der appearance and unsightly blossom, is the *Ophrys loeselii.*[252] I must thank you also for the tidings you give me of good Mr. Girardin and the expectation of his letter.

> I remain sir very respectfully
>
> Your obedient servant
>
> J. Corrêa de Serra

March. 10—1818.

CORREA TO GILMER   [*U.Va.*]

Norfolk 24 March 1818

Dear Sir and Friend

In Baltimore your letter of the 10th instant was given to me; the state of health and the removal here by the steam boat, have suspended my answer, but for a few days. I am very thankful to you for all your kindness, in the manner you wish to be paid for what i am in debt to you for Pursh's Flora, but the shortest is the best, and consequently i will remit to you a check for the sum one of these days.

I would be very happy if you settled here in this moment instead of being at Richmond, but this is a selfish momentary wish. Richmond will be the theatre of your glory and i hope your fortune and happiness.

My health is very bad. The climate of Norway except in a few transient moments, is settled in my bowels, if i am now free from cramps *a l'entrèe del estomac* of those that had tormented me last week, i am much

---

native of Europe and Asia to Mongolia. It has been naturalized in the eastern U. S. from Europe. Its early appearance in the mountains of Virginia as an immigrant species is interesting.

[252] Probably *Ophrys loeselii,* the genus *Listeria.* Its common names include Fen Orchid and Loesel's Twayblade, perhaps *L. australis* of modern manuals.

weaker.²⁵³   My head only (the thinking head i say) is tolerably well, but the skull is sometimes affected. Still i am confident i will be better in every respect in a few weeks, when there be a clearer sky and the season of fogs will be over.

I remark now that i have been always speaking to you of me, it is natural in every sick person.   You must believe that i am a well wishing steady friend to you and

Your sincere friend also

J. Corrèa de Serra

CORREA TO VAUGHAN   [*A.P.S.*]

Norfolk 27. March. 1818.

Dear Sir and Friend

Your favorers of the 16 and 19. instant, have reached me from Baltimore which place i left in the steam boat for this, after having been very sick there, in hopes that a milder climate and the medical assistance of Dr. Fernandes ²⁵⁴ would enable me to reach *fair and clear wheather.*   He has bled me from the arm, and after a gentle evacuation, has put me in the use of saporaceous to be followed by tonics.   This will keep me here several weeks, perhaps to the end of next month, consequently you will be so kind to forward me here every thing for me which may come to your hands.   Do not spare your letters, they are to me of the highest price.

---

²⁵³ C's affliction was probably the diabetes, from which he suffered more later.   C had a Portuguese physician in Norfolk, Dr. Fernandes, who he believed was the only man who could help him.   See C to John Vaughan, 27 March 1818, note 254, below.

²⁵⁴ Dr. John F. Oliviera Fernandes, Portuguese physician in Norfolk, corresponded with TJ and John Vaughan (*q.v.*). These letters indicate that he was a man of culture.   See letters in MSS. Div., LC.

That of the 16, and supplement about which your wishes have been satisfied, afforded me the pleasure which real friendship only can feel.

Edward [255] i left in the college,[256] about the institutions of which i must bestow praise, and are particularly fit for a young french mind. It is almost a continuation of the living and studies to which he was accostumed in the college of Belleville where he lived in France. I am very glad to hear that the letters for the Brazils are in Mr. M.s hands.[257]

I am most sincerely and affectionaly yours

J. Corrèa de Serra

[on second fold of sheet alone:]

I cannot tell you any thing of Mr. Walsh, i have put an normal wall of separation between him and me.[258] This intelligence keep to yourself.

JEFFERSON TO CORREA   [*L.C.*]

Monticello Apr. 10. 18.

Dear Sir

I set out tomorrow for Bedford, to return the first week in May. I note this to you because I have been

---

[255] Edward Joseph Correa da Serra (b. 1803), son of C by Esther Delavigne, a Frenchwoman, was legitimized not long before C's death. He was later an M.D. of Paris. See letters below, ch. IV, above, and Carvalho, 79–81. Edward apparently arrived in the U. S. during the winter of 1817–1818.

[256] Edward attended St. Mary's (Sulpician) College in Baltimore. C mentions in his letter to M. Deleuze of 13 May 1820 that Edward has been in attendance at the French College the Sulpicians have at Baltimore. C's friend, Father Babad, was a teacher there. See Smith, Robert C., A pioneer teacher: Father Babad and his Portuguese grammar, *Hispania* **28**: 337–339, 1945. The college is no longer in existence.

[257] Probably official letters to James Monroe which reached the U. S. through John Vaughan's shipping connections.

[258] For the wall C put between himself and his friend Walsh,

flattered with your visit in May, and Dr. Cooper promised me he would accept your kind offer of a seat in
your carriage. I wish you could be here some days
before the 11th of May, because on that day our Visitors meet and yourself and Dr. Cooper may, I am
sure suggest to me before hand something useful for
their consideration. the legislature has appropriated
15,000. Đ a year to an University. a commissioner [259]
from each Senatorial district (in number 24) [260] is to
meet at Rockfish gap on the 1st of Aug. and to report
a location for the University, the plan, the number of
professorships &c. to the next session of the Legislature,
who are to decide ultimately the nomination to that Executive of the 24. Commrs. is an excellent one, & I
have [no?] doubt of two thirds of their votes to make
the site of the Central College that of the University.[261]

mr Madison, judges Stuart, Holmes, Roane and Cabell,
mr Mason of Loudon, J. G. Jackson, mr Tazewell, all
of whom I believe you know, and myself, are of the

---

see ch. IV, above. Walsh had been shocked by a revelation of
C's about himself.

[259] For the story of the Commission and its meeting at Rockfish Gap in the Blue Ridge near TJ see Bruce, *History* 1: 209–
226.

[260] The actual twenty-one commissioners included James Madison of Orange, Archibald Stuart of Frederick, Spencer Roane
help him. See C to John Vaughan, 27 March 1818, note 254,
of Hanover, W. H. Cabell of Buckingham, A. T. Mason of
Loudon, and John G. Jackson of Harrison. Bruce, *History* 1:
211, names these and a number of others and states that four
more could not be present. One of the last may have been
Littleton W. Tazewell (1774–1860) of Norfolk. For the report
of this Commission see Honeywell, *Educational work,* 248–260.

[261] Though Lexington and Staunton as sites drew some
votes, the majority in favor of the Central College was over-
whelming. Actually of those TJ counted on, only Stuart voted
for his home town of Staunton, while others he evidently had
not counted on voted in favor of his location. See Bruce, *History* 1: 221.

Commissioners. so far, I think, is well; and as I know you take an interest in this institution, I inform you of it with pleasure, & with equal pleasure add assurances of my affectionate respect

Th. Jefferson

it would be quite a jubilee if mr Walsh could think his affairs would permit him to make your party here a trio.[262]

M. Correa

CORREA TO JEFFERSON   [*Mass.Hist.Soc.*]

Norfolk 10th of April 1818

Dear Sir

As i shall most probably very soon take a northern direction, which is pointed to me by what i have to do, i will in consequence be deprived of the pleasure i promised to myself of paying you in May the annual tribute of my personal respects; my pilgrimage to Monticello i must transfer to the autumnal months. But the American born Marrons [263] would lose the season of being sown, and i have the greatest wish to introduce them to you in the most favorable moment. You will find them in the little box that accompanies this letter. They ought to be planted directly in pots to germinate, to be transplanted next spring to a place where cattle cannot reach them, such as your kitchen garden. In

---

[262] Apparently TJ and many others never knew, or did not know for some time, of the break between C and Walsh. See ch. IV, above.

[263] For C's earlier mention of this kind of sweet chestnut, see C to TJ, 31 October 1817, note 228, above. For an account of modern disease-resistant varieties of the chestnut, see Smith, J. Russell, *Tree crops,* 127–155, New York, Devin-Adair, 1950. The chestnut blight has wiped out the great trees of TJ's time.

a few years they will furnish branches enough to inculcate a great number of chestnut trees, and this useful culture be introduced in your mountains. You know what a riches they are in Tuscany, Corsica and the Limousin in France. I have been here these three weeks with D'Fernandes, and will remain for a little longer, but not much. It is impossible to meet a more attentive nurse, and a more friendly and enlightened physician. My best compliments to Colonel and Mrs. Randolph. Accept the assurance of the high respect and veneration with which i am

Sir

Your most obedient sera-

Joseph Corrèa de Serra

CORREA TO GILMER   [*U.Va.*]

Washington 30 April 1818

Dear Sir and Friend:

I must be very sorry that you received so late my letter of the 24th of March, because that has deprived me so long of an answer from you, which have been as always a great pleasure to me. My health about which you are so kindly solicitous is thank God much recovered, and i am confident will strengthen every day. You know my diet, it is much changed, i drink dayly some wine, eat meat, and perhaps half the old ration of vegetables, with all that I do not feel any diminution of my patience.

Some weeks ago i wrote to Mr. Jefferson that i had better transfer my annual pilgrimage to the Holy land, to the summer or autumn. Perhaps you may in that season have nothing to hinder you from being one of the party. At all events i shall see you at Richmond, and that is an inducement to remain in that city some days, and you know that the Richmond that i anticipate and which perhaps neither of us will see is to me a fond cogitation and the hills on which it stands are even now a pleasant sight.

Till i read the second part of your letter i had not the least suspicion of your talent for poetry, so accustomed i was to your logical reasoning and geometrical precision, which in my opinion fit you so particularly for business and public life—What the deuce put you in mind of a rural establishment in the mountains, with herborisations and lectures and do nothing. That would be well enough for me provided these mountains were at the gates of Paris London or Rome, but for you, push yourself in your bar to be noticed and acquire fortune, making in the same time a provision of political real knowledge that make you useful to your state and to your nation, and give you a shining character in the histories of both. *Hae tibi erunt artes.*[264]

Since we mention herborisations, i must tell you that the supposed orchidery near Yo[u], is from the description you sent in one of your last letters either the Convallaria candensis,[265] or a beautiful little Pothos [266] that i observed in blossom yesterday morning in a creek about a mile and a half from the Capitol. What Flora that of the neighbourhood of Norfolk! not only a very early one, but the point of contact of the southern and

---

[264] Virgil, *Aeneid* **6**: 853. Loeb transl.: "These shall be thy arts," continuing "to crown Peace with Law, to spare the humbled, and to tame in war the proud."

[265] C almost certainly refers here to the **False Lily of the** Valley, *Maianthemum canadense,* judging from the specific epithet he uses.

[266] This is "Skunk cabbage," Symplocarpus, called Pothos in synonymy by [Obadiah Rich] in *A synopsis of the genera of American plants, according to the latest improvements on the Linnaen [sic] system: with the new genera of Michaux and others. Intended for the use of students in botany.* **17**, Georgetown, D. C., 1814.

northern systems of vegetation of the United States. I am disposed to believe that many of the plants there have not found place in Clayton's book, who living at the mouth of the Piankatank, lived in the middle of the northern system.[267]

If you answer this letter, or have anything to command, direct the letters to Philadelphia. Accept the assurance of the friendship and esteem with [which] i remain

Most sincerely yours

J. Corrèa de Serra

CORREA TO MADISON   [L.C.]

Philadelphia 5. September. 1818

Sir

I have just read your address to the agricultural society of Virginia [268] and must congratulate your state not only

---

[267] Clayton, John, (c. 1685–1773), *Flora Virginica, exhibens plantas, quas nobilissimus vir D.D. Johannes Clayton . . . in Virginia crescentes observat, collegit & obtulit D. Joh. Fred. Gronovii . . . Lugduni Batavorum . . . ,* 1762. Clayton lived in Gloucester County (now Mathews County) Virginia, on the Piankatank River, and supplied Gronovius with the data for *Flora Virginica.* The 1762 edition has a map showing that Clayton's botanical researches were confined to the regions between the Rappahannock and James Rivers, and the Blue Ridge. See *DAB.*

[268] Apparently C refers to *An address delivered before the Agricultural Society of Albemarle, on Tuesday, May 12, 1818. By Mr. Madison, president of the Society,* Richmond, printed by Shepherd & Pollard, 1818, 31 pp. There is a copy in Rare Book Div., LC. It is included in Madison, *Letters* (1865). In 1822, as president of the Albemarle Society, Madison wrote a circular letter to all Virginia agricultural societies, and referred to them as societies in other parts of the state. In 1803 he had become first president of a national society organized in Washington. I am indebted to Mr. Irving Brant, letter of 16 October 1951, for this information.

for the consequences which are still in the womb of futurity, and are not always proportionate to the best wishes, but for the rare example given by two subsequent chiefs of the nation, of improving the first and noblest of arts, after having administered the government of a great people. I remember the impression the improved plough of Mr. Jefferson made all over Europe, and am perfectly sure your efforts for agriculture will produce the same sensation. It is very happy for your nation to afford such examples in this moment to counterbalance the motives of discredit afforded by a very different sort of citizens, unworthy of belonging to the same nation. It is also to be hoped that some remedy will come from the same mountains to extirpate these bad weeds that injure your otherwise fair and hopeful crops.

The inclosed pamphlet,[269] is also relative to agriculture, though it has not the merit of your labours, to improve it. You will be so kind as to receive it as a mark of the high respect and veneration with which i am

Sir

Your most obedient servt.

J. Corrèa de Serra

CORREA TO JEFFERSON   [*L.C.*]

Philadelphia. 26. Septr. 1818.

Dear Sir

In the mountains of New Jersey i read in the newspapers that your Legislature had decided that the central

---

[269] This was almost certainly C's paper, On the nature and formation of the soil of Kentucky, which appeared in the *Trans. Amer. Philos. Soc.*, new ser., 1: 174–180, 1818, with the notation that it was read 21 April 1815. According to the Minutes of the Society, however, it was read on 3 March 1815 and approved for publication on 21 April.

college of your university was to be at Charlottesville.[270] Immediately on my return in Philadelphia i have witnessed the injustice done Mr. Cooper, by preferring to him a man poor in science, and unfit to increase his capital.[271] I congratulate you for both these events which contribute so materially to the fullfilment of your views for the instruction of Virginia. Mr. Cooper will bring there an immense store of useful knowledge accompanied with much philosophy and a great zeal for the dissemination of true science. I am much mistaken if his settlement in your state does not prove a remarkable epoch in the history of the litterary advancement of Virginia. He will set out for Monticello in a very few days and i will have the satisfaction of presenting him to you before the end of this month, because in going to pay you my annual visit, i intend to profit of his company. In the mean time accept the assurance of the sentiments which i have long vowed to you

Your most obedient servt.

Joseph Corrêa de Serra

CORREA TO GILMER   [*U.Va.*]

Washington 10th October, 1818

My dear Sir

The information you had received about my visit to Virginia was incorrect, and has deprieved me of the

---

[270] As noted in letter above, TJ to C, 10 April 1818, notes, the decision was made by the Commission appointed by the Legislature. The group met at Rockfish Gap on 1–4 August. The bills were not actually passed by the Legislature until 19 and 25 January 1819. See Bruce, *History* 1: 233–234.

[271] C probably refers to the fact that Dr. Cooper had not been elected to the chair of chemistry in the medical college of the University of Pennsylvania for which he had been a candidate (Malone, *Cooper*, 232). Robert Hare had been awarded the position. Cooper had on 7 October 1817 been elected professor

pleasure of seeing you, which i most sincerely regret. I would have gone to Virginia much earlier if the affairs which occurred had not fastened me in New York about a fortnight. The 24th of last month (the date of your letter) i left Alexandria for Frideriksburg, if you had remained a few days more in Albemarle i would have met you there. Patience and vegetable diet. Now i must remain in this garrison to do duty for winter except a few days of Philadelphia next week.

Your observations about Clarksburg and the glades,[272] answers as well for the glades of Pennsylvania, but these last begin to be settled as you will be in time by poor industrious families from the coldest parts of New England to which that montainous cold, will appear a delightful temperature. Your Virginians are too squeamish, and have been spoiled by the bounties of nature.

I have been accompanied by Judge Cooper, and all the journey has been a pleasant and useful bartering of vegetables for stones.[273] If it was possible to fix him in your university his vast acquirements would be very useful to the Virginian youth and to Virginia. Learning and love of science and of its diffusion, are as different as light and calorie, they are not always united. I have met through life many a phosphoric savant, who did not communicate heat. Judge Cooper has both.

May health and every happiness be your lot, this is the sincere wish of your friend and

Obedient servt.

J. Corrèa de Serra

---

of chemistry and law by the Visitors of the Central College, but when the more lucrative Philadelphia professorship seemed possible, TJ had stated that they would certainly not prevent Cooper's accepting it, much as they might deplore their loss (*ibid.*, 235).

[272] Presumably concerning settlements in Clarksburg, Virginia (now West Virginia).

[273] Cooper, mineralogist and chemist, drew out C's geological interest as Gilmer had drawn out C's botanical interest.

CORREA TO GILMER   [*U.Va.*]

Washington 26 Novber. 1818

Dear Sir and Friend

You must pardon me for not answering immediately your last letter, what i had in hand was of a more pressing nature. The chief object of it was to know my opinion of Florida lands, and if i understand you rightly, chiefly about the places where the purchase of the doubtful claim you have no difficulty to acquire, would be most valuable. You know i have never been in Florida my self, consequently my information is only from books which i read with excessive curiosity. Bartram's Travels [274] to whom i give no great faith, by having seen in our western excursion countries such as the Hiwassee and upper Georgia, which i found very different from his description. The other is Romans's description of Florida,[275] scarce book, of which one copy is in the library of the Philosophical society in Philadelphia. On this i rely more from a caracter of intrinsic evidence and truth imprinted in the whole work. If i remember well the lands to the south of Cape Caraveral along the water courses where they exist, and in the western coast except those that are in the same circumference and within the same latitude, are by far the most valuable by the nature of the productions, because not

---

[274] Possibly John Bartram, *Antiquities of Florida,* London, 1769, but almost surely William Bartram, *Travels through North and South Carolina, Georgia, East & West Florida, the Cherokee country* . . . , Philadelphia, 1791. Bartram's romantic descriptions of nature, used by Coleridge and others, make a masterpiece of art but certainly exaggerate the charms of the country.

[275] *A concise natural history of East and West Florida; containing an account of the natural produce of all the southern part of British America in the three kingdoms of nature, particularly in the animal and vegetable* . . . *By Captain Bernard Romans* . . . , New York, 1775.

only sugar but coffee itself will in all probability succeed. This is the only thing i can suggest to you, which indeed is not much.

I am sorry that we did not meet in Virginia, but *fata volentem ducunt nolentem trahunt* [276] and we must submit. My joy for the recovery of Mr. Jefferson is very great, and as you say the establishment of the University of which i entertain little doubt, could be a noble finale of such a noble life, but i wish him to enjoy the beauty of this finale, and that it would be the finale of his toils and not the finale of his life. Believe me most sincerely

Your constant well wishing friend

Joseph Corrèa de Serra

CORREA TO GILMER   [*U.Va.*]

Washington 28 December 1818

Dear Sir

I have received your letter of the 25th instant, and do not wonder at the opinion entertained in Virginia of Genl. Jackson. He was never a favourite of mine, his caracter is too like Bonaparte,[277] and i cannot imagine that he has the generalship of this last, because he has not had the same education. However of this i am

---

[276] Properly *ducunt volentem fata, nolentem trahunt,* Seneca, *Ad Lucilium Epistulae Morales,* Epistle **107**: 11. Loeb transl.:
Aye, the willing soul
Fate leads, but the unwilling drags along.

[277] General Andrew Jackson (1767–1845) had in the spring of 1818 led American troops into Florida, executed two captured Britons, and been disavowed by the U. S. Government (though Secretary of State J. Q. Adams defended him). In January, 1819, Congress engaged in a spirited fight as to whether Jackson should be censured or not. His supporters won. Others, notably Henry Clay, agreed with C that here was a potential dictator. See James, Marquis, *The life of Andrew Jackson,* 285–300, Indianapolis, 1938.

not a judge, but from history i have concluded that all these determined military men, are fitter for the beginning and old age of nations but not fit for those that are in their youthful epoch.

The plant about which you are perplexed, ligneous b[? or t?]all vine, with leaves of convolvulus, and fruit of Yucca is nothing else than the beautiful *Aristochia sipho*.[278]

I intend to visit Norfolk next spring, and am very glad that you are disposed to pay a visit to the Dismal swamp. If we could engage Col. Randolph it would be a most delightful party for me.

Your university has my best wishes. May providence protect this institution from the manifold dangers to which it is still exposed. I have been to speak in confidence much more sanguine about the futurities of your nation, than i am at present. It may still happen that the weeds may spoil the crop. You are as good moral as physical botanist, and with some attention are able to distinguish the genera and the species of them. For my part i am very sorry to see, in some respects rather discouraging symptoms.[279]

About what you say of your wishes of having letters from me, i assure you that i write with greater pleasure for nobody, write yourself, and few of your letters will remain unanswered.

Yours sincerely,

J. Corrèa de Serra

---

[278] *Aristolochia sipho,* or *A. macrophylla,* a kind of Birthwort, is a perennial plant or shrub remarkable for its odd-shaped flowers. It grows in most warm and temperate regions of the earth.

[279] C was definitely soured now by the privateers' preying on Portuguese commerce. For his official protests, see letter to John Quincy Adams, 23 November 1819, below; Agan, *loc. cit.;* Adams, C. F., ed., *Memoirs of John Quincy Adams . . . , loc. cit.,* **5** and **6**.

CORREA TO JEFFERSON   [*L.C.*]

Washington. 28. December. 1818.

Sir

I have lately received from you the report about the University of Virginia [280] for which i give you my best thanks. Though you had been so kind to communicate it to me at Monticello, and the leading ideas had remained in my mind, still a repeated and reflected perusal of it has still more impressed me with the soundness and fitness of the contents in all its parties. May your legislature adopt it, and may you enjoy the growth of this noble institution many years. It will be a most noble conclusion of the high services which you have rendered to America, because i consider an institution such as you have planned not only useful to yours and to the neighboring states, but as a stimulant to the other though distant states.

I have not left any occasion of knowing the state of your health, and am very glad to be informed to day by a letter from Gilmer that it is perfectly recovered.[281] Take now care of it for the sake of the work in which you are engaged; the legislature may decree, but no

---

[280] The report of the commissioners was printed and circulated among the Legislature by Joseph C. Cabell. See Bruce, *History* **1**: 226; for an easily accessible reprint, see Honeywell, *Educational work*, 248–260.

[281] In a letter to Lafayette, 23 November 1818, TJ states that he is just now recovering from an illness of three months "which have very much broken down" his health (*L&B* **19**: 268). In a letter to Henry Dearborn, 5 July 1819, he says that "the eruptive complaint which came upon me in August last was unquestionably produced by the bath of the warm springs which I tried on account of rheumatism. The cause of the eruption was mistaken and it was treated with the severe unctions of mercury and sulphur. These reduced me to death's door and on ceasing to use them I recovered immediately . . ." (*ibid.* **19**: 270–271).

body can execute it but the planner, i know your country.

Not to trouble you with microscopic observations, i inclose a bit of paper for Colonel Randolph, and remain always with the greatest respect and attachment

Your most obedt. faithful servt.

Joseph Corrèa de Serra.

Correa to Gilmer   [*U.Va.*]

Washington 12th Febry 1819

Dear Sir and Friend

A bad report is circulating in Washington which i expect may still prove untrue. They say that young Jefferson Randolph has been treacherously stabbed by his brother in law Bankhead.[282] If unfortunately it proves true what a sorrow to our venerable friend! To Col. and Mrs. Randolph! Be so kind, relieve me of this uneasiness, by writing to me the truth which you no doubt know. You are sensible that it would be a bad occasion of writing to them on indifferent topics.

I told Mr. Garnet [283] your proposal of visiting the dismal swamp this spring and my acceptance of it. He

---

[282] Charles Bankhead had married Anne Cary Randolph, TJ's granddaughter. Their place of residence was probably "Carlton," Albemarle County, Virginia. See Warren, Mrs. J. E., "Bankhead Family," *Wm. & Mary Quart.,* 2nd series, 9 : 303–313, 1929. For Bankhead's version of this affair, see his letters to TJ, 7 Feb. 1819, TJ Papers, LC. Thomas Jefferson Randolph (1792–1875), his grandfather's executor, an able financier, was later for thirty-one years a Visitor of the University of Virginia. See *NCAB.*

[283] James Mercer Garnet(t) (1770–1843), a plantation owner along the Rappahannock at "Elmwood," had been M.C. from Virginia for two terms and active in agricultural reform for many years. He was the founder of the Virginia State Agricultural Society and first president of the U. S. Agricultural Society. See *DAB.*

tells me that if we agreed to meet at his plantation on the Rappahannock, he would be of the party, and we could visit in our journey to Norfolk, the western shore of the Chesapeake, York, and Williamsburg. You know better how far that is convenient to us, and what help he could be to us if we conformed to his plan. If you do not find it convenient, i may let the proposal drop. But by all means make your calculation that your court sessions may not interfere, and i may know if the fortnight that i intend to remain with my Portuguese friends [284] at Norfolk, is to be placed before or after our herborisation. I must inform you that vegetation is more forward at Norfolk than in Richmond at least ten days if not a fortnight. Epigae repens [285] and many pretty plants were last year in blossom in the beginning of April, Gelsemium [286] in the hedges was in bloom toward the middle of the month, with almost all the cultivated spring flowers in the gardens.

Give me some account of your progress in life, you know the interest i take in your welfare and my good wishes for it. My health thank God is very good, and i hope it will keep. This winter has been very favourable to that end by its mildness.

Most sincerely yours

J. Corrèa de Serra

---

[284] Including of course Dr. Fernandes, his physician.

[285] *Epigaea repens,* trailing arbutus, an evergreen spring blooming plant.

[286] *Gelsemium,* the jessamine, of Loganiacae, is in this case the Carolina yellow jessamine, a woody twiner of the southern U. S.

CORREA TO MADISON   [*L.C.*]

Washington 12th. Febry. 1819

Dear Sir

I received in due time your letter of the 9th of last month, and with it the seeds of the Missouri orange,[287] for which i offer you my hearty thanks. They are already gone to Europe, where the greatest care will be taken of their germination and growth. The four that remain with you, will i hope vegetate and thrive in a congenial climate.

  Permit me to offer you another seed, which though not so scientifically curious, is nevertheless economically very important, and well worth the attention of a character like you, in his philosophical retreat. I send you a little parcel of Marons [288] of last crop, gathered from a young tree which thrives and begins to bear fruit, at Belmont [289] near Philadelphia. As they are american born i am sure they will thrive in Virginia. You know that in a large portion of Tuscany, almost all Liguria and Corsica they constitute the chief nourishment of the inhabitants, and that they are very easily propagated by engrafting their branches on the wild chestnut of which they are only a variety. I will be obliged to you if you send a few to Col. Randolph at Monticello, because i have no means of conveyance, which probably are very frequent with you.

-----

[287] Or the Osage orange, *Maclura pomifera.* See C to TJ, 10 April 1814, note 48, above.

[288] A European sweet chestnut. See letters above, C to TJ, 31 October 1817 and 10 April 1818; and TJ to C, 25 November 1817.

[289] The country seat near Philadelphia of Judge Richard Peters (1744–1828), eminent jurist and practical farmer. The *Memoirs* of the Philadelphia Society for the Promotion of Agriculture contain more than one hundred of his papers. See *DAB; Em. Phila.*

A bad report is prevailing in Washington about Jefferson Randolph having been treacherously stabbed by his brother in law, and very dangerously.[290] I wish it may be untrue, and even in doubt i cannot forbear feeling for my venerable old friend and family. Accept sir the assurance of my high esteem and respectful consideration

J. Corrèa de Serra

Turn the page

N. B. The Marons must be steeped in water at least four and twenty hours before they are sown. The season of sowing them in your climate must be this month and the next.

CORREA TO THOMAS MANN RANDOLPH [291]   [L.C.]

Washington. 1st. March. 1819.

Sir

Your letter of the 14th last came to my hands in due time, and would have been immediately answered, was it not for the many letters for Portugal and the Brazils, which admitted no delay, the ships which are the only mails for those countries being on the eve of departure.

I thank you exceedingly for the details you give me of the late sickness and actual state of health of Mr. Jefferson. It was natural for me to feel much uneasiness in hearing the reports that circulated, which received still the party colour on both sides, and were for that same reason alarming from both sides. As for me who besides the personal attachment, look on him as posterity will do, as a man whose ideas have given a particular direction to the future history of this coun-

---

[290] See C to Gilmer, 12 February 1819, note 282 above.

[291] (1768–1828), TJ's scholarly son-in-law. See letters above, C to TJ, 6 Sept. 1813, note 20, etc.

try, and by that means to that of mankind, i saw his threatened departure from amongst us, in the time that he was engrafting science on Virginia as a deplorable event. The institution he is about to settle is in my eyes of more consequence than perhaps he is aware of. Besides the influence of light and taste in the future Virginians, the emulation will do wonders in the other states, as i am perfectly convinced by my own observation, and it is not indifferent for the world what is the degree of mental improvement of a nation that is destined to act such a part in the world as yours. May he complete his work.

You do not tell me to whom i was to give the *Marons* [292] i destined for you, but luckily Mr. Todd [293] came here, and i sent them to Mr. Madison praying him to divide them with you. Do not forget soaking them, before committing them to the ground.

The plant yo[u] describe to me, that you found creeping in deserted walls and in the islands near Richmond bridge, is not the *Momordica operculata* [294] which i never met in America, but the *Sycios angulata* [295] which i have met every where in spots like those in which you found it, and answers perfectly well; those

---

[292] See C to James Madison, 12 Feb. 1819, note 288, just above, etc.

[293] John Payne Todd, son of Mrs. Madison, was born 29 Feb. 1792. From May, 1813, he spent two and a half years in Europe with the Peace Commission. From that time until the fall of 1819, when his mother attempted to maneuver him into marriage, very little is known of his exact whereabouts. Apparently he roamed considerably. See Anthony, Katherine S., *Dolly Madison, her life and times,* Garden City, N. Y., Doubleday, 1949.

[294] That is, a wild cucumber, or wild balsam apple. *Momordica operculata* is a synonym for *Luffa operculata* cogn. according to the Index Kewensis. Luffa is the genus to which the dishrag gourd belongs. It is not a native North American plant.

[295] Or *Sicyos angulatus,* one-seeded Bur-Cucumber.

that appeared seeds in clusters with *seta spinosa* [296] are not seeds but *Pepones monosperma*.[297]

I am sure our friend Gilmer has spoken to you of an herborisation which i intended to make in the Dismal swamp and around Norfolk in the first days of May, to which he has volunteered himself, and in which i would be exceedingly happy you would join us. You will see if you come more curious plants in a week, than in as many months among the vegetals of the Northern Flora to which you are accostumed[*sic?*]. Pray do if you can. The 4 of May i shall be in Norfolk.

Present my respects and congratulations to Mr. Jefferson, to your lady and accept the assurance of the high esteem and friendship with which i am

Your most attached friend and servt.

Joseph Corrèa de Serra

JEFFERSON TO CORREA　　　　　　　　　　[*L.C.*]

Monticello Mar. 2. 19.

Dear Sir

You have heard long ago that our legislature has passed the act for establishing their university at the central college. we had hoped they would have accompanied it with an additional donation for erecting the necessary buildings. in this we are disappointed; and therefore are obliged to apply our funds generally to the erection of buildings for the accomodation of the Professors & Students, before we engage the Professors themselves. this, if we receive no other aid from the

---

[296] Probably a descriptive term. It is not a real name.

[297] Like *seta spinosa,* this is probably a descriptive term. Today it describes a berry with a hard rind, though it was probably used in a general sense in C's time.

legislature will take 2 or 3 years, and will so long delay the opening of the university. but it has been proposed in the mean time to commence a classical school, as a nursery to prepare subjects for the scientific branches; and with this view to accept Dr. Cooper's offer to take charge of the higher classes pro tem. while for the lower ones we engage an Usher to set up a grammar school in Charlottesville on his own account; himself however to be our selection, & under our controul & patronage.[298] this proposition lies over to our next meeting.

I must now mention to you a subject so confidential that I must not only pray it may never be repeated to any mortal but that this letter may be burnt as soon as read. at a meeting of our visitors called the other day, I proposed to invite Dr. Cooper to come on immediately for the purpose of opening our classical school, and was mortified to find one or two members in doubt about employing him; alledging that they had heard he was in habits of drinking.[299] I unhesitatingly repelled the imputation, and, besides other presumpt[a?]tive evidence, stated my own observation of his abstemiousness during his short visit to Monticello, not venturing to

---

[298] This procedure had been determined upon at the final meeting of the Visitors of the Central College 26 Feb. 1819. As a working corporation the Central College was to end on 29 March 1819. See Bruce, *History* 1: 237.

[299] See "The Fight against Cooper," in Bruce, *History* 1: 200 ff. Actually Joseph C. Cabell, Chapman Johnson, and John H. Cocke were all opposed to Cooper's reappointment, for that is what it amounted to. Though Cabell and Johnson said they would yield to TJ if he had committed himself to Cooper, Cocke was not so inclined. In a now celebrated letter to Cabell of 19 Feb. 1819, TJ stated that "Cooper is acknowledged by every enlightened man who knows him, to be the greatest man in America, in the powers of mind, and in acquired information; and that, without a slight exception." TJ carried his point, and on 29 March Cooper was selected professor of chemistry, mineralogy, natural philosophy, and law.

take a glass of wine nor to drink of the common beverages of beer or cyder; and added that the state of his health threatened to render this abstinence necessarily permanent. Mr. Madison was equally urgent as myself, but we found it prudent to let the matter lie until the 1st meeting of the new board of visitors, on the 29th. inst. but, in this, three new members are added to four of the old ones and we know not therefore whether the majority of the new board may entertain the same views as that of the old one. some testimony may therefore be necessary to rebut this suggestion with them, & none would be more satisfactory than yours; and the more so as your intercourse with Dr. Cooper enables you to speak on your own knolege, and not on rumor. will you then write me a letter, as in answer to enquiry from me, stating what you know of our friend's habits of temperance, and write it so that you can permit me to read it to the visitors.[300] I would not have Dr. Cooper know anything of this enquiry because the very doubt is an injury. and if you wish to trust what you say no further than to myself alone, say so, and using your information for my own government only, will burn the letter as I have requested you to do this.

Ever and affectionately yours.

Th. Jefferson.

---

[300] See C to TJ, 22 March 1819, below.

CORREA TO DR. JACOB BIGELOW [301]   [*Mass.Hist.Soc.*]

Washington. 7 March 1819.

Dear Sir

I profit by the departure of Mr. d'Artiguenave [302] from this to your town to write to you a few words about Botanical negociations. Mr. Lamonroux professor at Caen,[303] whose noble work on the marine plants you have perhaps seen, wishes to have a botanical correspondence in America. Mr. Lamonroux has advanced that branch of science far beyond any present or past botanist. If that is convenient to you write me a word at Philadelphia where i will be in a short time, and this affair will be settled.

I am sure by this time you have investigated every corner of New England I wish you would do for the northern states what Mr. Elliot [304] is doing for the southern ones. Nuttall is now exploring the Arkansas country at my expence and two other friends,[305] we

---

[301] Dr. Jacob Bigelow (1786–1879), botanist and physician, held two chairs at Harvard. From 1815 he was professor of Materia Medica in the medical school, and from 1817 to 1827 he held the chair of application of science in the useful arts, established by Count Rumford. The author of *Florula Bostoniensis* (1814) and *American Medical Botany* (3 v., 1817–1820), he invented the term "technology" in connection with his teaching of mechanics. See *DAB*.

[302] See note 306 below.

[303] Jean Vincent Lamouroux (1779–1825), professor at the Academy at Caen, was a well-known botanist and geologist. See *Enc. Univ.*

[304] Stephen Elliott (1771–1830) of Charleston, S. C., whose acquaintance C had made in 1815. Elliott collected botanical material from his whole area, 1800–1809, but did not publish his *Sketch of the botany of South Carolina and Georgia* until 1821–1824. See *DAB*.

[305] Thomas Nuttall (1786–1859), British-born botanist, published in 1818 *The genera of North American plants and a*

shall have a good harvest before the end of the year.

All those persons of cultivated understandings who are in this town have been delighted with Mr. Artiguenave's exhibitions.[306] I am very glad your countrymen show the good sense and taste they are possessed of, in knowing how much, declamation is useful in a republican form of government, and by inviting him to your university.

Pray be so kind to remember me to all those excellent persons, that formed our society, and whom it is impossible to forget. They are so many that i avoid particular mentions for fear of omission. Judge Davis in the quality of a brother botanist,[307] the only one

---

catalogue of the species to 1817 (2 v., Philadelphia), with a flattering dedication to C. In 1821 appeared his *A journal of travels into the Arkansa Territory during the year 1819 . . . ,* Philadelphia, dedicated to his four sponsors, C, Zaccheus Collins, William Maclure, and John Vaughan. See ch. V, above. C had probably also supported the *Genera* financially. See Pennell, Francis W., Travels and scientific collections of Thomas Nuttall, *Bartonia* **18**: 1–51, 1936.

[306] Apparently Joseph Linna Artiguenave, author of *Quatrième séance de déclamation, morceaux divers, de prose ou de poésie, prononcés à Boston, par Joseph Linna Artiguenave, clève de l'Ecole Spéciale, de declamation, et artiste du Théâtre Français de Paris. Boston 1817* and of *Morceaux divers de prose ou de poesie, prononcés dans des séances de déclamation Française A New-York, par* . . . [n.d.]. The "Minutes of the Immediate Government of Harvard College" of 11 August 1817 had mentioned the preparation for a recitation of Mons. Artiguenave the next day. On 3 February 1819 he had performed in Philadelphia (see *Phila. Union. United States Gazette and True American,* adv.). In Washington he gave two performances at "Mr. Strother's Assembly Room," Strother's Hotel, on the evenings of 24 February and 5 March 1819 (see *City of Washington Gazette,* announcements of 20 Feb. and 3 March). The Ridgway Branch, Library Company of Philadelphia, owns copies of Artiguenave's two works mentioned above.

[307] John Davis (1761–1847), judge of the U. S. District Court for the district of Massachusetts for more than forty years, was

among the american lawyers, deserves commemoration in a letter to one of the brotherhood.

Accept the assurance of the esteem and friendly sentiments with which i remain

> Sir
>
> > Your obedt. faithful servant
> >
> > J. Correa de Serra

Dr. J. Bigelow

CORREA TO GILMER   [*U.Va.*]

Washington 11 March 1819

Dear Sir

In a week i leave this for Philadelphia, where i expect you will in proper time let me know the day you intend to meet me at Norfolk, that there may be no mischance of your not finding me there or i you. I have received a letter from Col. Randolph, which afforded me great satisfaction for the minute details he gave me of the health of Mr. Jefferson, which to my great contentment is perfectly reestablished, but he says not the least word about being of our company. He would be such an addition to the pleasure i promise to me from this excursion, that i carefully entreat you to employ every means in your power to engage him. It would not be so much out of his way, there is a regular steam boat, between Richmond and Norfolk, and there is no doubt he will be much pleased by exploring this *avant poste* of your southern vegetation. The trial of Bankhead will be over by that time.[308]

---

greatly interested in botany, mineralogy, and conchology. He was president of the Massachusetts Historical Society and treasurer of Harvard, 1810–1827. *DAB; NCAB.*

[308] See C to FWG, 12 February 1819, note 282, above; and Charles Bankhead to TJ, 7 February 1819, TJ Papers, LC.

Business has forced me to remain in this desolate city, after the dissolution of Congress. You cannot imagine what emptyness it presents me to the eye and to the mind.

Discessere omnes adytis arisque relictis
Dii quibus imperium hoc steterat [309]

Farewell

Most sincerely yours

J. Corrèa de Serra

CORREA TO JEFFERSON   [*L.C.*]

Washington 22d. March. 1819.

Dear Sir

I was very glad of what i knew, about your perfect convalescence and about the progress of the Virginian university, but it has been to me a great additional pleasure, to read it in your handwriting. Your health i am confident will with proper attention continue strong and i hope and wish, for a pretty long period too.

Serus in cœlum redeas diuque
laetus intersis — [310]

My anxiety about the ultimate success of your university is not quite so much allayed. I have studied with some degree of attention the litterary seminaries of America, and remarked the diseases to which they are liable in their beginnings, and under which most of

---

[309] This appears in Virgil, *Aeneid* 2 : 351–352, as "excessere omnes adytis arisque relictis / di, quibus imperium steterat . . . ." Loeb transl.: "All the gods on whom this empire was stayed have gone forth, leaving shrine and altar."

[310] Also quoted in letter of C to TJ, 31 October 1817 above (see note 227). Horace, *Carminum* 1 : 2, 45.

them lead afterwards a lingering existence. One of the most pernicious is the mediocrity of views in a great number of people and the mediocrity of science in those that aspire to be institutors, and who generally by the help of the others obtain their wishes. Thank God the first of these infirmities has now no place in Virginia among the acting gentlemen. The second i have seen with my own eyes to prevail in America almost every where. Immediately as a seminary of learning is instituted, people of great and contagious mediocrity, chiefly New Englanders squat in them, and the seminaries become ricketed in point of science. It is not that those states are deficient in men of great knowledge, but these they keep at home. The general prejudice in favour of clerical instruction produces everywhere the same evil. I could write a long and curious chapter of anecdotes of this general disease, that my eyes have witnessed in visiting your states, many of them still extant, and easy to ascertain. Mediocrity in all shapes, is any where naturally and strongly allied. They keep together, and help one another as by instinct. This dry rot not only enfeebles young seminaries, but will have power to put down even corporations seemingly robust, as for instance the Philadelphia Medical school, as your country will witness at no distant period. I was very glad you had thought of Mr. Cooper, to whom you could find no equal in America, in point of science and zeal to spread it, and in point of sound and manly morals too, fitter perhaps for the Virginian climate, than for that in which he now lives, but from my knowledge of mankind, as far as it goes, i am apt to believe that since the news of the spirited acts of your legislature have been known, as well as your intention which is not a secret, all the aspiring mediocrity has been speculating, and their first step will be to try by all means to put him out of their way. The three first years of my residence in America, it is incredible, the *but* with which such people particularly of a certain description mixed when they spoke of him to me, the praises which they could not well deny to his superior talents and knowledge. I have passed the last four years in acquaintance and intimacy with him, remarking the direct opposition, between his real character and all the *but* i had heard before. They had represented him as nearly an infidel, of a violent temper, and of intemperate habits, and i have found him only a bitter enemy of hypocrites, no violent man, but by no means an enduring one, and have not seen a single solitary instance of intemperance.[311] He will always have the cordial hatred and interested too, of all the litterary fireflies who shine only in the dark, and whom he has seldom the prudence to manage. God grant you may get over all the snares that will surround your new born university. I take the liberty of speaking my sentiments to you so freely, being sure that you will not be offended at it, knowing as you do the hearty interest i take in your great state school. In my eyes it is the institution that not only can ensure for the future the high standing of your state in the union but by raising emulation accelerate the progress of knowledge in the other states. Virginia by its central situation, size, resources, and above all the caracter of its white population, is and will always be in your continent, what France is to Europe; no change can happen in her without influencing all the other states of

---

[311] Of course this whole letter is a masterly compliance with TJ's request that C comment on Cooper's habits of temperance. See TJ to C, 2 March 1819, above.

that part of the world. Pardon me Sir this friendly *radotage* and believe me

Ever and affectionately yours

Joseph Corrèa de Serra

My best souvenirs
to Col. and Mrs. Randolph

ZACCHEUS COLLINS [312] TO CORREA [*Ac.Nat.Sci.Phila.*]

Dear Sir

I send one of your references, of Muhl. Cat. to Jessieu's Nat. orders [313] with a very few notices of plants omitted—These are for you, to finish[.] *Floerkea* [314] to me is yet doubtful—*Elliottia* [315] I know but little of

---

[312] Collins (d. 1831, *aet.* 67), a Philadelphia friend of C's from the latter's arrival in the U. S. in 1812, was interested in many phases of science. He was vice-president of the Philadelphia Academy of Natural Sciences, president of the Pennsylvania Horticultural Society, and an active member of the APS. C later refers to him as "the over modest Mr Z. Collins." See ch. III, above. Collins' botanical correspondence is now in the AcadNatSciPhila and the HistSocPenna.

[313] Almost surely a reference to the pamphlet C prepared for the use of his Philadelphia class in botany a few years before, *Reduction of all the genera of plants contained in the Catalogus Plantarum Americae Septentrionalis, of the late Dr. Muhlenberg, to the natural families of Mr. De Jussieu's system. For the use of gentlemen who attended the course of elementary and philosophical botany in Philadelphia, in 1815,* Philadelphia, 1815 [16 pp.]. See ch. V, above.

[314] *Floerkea* is what is today called *F. proserpinacoides* Willd., and called "False mermaid." Muhlenberg called it *F. uliginosa* or "Marsh Floerkea," in his *Catalogus, 36.*

[315] *Elliottia,* named after Stephen Elliott (*q.v.*), family Ericaceae. A deciduous shrub cultivated for its handsome racemes of delicate white flowers. Not hardy in the north.

except that it comes very near to Clethra [316] and I have placed it under Ericae[.] [317] Pachysandra [318] seems to be nearest Euphorbia[.] [319]

After you shall have regulated these matters send it to Dr. Cooper and believe

with high respect

Truly yours

Z. Collins

June 22.

His Ex'y J. Corrèa de Serra

[on reverse:]

copy of note to Mr Correa June 22, 1819

---

[316] *Clethra,* family Clethraceae, White Alder, shrubs or small trees grown for their handsome spikes of white fragrant flowers appearing in summer.

[317] Ericae is an older name for the family Ericaceae or Heath family.

[318] *Pachysandra* of Muhlenberg's *Catalogus,* 85, is the well-known *P. procumbens,* credited by Muhlenberg to "Ten. Missis." In some ways it would be difficult to place this *Pachysandra* in a natural system. Its present alliance is certainly not "nearest Euphorbia," though it is today accepted as a valid genus of the family *Buxaceae,* not too distantly related to Euphorbiaceae.

[319] *Euphorbia* is a well-known, world-wide, and polymorphous genus of the spurges, of the Spurge Family, Euphorbiaceae. Collins is speaking in very general terms here, and just what *Euphorbia* he refers to is hard to trace at this distance.

JEFFERSON TO CORREA   [*L.C.*]

Monticello June 30. 19

Dear Sir

In the hope of receiving the annual visit as hereto-fore, I think it necessary to advise you of my future motions lest I should lose the benefit of it as befell me once before. on this day week I proceed to Poplar Forest where I shall continue to the 1st of October, when the meeting of the visitors of the university will oblige me to return. perhaps that meeting may be an additional motive for fixing the time of your visit, as measures will then be taken of much interest to the institution on which you have been so partial as to rest some hope. we are going on with our buildings, and in the course of this and the next year we hope to have accomodations ready for all our professors and students. Those for the professors will be as handsome and comfortable as probably they could have any where. as the institution gains favor daily with the public, so our confidence grows in the patronage of the legislature and in the enlargement of their endowment. without this indeed years will be necessary to accomplish the buildings. we have some breakers ahead too which threaten some danger. the infatuated confidence in banks occasioned large portions to be deposited in them of the funds for the literary establishment and public works. how these banks will weather the present storm, we cannot foresee. their failure would produce heavy loss to our funds.[320] I salute you as ever with affectionate friendship and respect.

Th. Jefferson

M. Correa de Serra

---

[320] See Bruce, *History* **1** : 291 ff.

CORREA TO GILMER [*U.Va.*]

Philadelphia 6 August 1819

Dear Sir

It is now three weeks since i left you, and i left you in bad health,[321] can i request a line from you about the state of your convalescence? because i hope you are better, though i do not like to be ignorant of it. Hypotheses and hopes are not entirely satisfactory.

Had you been at liberty to come down to Norfolk with me, you would have been well pleased. What difference between that Flora and those of Richmond and Albermarle! The Callicarpa [322] that we have found in Georgia was in blossom in the woods, the Miegia [323] or Cane which we had left on the Santee, was though not in plenty at a little distance from the town, and several other southern acquaintances. In coming here i have found many new journals and books from Europe, and i find that the study of fossil remains of plants is now become fashionable; discoveries will no doubt be made in this new career. That puts me in mind that you live in a rich mine of such curious objects. Your coal mine in the slaty part of it offers number of vegetable impressions. Almost all the specimens that now attract the attention of European savans are from coal mines. Yours is one of the most singular in its formations, the coals being superimposed to granite, it was the first coal mine ever known of such a nature. How easy it would be to you to make a fine collection of such objects. It is very probable that many of them will be

---

[321] See Davis, *Gilmer,* 140.

[322] *Callicarpa,* of family Verbenaceae, the Beauty-Berry, an ornamental plant cultivated chiefly for its bright-colored berry-like fruit appearing late in the autumn.

[323] Name applied to American cane by C's friend Persoon (see ch. V, above) in 1803 and followed by C's protégé Nuttall (see *ibid.*).

different from those found in the old world. What begins to be looked of importance in Europe, will in a few years be looked as such in America, and you steal a march by beginning your collection now.

Pray do not forget the Salsola.[324]   A little box of it could be sent by one of the schooners that come frequently to Philadelphia, Judge Cooper will examine it, and this experiment will decide the question.

All these are advised and wished, the only thing that i earnestly request from you is a word about the state of your health.   I am

Most sincerely yours

J. Corrèa de Serra

CORREA TO COLLINS   [*Ac.Nat.Sci.Phila.*]

[September 1819] [325]

Dear Sir

In returning from my walk, i have found your kind note about Aublet,[326] for which I thank you, and accept your invitation, for going to look at it this afternoon.

---

[324] *Salsola kali,* the common Saltwort. There are fifty species of Salsola. *Salsola kali* is now a widespread weed along railroad rights of way.   For C's interest in it, see Gilmer to TJ, 8 October 1820: "'One of the last injunctions of our excellent & ever to be cherished friend Mr. Correa, was, that I should send a small quantity of the ashes of Salsola Kali to Dr. Cooper, that he might learn whether it contain as much Soda when growing remote from the sea, as when contiguous to it. . . ."   See Davis, ed., *Jefferson-Gilmer correspondence,* 71.

[325] So placed in the volume of botanical correspondence of Collins in the AcNatSciPhila.

[326] A reference to the four-volume work of Jean Baptiste Christophe Fusée Aublet (1720–1778), *Histoire des plantes de la Guiane francois . . . ,* 1775.   A set probably came to Philadelphia about this time.   William Maclure (*q.v.*), friend of both C and Collins, presented the work to the AcNatSciPhila in 1820, perhaps this very set.

But i have been invited by our friend Cooper to assist to his lecture on Geology, at the University at four o'clock.[327] Would it be convenient to you to be an assistant also, or to be in the hospital a little past five that i may wait on you there? I will put myself in your way whichever of the two you chuse

Most sincerely yours

J. Corrèa de Serra

Correa to Gilmer   [*U.Va.*]

Philadelphia 22 Septber. 1819
Dear Sir and Friend

I had long been sollicitous about your health, the state of which was not very satisfactory when i met you lately at Richmond. A letter which i wrote to you at Richmond inquiring about it, having remained without answer gave me still more uneasiness, and i was on the point of writing to Col. Randolph on this subject when i received yours from Albemarle, by which i see that you are convalescing there. Perhaps my letter is still at Richmond, by a mistake i made in the direction, which i adverted to, when it was gone. It was directed to Mr. William F. Gilmer, instead of Mr. Francis W. Gilmer, Counsellor at Law. It matters little now, only to make me more cautious for the future.

In receiving your letter i believed i could have been able to meet you in Albemarle by this time, but fate had ordered otherwise. It is necessary for me now to be near the seaports, and the pilgrimage to Monticello which had so many attractions for me, i will not be able to perform but in November, before i go to Washington. I write on that to Mr. Jefferson.

---

[327] Cooper has been professor of applied chemistry and mineralogy in the college department of the University of Pennsylvania since 6 December 1816. See Malone, *Cooper,* 230; and letters above, C to TJ, 31 Oct. 1817, and C to Gilmer, 10 Oct. 1818, with notes to both letters.

In the letter i wrote to you directed to Richmond, i proposed to you to make a collection of the impressions of organized bodies found in the coal district. It will be easy for you, and will be of importance to science. Are they the impressions of the same organized bodies of the coal mines of the old world or different? Many of the impressions in the old world are of American plants, many are still a problem being imprints of absolutely unknown ones. What are those of your country? This collection which i presume will be easy and little expensive to you, will be an object of value at the end of some years, because such is the nature of collection, *Tantum series juncturaque pollet*,[328] but also because the taste for natural history is rapidly increasing in your nation.

I hope to find you in Richmond, either in my going to, or coming from Monticello, intirely reestablished in your health. In the meantime accept my hearty wishes for your welfare.

Most sincerely yours

J. Corrèa de Serra

CORREA TO JEFFERSON   [*L.C.*]

Philadelphia 2 October. 1819.

Dear Sir

I am unluckily forced to differ my pilgrimage to Monticello, till the beginning of November, when i will pay my respects to you before i shut myself in Washington for the winter. In the present circumstances it would be highly imprudent in my situation to quit the sea shore and to go far from this city, New York and Boston, the three doors by which communications and orders can reach me.

---

[328] Horace, *Ars Poetica* 1: 242. Loeb transl: "such is the power of order and connection."

By this time your university meeting has taken place, and i hope the results are according to your wishes, and of course to mine. What i have witnessed of late in this medical school[329] has brought to my recollection the practice of many European Universities, which practice i am persuaded is one of the causes of their superiority. By a curious contrast it is more consonant to the American institutions and spirit than to ours. I shall lay it now before you and you will judge. I have seen it practised in Rome and at Naples (i believe it is also followed in the other Italian universities of the first order) and in Portugal where since the reform of the studies which was radical in 1774, it has proved the palladium of real science. This practise is what they call *Concorso* in Italy, Opposition in Portugal. Whenever a chair is vacant, solemn proclamations and advertisements are made through the nation, that the chair will be open to concourse in such a day. All the candidates present by the fixed time are admitted and duly registered. All the academical corporation whether professors or curators, are called to the opening of the text book, suppose the Bible for the Divines. A child with an ivory knife opens the book at random, and the first verses of the prior page, are given as a theme to the candidates, who are then shut in the library of the university and kept there with great

---

[329] The printed and MS. records of the University of Pennsylvania for this period contain no evidence of a public examination of candidates for professorships. There were letters of application from or recommendation of potential candidates. See Montgomery, T. H., *History of the University of Pennsylvania,* 487–488, Philadelphia, G. W. Jacobs, 1900. The MS. Trustees Minutes of the University refer merely to the election of faculty members according to the "Rules and Statutes" adopted in 1811 (and in force until 1826) which state simply that professors are to be elected by a majority of trustees present (not less than thirteen), and in no case at the same meeting at which they are nominated.

solemnity without interference of any body else of any denomination. They have the use of the books, pen and ink and paper. At proper fixed hours they are permitted to go home to rest. The morning after, they appear in the hall of concourses, which is generally the largest in the building, and open to all the public, and none of the academical corporation is permitted to be absent without proper and sufficient reasons. The candidates go to the chair one by one, and must speak an hour on the subject of the text, and give to the corporation the notes they had written in the library, because many men can better write than speak, and others possess the art of speaking, and think less. The professors then choose three, which they believe the best and from them the whole body academic chuses by plurality of voices.

You see by this exposition how the public opinion is *eclairèe* and dark intrigues bridled, and aristocratic influence limited. I need not, speaking to you, enter in more detailed considerations, because i am sure you see them all at a glance.

I beg you will present my best respects to Mrs. and Cl. Randolph, and to accept for yourself the assurances of the heartfelt respect and attachment, with which i am

Most respectfully and affectionately yours

Joseph Corrèa de Serra

P.S. I know that you buy books in France and England. I dare recommend to you to subscribe to the Revue Encyclopedique, a new journal begun January last, carried chiefly by members of the Institute. Nothing shows better how much French minds have gained by the revolution, and the fall of Napoleon. What prodigious century this nineteenth will be for human understanding! An essay [330] on prejudices by Simonde Sismondy [331] i am sure will strike you by its simplicity and depth, as it has struck me. It is in the Revue for April. The maturity, and judgment with which every branch of moral or natural science is treated, will rapidly increase the circulation of truth.

CORREA TO JOEL R. POINSETT [332]   [*A.P.S.*]

Dr. Sir

The last time I had the pleasure of being in yr Compy I spoke to you abt. Dr. Meade [333] who intended to be a candidate for the vacant Chair of Chemistry in yr

---

[330] *Revue encyclopédique, ou analyse raisonnée des productions les plus remarquables dans la littérature, les sciences et les arts,* par une réunion de membres de l'Institut et d'autres hommes de lettres . . . Paris 1819–   . Issue II (Ajril 1819) contains on pp. 78–114 an article signed S. C. L. S. de Sismondi, "Prejugé," which discusses prejudices in four classes and concludes with a "Table Analytique du Traité des Préjugés."

[331] Jean Charles Leonard de Sismondi (1773–1842), whose real name was Simonde, an agricultural economist, historian, and humanitarian, was a friend of Madame de Stael. He published in 1819 *Nouveaux principes d'économie politique.* Among his greater works are *Histoire des républiques Italiennes du moyen âge* (16 v., 1807–1817) and *Histoire des Français* (29 v., 1818–1842). See *Biog. Univ.*

[332] Poinsett(1779–1851), South Carolina diplomat and statesman, had been representative on special missions in South America in 1810–1814, and had spent a winter in Portugal before 1801. From 1816 to 1820 he was a member of the South Carolina legislature, and a member of the Board of Public Works. Another member of this board, Abram Blanding, an alumnus and trustee of the South Carolina College, was tremendously concerned with developing the sciences at the College and perhaps interested Poinsett in these matters. There is no record of Poinsett's direct association with Cooper's appointment. See Green, Edwin L., *A history of the University of South Carolina,* Columbia, The State Co., 1916; and Rippy, J. Fred, *Joel R. Poinsett, versatile American,* Durham, Duke, 1935.

[333] Presumably William Meade, M.D., an active scientist and member of the AcNatSciPhila. Meade had published at least

univy. of Columbia.[334] I did not then know that a very superior Candidate offered himself, whom it wd. be an honour & also a great advantage to yr Country to possess. Judge Cooper informs me that he shd find himself more to his taste in Columbia beginning immediately, than in Virginia when they have nominated him but to begin Feb. 1 or 2d.[335] Th[e] science & character of this Gentn. is above every praise & it is not with you that he needs recommendatn. but as you have told me that in the choice of Professors you had influence I believe I do service to you & to yr Country in letting you know he is a candidate.

Joseph Correa de Serra

J. R. Poinsett Esq   Phila 20 Octr. 1819.

CORREA TO MADISON   [Hist.Soc.Penna.]

J. Madison L. P. of the U.S.

Philadelphia 15th. Novber. 1819

Sir

Baron Stackelberg [336] Chargè des affaires of H. Swed-

---

one book on chemistry. See *Journal* of AcNatSciPhila, **1**: 219–493, 1817–1818.

[334] The South Carolina College (later the University of South Carolina) at Columbia.

[335] Cooper became professor of chemistry at the South Carolina College in January, 1820. In May, President Maxcy died, and Cooper became president *pro tempore*. In December, 1821, he was elected president of the college. Though Cooper for the first months still hoped for the appointment at Charlottesville, he soon settled into his position, which he held until 1834. See Malone, *Cooper*, 251–253.

[336] Baron Berndt Robert Gustaf Stackelburg was chargé d'affaires from 14 Nov. 1819 to 6 June 1832. See MS. Dept. of State, NatArch; and C's letter to Stackelburg (in French) of 8 December 1819, New York to Washington (HistSocPenna), concerning an apartment in Washington at Mrs. Wilson's. Apparently Stackelburg was to succeed C in the apartment.

ish My. bearer of this letter intending to visit your state wishes to have the honor of being introduced to your acquaintance, and i am proud that your goodness enables me to procure him this advantage. He will gain in seeing the men who honor this country, and you will receive much satisfaction in being acquainted with so accomplished a gentleman.

Agree the assurances of the high consideration and respect with which i am

>Sir

>>Your most obedt. faithful servt.

>>Joseph Corrèa de Serra

CORREA TO JEFFERSON   [*Hist.Soc.Penna.*]

>>T. Jefferson L. P. of the U. S.

Philadelphia 15th. Novber. 1819.

Sir

Baron Stackelberg Chargè des Affaires of H. Swedish My. near your Government, bearer of this letter, having shown disposition to visit your State i have believed that i could do no greater service to him, than procuring him an occasion to see you, and the honor of your acquaintance. You will also i am sure receive great satisfaction in being acquainted with so accomplished a gentleman. I shall be very glad if he sees the first stamina of your University, and your way of resting from labours for the present age, in working for the future ones.

You will accept the assurances of the high esteem and affectionate friendship with which i am

>Sir

>>Your most obedt. faithful servt.

>>Joseph Corrèa de Serra

CORREA TO JOHN QUINCY ADAMS [337]   [*Nat.Arch.*]

Recd 25 Nov.

Philadelphia 23d. Novber. 1819.

> Honble. John Quincey Adams
>
> Secretary of State

Sir

O [*sic*]

I have the honor of submitting to you the following facts and considerations.

During more than two years, i have been obliged by my duty to oppose the systematic and organized depredations daily committed on the property of Portuguese subjects, by people living in the United States and with ships fitted in ports of the Union, to the ruin of the commerce of Portugal. I do justice to, and am grateful for the proceedings of the Executive in order to put a stop to these depredations, but the evil is rather increasing. I can present to you if required a list of fifty—Portuguese ships, almost all richly laden, some of them East Indiamen which have been taken by these people during this period of full peace. This is not the whole loss we have sustained, this list comprehending only those captures of which i have received official complaints. The victims have been many

---

[337] Almost exactly a year before he did leave the U. S., C announced his attention of so doing and summed up, in more tactful language than he had always employed in the past in addressing the State Department, the grievances of his government and its agent. That he had a good case historians now acknowledge. For John Quincy Adams' personal feelings on the U. S. treatment of Portugal, see ch. IV, above. Also see Agan, *loc. cit.*, and *Memoirs of John Quincy Adams* **4** and **5**, *passim.*

more, besides violations of territory, by landing and plundering ashore, with shocking circumstances.

One city alone in this coast has armed twenty six ships, which prey on our vitals, and a week ago three armed ships of this nature, were in that port waiting for a favorable occasion of sailing for a cruize. Certainly the people who commit these excesses, are not the United States, but nevertheless they live in the United States, and employ against us the resources which this situation allows them. It is impossible to wiew[*sic*] them otherwise than a wide extended and powerful tribe of Infidels worse still than those of North Africa. The North Africans make prizes with leave of their government, according to their laws, and after a declaration of war, but these worse Infidels of whom i speak, make prizes from Nations friendly to the United States, against the will of the Government of the United States, and in spite of the laws of the United States. They are more powerful than the African Infidels, because the whole coast of Barbary does not possess such a strength of privateers. They are numerous and widely scattered, not only at sea for action, but ashore likewise to keep their ground against the obvious plain sense of your laws, since most generally wherever they have been called to the law, they have found abettors who have helped them to evade the laws by formalities.

I shall not tire you with the numerous instances of these facts but it may be easily conceived how i am heartily sick of receiving frequent communications of Portuguese property stolen, of delinquents inconceivably acquitted; letters from Portuguese marchants deeply injured in their fortunes, and seeing me (as often has been the case) obsessed by prayers for bread from Portuguese sailors thrown pennyless on these shores, after their ships have been captured.

The Executive having honorably exerted the powers with which your constitution invests him, and the evil he wishes to stop, being found too refractory, it would be mere and fruitless importunity if i continued with individual complaints except by positive orders. This Government is the only proper judge [here, a blot] of what constitutional disposition or arrangements may be established for the enforcement of the laws, and he alone has the means of obtaining them, which are constitutionally shut to any foreign Minister. I thrust[*sic*] in the wisdom and justice of this government that he will find the proper means of putting an end to this monstrous infidel conspiracy, so heterogeneous to the very nature of the United States.

Before such convenient means are established, the efforts of a Portuguese Minister on this subject (the only of importance at present between the two nations) are of little profit to the interests of His Sovereign. Relying confidently on the succesful [*sic*] efforts of the government to bring forth such a desirable order of things, i chuse this moment to pay a visit to the Brazils, where i am authorised by His Majesty to go. My age and my private affairs, do not allow much delay in making use of this permission, and i intend to profit of the first proper occasion that may offer. The arrangements for my departure, will require my personal exertions, and it will not be consequently in my power to make an early or long residence in Washington this winter. As soon as i shall be able i will present myself there to pay my due obeisance to the President of the United States, and my respects to you.

Accept the assurances of the high consideration and respect with which i have the honor to be.

Sir

Your most obedient servt.

Joseph Corrèa de Serra

Correa to Monroe   [L.C.]

Philadelphia 1st. January. 1820

                           President of the United States

Sir

By my letter of the 23d. November last to the Secretary of State,[338] you have been made acquainted with the reason that keeps me from repairing to Washington in the usual time. But though personally absent in this beginning of a new year, i feel myself in duty bound by the respect which is due both to the high place you fill, and the personal qualities i revere in you, to present to you my wishes and sincere vows, that all the events of the forthcoming year may add to the glory and prosperity of your administration, as well as to your individual and domestic happiness.

Permit me Sir to profit of this occasion to offer you my best thanks for the sentiments you so nobly and so morally expressed in your Message to Congress, about the violations of neutrality.[339] I hope they will be seriously acted upon, as well for your glory and the honor

---

[338] See C to John Quincy Adams, 23 Nov. 1819, immediately above.

[339] Monroe's annual message was delivered on 7 December 1819. For (partial) text see Hamilton, S. M., ed., *The writings of James Monroe*, 7 v., **6**: 106–113, New York, Putnams, 1890–1903. After several paragraphs on neutrality, Monroe states : It is of the highest importance to our national character and indispensable to the morality of our citizens that all violations of our neutrality shall be prevented. No door shall be left open to the evasion of the laws, no opportunity afforded to any who may be disposed to take advantage of it to compromit [*sic*] the interest or honor of the nation. It is submitted, therefore, to the consideration of Congress whether it may not be advisable to revise the laws with a view to this desirable result. . . ." For C's part in earlier neutrality legislation, see C to James Monroe, 22 December 1816, note 212; and ch. IV, above.

of your nation, as for a lasting good harmony, and common advantage of our two countries[.]

Accept the assurances of the most respectful veneration with which i remain

Sir

Your most obedt. faithful servt.

Joseph Corrèa de Serra.

CORREA TO GILMER [*U.Va.*]

Philadelphia 7 Janry 1820

Dear Sir and Friend

It is long since i have had any news of your health and of your occupations, and i wish to know something of both. I profit therefore of the voyage of Mr. Cleeman [340] to Virginia, where he intends to reside in Petersburg, in order to excite you to write a word. I write also to our friend the New Governor,[341] who i hope will from the actual time and circumstances have full occasion of showing his noble and upright soul. You also will have honorable occasions of appearing in public; you know my way of thinking.

I am very pleased at this occasion of introducing to one another two persons whom i so sincerely esteem, such as you and Mr. Cleeman, and am confident that in process of time you will find yourselves much pleased by this reciprocal acquaintance that i procure to both. I remain

Most sincerely yours

Joseph Corrèa de Serra

---

[340] Unidentified.

[341] Thomas Mann Randolph (1768–1828) (*q.v.*), TJ's son-in-law, was in 1819 elected Governor of Virginia by the House of Delegates.

Correa to Randolph [*L.C.*]

H. Exy. T. R.[*sic*] Randolph
Governor of Virginia

Philadelphia 7th January. 1820.

Dear Sir

I have seen with the most lively interest in the newspapers your election to the Chief Magistracy of your state,[342] but have avoided troubling you in the first moments of your entering your laborious task, well persuaded that you knew perfectly well my sentiments towards you, without any new utterance of them.

From the correspondence between you and the committee of election, i see that the electors and the elected are both conscious of the critical situation of the moment.[343]   Forgive me if i tell you that perhaps the danger exceeds their apprehension, though i am certain is not superior to their courage, nor to their will of making a noble defence of their rights, and it is more honorable to you to be elected in this moment and for this end, that[*sic*] if you had been chosen for life in other circumstances.

The pamphlet i send to you [344] is the joint production of the leading federalists of New York and New Eng-

---

[342] See C to Gilmer, 7 January 1820, note 341 above.

[343] Complimentary letters were exchanged on 11 December 1819 between TMR and the committees of the Legislature chosen to notify him of his election.   Both letters refer to states rights and the necessity for their preservation.   These letters were published in the *Richmond Enquirer* of 16 December 1819 and may have been reprinted in Philadelphia newspapers.

[344] Probably *Free remarks on the spirit of the Federal Constitution, the practice of the Federal Government, and the obligations of the Union, respecting the exclusion of slavery from the new territories of the United States,* Philadelphia, 1819.   See Adams, Alice D., *The neglected period of anti-slavery in America, 1808–1831,* 279–286, Boston, Ginn, 1908.

land, who sent the materials elaborated, to a writer in Philadelphia to be polished and [varni?]shed. All the meetings on that question here and elsewhere are moved by federal wires, in order to resuscitate the party under another form. They look at gaining the ascendancy on the southern states at the head of which is and must be Virginia. If they carry this point in Congress, the next will be (and they do not dissemble it) to wrest the slave states of the representation of the three fifths of the slaves. The same restriction that they propose for Missouri, will be proposed next year for Arkansas, and for all others. The slave states reduced to a minority in Congress, will afterwards very probably by some law of Congress in which they according to their system intend to concentrate all powers, even attempt to stripe [*sic*] you of your property of slaves. Read and you will see that even for this last step they are laying foundations. You will find that they mention even the demi-sovereignty of the particular states. The pamphlet if you have not seen it before this time, will uncover to you part of their scheme. As for me as i live here with many of them [it] is as clear as the day light.

Even these few words i would not have ventured to write to you, if i had not such a confidence in the bearer Mr. Cleeman,[345] partner of our Consul General, and whom i thrust[*sic*] intirely. I direct him to give both this letter and the pamphlet in your hands, and no other. By the post i shall write to you something of a more indifferent nature, and remain with the most sincere friendship and attachment

Sir

Your most obedt. faithful servt.

Joseph Corrèa de Serra

---

[345] As noted above, Mr. Cleeman is unidentified. The Portuguese consul general at this time was apparently Joachim

CORREA TO RANDOLPH   [*L.C.*]

Philadelphia 4th. February. 1820.

Sir

It is after some hesitation and reflection that i venture to write to you on the following subject. Knowing your mind and your principles, i shall limit myself to a short exposition of the matter, and to a request. You will better judge of its fitness, and i shall acquiesce perfectly in what you may find most proper to do.

You received two months ago a pamphlet on the violations of neutrality committed by american citizens unworthy of this name; [346] still that pamphlet does not contain the tenth part of the horrors committed, the author of the book having very judiciously omitted

---

Joseph Vasques of New York, who succeeded Joseph Rademaker in 1816 as *ad interim* appointee. Joachim Barrazo Pereira, who succeeded, did not arrive in the U. S. until some months later. See C to JQA, Secretary of State, 4 June 1820, NatArch.

[346] Many memorials protesting privateering and preying upon Portuguese commerce were addressed to Congress in this period. Of these the one to which C refers may be *An appeal to the Government and Congress of the United States against the depredations committed by American privateers, on the commerce of nations at peace with us. By an American citizen* . . . , New York . . . , 1819. This pamphlet, reviewed in periodicals in various parts of the U. S., fits C's description quite well. In an appendix it reprints extracts from newspapers concerning depredations committed, in the text Portuguese vessels are specifically cited, and a list of Portuguese vessels seized is given (p. 84). It is probably this pamphlet too which C sent to Palmela in England, asking him to see that Gifford of the *Quarterly* got the copy for review. C hoped Gifford's criticism would have effect in the U. S. See C to Palmela, 4 March 1820, listed below. C claims that the pamphlet sent to Palmela was composed of materials gathered by C himself and given their American garb by a professor in the University.

every thing which was not in american newspapers. I have in hand a vast pile of materials and my government has collected many more, of the most shameful nature, at which every honest american, and indeed every man whatever must shudder. A strong party and intrigue has rendered abortive any remedy that has been attempted, and if congress does not take a strong resolution, the character of your whole nation is undeservedly at stake for the avarice of a particular set, and its morality also, because the bad example of impunity of robbery is contagious. You see the fruits of this impunity in the Algerine city of Baltimore (the focus of all this evil) by the manner in which they have defrauded the bank of the U. S. their own city bank &c and i abstain from mentioning the increase of like immoralities in other parts of the Union, which i believe were unheard of before. These people understand very well how to paralize any attempt to counteract or punish them; which i well know by the sad experience of two years and a half chiefly employed in opposing them. I have recent and sure information, that they now intend to render nugatory and void of effect the recommendation against them by the President in his last message,[347] and hope to contrive by all their means, that in the crowd of other important business, congress may leave this point at rest and overlook it. Notwithstanding the memorial of the insurance companies of Boston, and what the most reputable real merchants of Baltimore have said in their memorial,[348] i am afraid their hopes will be accomplished, if there is no authority of weight that recalls to Congress that part of the President's message. I feel sorry that prudence forbids to commit the reasons of my fear to paper.

---

[347] See C to Monroe, 1 January 1820, note 339, above.

[348] See note 346 above. C refers to other memorials than that he encloses but along the same lines, of course.

In such circumstances i dare appeal to your feelings, and principles. Would it not be decorous and becoming the high character of Virginia as a state, to declare publicly her abhorrence of such practises, and recommend to her senators and representatives in Congress, to have this matter called up and that recommendation of the President's message attended to?[349] I can see no inconvenient[*sic*] but only honor to the state from such a step, and utility to the whole nation in putting a stop to such dishonorable practises, of which Virginia has been almost exempt.

Now the legislature of Virginia is in session and you are the Governor of the state. I have nothing more to say.

Mr. Graham[350] was presented to the King the 3d. of July last, and talked to him about the friendly dispositions of the U. S. That same evening a great complaint came to his Majesty of a ship of value which had sailed two or three days before from Rio Janeiro to Rio Grande being taken at a little distance by a Baltimore privateer under Artigan flag. The irritation is at its zenith though covered with politeness, as is the constant usage of Monarchies. In conscience it cannot be otherwise, when in full peace our ships are taken by american privateers under the flag of Artigas (who has not a square inch of seacraft) unless they be escorted by ships of war, which causes an extraordinary expense to government, and this be the requittal of a spotless

---

[349] Dr. W. H. Gaines of the History Division, Virginia State Library, who wrote a doctoral dissertation on T. M. Randolph, knows of no action taken by the Virginia General Assembly in response to this request of C's.

[350] John Graham of Virginia was commissioned minister plenipotentiary on 6 January 1819, accredited to the Portuguese court residing in Brazil. He left Rio de Janeiro on account of illness 13 June 1820. See *DAB* and *Register of the Department of State for 1874*, 92, Washington, 1874.

amicable conduct towards your nation, and of the manifested wishes of a more closely intimate connection and friendship. Relying on your caracter so well known to me, i send you a copy of my letter to the Secy. of State,[351] that you may see why i am not gone to Washington, and have determined to go to Rio-Janeiro. The King has lately been very generous towards me, giving me a highly honorable place near him of member of his council, inspector of finances and the star and ribband of the order of the Conception the first now in the kingdom. The public instruction in the Brazils is to be organized, and the actual ministers all my old acquaintances, wish and wait for my assistance. Would i not be a fool to prefer remaining here in the most unfriendly circumstances, rather than to go among my people, and be useful to them and to me? I will always remember with the most affectionate feelings Virginia and Monticello, Mr. Jefferson and you. In April next i will be with you there.

Accept the assurance of the heartfelt esteem and friendship with which i remain

Your Excellency's

Most sincere friend and servt

Joseph Corrèa de Serra

H. Ey. T. M. Randolph

---

[351] The enclosure was a copy of the letter of 23 November 1819, to J. Q. Adams given above, but differing slightly in phrase.

CORREA TO GILMER   [*U.Va.*]

Philadelphia 2d March 1820

Dear Sir and Friend

The day before yesterday i received your letter of the 25th February, and feel deeply obliged for the marks of real friendship it contained, which is most sincerely reciprocated by me. No doubt i shall pass in Virginia all the time that i will not be forced to employ elsewhere. You know what is my partiality to your state, and i have declared every where in America, that if i was to belong to the U.S. i would chose to be Virginian, nothwithstanding the mending the state requires to be what nature has destined it to be. The time of my departure i have fixed for the month of June but i do not know in what port i will embark,[352] perhaps it will be Norfolk. You will know it.

I remark that your letter is written by another hand, i hope it is not occasioned by bad health, pray give me a detailed account of its state. I wrote lately to our Governor,[353] pray ask him if he has received my letter, and inform me of it for my tranquility.

You say that this nation is now in days of humiliation, that is not the word, my friend, the days are of the greatest danger; i cannot write what i would readily say to you. Your state alone by its steadiness and caracter can only save itself and the whole, otherwise all is lost and a new scene will appear. Circumstances have given me occasion of knowing part of the plot and smelling the rest.

Judge Cooper has been frighted with good reason by some paragraph of a fanatical presbiterian magazine printed in Virginia.[354] Be so kind to tell me if these

---

[352] C's embarkation was delayed until November.

[353] See C to Gilmer, 7 Jan. 1820, note 341, above.

[354] Dr. John H. Rice (1777–1831), eminent Presbyterian divine who had supported TJ in the founding of the University of

people are really powerful and capable of doing him any harm.

Long ago you had been elected member of the Academy of natural sciences of Philadelphia, it had a very humble beginning.[355] The progress has been prodigious and their first volume [356] has been extolled in Europe by the most fastidious British reviewers, and by the most impartial and authoritative continental ones i have consequently asked a certificate of your election, which i send to you.

Keep your promise and write me often. Present my most affectionate souvenirs to our virtuous and noble Governor, who has been put in place in the moment of danger and honor, and i am sure will support his country, and gain a glorious caracter in your history.

I remain

Most affectionately yours

Joseph Corrèa de Serra

Virginia, was editor of the *Virginia Literary and Evangelical Magazine,* published at Richmond (see *DAB*). Rice expressed his opposition to Cooper's appointment in the issue of February, 1820 (3 : 49, 63–74) ; see Malone, *Cooper,* 239–244. Rice objected "to Cooper's frank materialism, to his declaration that religious opinions were immaterial, to his condoning even of atheism." These and other arguments presented to an essentially religious constituency had considerable effect among several sects, though the Presbyterians especially in both Virginia and South Carolina were offended by certain abusive remarks of Cooper's concerning orthodox Calvinistic theology. TJ himself was disgusted at the attacks on Cooper (see Malone, 243), especially as his own views coincided with Cooper's at many points, but the effect of the Presbyterian hostility was that Cooper never became a professor in the University of Virginia. Actually Dr. Rice was one of Gilmer's good friends. See Davis, *Gilmer,* 134, 284–285.

[355] Gilmer had been elected a corresponding member on 28 February 1815, according to the Minutes of the Academy. His address was given as Albemarle County, Virginia. His name was proposed by Reuben Haines and seconded by Robert Hare.

[356] *The Journal of the Academy of Natural Sciences of Phila-*

JEFFERSON TO CORREA [*L.C.*]

Monticello Apr. 11. 20.

Dear Sir

Since I had the pleasure of seeing you, I have learnt that you are about to leave us. considering myself only, this would fill me with regret; but my affection for you obliges me to suppress that selfish feeling, and to console myself with the assurance that you are appointed by your government to a high and important station, wherein you can do more good to your country. and more to our twin continents, in general. I received with great pleasure the assurance from a friend that you would visit us once more before your departure. that I may not again incur the misfortune of losing this last gratification by my visit to Poplar Forest now approaching, I take the liberty of mentioning that I leave this for that place, within a few days, and shall be again at Monticello about the 7th. of May, to continue here till harvest, say the 1st. of July. it would particularly grieve me were you to leave us without having seen our university in it's present advanced state. this is such as to give an idea of what it will be. we are enabled now to accomplish the buildings of the whole establishment (the library excepted) by the close of next year; and this being secured, it is impossible that the legislature, or it's constituents, can see with indifference such a suite of buildings standing compleat, and unoccupied. There exists indeed an opposition to it by the friends of William and Mary, which is not strong. the most restive is that of the priests of the different religious sects who dread the advance of science as witches do the approach of day-light; and scowl on the fatal harbinger announcing the subversion of the duperies on which they live. in this the Presbyterian clergy take the lead.[357]   the tocsin is sounded in all their pulpits, and the first alarm denounced is against the particular creed of Doctr. Cooper; and as impudently denounced as if they really know what it is. but of this we will talk when you see us at Monticello. in the mean time cura ut valeas, et me ut amaris ama [358]

Th. Jefferson

M. Correa.

CORREA TO SIR JAMES EDWARD SMITH [359]

[Hist.Soc.Penna.]

Sir J. E. Smith

Philadelphia 9 May 1820

Dear Sir and Friend

After so long an interruption of correspondence, though not in the least of friendship, it would seem natural that a sort of apology be made by the first who speaks. I will attempt that in another occasion, but in this one i do not find the necessity, since it is to introduce to you Mr. George Orde [360] of this city, who being already a

---

delphia published its first volume of several numbers in 1817–1818. The principal contributors, who wrote several articles each, were C. A. Lesueur, George Ord, Thomas Say, Thomas Nuttall, and William Maclure.

[357] See C to Gilmer, 2 March 1820, note 354, above, and TJ to Dr. Cooper, 14 August 1820, L&B **15**: 264–269.

[358] For TJ's earlier use of the same Latin, see TJ to C, 27 December 1814, note 91, above.

[359] Smith (1759–1828) (q.v.), naturalist and founder and president of the Linnean Society of London, had been C's friend and correspondent as early as 1795. See DNB and C's letters to Smith, 1795–1821, in the Linnean Society MSS. Since the present letter is the only one which seriously concerns C's American years (except that quoted in ch. V, above), it alone has been reproduced in the present volume.

[360] George Ord (1781–1866), naturalist and philologist, had in 1818 accompanied Thomas Say, Titian Peale, and C's friend, William Maclure, on a botanical excursion to Georgia and

well known Naturalist particularly in the Zoological part of the continuation of Wilson's american Ornithology, and several memoirs in the transactions of the Philadelphia academy of Natural sciences [361] have demonstrated, is now leaving this country for Europe with the only view of being introduced to the coryphees of the science he with so much real zeal cultivates, and increasing his already large stock of knowledge. Being well acquainted with his scientific and moral caracter for many years i am proud of introducing him to your acquaintance, sure that mutual friendship will arise from this introduction, and science will profit by it.
I am most sincerely and affectionately, and gratefully too

Your most obedt. faithful servt.

and friend

Joseph Correa de Serra

[note in a different hand:]

Sir James E. Smith's absence from London prevented me from having the satisfaction of seeing that eminent Botanist; consequently this introductory letter, voluntarily tendered to me by the learned and estimable writer of it, was retained as a memorial of his respect and friendship.

George Ord

Florida. Earlier he had been the field companion of the naturalist, Alexander Wilson (1766–1813), who mentions Ord frequently in his *Ornithology*. Ord himself edited the eighth volume and wrote all of the ninth volume of the work.

[361] Ord's essays in the *Journal of the Academy of Natural Sciences of Philadelphia* 1, 1818–1819, are Account of a North American quadruped, supposed to belong to the genus Ovis (8–13); An account of the American species of the genus *Tantalus* or *Ibis* (53–57); An account of the *Florida Jay,* of Bartram (345–347).

GILMER TO DABNEY CARR [362]   [*Va.St.Lib.*]

Richmond 10. Augt. 1820

I leave it to you my good friend to explain the phenomenon upon philosophical principles, but so it is,
that whenever I am oppressed at heart I sigh forth my
sorrows at you or my good brother [363] and I believe it
is that principle of my nature which now prompts me
to [write] [364] to you, in one of my saddest plights. on
yesterday morning I took an everlasting adieu of Mr.
Corrêa who from the first moment [of] our acquaintance
which was accidental & without introduction [or] recommendation, shewed the greatest kindness to me, &
has ever since honored me with his friendship. Tho' I
was much attached to him I had no idea that separating
from him could under any circumstances have pene-
trated so deeply. I had promised to accompany him to
Norfolk, but on the day of his departure [I] felt very
unwell & declined going, I went however to the steam
boat to see him embark. In the moment of parting as
we both knew for the last time, he put his arms round
my neck [&] shed tears upon me, & could not speak—
they start afresh into my eyes, as I recall one of the
most affecting scenes of my life. Little do they know of
him, or of human nature who regard him as a cold,
unfeeling, & insincere philosopher yet there are [   ] [365]
against the life of Socrates & murdered him by false
accusations. If he be insincere, what interest could
induce him in 1814 when I had just grown to be a

---

[362] TJ's nephew. See C to Gilmer, 21 July 1816, note 206,
above.

[363] Peachy Ridgway Gilmer (b. 1779). For his autobiography
see Davis, *Gilmer,* 360–373.

[364] The first of several words in brackets, the editor's conjectures as to words or phrases now gone from the crumbling
edges of this MS.

[365] The rest of this line, at the bottom of the page, has
crumbled away.

man, unknown, without fortune, or favour which could advance any object of his desire, to select me of all persons, on whom to lavish his kindness, & as far as I could receive it, his knowledge. I have travelled with him thro' many a forest, & over many a dreary road, and have found him in every situation the same amiable man. When I was once sick on our journey, he sat by my side & nursed me with parental kindness—I observed on his late return from Monticello that he could not think of his parting scene, without feelings that oppressed him, and his last adieu to me, can never be forgotten while memory holds a seat in this distracted globe. I have reason for the sadness I feel—I can never see my friend again—alas! nor ever his like. Pity & comfort me.

The same sentiments which inspire this regret, naturally lead me to take deep interest in the health of my good friend Mrs Carr. who was still unwell when I heard from you. Pray let me know how she is.

remember & love me

Your friend

F. W. Gilmer

CORREA TO GILMER   [*U.Va.*]

Washington 31 August 1820

Dear Sir and Friend

I leave Washington for Philadelphia the day after tomorrow and i will not loose sight of the land of Virginia without writing a few words to you. In the week i remained at Norfolk i wished every day that you had been with me. I have this time carried my herborizations farther than i have done before. You would have seen new genera of plants for instance

Watsonias Villarsias [366] &c. which we have not met in our excursions. The dismall swamp where i have been is not like Virginia, it is botanically a pattern book of the Carolinas and Georgia, even the Decumaria [367] which gave us so much trouble to determine climbs but not frequent on the trees. I have left Norfolk as healthy as i entered it, and am confident the same would have happened to you. In some of the next years you ought to pay that spot a botanical visit in June, which i guess is the properest month in the year to see it in its glory, and if our good dear Colonel would consent to be of the party, that spot would i am sure prove to you both an Eden. You will find there plenty serpents also, but none that tells tales, or explains the properties of plants, which would be an excellent companion for Botanists.

Be so kind to present my heartfelt remembrances to Colonel Randolph, and my compliments to the good company to which you introduced me in Richmond. I beg particularly that you will make my excuses to Mr. Gibbons,[368] whom i found already gone when i went here to repay him his kindnesses. He is the most ancient acquaintance i have in Richmond, and a pattern of that unaffected gentlemanly behaviour, which thanks to universal suffrage is evaporating so fast in

[366] *Watsonia* is a tunicate bulbous herb much like gladiolus. *Villarsias* is probably the floating aquatic now known as *Limnanthemum* of Gentianaceae. Exactly what C refers to has not been identified.

[367] A climbing shrub, with glossy foliage and clusters of attractive white flowers, appears in eastern North America and in China, and is native from Virginia to Florida and Louisiana. It prefers moist situations.

[368] Probably Major James Gibbon (1758/9–1835), the hero of the battle of Stony Point, who was for thirty-five years collector of internal revenue and of the port of Richmond. His home was at Fifth and Main Streets, northeast corner, facing west. His portrait, by John B. Martin, now hangs in the Virginia Historical Society. See *Va. Mag. Hist. & Biog.* 7: 239, 1900.

your country from Maine to Georgia.

From Philadelphia you shall hear more from me, in the meantime remember with what real attachment and esteem i am

Your obedt. servt. faithful friend

Joseph Corrèa de Serra

THE ACADEMY OF NATURAL SCIENCES OF PHILADELPHIA [369] TO CORREA   [*Ac.Nat.Sci.Phila.*]

The Academy of Natural Sciences of Philadelphia, sensible of the loss they are about to sustain in the departure of Mr. Correa de Serra from this Country, and filled with the deepest regret at the circumstance, cannot refrain from an expression of its feelings.

This institution, recently springing from inconsiderable beginnings, and pursuing its objects in a retired and unpretending manner, could scarcely have hoped during its short existence, to see its exertions recognized, both at home & abroad, in so flattering a manner.

In reviewing the several causes which have conspired to so auspicious a result, they believe, amongst the most prominent & substantial, to be the uniform attention to its proceedings by Mr Correa; it is he, who has countenanced by his presence and cheered by his encouragements & instructions, a society labouring under the combined disadvantages of youth & [in]experience.

Wishing, therefore, to testify its gratitude by a public avowal of its sentiments toward one so distinguished for the excellence of his character, as well as, for his celebrity in the scientific world—

---

[369] The Academy of Natural Sciences of Philadelphia, now possessed of a great building, elaborate natural exhibits, and a fine library, had been founded in 1812. C was elected to membership 8 February 1814, on nomination of Reuben Haines and the seconding of J. Shinn, Jr. See "Minutes," in the Library of the Academy. For C's activity in the Academy, see chs. III, IV, and V, above.

Be it resolved, That the Ac. of N.S. entertaining the highest sense of the character & services of Mr. Correa de Serra, feel the deepest regret on account of the expected departure, which will deprive [*sic*] of the example & support of so valuable a member—also

Resolved, That the Members of this Society, flattering themselves that the Academy may continue to maintain a place in the regards & affections of their fellow-member, do present to him their best & sincerest wishes, for his future happiness & welfare

Hall of the Ac. of N.S.

26 Sept. 1820

Resolved that a copy of the foregoing preamble & Resolutions signed by the Prest. & Secy. be presented to His Excellency M. Correa de Serra *by the Academy*** [370]

CORREA TO THE ACADEMY OF NATURAL
   SCIENCES OF PHILADELPHIA   [*Ac.Nat.Sci.Phila.*]

President and Members of the Acady. of Natl. Sciences of Philadelphia:

Gentlemen and honored Colleagues

The Address, which your kindness has directed to me, has afforded my heart one of the purest delights, he has ever enjoyed. My attachment to your society was a natural effect, the sincerity and steadiness with which i saw, you pursued science, i was happy to find myself a member of so honorable a society. My good wishes, which you are pleased to repay so superabundantly, where therefore natural and necessary feelings more than a virtue. By the recompense which you give me

---

[370] This copy is a paper laid in the "Minutes" of the Academy. These last three words are underlined or crossed out with a flourish.

by your resolution; what was sympathy till now, becomes an obligation for the future. Wherever i may live, I will keep dearly the remembrance of the merits and candor of the members of this society, together with that of their gratuitous kindness to me in this occasion. It is useless to add that i will feel happy, if I can concur by any means in my power to the success of their undertakings.

Accept the assurances of the gratitude and high esteem, with which I am,

Gentlemen,

Your obedt. faithful servt.

Joseph Corrèa de Serra

Philadelphia 3 October 1820 [371]

CORREA TO GILMER   [*U.Va.*]

Philadelphia 11 October 1820

Dear Sir and Friend

Our revered friend Judge Cooper will pass by Richmond in his way to Monticello.[372]   I believe you are already acquainted with him personally, because i have heard you speak of him in the high terms he deserves. At all events i am very glad to bring you both together. It is by my advice that he has taken the road he follows and so it is my duty to extricate him from every

---

[371] The above is a reproduction of the original, though a copy is written into the minutes of the Academy with certain changes in punctuation and spelling. C here as occasionally elsewhere writes the first person singular once with a small letter and immediately afterwards with a capital.

[372] Dr. Thomas Cooper had assumed his duties at the South Carolina College in January 1820. At this time he must have been returning to South Carolina after a visit to the north. See also ch. IV, above.

perplexity he may encounter in his way. If any such happens, i pray you to supply my absence, and give him the best advice.

My best thanks to Mrs. Bell [373] for the prescription of the cake, they will have for me henceforward a still higher merit, and the value i put on them, shall be certified and registered in her garden, from Brazils.

You know already how sincerely i am

Your friend and faithful servt.

Joseph Corrèa de Serra

I am as you see still here but for moments.

CORREA TO JEFFERSON   [L.C.]

Philadelphia 12. October. 1820

Dear Sir.

I cannot let go Judge Cooper to Monticello,[374] without once more before i leave your country expressing to you my strong attachment to you, of which you shall have constant proofs as long as i live.

---

[373] The name may be Ball as well as Bell, but there can be no satisfactory identification for the former. A Mrs. Bell, however, probably known to C as Mrs. John Bell (c. 1784-1847), born Mary Ann Walker, was prominent in social life and welfare work. She is described as being very pretty, and "a dame of much will power, as well as of quick and decided action." Her first husband died after 1820, and she married Edmund W. Rootes in 1822 and Dr. Robert Bolling Starke in 1837. See *Richmond portraits in an exhibition of makers of Richmond, 1737–1860,* 17, Richmond, Va., The Valentine Museum, 1949.

[374] In a letter to Cooper of 14 August 1820, TJ expressed the hope that Cooper would keep himself uncommitted for the time, in hopes that the University of Virginia might later employ him. See *L&B* **15**: 268.

He will inform you of the things, which i promised to write to you as he is thoroughly informed of them.[375] I respect your person and your repose too highly, to wish to meddle you in the least in this dirty affair. I am resolved to let things have their course, and time will insensibly bring on the proper reaction and due retribution. If in the end it proves an unprofitable and ruinous trade, let the parties now concerned bewail the consequences, which they themselves are the manu- facturers.

Mr. Vanhuxem [376] of Philadelphia accompanies Judge Cooper. He is one of the most thriving among the many proselites of science, which the nursery estab- lished by Mr. Maclure [377] in this city has already af- forded. Some of them and Mr. Vanhuxem amongst the others have gone to Paris at the fountain head of natural sciences, and with great profit. *Multa ferunt anni venientes commoda secum.* I can add also, *multa recedentes adimunt,*[378] because i see with pain that the beautiful and novel caracter which you had imprinted

---

[375] Apparently this paragraph refers to the Baltimore piracies against Portuguese commerce. See Agan, *loc. cit.,* and above, ch. IV.

[376] Lardner Vanuxem (d. 1848, *aet.* 56) was a donor to the museum and contributor to the *Journal* of the Academy of Natural Sciences of Philadelphia, 1817–1818. See *Journal* 1: 214–216; 2: 82, 182. Vanuxem followed Cooper to South Caro- lina, being designated as "Prof. Min. Col. of S. C." when elected member of the APS on 11 October 1822. He resigned from the South Carolina faculty 3 November 1827. See Green, *History of the U. of S. C.,* 39.

[377] William Maclure (1763–1840), already named several times above, was a Scottish-born scientist known as the father of American geology. A liberal patron of science for many years, he was from 1817 president of the Academy of Natural Sciences of Philadelphia.

[378] The two clauses come in sequence in Horace, *Ars Poetica* 1: 175. Loeb transl.: "Many blessings the advancing years bring with them; many, as they retire, they take away."

on your nation is fast wearing away. Posterity will discriminate easily what belonged to your mind, and what was natural to the soil, which is productive of rank weeds, rather smothering the fine crop[.] I know you well enough to suppose that though your historical caracter will certainly appear brighter, you may feel flattered from what i am saying.

My most cordial souvenirs to Colonel Randolph, and my respects [to] his Lady and family.

Most attached faithful friend and servt.

Joseph Corrèa de Serra

JEFFERSON TO CORREA   [*L.C.*]

Monticello Oct. 24. [1820]

Your kind letter, dear Sir, of Oct 12 was handed to me by Dr. Cooper, and was the first correction of an erroneous belief that you had long since left our shores. such had been Col: Randolph's opinion, and his has governed mine. I received your adieu with feelings of sincere regret at the loss we were to sustain, and particularly of those friendly visits by which you had made me so happy. I shall feel too the want of your counsel and approbation in what we are doing and have yet to do in our University. the last of my mortal cares, and the last service I can render my country. but turning from myself throwing egoism behind me, and looking to your happiness, it is a duty and consolation of friendship to consider that may be promoted by your return to your own country. there I hope you will receive the honors and rewards you merit, and which may make the rest of your life easy and happy. there too you will render precious services by promoting the science of your country, and blazing it's future generations with the advantages that bestows. nor even there shall we lose all the benefits of your friendship:

FIG. 5. Thomas Jefferson, by Thomas Sully, from the portrait in the American Philosophical Society.

for this motive as well as the love of your own country will be an incitement to promote that intimate harmony between our two nations which is so much the interest of both. nothing is so important as that America shall separate herself from the systems of Europe, & establish one of her own. our circumstances, our pursuits, our interests are distinct. the principles of our policy should be so also. all entanglements with that quarter

of the globe should be avoided if we mean that peace &
justice shall be the polar stars of the american societies.
I had written a letter to a friend [379] while you were
here, in a part of which these sentiments were expressed
and I had made an extract from it to put into your
hands, as containing my creed on that subject. you
had left us however in the morning earlier than I had
been aware. still I inclose it to you because it would
be a leading principle with me, had I longer to live.
during six & thirty years that I have been in situations
to attend to the conduct and characters of foreign nations, I have found the government of Portugal the
most just, inoffensive and unambitious of any one with
which we had concern, without a single exception. I
am sure this is the character of ours also. two such

---

[379] For a later statement and anticipation of the Monroe doctrine, see TJ to Monroe, 24 Oct. 1823, *L&B* **15**: 477–480. The
letter to which TJ probably refers in the present instance is
that to William Short of 4 August 1820, *L&B* **15**: 262–264:
"Mr. Correa is here, on his farewell visit to us. He has been
much pleased with the plan and progress of our University, and
has given some valuable hints in its botanical branch. he goes
to do, I hope, much good in his own country; the public instruction there, as I understand, being within the department destined
for him. He is not without dissatisfaction, and reasonable dissatisfaction too, with the piracies of Baltimore; but his justice
and friendly dispositions will, I am sure, distinguish between the
iniquities of a few plunderers, and the sound principles of our
country at large, and of our government especially. From many
conversations with him, I hope he sees, and will promote in his
new situation, the advantages of a cordial fraternization among
all the American nations, and the importance of their coalescing
in an American system of policy, totally independent of and
unconnected with that of Europe. The day is not distant, when
we may formally require a meridian of partition through the
ocean which separates the two hemispheres, on the hither side
of which no European gun shall ever be heard, nor an American on the other; and when, during the rage of the eternal wars
of Europe, the lion and the lamb, within our regions, shall lie
down together in peace. The excess of population in Europe,
and want of room, render war, in their opinion, necessary to

nations can never wish to quarrel with each other. subordinate officers may be negligent, may have their passions & partialities, & be criminally remiss in preventing the enterprises of the lawless banditti who are to be found in every seaport of every country. the late pyratical depredations which your commerce has suffered as well as ours, & that of other nations seem to have been committed by renegado rovers of several nations, French, English, American which they as well as we have not been careful enough to suppress. I hope our Congress now about to meet will strengthen the measures of suppression. of their disposition to do it there can be no doubt; for all men or moral principle must be shocked at these atrocities. I had repeated conversations on this subject with the President while at his seat in this neighborhood. no man can abhor these enormities more deeply. I trust it will not have been in the power of abandoned rovers, nor yet of negligent functionaries to disturb the harmony of two

---

keep down that excess of numbers. Here, room is abundant, population scanty, and peace the necessary means for producing men, to whom the redundant soil is offering the means of life and happiness. The principles of society there and here, then, are radically different, and I hope no American patriot will ever lose sight of the essential policy of interdicting in the seas and territories of both Americas, the ferocious and sanguinary contests of Europe. I wish to see this coalition begun. I am earnest for an agreement with the maritime powers of Europe, assigning them the task of keeping down the piracies of their seas and the cannibalisms of African coasts, and to us. the suppression of the same enormities within our seas ; and for this purpose, I should rejoice to see the fleets of Brazil and the United States riding together as brethren of the same family, and pursuing the same object. And indeed it would be of happy augury to begin at once this concert of action here, on the invitation of either to the other government, while the way might be preparing for withdrawing our cruisers from Europe, and preventing naval collisions there which daily endanger our peace. . . ."

nations, so much disposed to mutual friendship, and interested in it. to this, my dear friend, you can be mainly instrumental, and I know your patriotism & philanthropy too well to doubt your best efforts to cement us in these. I pray for your success, and that heaven may long preserve you in health and prosperity to do all the good to mankind to which your enlightened and benevolent mind disposes you of. the continuance of my affectionate friendship with that of my life and of it's fervent wishes for your happiness, accept my sincere assurance.

Th. Jefferson

CORREA TO GILMER   [*U.Va.*]

New York 9th November 1820

Dear Sir and Friend

To morrow in the Albion packet i sail for England, and from thence in January i will sail for the Brazil, where i will be in the beginning of March. It is impossible for me to leave this continent without once more turning my eyes to Virginia, to you and Monticello. I leave you my representative in that state, and near the persons who attach me to it, and i doubt not of your acceptance of the charge. Mr. Jefferson, Col. Randolph and his excellent lady and family, the family i am most attached to in all America, will receive my adieus from you. Do not forget also that pure and virtuous soul at Montpellier and his lady. You will i hope live long my dear friend, and you will every day more and more see with your eyes, what difference exists between the philosophical Presidents, and the whole future contingent series of chiefs of your union. You know the rest of my acquaintanceship in your noble State, and the degrees of consideration i have for each, and you will distribute my souvenirs in proportion.

At my return in Philadelphia i found a letter from your brother in law Mr. Minor of Ridgeway [380] dated the 5th of July, to inform me as secrt. of the Agric. Soct. that they had been so good as to elect me one of their body, and that they would be glad of receiving some communication from me. I found at the same time as many orders to execute and dispatches to answer, with plenty of troublesome trifles to expedite, and i am now ashamed to write; i beg you will be my letter, and you can tell him that i will send better proofs than compliments of the price i attach to their kindness. I was in Virginia so long after the letter that chuse just the moment of my departure, in order to arrive in Philadelphia, and could have personally answered if i had known it.

Glory yourself in being a Virginian, and remember all my discourses about Va. It is the lot i would have wished for me if i was a North American, being a South American i am glad to be a Brazilian, and you shall hear of what i do for my country if i live.

Cras ingens iterabimus aequor,[381] but everywhere you will find me constantly and steadily

Your faithful and sincere friend

Joseph Corrèa de Serra

---

[380] Peter Minor of Ridgeway, Albemarle County, Virginia, was first secretary of the Board of Visitors of the University of Virginia. See Bruce, *History* 1: 238. The Agricultural Society of Albemarle County's "Minute Book" shows that C was proposed as an honorary member by P. Minor (secretary) and Thomas Mann Randolph on 11 October 1819, and was elected on 8 May 1820. C was reelected on 10 October 1820. See *Annual Report of the American Historical Association* 1: 263–349, 1918. The original "Minute Book" is now in the VaHist Soc.

[381] Horace, *Carmina* 1: 7, 32. Loeb transl.: "Tomorrow we will take our course over the mighty main."

CORREA TO VAUGAN   [*A.P.S.*]

New York 9 November. 1820

Dear Sir and Friend

I received yesterday your letter of the 7th instant, to which i cannot better answer, than shewing you as long as i shall exist, how much i feel all your worth, and how much i am attached to you. That feeling you will i hope find alive in me at all times, and will make both in you and me some compensation for an unavoidable absence. For the rest i recommend again to you to take care of your health, of which you have made no mention in your letter. Edward [382] is very grateful to your souvenir. Mr. R. P. Brown and Mr. Dickey [383] have done every thing you have recommended to them in my behalf. As for the newspapers about which you ask, i include here the receipt of the Union,[384] you will see by that what is due for it and must be discontinued. I have given to Mr. Barrazo [385] the receipt of Edes [386] of Baltimore for the Federal republican, which is paid to the end of this year and must be discontinued. The only ones that i chuse to continue are the National in-

---

[382] C's son Edward (*q.v.*).

[383] Probably R. Dickey, merchant, and possibly Richard Brown, sloopmaster, or Robert Brown, shipwright, according to Longworth's *American Almanac, New-York Register and City Directory,* 1820–1821. All other Dickeys are carpenters, cartmen, and shipwrights.

[384] The Philadelphia *Union. United States Gazette and True American,* founded 1818.

[385] In an official note of 4 June 1820 to Secretary of State John Quincy Adams (MSS. Dept. of State, NatArch), C stated that the new Consul General for Portugal in the U. S., Mr. Joachim Barrozo Pereira, had arrived in Philadelphia.

[386] Benjamin Edes (1784–1832) published the *Federal Republican* in Baltimore.

FIG. 6. John Vaughan, by Thomas Sully, from the portrait in the American Philosophical Society.

telligencer [387] for the country which is paid till the middle of April next, and the National gazette for the country [388] if it continues; the daily i do not intend to

[387] The *National Intelligencer* was the Democratic organ published in Washington, D. C.

[388] The journal of that name founded in Philadelphia on 5 April 1820 by William Fry, not the more famous *National Gazette* of 1791–1793. See Brigham, C. S., *History and bibliography of American newspapers, 1690–1820*, 2 v., Worcester, Mass., Amer. Antiq. Soc., 1947.

take. For the present i do not engage in Niles's register,[389] but i wish by all means to continue the North American review.[390] All the papers to my account you will have the goodness of giving to Mr. Barrozo, who will take proper care to transmit them to me. The transport of my baggage to Rio Janeiro i recommend conjointly to both.[391] I will take proper care to send you money for all these little expences, before what i left is finished.

Again i repeat take care of your health, you trifle much with it.

My best souevenirs to all the Misses Drake,[392] and my respects to Mr. Lorick.[393]

Yours for ever most sincerely

Joseph Corrèa de Serra

---

[389] *Niles' Register,* founded in Baltimore in 1811 by Hezekiah Niles, who edited it for twenty-five years, was the news magazine of the U. S. until 1849. See Luxon, N. N., *Niles Weekly Register, news magazine of the nineteenth century,* Baton Rouge, L. S. U., 1947.

[390] *The North American Review* (founded 1815) was, of course, the well-established Boston literary and critical periodical.

[391] C was sailing for England and then planned to reembark there for Brazil, but the political movements in Portugal and Brazil changed his plans. See ch. VI above.

[392] See letter of 27 September 1813, C to John Vaughan. The Misses Drake, with whom C and his son boarded in Philadelphia, are frequently mentioned in his letters. See note 41 after letter mentioned above.

[393] Severin Lorich, or Lorick (d. 1837), Swedish and Norwegian Consul, Chargé d'Affaires, and Consul General, lived in Philadelphia. He was elected a member of the APS on 16 July 1824. See *List of Members APS;* Desilver, R., *Phila. Index & Dir. 1823;* Whitely, *Phila. Reg. 1820, 1821.*

CORREA TO VAUGHAN [*A.P.S.*]

London 23d. April. 1821.

Dear Sir and Friend.

Since my arrival in England, i could have to be sure
written to you, and if i had done it as frequently as i
have thought of you, you would have been overwhelmed
by my letters. But besides my Aernal sin of disliking
to write letters except from necessity, there have been
now many other concurring causes. I have been in a
continual vortex and hurry both in England and in
France, not only by the society of old friends, but
sometimes by ticklish and perplex business. Thank
God all is over, and nothing remains now to be done
than to call at Head quarters, which will be very shortly.
Your excellent brother [394] to whose benevolence i am
very much obliged will forward you by ship a longer
letter than this, and letters, for Mr. Amado,[395] Mr.
Barrozo,[396] Mr. Duponceau,[397] Dr. Mease,[398] Reuben

---

[394] William Vaughan (1752–1850), merchant and author,
was one of the builders of the port of London and was a writer
and recognized authority on docks and canals. He was the
brother of John and Benjamin (see *DAB* and *DNB*) Vaughan.
William was a Fellow of the Royal Society, the Linnean Society,
and the Royal Astronomical Society. See *DNB*.

[395] On 6 November 1818 C informed Secretary of State
Adams that Mr. José Amado had arrived as Secretary of Lega-
tion for the Portuguese mission. See MSS., Dept. of State,
NatArch.

[396] See C to John Vaughan, 9 November 1820, note 385, above.

[397] Peter S. DuPonceau (1760–1844), lawyer and author,
French-born and ecclesiastically educated, accompanied Baron
von Steuben to the U. S. in 1777. He became a citizen of
Pennsylvania in 1781, and was an authority of constitutional,
international, and maritime law. He had as clients many diplomatic and consular agents. Later he was president of the APS.
See *DAB; Em. Phila.;* and C to DuPonceau, 12 Jan. 1822, below.

[398] Dr. James Mease (1771–1846), Philadelphia physician,

Haines; [399] Edward of whose behavior in the world i have great reason to be satisfied begs to be recalled to your memory, and i take the liberty of inclosing here three letters he writes to his friends. You know better than i do who are my friends and who are not in Philadelphia, so i leave at your disposal and justice the distribution of my souvenirs, and leave details for the letter which is to go by your brother. The only thing i had better not to forget now, is that i have had the satisfaction of signing his certificate for member of the Royal Linnean Society, and in a few days i will have the pleasure of voting for him. He is here generally more than esteemed because he is generally cherished. I believe this was a legacy your father left to all his children. Mr. Orde [400] is going in such a hurry just in the time the Brazil packet is about to depart, that i must again refer to my next letter. I need not mention my feelings towards you, not the assurance of finding me always

Yours most truly and affectionately

Joseph Corrêa de Serra

---

scientist, and author, had published in 1807 his *Geological account of the United States.* See *DAB.*

[399] Reuben Haines of Philadelphia, mentioned above, was instrumental in forming the first fire-fighting company in the city and was active in the Academy of Natural Sciences. See Mease, J., *A picture of Philadelphia,* 138, 357, Philadelphia, 1811; *Journal* of AcNatSciPhila 1, 1818, Roster of Officers.

[400] For George Ord, see C to Sir James Edward Smith, 9 May 1820, above. Ord had gone abroad in May, 1820.

[401] Eduardo José Correia de Serra, to give his full Portuguese name, is discussed above. He had spent about three years with his father in America and at the age of eighteen was accompanying the aged statesman back to Portugal. Except for the years in the U. S., Edward had apparently lived all his life up to that time in France. On 21 Nov. 1821 C petitioned his king that his son be declared his legal heir (see ch. VI, above), and the request was granted on 5 February 1822. See Carvalho, 79–80, 81.

EDWARD CORREA TO VAUGHAN   [*A.P.S.*]

London June 26 1821

Sir

In writing you the present letter I have been helped by more than one reason. 1st that my letter would not be troublesome to you, as you assured me when we went away. 2d that you perhaps wish to hear from us; and 3d that if you were to wait till Mr Correa [401] should write, this happens so seldom, that he and I might have time to die before you should know wether we were sick. these sir as you perceive are powerful reason, and I hope that on account of them my boldness will be forgiven. We have here the finest weather possible; it is the end of June, and fires are kept up as in January. this indeed is very tolerable when the sun shows his agreable visage, but since I came to England, I truly can't guess what the sun has been about. he appears three or four times a month, and then hides himself again. how different must it be in Philadelphia. as for the rest this country is certainly the most powerful of all in all respects. the arts show themselves every where in their highest perfection, and this is surely their country. Mr [Sangueret?] who as you know came to England, paid us a visit with Mr. Oliver [402] who also came in the same ship. and knowing nothing about London and wishing to see all the fine thing it was said to contain, they wanted (I mean Mr [Sangueret?] and his lady) a Cicerone, and this office Mr Oliver and I fulfilled by turns. they are

---

[402] The *S* and *r* in the name Sangueret are extremely doubtful, but even then no name resembling this occurs in the sailing list of the *Albion* published in the *New York Evening Post*, November 11, 1820 (which states that the ship sailed "yesterday morning"). The list is incomplete, for Edward Correa is not mentioned, though the Abbé and "servant" (Adam Cain) and "W Oliver, of Philadelphia" are.

going to leave London for Paris in two or three days. they are exasperated against the English Sky, and no doubt they ought to be since Mr [Sangueret?] has the goodness to compare it to that of Italy, and the lady to that of America. Mr [Sangueret?] was a few days ago, as well as Mr. Correa and his nephew invited to dine at Mr W. Vaughan's; [403] and you, Sir, during the dinner engrossed no small share of the conversation. Almost all the guests knew you. "The great Babe" as he is called here is still pushing on all the baubles of his pretty play thing the coronation.[404] Some members in Parliament have already called it by its right name, that is a childish ceremony of which the people have to bear the cost, which they can but ill afford in these narrow times. the King does not seem to mind this much. the Queen already begins to claim her rights to the ceremony, and certainly she has, for she has been willingly or no acknowledged queen to all intents and purposes. She gets the revenue of a queen, and in fact if they refuse her what she asked I cannot guess under what pretence it can be. I myself saw the preparations for the coronation, and inquiring of my guide whether there was room for the queen, he answered me in the affirmative. is she then to be crowned exclaimed I! Whether she will or [no] answered the man, we know nothing about, only we have been told to make room for her. this shows you, sir, how this business is conducted here. the sums spent are immense, and I will try to give you an idea in what manner. The old crown of the kings of England was of gothic shape and conse-

---

[403] William Vaughan's city residence was at 70 Fenchurch Street. See *DNB*.

[404] George IV (1762-1830) had succeeded his father, George III, on 29 Jan. 1820, but his coronation did not occur until 1821. His queen, Caroline, he had already attempted to divorce on grounds of adultery. She in turn attempted to force her way into the Coronation. She died soon after, in August, 1821.

quently not fashionable. therefore it could not fit the dandy. this he represented to parliament. the demand was too just not to be complied with: a new crown was made which being massive gold, and litterally covered all over with Diamonds, has become so heavy that it will only be used for the ceremony of crowning, then taken off and the old one is to be placed in its stead, and worn during the rest of the day. thus are fifty or sixty thousand pounds spent for a bauble which is to be used for about five minutes. and this is done at a time in which the parliament talks of economy, and of alleviating the great burthen of taxes imposed on the people. Such is England.

Mr Correa health has been impaired by all the vexations following the disappointments occasioned by the running to and fro of our King.[405] I hope however that it will soon be at an end, for the king will soon be in Lisbon. We are waiting every day for the news of this agreable event, in order to start, and join him. I am sorry that I cannot write to every body at the same time. but this is impossible. I entreat you sir but especially to the Misses Drake, and Mrss Lorick and Barrozo. and to you, sir, I offer all that the present mode of communicating can permit, which is the assurance of the high respect and esteem entertained for you by your humble and devoted servant.

E. Correa De Serra.

Jo. Vaughan Esqr. Philadelphia.

---

[405] João VI, or John VI, mentioned above, had succeeded to the Portuguese throne, then in Brazil, on 20 March 1816. He reached Portugal on 3 July 1821. See Cunha, *Eight centuries of Portuguese monarchy,* 122.

CORREA TO PETER S. DUPONCEAU [406]

[*Ac.Nat.Sci.Phila.*]

Lisbonne 12 Janvier. 1822.

Monsieur et respectable ami

Le retour de mon ancien domestique [407] a Philadelphia, m'offre une occasion que je veux perdre de me rapeller a votre souvenir, et de vous temoigner celui qe je garde de votre amitiè et de votre bonté pour moi. Vous aurez crû peut etre par mon silence de quatorze mois qe j'avois oublié le parfait honnete homme qui demeure au coin de Chesnut et Sixth street,[408] avec qui j'ai passé tant de momens heureux dans la communion dela paix et du savoir, mais ces souvenirs chez moi ne s'effacent pas, comme s'effacent ceux des torts meme considerables qu'ont eu et continuent d'avoir des gens qui vivent dans la meme ville, et qui me font pitié.

Depuis qe je ne vous ai pas vû, qe de choses se sont passées! et qe de scènes ont parû devant mes yeux, et dans combien d'elles il m'a fallû etre acteur! Je pourrois dire a la Kotzebue, *L'annèe la plus memorable de ma vie,*[409] et en faire un livre qui ne seroit pas sans interet, mais il ne fairà pas le sujet meme d'une lettre. Lorsqu'il faut agir ou mediter sur ce qui est a faire il n'y a pas lieu a outre occupation. Depuis mon arrivée en Angleterre jusques aujourdhui tout mon tems a eté pris par les affaires de notre revolution, tant pour le bien de ma nation, qe pour le caractere qe je souhaitte avoir parmi ceux qui doivent me juger dans la pos-

---

[406] See C to John Vaughan, 23 April 1821, note 397, above.

[407] Adam Cain, C's servant for many years. See C to John Vaughan, 13 Jan. 1822, note 413, below.

[408] DuPonceau lived at 199 Chestnut Street, the northeast corner of Sixth and Chestnut.

[409] The Title of the French translation of Kotzebue's *Das merkwürdigste Jahr meines Lebens* (Berlin, 1801), which was published in Paris in 1802.

terité, et je crois avoir eu quelque seccès. A present je suis surchargé de travail, amis j'ai le douce recompense d'etre regardé par les reformateurs et par ceux qe l'on reform, comme un homme qui n'a d'autre parti qe le bien de son pays, A la satisfaction d'une conscience sûre. Aussi me l'ont ils temoigné dela maniere la plus flatteuse dans la seance des Cortes du 18 Aout dernier, le Roi par un message au Congrés par le Ministre dela Marine exposant mes services dans l'ancien tems, et dans le moment actuel, et son desir qe l'on verifiat les recompenses qu'il comptait m'accorder et la response des Cortes qui me les accorderent sur le champ unanimement et par acclamation; le coté droit aussi bien qe le coté gauche, en y ajoutant qe c'etait de toute justice. C'est un example tres rare, et un tel jour paye bien des années de souffrance.

Mais c'est trop vous parler de moi. Oserai je me flatter mon respectable ami qe vous voudrez bien me donner de vos nouvelles, et meme bien detaillées? Il me semble qe je vois cherchant a *gramatiser* quelque nouvel echantillon de langu22age Indien qe l'on vous à envoyé de bien loin.[410] Je vois d'ici votre sallon du coin dela rue et Madamae et Monsieur Garasché [411] et vos petits enfans. Mille benedictions de ma part sur toute la famille. N'oubliez pas je vous prie de faire ressouvenir de moi l'estimable Mr Mal Enfans.[412] Il

---

[410] DuPonceau was an authority on Indian languages. For example, *A grammar of the Massachusetts Indian language by John Eliot,* a new edition with notes and observations by DuPonceau was published in Boston in 1822.

[411] Presumably Mr. and Mrs. Gabriel Garesché (note difference in spelling), a merchant and his wife who lived at 199 Chestnut, the same address as DuPonceau had. See Philadelphia Directories for 1820, 1821, 1822, in HistSocPenna.

[412] Again unidentified, unless C refers to Pierre L'Enfant, which seems far-fetched. It is probably a pet name for a member of DuPonceau's family. Unfortunately the biographical materials concerning DuPonceau in the APS do not include such things.

n'est pas probable que nous ayons jamais occasion de faire ensemble des promenades philosophiques, mais rien ne m'empecherà jamais de conservir le souvenir tres vif de votre merite et de vos qualités, et d'etre avec la plus sincere amitié et consideration

Monsieur

Votre tres attaché servt. et ami

Joseph Corrèa de Serra

/Mr Du Ponceau/

CORREA TO VAUGHAN   [*A.P.S.*]

Lisbon. 13th. January 1822.

Dear Sir and Friend.

Adam returning to Philadelphia,[413] i charge him to give you this letter. He has been to me a good servant for whom i am obliged to you that gave him to me, and i have been i believe a kind master for him. All sorts of happiness may accompany him. I give him a bill on Philadelphia for Mr. Hutcheson [414] for three months wages after his arrival that he may find at leisure a place that fits him, and as i must be in your debt for the eight dollars a month that you have given his wife and other expences that you have made on my account, i beg you to draw a bill on me for the amount of my debt payable at three days sight after deducting the hundred dollars that i left, to occur these expences

---

[413] The passport of three passengers who disembarked from the English packet, *Duke of Marlborough,* in Portugal on 6 August 1821 shows C, aged 71, "Eduardo Correia da Serra, seu Secretario," 18, and Adam Cain, C's servant, aged 28 years. See Carvalho, 75.

[414] There were various prominent *Hutchinsons* in Philadelphia in this period. See Mease, *Picture of Phila.,* 365; Paxton's *Annual Phila. Dir.* 1820; Desilvers's *Phila. Index and Dir.* 1823.

which i could not then suppose would last such a length of time.

Poor Dr. Edward Barton.[415] arrived here in October last, and brought me letters from you and from the Philosophical society. I could not see him because i was at Caldas [416] fifty miles from taking the mineral waters there, my health having been very much impaired by the exertions both of body and mind since i arrived in Europe. I wrote to him in order to change his wild scheme of going to Hyéras,[417] and to retain him within my influence either at Madeira or Setubal [418] eighteen miles to the south of Lisbon which is by its situation a true *serre chaude* [419] and where as well as at Madeira i could have been very useful to his comfort, but he was determined to go. Mr. Hutcheson tells me that he has no hopes of ever more seeing him. I am very sorry because i sincerely loved him, and wished him well.

Your worthy brother i saw in London, but could not enjoy his company so much as i wished. He comes but seldom to the meetings of the Royal Society where i could have him half way, and what i was doing in London gave me scanty occasions of calling at the city. I wished visited him at his country house which is very pleasantly situated, and which he keeps with the grounds in very good order.[420]

---

[415] Edward Barton, M.D., had been recording secretary of the AcNatSciPhila in 1818. See *Journal* 1, 1818, Roster of Officers. A native of England, he came to the U. S. as a young man. After he took his medical degree at Philadelphia he was "visited" by a pulmonary affliction. He died in Genoa in 1821. See Thacher, James, *American Medical Biography* 1: 153–156, 1828.

[416] Caldas da Rainha lies near the coast above Lisbon.

[417] Hyéres, near Marseilles, on the coast of southern France.

[418] The district across the Tejo from Lisbon, to the south.

[419] That is, a hothouse or greenhouse.

[420] Vaughan's country house has not been located.

At Warrington i did not forget that it was the place where you had passed your youth,[421] and i felt how much you had gained on my affection. My good friend it will be impossible to me to forget your real worth, and your unaffected goodness as long as i live. Give me but occasions of showing you my friendship and attachment to you and you will make me happy.

You will receive with this letter my answer to the Philosophical Society for the great and unexpected honor of their letter which Dr. Edward Barton brought me.[422] The excuse for such a delay in my answer is in having received it ten full months after its date, and no proper occasion of sending an answer having occurred after that. I know all the value of their approbation, and expect they will see tokens of my gratitude, when occasion is offered.

As you know better than myself who are my real friends in Philadelphia, you may distribute amongst them my compliments, but i am persuaded that the Wistar, Meredith, and Mease families, the over modest Mr. Z. Collins, friend Reuben Haines[423] and a few others amongst whom i must in justice mention young Mr. Patterson[424] deserve my particular acknowledge-

---

[421] The Vaughan brothers were educated in part at an academy at Warrington, Lancashire. See *DNB,* William Vaughan.

[422] On 1 December 1820, the secretary of the APS was instructed to direct a letter to C, "expressive of the high regard of the Society, & their regret at his departure from this country." See Early Proceedings of the APS, *Proc. Amer. Philos. Soc.* **22**: (119) : 498, 1885.

[423] The Wistars, Dr. Mease, Collins, and Haines are identified above. Among many prominent Merediths was Samuel (1741–1817), Treasurer of the U. S. William Morris Meredith (1799–1873) was a prominent lawyer.

[424] Probably Robert M. Patterson (*q.v.*), professor in the University of Pennsylvania, as his father had been, and president of the APS from 1819. C had introduced him in October, 1811, to Sir J. E. Smith. See letter in LinnSoc, London.

ment for their sincere kindness to me.

Miss Drake and all her Family i will never forget for their worth and excellent quality, which i witnessed in so long a residence with them. I wish you would indicate to me some means of shewing how much i esteem them and wish them well.

You know i could not keep you company in your Sunday worship during the daylight, but i will thank you for presenting my best respects to Mrs Manigault [425] where we met the same day without difference of opinion.

To tell you something about me, it is enough to say that my reception from the king as well as from the Cortes has far exceeded my sanguine expectations, and a day such as the 18th. of August last as recorded in the journal of the Cortes, and even briefly in the official newspapers of government is enough to repay many years of sufferings and persecution. Of twelve Ministers plenip, and ambassadors that were in actual service twelve months ago, i am the only one which has been recompensed, though all are out of place now. The king has kept me in place and pay till i have entered the new place which is for life, and only last month my letters of recall have been sent to your government. Henceforth there will be in the U.S. only a Portuguese Charge d'affairs.

You know my excellent friend what are my sentiments and feelings towards you, consequently i need not tell more than that i am

Wholly and sincerely yours

Joseph Correa de Serra

---

[425] Mary S. Manigault, widow, NW corner Ninth and Spruce Streets, is the only Manigault mentioned in Desilver's *Phila. Index and Dir.*, 1823.

P.S. Do not forget my compliments to the truly worthy Judge Tilghman [426]

EDWARD CORREA TO VAUGHAN   [*A.P.S.*]

Lisbon January 19th 1822

Honoured Sir

It was with no less pleasure than surprise that I received your little remembrance dated from the 30th of October last: It was not expected, and was for that reason the more heartily welcome. We are still in Lisbon, Sir, and I painfully forsee that I will remain in it much longer. What a terrible place it is! figure yourself the palace of the goddess of filthiness, and still you will have but a weak idea of the comforts of this place. no kind of industry in the people, an immense bulk of ignorance and superstition entertained by a multitude of monks, priests, and friars, whose interest it is to keep the lower class in them the longer possible. this makes me regret the sweet and quiet Philadelphia, where superstition is so far from being enjoined by monks and friars, that I should think it had rather gone to the other extreme. Where cleanliness is so great that some people think it rather dull on that account. Those people here on the contrary seem to have no kind of Idea of what is comfort and ease. they have built their capital city on three hills, so steep and so sharp that it litterally required goats' feet and humour to be able to walk in Lisbon. the only thing that can a little make amends for all the disagreable ideas that arise in you at the sight of Lisbon, is the fineness of its atmosphere, the purity of the air you breathe, and the mild-

---

[426] William Tilghman (1756–1827), Chief Justice of the Pennsylvania Supreme Court, was from 1824 president of the APS. See *DAB; Em.Phila.*

ness of the climate. few houses have here chimneys.
we are now in december and the weather is nearly the
same as in April in America, strong winds, strong
rains, very little or no cold at all—it is beautiful. All
what nature has made here is very fine. whatever the
inhabitants lay their hands on is sure to be spoiled.
this is to be sure the most shameful compliment that
can be made to a nation, but I am truly sorry to tell that
they deserve it, and there is in it nothing but true.
there is in this nation as well as in all those that have
long been governed by the despotism of priests, a certain air of faded grandeur which at the first sight occasions painful sensations. the palace of the inquisition
is now occupied by all sorts of public offices, one of
which is the department of foreign affairs of which I
am an unworthy member: it is truly pleasing to see how
this ancient temple of cruel superstition transformed in
a truly bee hive where all the interests of the state go
to present themselves to be despatched. just opposite
the front door of it is to be built a constitutional monument of which the King himself has placed the first
stone. The prisons of this infernal place have been
thrown open, an whoever chooses may go and visit
them. There was a great curiosity entertained to see
the instruments used for the most christian and chari-
table purpose of torturing. the inquisitors have hidden
them, nobody knows where they are. When the prisons
were thrown open, there were names written on the
walls, some of very illustrious personages, such as
Camoes,[427] there were also writings inscriptions verses,
etc. this was too dangerous, the inquisitors have got
the walls white washed. some newly murdered bodies
are said to have been found in the subterraneous prisons.
oh Portuguese why were you such prigs as not to open

---

[427] Luis de Camoens (1524–1580), Portuguese epic and lyric
poet.

the doors all at once and break in as the Spaniards did at the moment of their revolution? how do you know what these demons did in the hell they inhabited at their first hearing the beating of the drums that announced your revolt? certainly this should have been their first effort however this was not done, God bless them and send them peace, they are good people the Portuguese.

I should like to know how all goes on in Pine street how many marriages have taken place in all of friend Miss Margaret Drake's family, how is Mary's knee how is her tender sweet heart and my friend Guerra.[428] I dare not ask you all this, sir, but order your nephew to write it to me, I am sure he owes me more than one letter. Mr. Correa's health continues to be weak as it ought to be at seventy one years of age, however I perceive as yet nothing alarming. mine continues to be strong as it ought to be at eighteen, however nothing is easier to me than to weaken it when I choose. I hope yours, sir, continues still to leave you that activity which seemed always to be noxious to it and at the same time was so useful and beneficial to all those whose welfare occasioned it. our poor Dr. Barton was here.[429] On the very day he came we were on the eve of making a little incursion in the interior of the country, he knowing it sent us a letter but could not see us for we started the day after and he in the time of our absence left Lisbon for Provence in this manner we were deprived of the pleasure of seeing him: I am very much afraid lest the occasion should not present itself again. I hope sir he will have the pleasure of visiting you again in America, Perhaps myself I may

---

[428] Guerra and Mary are unidentified. Miss Margaret Drake's boarding house, where Edward and his father lived, is mentioned several times above.

[429] Dr. Edward Barton. See C to Vaughan, 13 Jan. 1822, note 415 above.

some day or other be sent there by my fate in any case
and at any rate, I beg you, sir, to accept the assurances
of the profound respect of your humble and obedient
servant

and as I dare style myself your

young friend

E. J. Correa de Sérra

EDWARD CORREA TO VAUGHAN   [*A.P.S.*]

Paris January 8 1823.[430]

Honoured Sir

having now an occasion of writing to America I do
not wish to let it escape without letting you know what
has become of Mr. Correa and myself. of this last
personage, perhaps you do not care much to know any
thing. the ruler of the universe having however infused into my mind a, no slight share of vanity, I can't
help thinking that hearing of me, will be agreable to
others. as speaking of me is agreable to myself, and to
speak truth, to any being in the creation. be it as it
may, Mr Correa is now in Portugal covered with honours, incumbered with the weight and the obligations
imposed upon him by seven or eight places given to him
either by the king or by the Cortes. At seventy three
years of age, one may be excused, for not possessing
all the quickness and activity which he might have
possessed and even to an imminent degree in his
younger days. and for this reason Mr Correa whose
chief virtues have never been either too great quickness
or activity in affairs, finding himself overburthened with
business, has found the precious means of having great
many places at the same time, of fulfilling but very few
of the functions of them, and still of getting new ones

---

[430] The date line may be in a different hand.

every day. this I own to be rather extraordinary, but believe me, we travellers see wonders, and I don't use at all of the privilege which is generally granted to the class of men in which I just now ranged myself. Notwithstanding this rare discovery it is painful to me to see a man so miserable, for all the honours and riches of this world could not give him the most precious of all goods, namely, health. he is still tormented by the cruel diabetes which seized him since his second passage from france to England. this in truth is not, and ought not to be called a desease, it is really an infirmity of an old man. It being of the mildest sort, it would but very little derange him, if he had not the fatal illusion of curing it. the remedies which he opposes to it are worse than the ill itself, and consequently he destroys by them the little strength which remains in his body, and the despondency occasioned by the little effect which he has produced by remedies in which he placed his whole confidence, causes him to be always sad and full of grief. As to the rest of his affairs go even too well for him, which though it seems a paradox, you will readily understand when i tell you that he is, member of the king's counsel, member of the counsel of the treasury, member of the committee of the royal academy of Lisbon, that he has lately been named deputy to the Cortes, member of the commission to try the queen, member of the commission of agriculture, member of the commission of Diplomacy, member . . . member . . . &c&c. this would tire one, young and active; this will kill him old, sick and indolent if he had not made the rare discovery which I told you before. As for my part, I had been named to a place very honourable and lucrative, but which did not at all please me. the functions of it did not oblige me either to more or less than the entire sacrifice of the pleasure which I took to reading, and to the sciences. my mental faculties though not great were soon tired by the empty and uninteresting occupations to which I was obliged to apply my whole attention. I was one of the under-secretaries of the Minister to the foreign department. A Swedish frigate entered the port of Lisbon, and the commander of her complained that they had fired from the port one less gun than they ought to. excuse the expression, but really what the devil was that to me. however I worked like a turk for a whole fortnight to the reparations which were made to the Swedish commander. one John Cornuto[?] a Spaniard entered Portugal, and the poor fellow could give no account of himself, and there I was again wasting ink and pens scribling papers. tired of all this I gave my decision I chose rather to study medecine; profession, at least, where I will be master of myself. for this purpose I came to Paris where I am now, and from where my letter is dated. I have made an acquaintance with a few American students, all from Philadelphia. such as the son of Dr. Coxe.[431] the son of the reverend Dr Staughton.[432] the son of Mr Kitchen [433] and some others. I find myself very happy at least for the present, and from time to time my heart tells me, "happy is he who is independants of kings and governments." Mr Correa envies my fate very much, and were his matter to permit him to come finish his days

---

[431] Probably a reference to Dr. Edward Jenner Coxe, son of John R. Coxe, M.D. (d. 1835; elected member of the APS in 1799). See Paxton's *Phila. Dir.* 1819.

[432] William Staughton, D.D. (d. 1829, *aet.* 59) was pastor of the Sansom Street Baptist Church in 1823 (Desilver's *Phila. Index and Dir.,* 1823) and was elected a member of the APS on 15 July 1808.

[433] Dr. James Kitchen graduated from the medical school of the University of Pennsylvania in 1822 and soon after his graduation went abroad, spending two years in travel in England, Scotland, Holland, and France. He returned to Philadelphia in 1824 and established his practice at 37 Spruce Street. See Thomas, A. R., In memoriam James Kitchen, M.D., *The Hahnemannian Monthly* **29**: 652–659, 1894.

in Paris, he would joyfully leave all his fetters and come botanize in the *Gardin des plantes.*

Our carriages, books, and furniture arrived to Lisbon two months ago, bearing all the marks of having travelled without their masters.

My time does not permit me to write more, or I should have written to the good Misses Drake. I should wish very much to have made a gross fault of impoliteness in my giving them the name of their father, but if I have, they will excuse me without waiting till I should beg pardon, for far from doing such thing I will on the contrary be very glad, for their sake, of finding myself guilty of such ungentlemanly conduct. by the news which I get of America through the canal of my American acquaintances, I hear that your health is pretty nearly the same, at least up to the last news. I could end this like a sermon, by holily wishing you the continuation of it, but you know me to well, Sir, to render this precaution necessary in order to persuade you of the interest which I bear to your welfare and conservation, and of the respect with which I am your humble servant

E. Correa de Serra

EDWARD CORREA TO VAUGHAN   [*A.P.S.*]

Paris July 1st 1823

Honoured Sir

It was with a very great pleasure that I received your unexpected letter of the 26th of April last which was brought me by Dr. Coxe of Philadelphia.[434]   to write to you was for me a duty since I could do it with facility, but indeed sir, your writing to me was a great favor,

---

[434] See EC to Vaughan, 8 January 1823, note 431, above.

for you must have plenty other affairs than thinking about such a worthless fellow as myself. however you appeared to think differently, and I renew my thanks to you for your kindness. Mr Correa is now deputy to the cortes of Portugal and there as every where else he shows that simplicity of manners and originality of mind which caused him to be called by some American writers the Franklin of Portugal. his health is altogether as good as can be expected from his age (73), and if he do not continue to surround himself with Phisicians as he used to, I have a good hope that he has yet many years before him. the art of letter writing is a difficult one, will you permit me, sir, with all the respect I owe you, to tell you that you committed an enormous error in your last to me? I mean neither more nor less than that you told me nothing of the thing I most desired to know, namely your Health. from your telling me nothing about it, I ought to have concluded that you were well, but still I might have been mistaken. happily the evil is not of an irreparable nature.

There was once a time in which I was thought by some of my friends to be a tolerable politician. Young dogs got fresh experience every day, and I have found since, that of all trades and professions, of all the speculations which are capable of busying a common understanding politics are the worst. some years ago Mr Jefferson devoted all his time to the reading of newspapers, nothing pleased him so much as a newspaper. now (or at least when I was there,) not a single newspaper is found in his house. still when he can catch hold of one his old mania comes back again and sticks him close to it. so it is with politicians, though they have been times and of time belied in their foresight of future events, though they have sworn so many times that they never should meddle any more with politics, still let there once be wind and a fair occasion, and they'll run after the bubble. The affairs of Spain and Portugal are according to me in a desperate situation, the efforts of the gentlemen of the holy alliance will be too strenuous and they have too many partisans in all countries not to be attended with success. in a country where one fifth of the population is of monks and friars, one eighth of noblemen and another fifth and more of their vassals, what is there to be expected for the cause of liberty? it is the interest of the nobility that people should be slaves, people are never better than slaves but when they are ignorant, but it is the interest of rich monks that people should be ignorant, so that these two classes agree together for the better exertion of their individual tyranny. there is however a consolation, enlightenment is a bamboo in fact a bow will bend, but the more it has been curved and the more powerfull will be its succeeding expansion. similar will, I think be the case with the Peninsula, the powers developped against young liberty are to strong for its infantine strength, but it will then grow secretely in its prison and will at last come out as an irresistible torrent.

Whilst I was forgetting myself in the sublimer regions of high politics I might have talked or written for hours and hours if a cooler reflexion had not made me think that I was tiring you and more probably making myself ridiculous, for what is there more so than for a beardless young fool to discuss with a doctoral and pedantic tone on subjects which men older and more experienced than he, enter only with great precautions. the sublimest degree of bravery which is thought of by young moths is to go at night to burn their wings in every candle they meet. young dogs do something else against every casks; the ones kill themselves and the others get flogged.

I am sorry to hear that the Misses Drakes beg to be remembered to me. I am not such a monster as for them to dread trusting me with a line or two of their hand writing. Some one or other of them used to think differently before. However as I am not a member of the holy alliance I will only complain, and to push (or more englishly) to carry my forbearance further I will entreat you to assure them that notwithstanding their negligence I pray them to continue to consider me as one of their best friends, and as for you, honoured sir, I think it almost useless to repeat for you know it well that I am always your humble and devoted servant

> E. Correa de Serra

I have written to Md Godon.[435]   She does not answer me probably for want of occasions to send the letter. you could remedy to that if you only passed once in an age into her shop.

EDWARD CORREA TO GEORGE ORD [436]   [*A.P.S.*]

> Paris 10th of October. 1824.

Sir

having received through your means the expressions of regret and condolence which the learned members of the Philosophical Society of Philadelphia with the regard, sympathy and at the same time with the urbanity which characterized throughout all the world, men of distinguished talents, have directed to me on

---

[435] "V. Godon, storekeeper, *32 South 4th*" is listed in Paxton's *Annual Phila. Dir.,* 1819, the only Godon listed.

[436] The letter is addressed to Ord as "Secretary of the Philosophical Society of Philadelphia." It is a reply to the expression of sympathy ordered to be written at a meeting of the APS of 19 March 1824, at which the Abbé's death was announced. See *Proc. Amer. Philos. Soc.* **22** (119) : 527, 1885.

account of the death of my father Joseph Correa da Serra whom they had honoured with making him one of themselves, I request you, Sir, to present the learned assembly my sincere thanks and my grateful acknowledgements for their remembrance. the more so as great many and the most part of the learned members who, friends to my deceased father, have more than one title to my respect and who are personally known to me.

I embrace the same opportunity to request you to accept the assurances of the respect with which I remain

Sir

Your humble Servant

E. J. Correa da Serra

JEFFERSON TO JOHN P. EMMET [437]   [*L.C. and U.Va.*]

[Monticello, 27 April, 1826]

Dear Sir

It is time to think of the introduction of the school of Botany into our institution. not that I suppose the lectures can be begun in the present year, but that we may this year make the preparations necessary for commencing them the next. for that branch, I presume, can be taught advantageously only during the short season while nature is in general bloom, say during a certain portion of the months of April and May, when, suspending the other branches of your department, that of botany may claim your exclusive attention. of this however you are to be the judge, as well as what I may now propose on the subject of preparation. I will do

---

[437] John Patton Emmet, M.D. (1797–1842), first professor of natural history at the University of Virginia, was the son of Thomas Addis Emmet, and therefore nephew of the more famous Robert Emmet, Irish patriot and martyr.

this in writing while sitting at my table & at ease because I can rally there, for your consideration, with more composure than in extempore conversation my thoughts of what we have to do in the present season.

I suppose you were well acquainted by character if not personally, with the late Abbé Correa, who past some time among us, first as a distinguished Savant of Europe and afterwards as Ambassador of Portugal, resident with our government. profoundly learned in several of the branches of science he was so above all others in that of Botany; in which he preferred an amalgamation of the methods of Linnaeus and of Jussieu to either of them exclusively. our Institution being then on hand in which that was of course to be one of the subjects of instruction, I availed myself his presence and friendship to obtain from him a general idea of the extent of the ground we should employ, and the number and character of the plants we should introduce into it. he accordingly sketched for me a mere outline of the scale he would recommend, restrained altogether to objects of use, and indulging not at all in things of mere curiosity, and especially not yet thinking of a hothouse or even a Green-house. I enclose you a copy of his paper, which was the more satisfactory to me as it coincided with the moderate views to which our endowments as yet confine us. I am still the more satisfied as it seemed to be confirmed by your own way of thinking, as I understood it in our conversation of the other day. to your judgment altogether his ideas will be submitted, as well as my own, now to be suggested as to the opening of the present year preparatory to the commencement of the school in the next.

I. our 1st operation must be the selection of a piece of ground, of proper soil & site, suppose of about 6 acres as Mr Correa proposes, in chusing this we are to regard the circumstances of soil, water, and distance.

I have diligently examined all our grounds with this view and think that on the public road, at the upper corner of our possessions, where the stream issues from them, has more of the requisite qualities than any other spot we possess. *170 yards square taken at that angle would make the 6. acres we want but the angle at the road is acute, and the form of the ground will be trapezoid, not square. I would take therefore, for it's breadth, all the ground between the road and the dam of the brick ponds, extending Eastwardly up the hill as far & wide as our quantity would require. The bottom ground would suit for the garden of plants, the hillsides for the trees.

2d operation. inclose the ground with a serpentine brick wall 7. f. high. This wd. take about 80 M bricks &nd cost 800D, and it must depend on our finances whether they will afford that immediately or allow us, for a while, but an enclosure of posts and rails.

3d operation. Farm all the hill sides into level terraces of convenient breadth curving with the hills, and the level ground into beds & allies.

4th operation. make out a list of the plants thought necessary and sufficient for the botanical purposes, and of the trees we propose to introduce, and take measures in time for procuring them.

As to the seeds of plants, much may be obtained from the gardeners of our own country. I have moreover a special resource—for three and twenty years of the last twenty five, my old friend Thouin [438] Superintendent of the garden of plants at Paris has regularly sent me a box of seeds, of such exotics to us, as would suit our climate, and containing nothing indigenous to our country. These I regularly sent to the public and

---

[438] For the friendship of TJ and Thouin, see C to TJ, 6 March 1812, note 9.

private gardens of the other states, having as yet no employment for them here. but during the last two years this envoi has been intermitted, I know not why. I will immediately write and request a recommencement of that kind office, on the ground that we can now employ them ourselves. they can be here in early spring.

The trees I should propose would be exotics of distinguished usefulness and accomodated to our climate, such as larch, cedar of Libanus, Cork-oak, the Maronnier, Mahagany the Catachu or India rubber tree of Napul [30°] Teak tree or Indian oak of Burman [23°], the various woods of Brazil &c.

The seed of the Larch can be obtained from the tree at Monticello, cones of the Cedar of Libanus are in most of our seed shops, but may be had fresh from the seeds in the English gardens. the Maronnier and Cork oak, I can obtain from France. there is a Maronnier at Mount Vernon, but it is a seedling, and not therefore select. the others may be got thro' the means of our Ministers and Consuls in the countries where they grow, or from the seed shops of England where they may very possibly be found.

Lastly, a gardener of sufficient skill must be obtained.

This, dear Sir, is the sum of what occurs to me at present; think of it, and let us at once enter on the operations.

Accept my friendly & respectful salutations.

Th. J.

Doctr. Emmet
    Professor of Nat. Hist at the Univty. of Virginia

* To wit 19,360 sq. yards = 4. acres for the garden plants
            9,600 d° — — — = 2 a^c – for the plantn of trees

_____

29,040   = 6. a^c – in the whole.

A CHECKLIST OF CORREA'S EXTANT LETTERS WRITTEN DURING HIS AMERICAN PERIOD TO FOREIGN CORRESPONDENTS

With one exception, these letters are not reproduced in this study. At the right in each column is given the location of the printed letter or, if it survives only in manuscript, of the repository. In most instances the place to which the letter is directed is not given in the printed form. For the abbreviations, see above pp. 91–92, note 1.

1812

May 15	to Conde da Barca Philadelphia to—	Carvalho, pp. 163–164
May 29	to Conde da Barca Philadelphia to—	Henriquez, p. 110
June 27	to Conde da Barca Philadelphia to—	Henriquez, pp. 110–111
October 11	to F. José Maria de Brito New York to Paris	Carvalho, pp. 164–166

1813

February 12	to Marquez de Funchal Philadelphia to—	Carvalho, pp. 166–170
May 24	to M. Delessert Philadelphia to Paris	Library of the Institute of France, Paris
June 5	to F. José Maria de Brito New York to—	Carvalho, pp. 170–174
June 6	to [F. José Maria de Brito?] New York to—	Carvalho, pp. 174–176
October 24	to Conde da Barca Boston to—	Carvalho, pp. 176–178 Henriquez, pp. 112 ff.
November 15	to Conde da Barca Boston to—	Carvalho, pp. 178–179
November 18	to Dr. J. E. Smith Boston to London	Linnean Society, London

1814

April 28	to Messrs. LeRoy, Bayard & McEvery Philadelphia to [Paris?]	HistSocPenna, Philadelphia
May 31	to M. Benj. Delessert Philadelphia to Paris	Library of the Institute of France, Paris

1815

April 26	to [Conde da Barca] Philadelphia to—	Carvalho, p. 53(part) Henriquez, pp. 114–115
November 4	to Conde da Barca Philadelphia to—	Carvalho, pp. 179–181 Henriquez, pp. 116–117
November 15	to Conde da Barca [Philadelphia?] to—	Carvalho, p. 54(ref. to)

1816

February 9	to Conde da Barca Philadelphia to—	Carvalho, pp. 182–183
June 27	to M. Richard Philadelphia to Paris	Library of the Institute of France, Paris
December 2	to [Conde da Barca] Washington City to—	Henriquez, pp. 115–116
December 24	to [Conde da Barca] Washington to—	Carvalho, p. 62(ref. to) Henriquez, pp. 118–120

1817

n.d.	to Conde de Palmela	Carvalho, p. 73(ref. to)

1818

June 1	to Snr. Tomaz Antonio [1] Vila Nova Portugal Philadelphia to Rio	Carvalho, pp. 183–185
October 22	to Snr. Tomaz Antonio Vila Nova Portugal Philadelphia to Rio	Ministry of Education and Health, Rio
December 6	to Snr. Tomaz Antonio Vila Nova Portugal Washington to Rio	Carvalho, pp. 185–186

1819

February 18	to Snr. Tomaz Antonio Vila Nova Portugal Washington to Rio	Carvalho, pp. 186–188 [there are two letters of this date in the Ministry of Education and Health, Rio]
March 29	to Snr. Tomaz Antonio Vila Nova Portugal Washington to Rio	Carvalho, pp. 188–189
March 31[21?]	to Snr. Tomaz Antonio Vila Nova Portugal Washington to Rio	Carvalho, p. 189
[April or May] 8	to Snr. Tomaz Antonio Vila Nova Portugal Washington to Rio	Carvalho, p. 190
May 14	to Snr. Tomaz Antonio Vila Nova Portugal Philadelphia to Rio	Carvalho, pp. 191–192
August 1	to Snr. Tomaz Antonio Vila Nova Portugal Philadelphia to Rio	Carvalho, pp. 192–193
September 2	to Snr. Tomaz Antonio Vila Nova Portugal Philadelphia to Rio	Carvalho, pp. 194–195

---

[1] All the letters to this court official are to be found in the Ministério da Educação e Saúde, Rio de Janeiro. A few of these and of the other letters appear in print in slightly abbreviated form.

CHECKLIST OF CORREA'S EXTANT LETTERS

1820

March 4	to Conde de Palmela Philadelphia to—	Torre do Tombo
April 30	to Snr. Tomaz Antonio Vila Nova Portugal Philadelphia to Rio	Carvalho, p. 196
May 9	to Sir J. E. Smith [reproduced above]	HistSocPenna, Philadelphia
May 13	to M. DeLeuze Philadelphia to Paris	Museum of Natural History, Paris
June 9	to Snr. Tomaz Antonio Vila Nova Portugal Philadelphia to Rio	Carvalho, pp. 196–197
June 14	to Snr. Tomaz Antonio Vila Nova Portugal Philadelphia to Rio	Carvalho, p. 198
July 4	to R. A. Salisbury Philadelphia to [London?]	Linnean Society, London
October 22	to Snr. Tomaz Antonio Vila Nova Portugal Philadelphia to Rio	Carvalho, pp. 198–199

Afterword

Léon Bourdon

In the last days of the year 1815, an announcement was made at the royal court in Rio de Janeiro that Brazil had been raised "to the prerogatives and dignity of kingdom united to the Kingdoms of Portugal and the Algarve."[1] This measure, irrevocably abolishing the colonial regime in this part of the world, led to most felicitous consequences for political and economic relations between the United States and Brazil, as U.S. plenipotentiary minister Thomas Sumter emphasized at an audience with the Prince Regent, who was soon to become King John VI.[2] This new state of affairs was particularly welcome in the aftermath of the Treaties of Vienna and Ghent, which in re-establishing peace in America and Europe had opened favorable prospects for the recovery and development of international trade. Thus, Sumter felt justified in deploring the fact that diplomatic relations between Washington and Rio de Janeiro had "been left for more than five years on a footing of inequality."[3]

---

[1] *Carta de lei* of December 16, 1815, published in *Gazeta do Rio de Janeiro* on January 10, 1816, but known in Court circles since December 17.

[2] John VI succeeded his mother, Maria I, who, incapable since 1792 of undertaking the responsibilities of the throne, finally died on March 20, 1816.

[3] Thomas Sumter to James Monroe, December 29, 1815, Rio de Janeiro, NA, DS, Diplomatic Dispatches—Brazil, I-A, pp. 139-50.

The United States had been represented in Rio since 1810 by a high-level and zealous diplomat who took his mission seriously. Portugal and thus Brazil had since 1805 kept in Washington a mere general consul chargé d'affaires, José Rademaker, a man of precarious health and cantankerous disposition. Rademaker had no contact whatsoever with federal authorities, and his dispatches to Rio were so distressingly inane that no one bothered to answer them. The Prince Regent, when Thomas Sumter discreetly pointed out Rademaker's failings, replied, "Oh, that minister is good for nothing! I must send a wise and prudent man to your country."

The Prince Regent was undoubtedly thinking of José Corrêa da Serra. Corrêa da Serra had in 1812 left Paris, where he had felt himself exposed to harassment by the Napoleonic police, for the life of a private citizen in Philadelphia, where he rapidly became acquainted with the American scene. In January 1816, Corrêa da Serra was appointed to the Washington position.[4]

No other choice could have been more appropriate. Brazil had much to gain from commerce with the United States, which had the capacity to consume a large quantity of Brazil's sugar and cotton in its vast domestic market and which could export advanced technology to aid the emerging industries being established by Brazilian entrepreneurs. In the twenty years Corrêa da Serra had spent away from his native land in both private and official capacities, he had sent to Lisbon and Rio de Janeiro a steady stream of practical information gathered in England, France, and the United States, information that had been very well received. Furthermore, Corrêa da Serra's scholarly reputation would promote his nation's prestige. A member of the American Philosophical Society and the Academy of Natural Sciences, he was on the best of terms with the American political and cultural elite. His accomplishments were to earn him a prominent position among the diplomats recognized in Washington, which in turn enhanced his ability to serve Luso-Brazilian interests.

As the year 1816 began, no issues, major or minor, clouded relations between the Portuguese Crown and the government of the United States. American relations with other nations had not been as untroubled. The United States had been on the verge of a rupture with France in 1798-1799. Relations with England were still problematic, despite the conclusion of the War of 1812. In addition, from the time of the Louisiana Purchase in 1803, the United States had been led by its expanding designs on Florida to consider the possibility of open war

---

[4]MHN, MS. 2442, exact copy.

with Spain. With Portugal and Brazil, in contrast, the United States had maintained consistently peaceful relations, which nothing seemed to seriously disturb, not even the recent incident of the *General Armstrong*, the American privateer sunk in September 1814 by British forces in Azorean waters off Fayal. Thus, although Corrêa da Serra began drafting detailed reports on the situation in the United States as soon as his credentials were presented in Washington, the Foreign Affairs Department in Rio de Janeiro, which was mainly concerned with protocol, confined itself at first to sending him superbly calligraphed chancellery letters reporting the happy or unhappy events affecting the royal family, letters intended to be handed to President Madison in private audience. In Corrêa da Serra's own words, the Portuguese legation in Washington was considered by Rio de Janeiro to be a "mission of pure pomp."[5] However, things were soon to take a very different turn.

For several months, the insurgent government of Cartagena, of the "Congress of Mexico," and, most importantly, of the United Provinces of Rio de la Plata, had been issuing letters of marque to American adventurers. These individuals, most of whom sailed out of Baltimore, had taken advantage of the war in Europe to dominate the Atlantic trade. By the present time, however, they had been reduced to going after Spanish vessels, which they brought into American ports to be sold. This enterprise was in blatant contravention both of the conventions of international law and of the 1794 and 1798 American neutrality acts. When these offenders were sufficiently clumsy as to be intercepted, however, they were routinely acquitted by the district courts, which were swayed by the popular attitude of extreme hostility toward Spain.

At this juncture, Virginia district court judge St. George Tucker, who was hearing the case against the *Romp*, a privateering vessel sailing under the Buenos Aires flag, relayed to Corrêa da Serra the instructions given by shipowner Thomas Taylor to the ship's master, one Captain Fisk. Fisk had been instructed to pursue Portuguese ships in addition to Spanish, in the event that the Portuguese king took a hostile stance against the La Plata insurgents. Additional evidence indicated that several other privateers, including the *Independencia del Sur* and the *Montezuma*, had received similar instructions.

Although to the best of his knowledge no Portuguese ship had been attacked by these privateers, Corrêa da Serra thought it unnecessary to

---

[5]Corrêa da Serra to the Conde da Barca, May 31, 1817, Washington, TTL, NE, Portuguese Legation to the United States, Box 3, no. 83.

wait until the threat materialized before taking action. Therefore, in mid-December 1816, he addressed a note to Secretary of State James Monroe in which, after pointing out that "Mr. Taylor is an American Citizen, the ship *Romp* was an American ship, no doubt only fictitiously alienated since the captain continued the same and the bulk of the crew remained composed of American citizens," he protested the fact that such ships might assail the nationals and property of Portugal, a country at peace with the United States. Blaming the situation on "the insufficience of the existing laws and the many evasions they afford to guilty persons, particularly if assisted by chicanery," he suggested "the proposition to Congress of such provisions by law as will prevent such attempts for the future." To avoid the appearance of unduly interfering in the internal affairs of the United States, he submitted the note's text in advance to Monroe. Monroe, having promptly obtained Madison's approval of its contents, judged the note to be in accordance with American policy and declared his willingness to receive it formally. The note, dated December 20, 1816,[6] was sent to the State Department on December 22.

Corrêa da Serra, aware of the audacious appearance of such an unusual request, thought it advisable to justify it to the government in Rio de Janeiro. In a letter dated December 28 and addressed to the Marquis de Aguiar, the State Secretary for Foreign Affairs, he declared that if he had behaved in a quite different manner from that adopted by the ministers of France, England, and most notably Spain, all of whom had reason to complain of American privateers' depredations, it was because his diplomatic colleagues dealt with the American government as if the President were a European-style monarch, one capable of making authoritarian decisions on his own initiative. In actuality, under the Constitution the President had only "the executive power of the laws." The only course to pursue was the one he had followed: to suggest that in the interests of justice, Congress should amend or supplement the existing neutrality laws in order to give the President the power to intervene independently in cases of this sort.[7]

When he wrote the preceding words, Corrêa knew that he was following a proper course. A day earlier, on December 27, he had been informed by Monroe [8] that Madison had sent a message to Congress on

---

[6]Corrêa da Serra to James Monroe, December 20, 1816, Washington, NA, DS, Notes from the Portuguese Legation, I.

[7]Corrêa da Serra to the Marquis de Aguiar, December 28, 1816, Washington, TTL, NE, Portuguese Legation to the United States, Box 3, no. 72.

[8]James Monroe to Corrêa da Serra, December 27, 1816, Washington, NA, DQ, Notes to Foreign Legations, II, pp. 193-94.

December 26 "with a view of obtaining such an extension by law of the Executive Power as would be necessary to preserve the strict neutrality of the United States in the existing war between Spain and the Spanish colonies, and effectually to guard against the danger in regard to the vessels of the king of Portugal."[9] The bill presented to Congress, *An Act more effectually to preserve the neutral relations of the United States,* stipulated, among other provisions, that customs agents would be authorized and even encouraged to prohibit the entry into or departure from any United States port of any ship of which the nature of the cargo or the importance of the crew aroused suspicion that its true mission was to commit hostile acts against the subjects or property of any prince, state, colony, province, or people with whom the United States was at peace, this prohibition to remain in effect until such time as the President made a decision in the matter. This represented a remarkable innovation in that it introduced the concept of preventive measures left to the discretion of the Executive Branch.

In Corrêa da Serra's informal words, "this law didn't pass easily."[10] Debate on the bill began in the House of Representatives on January 14, 1817, and in the Senate on January 29. After many interventions and amendments and much reshuffling, the bill was passed on March 3, the day Congress went into recess. Several speakers questioned the constitutionality of the proposed increase in the executive branch's powers. The project was generally thought to have been initially proposed to the State Department by the minister of Spain, Luis de Onis, and most of its opponents were eager not only to manifest their sympathies for the cause of the Spanish colonies' independence, but also to protest against pressure exerted on the American government by a foreigner. Luis de Onis was the subject of a number of violent verbal assaults in the course of the debate.[11] Although Corrêa da Serra's role

---

[9]Message of James Madison to Congress, December 26, 1816, Washington, in *The Debates and Proceedings in the Congress of the United States,* 14th Congress, 2nd session, col. 40.

[10]Corrêa da Serra to the Marquis de Aguiar, April 3, 1817, TTL, NE, Portuguese Legation to the United States, Box 3. At this time, Corrêa da Serra was unaware that the Marquis de Aguiar had died on January 27, 1817, and that the State Secretariat for Foreign Affairs was provisionally occupied by João Paulo Bezerra.

[11]The transcript of the Congressional debate on the bill is included in *The Debates and Proceedings in the Congress of the United States,* 14th Congress, 2nd session, col. 477-78, 716-70. The text of the law is given in *The Public Statutes at large of the United States,* III, pp. 370-71.

in this matter was well known — his note of December 20 had been forwarded by Monroe to the House and Senate Foreign Affairs Committees, and he had, by his own account, discussed the matter with John Forsyth and James Barbour, the chairmen of the committees — it was at no time even alluded to. Several leading opponents of the new legislation even told Corrêa da Serra in private that they regretted that their vote on the issue could not reflect their high regard for the Portuguese nation. Such gestures indicate the extent of Corrêa da Serra's personal prestige in Washington's political circles.

With Congress in recess, Washington would soon be nearly deserted until the following fall, and Corrêa da Serra left the capital to spend the hot season in Philadelphia. It was there that he received on April 28 a letter from Norfolk regarding an Englishman, Charles Bowen, who had recently arrived from Barbados on the *Herald*. Bowen, a businessman in Recife, was spreading word that a successful republican revolution had taken place in that city, whence he had departed on March 13. He further claimed that he had been charged by the rebels to prepare the American government to receive the emissary whom they were about to send to the United States. The very next day Corrêa da Serra returned to Washington, arriving on May 1.[12]

Charles Bowen was received on May 2 by the new Secretary of State, Richard Rush, who had been appointed to replace James Monroe, recently inaugurated as President. Alarmed by rumors circulating about attempts to purchase arms and ammunition for the rebel forces, Corrêa da Serra on May 13 sent the State Department a note in which he stated that being "thoroughly convinced of the upright and dignified principles of the President and of the sound maxims on which the actual Government of the United States is proceeding," he refused to "harbour the least uneasiness about the line of conduct which they will follow in the threatened case of the arrival of any adventurer who may style himself accredited agent of the rebels of Pernambuco." Nevertheless, he went on to say, he felt unable to "entertain any degree of security about the conduct which the greedy and immoral part of the commercial citizens, particularly in New York and Baltimore, will pursue in the actual unfortunate circumstances," and he felt compelled to confess that "the lukewarm acts of some of the United States officers

---

[12]Corrêa da Serra to the Conde da Barca, May 31, 1817, Washington, TTL, NE, Portuguese Legation to the United States, Box 3, 83. Corrêa da Serra had also read the article published in the *Norfolk Daily Herald* of May 24, 1817, under the headline "Highly important! Revolution in Brazil!"

in the seaports in past occurrences of a like nature" did not give him "that full confidence in them that he could wish to have." He declared himself firmly convinced, however, that "if the President was pleased to have them put in mind of the vigilance he requires from them in order to answer his own feelings on this subject, such a step would avoid negligences on their part and continue uninterrupted the good harmony between Portugal and the United States."[13]

Although Monroe, to whom Rush immediately conveyed this note, was somewhat taken aback by it, Corrêa da Serra was invited to visit the State Department on May 15. Corrêa da Serra began with a complaint that two ships loaded with arms had recently been sent from Baltimore to Recife. To this Rush replied that neither the law of nations nor any U.S. legislation forbade this type of commerce. (In the language of the day, the term "the law of nations" was used to refer to international law in general, and also to a concept of international law as stemming from natural law.) On the subject of his note, Corrêa da Serra pointed out that it gave the American government an excellent opportunity to affirm its doctrine concerning rebellious movements affecting other nations. Rush dryly countered this point, saying that the doctrine in question, as was clearly illustrated by past American actions, was to refrain from intervening in any manner whatsoever in matters of this nature. Obviously disconcerted, Corrêa da Serra explained that "he spoke in his personal, not in his public capacity," and that "his remark grew out of the warm attachment which he felt and would ever feel to the United States." In spite of being assured by Rush, "by a manner the most respectful and conciliatory," that he was convinced that Corrêa da Serra had been "actuated by no other than a friendly spirit," the meeting came to a rather chilly end. Rush was irritated by the "advisory" tone assumed at times by Corrêa da Serra, while the latter was left deeply disappointed by the position adopted by Rush, one that he thought too evasive to be satisfactory.[14]

It was thus urgent to appeal directly to public opinion in order to discourage various unscrupulous merchants who, influenced by enthusiastic reports of events in Recife published from late April on in such newspapers as the *Baltimore Patriot* and the *Norfolk Herald Office,*[15] were only too inclined to support the cause of the Brazilian

---

[13]Corrêa da Serra to Richard Rush, May 13, 1817, Washington, NA, DS, Notes from the Portuguese Legation, I.

[14]Rush informed Monroe on June 14, 1817 of what had been said in this interview, LC, Monroe Papers, XXV.

[15]*Baltimore Patriot,* April 29 and 30, 1817, and *Norfolk Herald Office,* April 24, 1817.

"patriots." Corrêa da Serra wrote, or at least inspired, clarifications published by the *National Intelligencer* on May 12 and 16, 1817, stating that "the port of Pernambuco was strictly blockaded by a Portuguese squadron," and that "it was not thought the conspirators can succeed for any time in opposition to the royal authorities." In addition, he arranged to have the *National Intelligencer* insert in its May 19 issue an "Official Notification of the Legation of Portugal" reminding the public that "the only passports considered as legal for the admission of foreigners in the dominions of His Majesty the King of Portugal are those signed by the Ministers Plenipotentiary in the countries from which these foreigners come, and those not affording such legal documents shall be considered as vagabonds and expelled as such."

On that same day, May 19, Washingtonians learned through a story in the May 15 Boston *Daily Advertiser* that the emissary heralded by Bowen had arrived aboard the *Gipsy*. The party from Recife consisted of "his Excellency António Gonçalves da Cruz, minister from the new government of Pernambuco to the United States, and suite," the "suite" comprising a legation secretary and a private secretary. Corrêa da Serra, distressed by this information, addressed a new note to the State Department on May 20, stressing the criminal nature of rebellions like that taking place in Recife and the dangers that movements of this kind represented to all established governments. "What would have become of this United States," he pointedly asked, "if Shays' principles and revolt had prospered? What if the Western revolt had not been put down? Your great and good Washington shewed in that critical moment by his personal services how much he detested anarchy and treason under whatever veil it might appear."[16] But this example, intended to appeal to the hearts of all true Americans, failed to move Rush, whose apparently voluntary silence Corrêa da Serra found quite troubling.

Immediately on his arrival, António Gonçalves da Cruz, assisted by his legation secretary Domingos Malaquias de Aguiar Pires Ferreira, published in the May 17 *Boston Patriot*, under the headline "The Brazilian Republic," a long refutation of the reservations about the rebels' capacity for resistance that had been voiced in the May 12 *National Intelligencer*. "As to the permanent establishment of the

---

[16]Corrêa da Serra to Richard Rush, May 20, 1817, Washington, NA, DS, Notes from the Portuguese Legation, I. On Shays' Rebellion of 1786-1787 in Massachusetts see J. P. Warren, *The Confederation and the Shays Rebellion,* in *American Historical Review,* XI (1905-1906), pp. 42-67. On the Western Revolt of 1800-1802, which affected the Mississippi region, see W.F. McCaleb, *The Aaron Burr Conspiracy*, 1903.

republican government," the writer asserted, "there cannot be the least doubt."

Corrêa da Serra may have known about the *Boston Patriot* article as early as May 21. These efforts to cast doubt on the existence and efficacy of the Recife blockade and to disparage the naval power of the King of Portugal greatly distressed him. In addition, persistent rumors about the enormous sums of money that the rebels had at their disposal encouraged a number of American shipowners to be willing to trade with them, especially since marine insurers did not appear to be overly restrictive in this matter. So, without benefit of the Rio de Janeiro ministry's advice, and aware that he was once again transgressing normal diplomatic practice, Corrêa da Serra arranged to have inserted in the May 22 *National Intelligencer* a new "Official Notification of the Legation of Portugal" warning the public that "the port of Pernambuco and the adjacent coast are effectually blockaded by the ships of war of H.M.F. Majesty" and warning "American ships not to venture navigating to these parts because the law of nations relating to strict blockades will be rigorously enforced."

Annoyed by Corrêa da Serra's unusual initiative, Richard Rush sent him a dryly-worded note on May 24: "Having read a publication purporting to be from the Legation of Portugal whereby the port of Pernambuco and adjacent coast are declared to be effectually blockaded by the ships of war of His Most Faithful Majesty, I take the liberty to ask whether the publication alluded to has the sanction of your authority."[17] Corrêa da Serra answered this note the following day, May 25, in no less dry a tone: "I am superabundantly certified of the blockade of Pernambuco, and it is my strict duty, in sight of what is going on in some ports of the United States, to obviate what is clearly contrary to the interests of my Sovereign and may even prove ruinous to many citizens of the United States, by giving to this blockade the greatest possible notoriety."[18]

Richard Rush's long response of May 28, from the opening lines on, subjected Corrêa da Serra to a severe condemnation of his actions: "Settled and approved usage, founded upon reasons too familiar to be dwelt upon, required that whatever communication you had to make relative to the alleged blockade of Pernambuco and upon whatever foundation it rested, should have been made to this government and not promulgated without its knowledge through the medium of a

---

[17]Rush to Corrêa da Serra, May 24, 1817, Washington, NA, DS, Notes to Foreign Legations, II, pp. 228-29.

[18]Corrêa da Serra to Rush, May 25, 1817, Washington, NA, DS, Notes from the Portuguese Legation, I.

newspaper." Corrêa da Serra might have expected, after such censure, an injunction to repudiate the May 22 notice. However, to his great surprise and satisfaction, he detected a much modified tone in the closing lines: "As you communicate to this government the existence of the blockade in question, the information will naturally be respected as resting upon your own responsibility alone."[19]

The existence of the Pernambuco blockade, then, was not denied. In his May 31 dispatch to Rio de Janeiro, Corrêa da Serra, while congratulating himself for having "managed the enterprise in the best interests of His Majesty," expressed his conviction that the last sentence of Rush's note had been included at Monroe's insistence. "Rush," he added, "who is as Jacobin as the rebels, is furious at not having been able to force me to issue a retraction."[20] Sharing the Secretary of State's anger, the "pack of Jacobin gazettes" attacked Corrêa da Serra, "biting every day with their fangs." But as the government did not contradict the announcement of the blockade, the gazettes were reduced to "chewing on their prey without being able to swallow." Thus, "the results surpassed all expectations," and although the moderate *National Intelligencer* suggested on May 27 that "the notice of the blockade of the port of Recife is certainly premature," insurance carriers in Philadelphia and even Baltimore refused coverage to ships bound for the Pernambuco coast. This fact so impressed the level-headed merchants that they cancelled all shipments of arms and ammunition to the rebels.

Pleased with these results, Corrêa da Serra returned to Philadelphia on June 3 without even acknowledging the receipt of Rush's note. That same day Rush wrote to Monroe, "The Portuguese minister left town. I infer that all correspondence upon the subject of the blockade is at an end. Best so perhaps."[21] It was undoubtedly better that way. Fearing that Jefferson and Madison might have gotten a bad impression from this incident, Rush, with Monroe's full support, sent a long letter to Madison on June 14, and asked him to convey it to Jefferson. In it, he gave a detailed account of the notes exchanged with Corrêa da Serra on the subject of the blockade, deploring the fact that their relations had not been wholly based on mutual trust.[22] Jefferson's reaction to this

---

[19]Rush to Corrêa da Serra, May 28, 1817, Washington, NA, DS, Notes to Foreign Legations, II, pp. 229-31.

[20]Corrêa da Serra to the Conde da Barca, May 31, 1817, Washington, TTL, NE, Portuguese Legation to the United States, Box 3, no. 83.

[21]LC, Monroe Papers, XXIV.

[22]Rush to Madison, June 14, 1817, Washington, LC, Monroe Papers, XXV.

letter is not known, if in fact it was transmitted to him. Madison, despite the fact that in his answer of June 27 he expressed his basic approval of Rush's conduct in the matter, did not disguise his opinion "that Mr. Correa may feel some conflict in the present position between his two characters of philanthropist and plenipotentiary and that he may infer some indulgence towards the latter from a respect to the former: conciliation can in no case be more properly intermingled."[23] Rush, then, when on June 18 he sent Sumter the dossier on the affair, was able to write that "alth' Mr. Correa's conduct was deemed irregular and injustifiable, none other than harmonious intercourse continues to exist between the government and himself."[24]

António Gonçalves da Cruz, meanwhile, took great pains to present himself in a favorable light. In response to an article in the May 28 *Boston Daily Advertiser* insinuating that "the new minister from Recife will meet a cold reception at Washington," he arranged to have inserted in the May 20 *Boston Patriot* an article overflowing with his own praise and with allusions to the advantages which would accrue to American commerce from Pernambuco's independence, which was presented as a forerunner of the impending emancipation of the rest of the Americas "to the remotest regions of Patagonia." The May 28 *Essex Register* noted that the "venerable patriarch" John Adams had received Gonçalves da Cruz in his Quincy retreat "with the same spirit which distinguished his patriotic virtue in the great cause of the American revolution." He was aided in this campaign by a Frenchman by the name of De Grand, who "guided all his movements." [25] Despite these efforts, Gonçalves da Cruz never succeeded in arranging to be received by Monroe. Quite to the contrary, Monroe instructed his main advisor for South American affairs, Caesar Augustus Rodney, to inform Gonçalves da Cruz that, under the existing circumstances, the United States would more effectively serve the cause of the Brazilian provinces' independence by remaining neutral.[26] The United States

---

[23]Madison to Rush, June 27, 1817, Montpelier, *Madison Writings,* VIII, pp. 394-96.

[24]Rush to Sumter, July 18, 1817, NA, DS, Diplomatic instructions all countries, VIII, pp. 142-43.

[25]On Pierre Paul François de Grand, "a French businessman" established for some time in Boston, "a very active, obliging merchant who knows how to bestir himself," see B.G. Dupont, *Life of Eleuthère Irénée Dupont,* X, pp. 78-79, 88-89.

[26]This interview took place in Philadelphia on June 5, 1817, and Rodney reported it to Monroe in a letter dated June 6, LC, Monroe Papers, XXV.

would be able then, without any interference by England, to supply them with whatever goods they needed with the exception of arms, which were refused to all belligerent parties. It was thus not on a strictly official level that on June 18, one day after an audience the private nature of which was that same day proclaimed in the *National Intelligencer*, António Gonçalves da Cruz had sent to Rush some documents concerning the events at Recife along with "some brief remarks on the favorable disposition displayed by the various regions of Brazil towards the independence of the country."[27] These propaganda pieces, however, were undermined by the alarming news then reaching Washington of the growing internal resistance to the rebellion and, more importantly, the external threat posed by the imminent dispatching of two corps of troops from Rio de Janeiro and Bahia.[28] In addition, as early as June 23, the very radical *Baltimore Patriot* reported that, although "on his visit to the seat of government M. da Cruz was received by the heads of departments in a manner grateful to his feelings, this gentlemen does not expect to be recognized as minister under the existing circumstances of his country."

By this date, the rebels had been forced out of Recife more than a month earlier, although this information did not reach Washington until mid-July 1817.[29] Trumpeting violent accusations against "the royal beast of Rio de Janeiro, the devouring monster of the Brazils, the Portuguese Sardanapalus" and against the Conde dos Arcos, the "satrap, vizier or padishah of Bahia," while expressing pity for "the four millions of human beings who are groaning under the arbitrary power of the degenerate house of Braganza,"[30] the radical gazettes obstinately contested, using the worst sophistries, all testimony about the disaster at Recife.[31] Abandoning the diplomatic team with which he had until then surrounded himself,[32] António Gonçalves da Cruz

---

[27] These texts are included in the *Documents Históricos* published by the Divisão de Obras Raras of the Biblioteca Nacional de Rio de Janeiro, CIX — 1817 Revolution, pp. 238-66.

[28] *Boston Daily Advertiser,* June 7, 1817; *Essex Register,* June 9; *Baltimore Patriot* and *National Intelligencer,* June 13.

[29] The *National Intelligencer* of July 15, 1817, published a letter from Pernambuco, dated May 25, announcing that "on the 20th at night the Patriot army evacuated the Town."

[30] *Aurora,* August 12, 1817.

[31] *Essex Register,* July 23 and August 6 and 13, 1817; *Aurora,* August 2, 1817.

[32] Corrêa da Serra to the Conde da Barca, July 25 and August 30, 1817, Philadelphia, TTL, NE, Portuguese Legation to the United States, Box 3, nos. 88 and 90.

assembled a handful of refugees from Pernambuco and continued the struggle, involving himself with adventurers of all kinds — radical Americans, Bonapartist French émigrés, and, most importantly, "insurgents" from Bolivia, Venezuela, New Grenada, and La Plata[33] — "all of them debris" as Corrêa da Serra wrote, "of rebellions in all corners of the world, and who, united by the secret ties of an infernal conspiracy, attempt to stir up agitation everywhere, beginning with Brazil."[34]

"Knowing this country," he continued, "I did not want to waste my time composing protest notes which would soon vanish like smoke, and I thus thought it more useful to the service of the King to concentrate on persons who might have the capacity, and more importantly the inclination, to help me" — the "reasonable ones," in Corrêa da Serra's own words, as opposed to the "politicians" — "gathering them at several dinner parties which continued as animated conversations well into the night." These contacts undoubtedly increased after James Monroe decided in early January 1818, having realized the inadequacies of the law passed on March 3, 1817 to suppress the actions of ships armed in Baltimore under the insurgent flag, to propose to Congress legislation which would take the place of all the neutrality laws promulgated in the previous twenty years. "This elevated me," Corrêa da Serra remarked, "to the honour of being insulted by the impudent gazettes of the Jacobin party."[35]

The editor of the *Aurora*, the vitriolic pamphleteer William Duane, had in fact attacked Corrêa da Serra in a series entitled "Features of Politics" in the January 15, 16, and 17, 1818, issues of his journal.[36] Following what he presented as a "translation as carefully executed as possible" of Corrêa da Serra's December 20, 1816 note on the necessity of amending the American laws of neutrality, Duane criticized the

---

[33]Corrêa da Serra to Luís do Rêgo Barreto, December 15, 1817, BNR, MS I-3, 14, 8.

[34]Corrêa da Serra to João Paulo Bezerra, March 5, 1818, Washington, TTL, NE, Portuguese Legation to the United States, Box 3, no. 105.

[35]Corrêa da Serra to João Paulo Bezerra, February 5, 1818, Washington, TTL, NE, Portuguese Legation to the United States, Box 3, no. 104.

[36]On this individual, as much feared as he was attacked, see Allen Calling Clark, "William Duane (1760-1835)," in *Records of the Columbia Historical Society,* XX (1906), pp. 14-62. John Quincy Adams states, in his *Memoirs,* IV, pp. 505-6, that the *Aurora* was "the most slanderous newspaper in the United States."

"Audacity" with which Corrêa da Serra had attempted to "dictate new laws" to the government of the United States. "A man like the Abbé Correa," he concluded, "may be a most respectable private friend, but when he comes on the diplomatic tapis and presents such a lecture upon government to the chief magistrate of a free people, respect instantly ceases, and the association of inquisitor and politician immediately call upon our apprehensions along with our indignation." Countering this abusive tirade with an article published under the byline "North-American," which undoubtedly owed much to Corrêa da Serra himself,[37] the January 28, 1818 issue of the *Democratic Press* vigorously protested the "torrents of ribaldry spouted forth" by William Duane. The article's author noted that the alleged "translation" of Corrêa da Serra's note had been made not from the original text itself, which had been written in English, but rather from a translation into French appearing in the Paris *Moniteur* of July 19, 1817.[38] The *Aurora*'s translation had been "carefully executed" only "in regard to the purpose for which it was published." Eight well-chosen examples from Duane's article served to demonstrate that "as a translation, it wore an equivocal character of bad faith." Under the circumstances, it was unnecessary to "proceed farther in the vindication of the minister of Portugal, as in fact he needs none for those who can seize the spirit of his letter and who are versed in the laws and usages of nations." However, on February 5, under the headline "Something new in Diplomacy," the *Baltimore Patriot* again attacked "that philosopher, that modern Socrates, to wit the mock representative of that pious and humane king John of Portugal," and, not shrinking from incitements to violence, invited the citizens of Baltimore to demonstrate, should he venture through their city, just how they appreciated the honor of his presence among them.

In Washington, by contrast, Corrêa da Serra was on very good

---

[37]The *Baltimore Patriot* of March 16, 1818 made reference to the "the priestly article which the Abbé Correa da Serra fulminated against the editor of the *Aurora* in the *Democratic Press* of the 28th January ultimo."

[38]In fact, Duane had made his re-translation not from the French translation of the *Moniteur,* but from the Portuguese translation of the *Gazeta do Rio de Janeiro,* or even possibly from the Spanish translation of the *Gazeta de Madrid,* where the President's "wisdom" in the English original is translated as "prudencia," a word that Duane improperly renders as "prudence," as "A Portuguese Republican" notes in his April 11, 1818 article in the *Baltimore Patriot* entitled "The Abbé Corrêa da Serra."

terms with John Quincy Adams, who had replaced Richard Rush at the State Department in September 1817. Adams did not hesitate to drop in on Corrêa da Serra when passing by his house, and indicated that he would rather host the ambassador at home "as a familiar acquaintance to talk literature and philosophy, as a domestic inmate to gossip over a cup of tea"[39] than meet him at the office. This sustained cordiality was a determining factor in Corrêa da Serra's decision to forward to the State Department on March 8, 1818, a note which he had delayed sending for the previous few months for fear of overstepping his bounds.[40] The note referred to the capture on the open Atlantic Ocean in December 1816 and March 1817 of three Portuguese vessels by privateers from Baltimore, one of which had been christened, significantly, the *Buenos Ayres Patriot.* In the note, Corrêa da Serra stated that "the perfect amity which H. M. the King of Portugal entertained to the United States propensed Him that this Government would be willing to give satisfaction and indemnisation for this injury done to His subjects and insult offered to His flag by those unworthy american citizens." [41] Adams, however, rejected the claim in his response of March 14, on the grounds that "the government of the United States having used all the means in its power to prevent the fitting out and arming of vessels in their ports to cruise any nation with whom they are at peace, cannot consider itself bound to indemnify individual foreigners for losses by captures on which the United States have neither control nor jurisdiction." Adams also attempted, in turn, to raise from the Azorean sea floor the ghost of the *General Armstrong,* "upon which the minister of the United States at Rio de Janeiro has been long and hitherto without success claiming satisfaction to the United States and indemnity to their citizens for injuries and losses sustained by them within the territorial jurisdiction of the Portuguese government."[42]

---

[39]John Quincy Adams, *Memoirs,* November 23, 1817 and April 8, 1819, IV, pp. 23, 326.

[40]Corrêa da Serra to João Paulo Bezerra, March 26, 1818, Norfolk, TTL, NE, Portuguese Legation to the United States, Box 3, no. 106.

[41]Corrêa da Serra to John Quincy Adams, March 8, 1818, Washington, NA, DS, Notes from the Portuguese Legation, I. As the "List of the Portuguese prizes" which serves as an appendix to this note makes clear, these ships were the *Senhor do Alívio,* the *Marquês de Pombal,* and the *São João Protector,* all captured near the Azores while en route from Brazil to Portugal.

[42]John Quincy Adams to Corrêa da Serra, March 14, 1818, Washington, NA, DS, Notes to Foreign Legations, II, p. 315.

Although he waited a long week before icily acknowledging receipt of the State Department note, accompanying his acknowledgment with a justification of the Portuguese authorities' attitude in the *General Armstrong* affair,[43] Corrêa da Serra had almost certainly received the note the day it was sent.[44] The State Department's brusque dismissal of his claim, coming after John Quincy Adams had in a private interview led him to expect "as favorable and conciliatory an answer as he should be able to give,"[45] acted on Corrêa da Serra's touchy sensibility, already irritated by "the hurt it receives from the sudden changes of temperature" of the Pennsylvania spring,[46] to drive him "almost into a fit of that melancholy madness"[47] to which he felt himself more and more susceptible as the years passed. He abruptly left Washington for Baltimore on March 15.[48] From there, he took his first-ever voyage on a steamboat — as he put it, "an expeditious and sheltered means of conveying me two degrees more to the south to encounter a warmer climate"[49] — to Norfolk, Virginia, where he put himself under the care

---

[43]Corrêa da Serra to John Quincy Adams, March 23, 1818, Norfolk, NA, DS, Notes from the Portuguese Legation, I.

[44]It was undoubtedly intentional that, in the abovementioned note of March 23, Corrêa da Serra was vague in his statement that John Quincy Adams's March 14 note had "reached (his) hands a few days ago."

[45]John Quincy Adams, *Memoirs,* March 6, 1818, IV, p. 61.

[46]Corrêa da Serra to John Quincy Adams, March 18, 1818, Baltimore, NA, DS, Notes from the Portuguese Legation, I.

[47]In his *Memoirs,* April 8, 1819, IV, p. 326, John Quincy Adams alludes to the crisis which had affected Corrêa da Serra "last spring."

[48]The date "the Sunday the 15th ultimo" is mentioned in a venomous article contained in the March 16, 1818 issue of the *Baltimore Patriot* which reports that "the abbé Correa da Serra passed through Baltimore with great rapidity and precaution, dreading the friendly reciprocal civilities of all those persons who he styled pirates in his official note of the 20th December, 1816." This article triggered the disapproval of the *Aurora* itself, in its issue of March 17, 1818. It should be noted that, contrary to what the *Baltimore Patriot* reporter seemed to think, Corrêa da Serra was not returning to Philadelphia, but had, rather, just embarked for Norfolk.

[49]Corrêa da Serra to John Quincy Adams, March 18, 1818, Baltimore, NA, DS, Notes from the Portuguese Legation, I.

of João Francisco de Oliveira Fernandes,[50] an émigré Portuguese physician and friend who had treated him in earlier episodes of this sort. His departure from Washington was also, and perhaps primarily, motivated by a fear of being personally attacked, as Luis de Onis had been, during the debate on proposed neutrality legislation scheduled to begin in the House of Representatives on March 18. This fear proved unfounded. Norfolk was close enough to Washington to receive echoes of the flattering references to Corrêa da Serra made by several speakers on the first day of the debate. Most notably, John Edward Smith and John Forsyth called attention to the fact that the "remonstrance" contained in Corrêa da Serra's note of December 20, 1816, "a garbled representation of which had been published," had been in fact "couched in respectful terms, such as appeared proper and consistent with a correct view of his duties as a foreign minister." Even the Whiggish Henry Clay made a point of praising Corrêa da Serra as "a man whose country could not have shown a greater respect for the United States than by deputing him as its representative to this Government."[51]

Despite such enthusiastic expressions of support, Corrêa da Serra was quick to react,[52] albeit briefly, to a provoking article in the April 11 *Baltimore Patriot*, in which a "Portuguese republican," doubtless António Gonçalves da Cruz, declared that "the true philosophers are sorry that his picture in the Philadelphia Museum is not placed in the department of the wild beasts as being the most worthy of the portraits

---

[50]On João Francisco de Oliveira Fernandes, the former physician of the royal palace in Lisbon, who, after being condemned in 1803 for insubordination to power as a result of his attempted kidnapping of Dona Eugénia Maria, the illegitimate daughter of the prince regent, later King John VI, had established himself in Norfolk, where he practised his calling with great success, see A. Balbi, *Essai Statistique sur le Royaume de Portugal*, II, p. XIX, and Ângelo Ferreira, *Dom João VI, Príncipe e Rei - A Bastarda*, pass.

[51]*Debates and Proceedings in the Congress of the United States,* 15th Congress, 1st session, March 18, 1818, Col. 1409, 1414, 1421.

[52]In a letter to the Conde de Palmela, of which only an undated transcription included in a copy of a letter to Villanova Portugal, also undated, is available, TTL, NE, Portuguese Delegation in the United States, Box 3, Corrêa da Serra asks that he be relieved of his post in order to live "o pouco que (lhe) resta em algum socego livre da contínua mosquitada deste partido jacobino." The context seems to indicate that these letters were written in mid-April, 1818. This request was not pursued any further: cf. Corrêa da Serra to Vilanova Portugal, February 18, 1819, Washington, in *Brasil Histórico*, no. 17, May 1, 1864.

of tyrants, their agents and executioners." Feeling progressively strengthened by Dr. Fernandes's advice to "drink daily some wine, eat meat and half the old ration of vegetables,"[53] he returned to Washington as soon as the new neutrality act was passed on April 20.[54] John Quincy Adams found him "in high spirits and entirely released from his terrors and ominous conjectures."[55] On May 6, Corrêa da Serra went back to Philadelphia.[56]

All political activity being suspended because of Congress's recess, as always at that time of year, Corrêa da Serra devoted most of his efforts to penetrating the mysteries of the secret meetings of the Pernambuco veterans,[57] which were steadily increasing in number.[58] His investigation was feasible thanks to information provided by Domingos Malaquias and one Rousado, whom he had with minimal effort brought back into the fold. More importantly, he undertook to oppose the increasing privateering — actually piracy — which, with the support of the Pernambuco veterans, was striking increasingly damaging blows to Portuguese commerce in the Atlantic trade routes. At the outset, most privateers armed in Baltimore had been provided with letters of marque by Juan Martin Pueyrredón, "Supreme Director of the Provinces of La Plata."[59] Pueyrredón had since that time lost all the prestige he had enjoyed in the eyes of both the "rabble of the

---

[53]Corrêa da Serra to Francis Gilmer, April 39, 1818, Washington, cited in R. Beale Davis, *op. cit.*.

[54]Corrêa da Serra to John Quincy Adams, April 24, 1818, Washington, NA, DS, Notes from the Portuguese Delegation, I.

[55]John Quincy, Adams, *Memoirs,* May 3, 1818, IV, p. 86.

[56]Corrêa da Serra to Vilanova Portugal, May 5, 1818, Washington, TTL, NE, Portuguese Delegation in the United States, box 3, 108.

[57]Domingos Malaquias had come to live at the lodgings of Corrêa da Serra "que o incumbira dos seus arranjos domésticos." As to Rousado, originally from Recife, one of the few Portuguese established in the United States who had initially supported to the rebellion, it was at his house that António Gonçalves da Cruz had lived. The liaison was thus established. Cf. *Documents Historicos, CVIII*— "Revolução de 1817," p. 131, and BNR, MS I-3, 33.

[58]Corrêa da Serra to Vilanova Fernandes, July 13, 1818, Philadelphia, TTL, NE, Portuguese Delegation in the United States, Box 3, no. 110. "Os demónios de Pernambuco que aqui estão receberam reclutas..."

[59]Cf. J.C. Rappo de la Reta, *Historia de Juan Martin Pueyrredón,* Buenos Aires,1949.

disorganizing party" and those in high places.[60] His reputation's decline benefited his rival, José Artigas, "Commander of the Eastern Forces,"[61] who, after Montevideo was taken by the Rio de Janeiro forces in January 1817, had saved the insurgents' honor by sustaining the Uruguayan campaign with a heroic handful of supporters ready to make any sacrifice. Most of the so-called "privateers" decided, therefore, to procure their letters of marque from Artigas. Instead of only occasionally and half-heartedly attacking Portuguese vessels, they began chasing them systematically. The growing scarcity of Spanish vessels in the Atlantic further encouraged this enterprise. The magnitude of this increased activity is indicted by the fact that thirty or so of these privateers,[62] armed with roughly three hundred cannons and manned by over 2,000 men — a "fleet comparable to that of the Barbary pirates" — managed to capture approximately one hundred merchant vessels sailing under the Portuguese flag.[63]

Corrêa da Serra's main occupation was, then, as Vilanova Portugal suggested in a letter dated April 10, 1818[64] which reached Washington

---

[60]Corrêa da Serra to Vilanova Portugal, June 1, 1818, Philadelphia, TTL, NE, Portuguese Delegation in the United States, box 3, 109.

[61]Cf. Facundo A. Arce, *Artigas, heraldo del Federalismo rioplatense, Paraná, 1950.*

[62]The number of these "privateers" is apparently higher, but this is due to their changing names from one expedition to another, or even in the course of a single campaign. See the "List of Patriot privateers fitted out in the United States, corrected to September 1818," published in *An Appeal to the Government and Congress of the United States,* pp. 83-84, and the "Lista autentica dos navios corsários incluindo só aquelles de que há certeza absoluta" appended to Corrêa da Serra's dispatch to Vilanova Portugal, December 3, 1818, Washington, TTL NE, Portuguese Delegation in the United States, box 3, 115. The list given by Ch. C. Griffin, in his article Privateering from Baltimore, in *Maryland Historical Magazine,* XXV (1940), pp. 8-9, is, with only twenty-one names, quite incomplete.

[63]The *Irresistible* was the leader in number of Portuguese ships captured, with twenty-nine. The majority of the other privateers captured at least three, if not four, each. In the list of captures for the *Fortuna,* there are three ships whose cargoes attained the value, quite exceptional, of $750,000.

[64]TTL, NE, Secretariat of State, Packet 90.

at the end of August,[65] to do everything in his power to arrange not only the punishment of the privateers but also the restoration of the captured ships and their cargoes to their rightful owners on reaching American ports. This, however, could only be achieved by appealing to the district courts. Since Corrêa da Serra refused to involve himself with the "repugnant chicanery" of the privateers' treatment at the district court level, he entrusted this pursuit to the general consul, and, through him, to the vice-consuls whose areas of jurisdiction included the ports in question. The popularity of the privateers operating under Artigas's authorization was so great, however, that the radical press glorified their piracies as "highly meritorious and outstandingly brilliant acts." Despite the competence and authority of such attorneys as David Hoffmann and Thomas Cooper, the first lawsuits, the most notorious of which included the *Globo* captured by the *Irresistible* (tried at Charleston) and the *Monte Alegre* and the *Dom João Sexto* captured by the *Fortuna* (tried at Baltimore), were decided in favor of the captors.[66] It was therefore without much confidence, and only "in compliance with formal orders" from Rio de Janeiro,[67] that Corrêa da Serra presented to John Quincy Adams a complaint against the *Irresistible*, which had on several occasions committed depradations off the coast of Brazil.[68]

Attempting to discover the reasons for these legal setbacks, Corrêa da Serra concluded that the problem lay not so much in local pressure as in the inadequacies of the "somnolent and lame" neutrality law enacted in 1818,[69] which left loopholes in enforcement. In supporting the

----

[65]Corrêa da Serra to Vilanova Portugal, September 16, 1818, Philadelphia, TTL, NE, Portuguese Legation to the United States, Box 3, no. 112.

[66]On the *Globo* affair, see the *Charleston Gazette,* issues of September 10 and November 25, 1818, and *An Appeal . . . ,* p. 170. On the incident of the *Dom João Sexto* or, rather, of that Portuguese ship that Corrêa da Serra thought justified in identifying as such, see *Niles' Weekly Register* of December 19, 1818. On the *Monte Alegre* affair, see the "libel," or complaint, of the consul José Joaquim Vasques, September 18, 1818, NA, Admiralty Records, District Court of Baltimore.

[67]Vilanova Portugal to Corrêa da Serra, August 13, 1818, Rio de Janeiro, TTL, NE, Secretariat of State, Packet 90.

[68]Corrêa da Serra to John Quincy Adams, December 11, 1818, Washington, NA, DS, Notes from the Portuguese Legation, I.

[69]The text of the 1818 neutrality act is included in the *Public Statutes at Large of the United States of America,* III, p. 144, ch. 88.

passage of the new law, the "Jacobin rabble" had "nibbled away" the substance of the 1817 law. Corrêa da Serra considered the earlier law — "his law," as he self-aggrandizingly called it — more effective.[70] Although emphasizing the fact that the earlier law, which had been voted in for a two-year duration, was still in force,[71] Adams let him know that it had for all practical purposes been abrogated and replaced by the 1818 law.[72]

The only remaining line of approach was to attack the very root of the evil. Corrêa da Serra, having learned that the Count of Palmela had in November 1818 recommended to the plenipotentiary envoys at the Congress of Aix-la-Chapelle that they outlaw Artigas's privateers on the grounds that Artigas lacked jurisdiction over any port where he might arm them or receive their booty, wrote a long memorandum dated March 17, 1819 in support of this position, personally conveying it to Adams. In it, he observed "solemnly, and officially too if necessary, that Artigas and his followers have been expelled far from the countries that could afford them the least means and power of navigating and consequently have no right to fight by sea."[73] Adams perused this document in a rather tight-lipped manner; afterwards, he discreetly advised Corrêa da Serra not to press this matter further. The American government, he said, had no choice but to refuse a call to deprive Artigas of his rights as a belligerant party, and thus could not consider it illegal for ships to sail under his authority.[74]

Several signs, however, indicated that a change in attitude was imminent. Heretofore, only the radical press had covered the arrival in American ports and sale of captured ships, treating it as a normal occurrence or even a cause for celebration. Now the moderate press was

---

[70]Corrêa da Serra to Vilanova Portugal, December 3, 1818, Washington, TTL, ME, Portuguese Legation to the United States, Box 3, no. 115.

[71]Corrêa da Serra to John Quincy Adams, February 4, 1819, Washington, NA, DS, Notes from the Portuguese Legation, I.

[72]John Quincy Adams to Corrêa da Serra, February 8, 1819, Washington, NA, DS, Notes from the Portuguese Legation, II, p. 352.

[73]Corrêa da Serra to John Quincy Adams, March 17, 1819, Washington, NA, DS, Notes from the Portuguese Legation, I.

[74]Corrêa da Serra to Vilanova Portugal, March 23, 1819, Washington, TTL, NE, Portuguese Legation to the United States, Box 3, no. 129.

also covering the story, but with indignation.[75] Local authorities were no longer refusing to arrest and prosecute the privateering captains who had plied their trade most blatantly,[76] and several district courts were less grudgingly restoring the captured vessels and cargoes to their original owners.[77] However, these encouraging signs were soon negated by the legal maneuvers of expert attorneys acting for the privateers. In April 1819, for example, a court overturned sentences it had previously handed down.[78] Thanks to "chicanery, intrigues, and cabals," the privateers were merely given insignificant fines, or simply released, as

---

[75]See, among many other sources, the *National Intelligencer* of February 23, 1819, and, most importantly, *Niles' Weekly Register* of April 17, 1819, which included a long article entitled "Privateering and Piracy."

[76]Such was the fate of Ford, captain of the *General Artigas,* of Cathel, captain of the *Republican,* and of Clark, captain of the *Fortuna,* as well as of the colorful José Almeida, the Azorean captain of the *Luisa,* who had placed himself at the service of Artigas.

[77]Thus were the *Dom João Sexto,* the *Monte Alegre,* and the *Sociedade Felix* restored to their owners. See Corrêa da Serra to Vilanova Portugal, March 29, 1819, Washington, in *Brasil Historico,* no. 21, May 29, 1864.

[78]This was the case with the *Monte Alegre,* as John Quincy Adams "found out through the newspapers," as he put it to in a letter to Maryland district attorney Elias Glenn, April 12, 1819, Washington, NA, DS, Domestic Letters, XVII, no. 283: "From the public newspapers it is known that the district court, after having decreed the restoration of the *Monte Alegre* to the Portuguese owners, rescinded that decree, and that the cause now remains open, it is not distinctly understood for what object. . . ." This affair would be debated for a long time: see the "Relatorio do aprezamento e estado de reclamação do navio denominado *Monte Alegre,"* appended to a letter from Palmela to Corrêa da Serra, October 17, 1820, Lisbon, TTL, NE, Complaints, Packet 93, and the "Relatório dos acontecimentos do navio português *Monte Alegre,"* appended to a letter from Silvestre Pinheiro Ferreira to José Amado Gebou, November 14th 1821, TTL, NE, Secretariat of State, Packet 90.

was the infamous John Daniels, captain of the *Irresistible*, in May 1819.[79]

Determined to take action, Corrêa da Serra began in early June 1819 to work out a surruptitious plan which, in his eyes, was "perhaps the only one which would ensure peace." He expounded the main elements of this plan in a dispatch sent on June 25 to Vilanova Portugal: "Just before Congress convenes, a small book that I am now secretly writing will come out, detailing all the iniquities which have so assiduously resisted exposure until now, in addition to the unfavorable consequences to Americans that all of this will bring about, the latter aspect being for them the most important consideration. It will be secretly printed in a place far from where I am, and will be given a wide distribution at that time, so much so that this government will feel called to take the lead in the struggle against the privateers, or be vilified instead by the opposing parties, something that doesn't quite fit their desires."[80]

This anonymous hundred-page pamphlet was entitled *An Appeal to the Government and Congress of the United States against the depredations committed by American privateers on the commerce of nations at peace with us,* "by an American Citizen," printed "for the Booksellers," New York, 1819. It was not written as a polemic pamphlet, but rather as a legal work. Throughout its eight chapters — in the writing of which Corrêa da Serra (for he was undoubtedly the author[81]) had help from a "University professor," very likely his friend

---

[79]Corrêa da Serra to Vilanova Portugal, June 25, 1819, Washington, TTL, NE, Portuguese Legation to the United States, Box 3, no. 131. John Daniels was acquitted in May 1819 because the indictment, "clumsily" written by district attorney Elias Glenn, was based on the 1817 law which, being valid for only two years, had in any case become inoperative by March 3, 1819. See the "Excerpt from a Washington paper of May 29, 1819, relating the indictments of Baltimore," in *An Appeal to the Government and Congress of the United States,* p. 85.

[80]TTL, NE, Portuguese Legation to the United States, Box 3, no. 131.

[81]That Corrêa da Serra is behind the signature "American Citizen" is established by the fact that, to his dispatch to Vilanova Portugal, December 9, 1819, New York, TTL, NE, Portuguese Legation to the United States, Box 3, no. 134, he appended the Portuguese translation of Chapter Eight of *An Appeal . . . ,* pp. 66-71, the distribution of which had only recently begun.

Thomas Cooper[82] — there are references to statements by "the wisest citizens of the Union on the relations of their country with nations at war," to the interpretation of international law concerning the obligations of a neutral state, to the various dispositions of English and French laws on privateering and piracy, and, finally, to the omissions in the drafting and pusillanimity in the enforcement of the American laws designed to prevent the illegal arming and criminal depredations of pirates. The part of the text Corrêa da Serra considered the most convincing, at least to the public at large, was an appendix of twenty or so pages of small print which consisted of judiciously selected excerpts from the American press of all shades of the political spectrum, reporting an impressive series of attacks made with near impunity in the previous two years against the subjects and property not only of neutral powers, but also of friendly ones, and in some cases even of American citizens, by American ships armed in America under an insurgent flag. At the end of this enlightening enumeration, one could not but hope, as Franklin had, "not to see a new Barbary prosper along the coastlines of the United States."

The text of this *Appeal* was circulated widely in the first days of December 1819 in those sectors of public opinion where it was likely to find adherents.[83] Even before then, Corrêa da Serra had informed John Quincy Adams in a long note dated November 23, 1819, and drafted in intentionally solemn terms,[84] of his intention to leave the United States. Given the impunity with which "brigandages" were being committed against Portuguese interests by privateers armed in the United States, "a wide extended and powerful tribe of infidels worse still than those of North Africa," and considering that "the Executive having honorably

---

[82]Thomas Cooper (1759-1839), born in England, professor of chemistry and mineralogy at the University of Pennsylvania (which explains in part his intimacy with Corrêa da Serra), was well-versed in judicial matters, which enabled him to occupy a seat as a district court judge in that state. As mentioned above, Corrêa da Serra had already made use of his counsel at the time of the *Monte Alegre* lawsuit. See also Dumans Malone, *The Public Life of Thomas Cooper,* Columbia, 1961.

[83]In a dispatch to Vilanova Portugal, March 31, 1820, Philadelphia, TTL, NE, Portuguese Legation to the United States, Box 3, no. 151, Corrêa da Serra congratulates himself on the fact that "este livro tem feito muito serviço e deixa a perfídia dos que governçao agora muito ao descoberto até no seu público..."

[84]Corrêa da Serra to John Quincy Adams, November 23, 1819, Philadelphia, NA, DS, Notes from the Portuguese Legation, I.

exerted the powers with which the Constitution invests him, the efforts of a Portuguese minister on this subject — the only of importance at present between the two nations — are of little profit.'' He had therefore decided "to profit of the first proper occasion that may offer to pay a visit to the Brazils.''

Three weeks before the start of the new Congressional session, which was scheduled to open on December 6, 1819,[85] and immediately before he was to "join battle,'' as he then put it, Corrêa da Serra was to abandon his post! Was he relapsing into one of those fits of melancholy that had so often felled him in the past?[86] On the contrary, he was in full control of his capacities, and had extensively deliberated when he made this decision, as he made clear in the dispatch sent to Vilanova Portugal on December 9, 1819, from New York: "As the time for the Congressional session was drawing near and since I had constantly alluded to my imminent return to Brazil, I thought that I ought to use my trip in the service of the King. I took my leave from my Washington house, and I know that the news of that has spread. My presence hinders the efforts pursued there by those willing to work for us,[87] and my absence serves them. . . . Giving the impression that I am far away, sullenly preparing for my journey,[88] strengthens whatever they will do.''

Clearly accustomed to Corrêa da Serra's abrupt changes of mood, of which he has left an eloquent description,[89] Adams did not answer the note of November 23. At least there is no further reference to this matter in his *Memoirs.* It is not inconceivable — and Corrêa da Serra

---

[85]See also *Journal of the House of Representatives of the United States,* 16th Congress, 1st Session, p. 7.

[86]Such was the most widely accepted interpretation of Corrêa da Serra's gesture, as William Short expressed in a letter to Jefferson on December 1, 1819, cited in R. Beale Davis, *The Abbé Correa, op. cit.*

[87]As he stated to Vilanova Portugal in a dispatch dated September 6, 1820, Wilmington, TTL, NE, Portuguese Legation to the United States, Box 3, no. 149, Corrêa da Serra had learned how to surround himself with active supporters who, initiated by him "nesta chimica com que se pode obrar em democracia,'' rendered him the most remarkable services, and whose names he could not reveal for fear that he might compromise them, since he had not been provided with any cryptographic system.

[88]Note that this dispatch was sent from New York. Corrêa da Serra had gone to this city in order to give the impression that he was getting ready to embark for Brazil.

[89]John Quincy Adams, *Memoirs,* April 8, 1819, IV, pp. 326-27.

would not been the last to have thought it so[90] — that reading the *Appeal* may have been partly responsible for James Monroe's last-minute insertion at the end of his December 7, 1818 message to Congress of a paragraph in which he recommended stiffening the laws against the excesses of the privateers.[91] Corrêa da Serra thought it appropriate to thank the American president warmly for this in his New Year's greetings.[92] After Adams had asked Attorney General William Wirt on January 28, 1820 for "the favor of (his) opinion to be transmitted to the Committee of Foreign Relations on the defects in the laws against piracy,"[93] the discussion of two bills was initiated in Congress.[94] Passed on May 15 and entitled *An Act designating the ports within only foreign armed vessels shall be permitted to enter* and *An Act to make further provisions for punishing the crime of piracy*, these laws authorized the President to use land-based as well as naval armed forces to guarantee their enforcement.[95]

Despite his skepticism about the adequacy of these laws, to which he still preferred "his own law,"[96] the 1817 neutrality act, Corrêa da Serra was forced to recognize three months later that the effects of these laws far surpassed his expectations.[97] Their effectiveness lay in the fact that privateers were not able to sell their prizes with impunity in even the more remote parts of the coast of the United States, and also that the punishments for such crimes were becoming increasingly severe. This was clearly demonstrated, several acquittals and lenient sentences

---

[90]He stated this categorically in his instructions to José Amado Grehon, September 21, 1820, Philadelphia, TTL, NE, Portuguese Legation to the United States, Box 3, no. 391.

[91]See *Journal of the House of Representatives*, 16th Congress, 1st Session, p. 15.

[92]Corrêa da Serra to James Monroe, January 1, 1820, Philadelphia, cited in R. Beale Davis, *The Abbé Corrêa . . .* , *op. cit.*

[93]NA, DS, Domestic Letters, XVII.

[94]*Journal of the House of Representatives,* 16th Congress, 1st session, pp. 246-80, 453-54; *Journal of the Senate,* 16th Congress, 1st session, pp. 286-87, 346, 350-51, *et seq.*

[95]See *The Public Statutes at large of the United States* III, pp. 510-14, 597-600.

[96]Corrêa da Serra to Vilanova Portugal, June 9, 1820, Philadelphia, TTL, NE, Portuguese Legation to the United States, Box 3, no. 148.

[97]Corrêa da Serra to Vilanova Portugal, September 6, 1820, Washington, TTL, NE, Portuguese Legation to the United States, Box 3, no. 149.

notwithstanding, by the death sentences and executions of roughly thirty privateers in Baltimore, Richmond, Boston, Charleston, Savannah, and New Orleans.[98]

The moderate press reported these punishments with commentaries that were for the most part favorable.[99] The radical press, of course, raised indignant protests. As might be expected, the *Aurora* unleashed its wrath against Corrêa da Serra, whom it accused of being the instigator of these verdicts. One could read in the May 10, 1820 issue: "What avail the artifices and the inconsistency of that philosophy which can unite in an abbé and an ambassador the fell malignity of hostility to man under the triple masquerade of the priest philosopher and agent of despotism?" And in that of May 20: "About thirty persons have been executed. The abbé Corrêa must now be satisfied. There are ten for his philosophy, ten for his piety, and ten for his diplomacy!"

A few days later, on June 6, 1820, the same publication spread the rumor that "a certain philosophical ambassador is recalled and will proceed to Brazil," suggesting that "the people who were catechised and disciplined in 1816 have discovered that there was something in his philosophy that squinted." Corrêa da Serra was in fact far from having fallen out of favor in Rio de Janeiro, nor had he become *persona non grata* in Washington. His departure was of his own volition, his decision undoubtedly influenced by his distress at the "constant stings by the radical mosquitoes" and perhaps also by the offer of a high honorific position and an important political post in Brazil.[100] Knowing that he understood "the levers and pulleys of the singular machine" that was the United States, since he had "nearly carried out and concluded what

---

[98]See *Niles' Weekly Register,* March 11 and 25, April 8 and 15, May 22, and June 5, 1820.

[99]See the *National Intelligencer* of April 5, 1820: "The fate of those unhappy culprits will, it is to be hoped, check the progress of that barbarous and impunitive plunder which has so long spread danger and death upon our seas and corrupted our seamen and dishonoured our country."

[100]Corrêa da Serra had been named Commandant of the Order of Nossa Senhora da Conceição de Vila Viçosa, and he had just learned that he was being considered as a prospective member of the Finance Council of Brazil. See his letter to Joseph Deleuze, whom he had known well in the past, at the Museum of National History of Paris, May 13, 1820, Philadelphia, MHN, MS 1686, no. 370: "Soon I will leave this country to go to Brazil where old friends request my presence and where my Master has just established me beyond my remotest wishes and has just decorated me in the Oriental way."

he had set out to do in order to punish and abolish piracy," he felt confident, based on what he had been given to understand,[101] that his master the King would permit the seventy-two-year-old Corrêa da Serra to allow someone else to "take advantage of the momentary opportunities that would arise" in the wake of his departure.[102]

The term "momentary" was not used idly, Corrêa da Serra added. "Between two recently established powers whose relations are not yet fixed and matured, collisions are bound to be frequent, as time will show." It was precisely because of this adverse possibility that he prolonged his stay in the United States for an additional nine months. During this time, he set out to conduct one last battle, the success of which he hoped would crown his career.[103]

When Corrêa da Serra went in late July 1820 to make his farewell visit to Thomas Jefferson at Monticello,[104] he and "his great friend" the former president held long and intimate conversations on many political issues. Jefferson described to Corrêa da Serra a project inspired by his thoughts on such works as Thomas Paine's *Common Sense*[105] and, most importantly, *L'Europe après le congrès d'Aix-la-Chapelle* by

---

[101]Pedro Machado de Miranda Malheiros to Corrêa da Serra, May 29, 1819, Rio de Janeiro, MHN, no. 2442.

[102]Thus would be achieved what Corrêa da Serra had hoped for in his letter to Vilanova Portugal, February 18, 1819, Washington, in *Brasil Histórico,* no. 17, May 1, 1864.

[103]At the end of March and beginning of May 1820, Corrêa da Serra informed Vilanova Portugal that he would leave for Brazil in June, and he confirmed his plans in the middle of that same month. But at the beginning of September, after a silence of three months, he wrote to him that, intending to have "levado perto da conclusão o desastrado negócio dos piratas," he was delaying his departure. See Corrêa da Serra to Vilanova Portugal, March 31, May 4, June 14, and September 6, 1820, TTL, NE, Portuguese Legation to the United States, Box 3, nos. 147, 149, 151; see also *Brasil Historico,* no. 25, June 26, 1864. Corrêa da Serra was not to leave the United States until mid-November 1820.

[104]Corrêa da Serra made every year what he called his "pilgrimage to Mecca" or "to the Holy Land," his visit to Jefferson at Monticello, where a room was permanently reserved for him.

[105]*Common Sense* was written in 1776. See *Paine Writings,* , 1967, p. 88.

the Abbé de Pradt.[106] The project's objective was "the organization of the American hemisphere in a system totally and reciprocally independent from that in place in the European hemisphere." To Jefferson, it was clear that this system could not but be placed under the aegis of the United States.[107] Corrêa da Serra managed to soften this too-rigid approach by appealing to ideas which he strongly endorsed and had previously formulated in other contexts. He underlined the importance of the role which, in this system of the Americas, should be assigned to Brazil. As he emphasized, "our two governments are the only ones of America that are acknowledged by all mankind and each of them will be always the paramount power in its respective moiety of this hemisphere," so that "when America is to be ruled by a system of herself, these two governments will always be the directorial ones of the whole system."[108] Jefferson was persuaded by these arguments to abandon the idea of putting this system under the exclusive or preponderant leadership of the United States, instead assigning to Brazil a role of theoretically equal responsibility. He stated that he would "rejoice to see the fleets of Brazil and the United States riding together as brethren of the same family and keeping down the piracies of the American seas."[109] Following up on this idea, Corrêa da Serra proposed to John Quincy Adams that the question of the indemnities and compensations accruing to the victims of piracies not be taken up in court, but rather be adjudicated by commissioners designated by both governments "with full powers to confer and agree in what reason and justice demand."[110]

---

[106]According to this work, published in 1819, "across the seas rises, like Carthage facing Rome, a power which tends to form an American system exclusive of all European influence."

[107]On this aspect of the genesis of the Monroe doctrine, see T.R. Schellenberg, "Jeffersonian Origins of the Monroe Doctrine," in *Hispanic American Historical Review,* XIV (1934), pp. 1-11.

[108]Corrêa da Serra had recently used these terms in a note to John Quincy Adams, March 17, 1819, Washington, NA, DS, Notes from the Portuguese Legation, I. However, in an earlier letter to Madison, July 10, 1816, Philadelphia, cited in R. Beale Davis, *The Abbé Corrêa . . . , op. cit.,* he had used nearly the same terms: "Our nations are now in fact both American powers and will be always the two paramount ones, each in his part of the New Continent. . . ."

[109]Jefferson to William Short, August 4, 1820, Monticello, in *Jefferson Writings,* XV, pp. 262-64.

[110]Corrêa da Serra to John Quincy Adams, July 10, 1820, Wilmington, NA, DS, Notes from the Portuguese Legation, I.

On none of these points did Corrêa da Serra obtain satisfaction. James Monroe, to whom Adams submitted the idea of a joint commission, rejected it on the grounds that its acceptance would mean that the United States would be admitting responsibility for the affair in advance and without proof.[111] As for the suggested cooperation between the two fleets to suppress the privateers, he feared that the net effect would rather be "to tie to a certain extent the United States with Brazil against the Spanish American colonies, the governments of which, although clearly still badly organised, would soon be in a position to merit full recognition."[112] Adams tried to explain these positions, with the utmost respect and without causing Corrêa da Serra to be "disturbed in his romancing,"[113] in two meetings he set up on August 21 and 28, 1820, shortly after the diplomat returned to Washington.[114] Even so, on the eve of the journey that, as he then thought, would take him to Brazil, Corrêa da Serra remained convinced that his substitute as chargé d'affaires, José Amado Grehon,[115] to whom he was leaving very detailed and precise instructions,[116] would be able to "reduce the question to a single point: the commitment made by the United States leaders to name commissioners who, jointly with His Majesty's ministers, will assess the damages inflicted on the latter's subjects."

Nothing of what might reasonably have been expected, however, was to come to pass. It was not in Rio de Janeiro that Corrêa da Serra lived out his last days, but in Lisbon, to which city the liberal revolution had recalled the King of Portugal. Brazil, in effect reduced back to a colony by this new state of affairs, no longer merited the status of partner in the eyes of the United States. Corrêa da Serra's mission was, then, stalled, if not an outright failure. It cannot be denied, however,

---

[111]Monroe to John Quincy Adams, July 24, 1820, Highland, and August 3, 1820, Albermarle, in *Monroe Writings,* VI, pp. 141, 147.

[112]Monroe to John Quincy Adams, August 11, 1820, Albemarle, in *Adams Writings,* VII, p. 63 n.

[113]John Quincy Adams, *Memoirs,* September 19, 1820, v, p. 175.

[114]John Quincy Adams to Monroe, August 21 and 30, 1820, Washington, in *Adams Writings,* VII, pp. 63, 68.

[115]José Amado Grehon had been named secretary of the legation in July 1818. In spite of his early "more than singular display of a haughty superiority," he soon would bow to the exceptional prestige that Corrêa da Serra seemed to enjoy in every circle.

[116]Instructions dated September 25, 1820, Philadelphia, TTL, NE, Portuguese Legation to the United States, Box 3, no. 391.

that in the matter of Atlantic piracy, he played a considerable role in dispelling the smug self-satisfaction in which the United States seemed to immerse itself, especially since the inauguration of Monroe, the first of the "politician-presidents." It must also be emphasized that, thanks to his valuable intimacy with Jefferson and Madison, the last two of the "philosopher-presidents," Corrêa da Serra had the privilege of intervening personally and actively in the elaboration of two fundamental and interrelated concepts: the doctrine of American neutrality and the emerging identity of the American hemisphere. These concepts were to form the basis for American foreign policy for a full century. For these reasons alone, Corrêa da Serra's name deserves to occupy an illustrious place in the history of Luso-American diplomatic relations.

List of Archives

BNR	Biblioteca Nacional, Rio de Janeiro
LC	Library of Congress, Washington
MHN	Museum d'Histoire Naturelle, Paris
NA	National Archives, Washington
TTL	Biblioteca da Torre do Tombo, Lisbon

INDEX

The letter *n* after the arabic page number indicates of course that the subject is alluded to in a note on that page. No additional page number is given, however, if the subject is also referred to in the text.

Academy of Natural Sciences of Philadelphia, 292-293, 307n; Gilmer elected to, 285n; *Journal of,* 285-287n

Adams, John, 345

Adams, John Quincy, 56, 59-60n, 68, 75n, 118n, 156n, 204n, 244-245n, 273-275, 280n, 303n, 306n, 349n, 350n, 352, 354, 356n, 358n, 359n, 363n, 364n

Aguiar, Marquis de, 50n, 338, 339n

Aigster, Frederick, 144n

Allan, Paul (or Peter), 121n, 194n

Almeida, José, 356n

Amado, José, 306n, 360n, 364n

American Philosophical Society, 112n, 124n, 149n, 312n, 315n; as depository for Lewis and Clark MSS., 196n; expresses sympathy on C's death, 366; library of, 243

Armstrong, General John, 118n

Arrowsmith, A., *A map of the U.S. of N.A.,* 174n

Artigas, José, 54, 213n, 282, 353

Artiguenave, Joseph Linna, 256n

Aublet, Jean Baptiste Christophe Fusée, *Histoire des plantes de la Guiane françois . . .,* 265n

Babad, Father Peter, 98-99n, 234n

Bagot, Lord, 128n

Bankhead, Anne Cary Randolph, 247n

Bankhead, Charles, 247n, 250, 257n

Banks, Sir Joseph, Bart., 15n, 17n, 79

Barca, Araujo da, Count, 60, 85n, 337n, 340n, 346n

Barlow, Joel, 21, 27n, 115n, 118n

Barrazo Pereira, Joachim, 280n, 303n, 306, 310

Barton, Benjamin Smith, 85n, 165n, 179n, 192n, 195, 200, 230n

Barton, Mrs. Benjamin Smith, 179n, 192

Barton, Dr. Edward, 314n, 315, 319

Bartram, John, *Antiquities of Florida,* 243n

Bartram, William, 79, *Travels,* 243n

Bell, Mrs. John (Mary Ann Walker), 295n

Biddle, Nicholas, 31n, 38n, 66, 118n, 121, 124, 194n, 200

Biddle, Mrs. Nicholas, 126

Bienville, de, and Iberville, journals of, 170

Bigelow, Dr. Jacob, 39n, 83n, 255n

Binns, John, 173n

Blainville, Henri Marie Ducrotav de, article in *Journal de physique,* 201n

Bochart, Samuel, *Hierozoicon,* 141n

Bonaparte, Madame Jerome (Betsy Patterson), 24n

Bonaparte, Napoleon, 20n, 130, 134n, 152n, 156, 193, 244, 269

Bowen, Charles, 340

Borbon, Infante Don Carlos Maria Isidro de, 175n

Botanical names mentioned: *Aristolochia sipho,* or *A. macrophylla,* 245n; *Callicarpa,* of family Verbenaceae, 264n; *Clethra* of family Clethraceae, 262n; "Convallaria candensis" (*Maianthemum canadense*), 238n; Decumaria, 291; *Elliottia,* family Ericaceae, 261n; Epigaea repens, 248n; *Euphorbia,* Spurge family, Euphorbiaceae, 262n; Floerkea, today *F. proserpinacoides* Willd., 261n; *Gelsemium,* of Loganiacae, 248n; *Maclura pomifera,* 128n, 249n; Miegia 264; *Momordica operculata,* 251n; *Ophrys locselii,* genus Listeria, 232n; Orobanche, 207n; *Pachysandra,*